Republic of Indians

EARLY AMERICAN STUDIES

Series editors:
Kathleen M. Brown, Roquinaldo Ferreira,
Emma Hart, and Daniel K. Richter

Exploring neglected aspects of our colonial, revolutionary, and early
national history and culture, Early American Studies reinterprets
familiar themes and events in fresh ways. Interdisciplinary
in character, and with a special emphasis on the period from
about 1600 to 1850, the series is published in partnership
with the McNeil Center for Early American Studies.

A complete list of books in the series is available from the publisher.

Republic of Indians

Empires of Indigenous Law in
the Early American South

Bradley J. Dixon

PENN

UNIVERSITY OF PENNSYLVANIA PRESS

PHILADELPHIA

Research in this volume was funded by
the Society of Colonial Wars Fellowship
in Memory of Kenneth R. LaVoy Jr.

Published by
University of Pennsylvania Press
Philadelphia, Pennsylvania 19104-4112
www.pennpress.org

Printed in the United States of America on acid-free paper
10 9 8 7 6 5 4 3 2 1

Hardcover ISBN: 978-1-5128-2642-5
eBook ISBN: 978-1-5128-2643-2

A Cataloging-in-Publication record is
available from the Library of Congress

To my mother and father and to the memory of my grandparents.

CONTENTS

"A Residencia for the Dead"

In the spring of 1656, rumors of invasion reached the ears of officials in two colonial capitals.[1] In James City, the news that hundreds of "western and inland Indians," the Richahecrians, were encamped near the Falls of the James River startled the members of the Grand Assembly of Virginia.[2] In San Agustín, word of the fall of Jamaica to an English amphibious attack rattled the nerves of Don Diego de Rebolledo, Florida's royal governor, who feared his colony was next. Though part of distinct empires with their own histories and separated by a distance of hundreds of leagues, the planters in the assembly and the governor, wearing his habit from the Order of Santiago, had the same response: they summoned the Indians to save them.

In Virginia, in March 1656, the call went to Totopotomoy, *weroance* (chief) of the Pamunkeys, who mustered his bowmen and hastened to a council of war to discuss strategy with the English commander, Colonel Edward Hill. Since 1646, the Pamunkeys and the rest of the Powhatans had been tributary subjects of the English, pledged by treaty to the defense of Virginia. The treaty's architect was Necotowance, *mamanatowick* (paramount chief) of Tsenacomacoh, the "land that was dwelt upon closely together," as the Powhatans called the Tidewater.[3] Necotowance made the agreement to end a terrible war, but in time the "articles of peace" between the Powhatans and the English became the foundation of something more. After concluding the treaty, Necotowance brought his tribute of beaver pelts into the capital and vowed to honor the king of England as long as the sun and moon endured. Within a year, he was no more. The paramount chiefdom transformed and individual leaders from the nations of Tsenacomacoh, *weroances* like Totopotomoy, took charge after swearing allegiance yet again. Now, they came to defend Virginia. When at last Totopotomoy and his warriors reached the Falls of the James to meet the invaders, reckless English soldiers opened fire during a peaceful parley. In the sudden attack, the militiamen murdered five Richahecrian leaders who, moments before, had offered gifts and promise of trade. The swift Richahecrian counterattack broke the English ranks, but Totopotomoy stood firm and rallied his men in pursuit of the enemy until a musket ball left him slain on the field. The Pamunkey *weroance* died at what Virginians remembered long after as the Battle of the Bloody Run. There, Totopotomoy proved his "fidelity" to an elusive ideal of united common-wealths, Indigenous and English. Across the Atlantic, a poet immortalized him in verse.[4]

In Florida, meanwhile, the order to mobilize the Indigenous militia went out to the council-houses in all the towns in the three provinces of Guale/Mocama (coastal Florida and Georgia), Apalachee (western Florida around modern-day Tallahassee), and Timucua (coastal and central Florida), where altogether at least fifteen thousand Indigenous people lived.[5] In Timucua, the governor's stipulation that the officers of the militia would have to carry their own supplies triggered an explosive response. The commanders were the chief men of their towns, "who amongst us," wrote one Franciscan friar, "are like nobles [*hidalgos*] and gentlemen and senior councilors."[6] Timucua elites refused to go "loaded as if they were mules or horses" and said "they had Vassals that could go with loads."[7] As they told the friars "they were not slaves" but vassals of the king of Spain.[8] Timucua *holahtas* (chiefs) revolted in defense of the privileges the Crown guaranteed them as the aristocracy at the head of Florida's Indigenous commonwealth, *la república de indios*, the "republic of Indians." Expelling the governor's soldiers—and killing the worst offenders against their rights—the Timucuas enlisted Florida's missionary Franciscans in a multipronged, transatlantic petitioning and lobbying campaign all with the goal of throwing the governor, whom the friars derided as "that creole from Cartagena," out of office.[9]

The tumultuous events in the spring of 1656 were unusual but the role of Indigenous leaders was not. Some Native peoples across the early American South understood themselves to be joined with European colonizers in larger polities, each jealously guarding their own bodies of liberties under royal sanction. Although the English failed Totopotomoy in 1656, Indigenous leaders like him were not always without European allies in America or across the Atlantic. Over her long tenure, Totopotomoy's wife and successor, the *weroansqua* (female chief) Cockacoeske, would curry favor with local Virginia grandees and seek allies at the royal court of "the Great King of England" her "very good friend," and "real Defender."[10] Cockacoeske, in time, rewrote Virginia's covenant with the tributaries, an exploit reported not in verse but mundane prose by the government's official London newspaper.[11] Cockacoeske was as savvy as any court insider and, like many Indigenous leaders of her day, maneuvered in imperial politics to advantage.

The state of play could shift rapidly, with Indigenous leaders making one set of allies one day and turning to others the next. In Florida, while the Timucuan elite found formidable partners in the Franciscans in 1656, the lords of Apalachee seized the same moment to get the better of the very same friars in the ever-shifting politics of empire.[12] The stakes in such political moves were high—winning royal favor, taking back power from colonizers, defending their people and their lands—and the tactics could be cutting. For these astute political players, it was all part of the game.

Frantically defending themselves against the Apalachee leaders' detailed allegations of abuse at their hands, the Franciscan chapter of Florida unwittingly left us an apt metaphor for the historian's craft. Recorded in the governor's hasty inspection tour of Apalachee, all part of a vain attempt to defeat the combined Indigenous-Franciscan campaign for his ouster, Apalachees' complaints about missionary corruption stretched back over years, naming some friars long since laid in their graves. Governor Rebolledo, the friars told the king, "did not content himself to blame the living, but he proceeds to investigate [*residenciar*] the dead."[13] The word the friars used was deliberate, conjuring visions of a *residencia*, the formal review of an official's conduct at the end of his term of service.[14] (The English had nothing quite so elaborate, although Edward Hill was cashiered from all his offices after the fiasco at the Bloody Run.)[15] Florida's governors dreaded the day news of their *residencia* was nailed to the church door in San Agustín and posted throughout Florida's Native American provinces. The reason was that the typical *residencia* invited anyone with a grievance—a soldier he had passed over for promotion, a creditor he still owed a debt, or an Indigenous chief still furious over his high-handed treatment—to lodge one last complaint.

This book contains the findings of my own "*residencia* for the dead," a wide-ranging inquiry into the conduct of two European empires, English and Spanish, in the early American South over the span of more than a century. The list of witnesses summoned from archives in Europe and North America includes traders, friars, soldiers, colonial governors, monarchs, and most of all, Indigenous people. They come from all ranks and walks of life. Some speak from cells, like the Weanoke chief imprisoned for debt in Virginia or the two men from Mocama confined in Havana's El Morro fortress for nearly a decade after a failed rebellion. There are *caciques* (chiefs) and *weroances*: Totopotomoy and Cockacoeske of Pamunkey; Harquip and his fellow *manguys* (councilors) of the Chickahominies; Santiago the *mico* (chief) of Tolomato just north of San Agustín; Ana Estasia, chief of Tupiqui on the Georgia coast; and Thomas Hoyter, "king" of the Chowans in North Carolina. Some boldly addressed their words to distant European monarchs. The names of many more were not recorded. What they have to say comes through instead in brief notations from council records, royal decrees, and in the text of laws in colonial statute books.

The investigation reaches a surprising conclusion. By the mid-seventeenth century, some Native Americans in the South were not only protected subjects of imperial governments but active participants in politics, even to the point of writing their political demands into colonial law.[16] Their testimony, especially in the petitions they sent to colonial officials and to the Crown, reveals that some Southern Natives—in particular so-called "mission Indians," "Settlement Indians," and tributaries—embraced the status of imperial subjects and vassals and used it to push for incorporation in larger polities in which they had a say and that they were themselves instrumental in creating.[17] What they secured were commonwealths of their own, a republic of Indians, joined together with European colonizers by a shared law and shared allegiance to the same crown. When they marched to battle, rather than marching to the defense of colonies, Totopotomoy or the Timucuas were defending their own republics.

The ideal of the "republic of Indians," an Indigenous commonwealth standing side by side and yet bound with the colonial polity, was a feature of what we might call the American South's "Latin American" phase.[18] During my version of the "long" seventeenth century (ca. 1585–1715) the patterns of politics in the early American South were an extension of Latin America's. Or, more precisely, the political culture in the South among the peoples described in this book, was more Spanish and Indigenous in flavor than English prior to the turn of the eighteenth century. Borrowing "republic of Indians," a Spanish term with a rich and controversial historiography, to describe a kind of political system that emerged even in an English colony like Virginia, does not mean I think they were exactly the same thing.[19] Conversion to Christianity, for one, was not always requisite for membership, certainly not in the English empire, where a Native leader once praised King Charles II for commanding "that us the heathen and Natives of the Land: Should enjoy Common justice and Equity as well as the Rest of your subjects in these parts."[20] But what these regimes had in common make the model helpful for seeing the history of empires throughout the Americas in a new light.

The republic of Indians in places across the South—indeed, across the hemisphere—was a system that protected Indigenous custom and jurisdiction, and afforded leaders access to political participation through petitioning and lobbying, making it possible for these Native vassals and subjects to prompt changes in law.[21] There were many republics—some at the level of individual towns, some comprising individual nations—which in turn fit into the larger "republic of Indians," a "composite of communities" distinct from the republics of Spaniards or from the colonial governments of the English.[22] Within the republic of Indians the small republics comprising it often won special exemptions, favors, and privileges that belonged exclusively to them.[23] By the eighteenth century, Virginia's colonial law reflected—if on a smaller scale—a patchwork of privileges similar to what prevailed among Indigenous communities in the Spanish Empire at the time. One digest of Virginia law from the 1730s singled out three key Indigenous groups by name as holders of special liberties and exemptions above those to which tributary Indians were already entitled.[24] We might say, then, that the republic of Indians was another "emergent property," of the larger collision between Indigenous peoples and European colonizers across the Americas.[25]

As a category of analysis or a model, the republic of Indians serves as a convenient shorthand for what were, in fact, a multiplicity of understandings of what was, in each colony, really a similar system. On the one hand, the republic of Indians represents the place Europeans expected colonized Native peoples to occupy within empires—as subordinate and loyal subjects or vassals. Spaniards and Englishmen in the South founded colonial outposts with very different objectives in mind, yet Indigenous peoples were central to their aims. "Spanish" Florida was a military base, funded with a subsidy from the Crown, a good portion of which was in turn invested as gifts to local Native rulers who sent the labor and foodstuffs to San Agustín that kept the colony viable. Virginia and the Carolinas, meanwhile, whatever their high ideals at the outset, were profit-seeking ventures that became settler colonies. In time, the most valuable commodities Indigenous people possessed were their lands and their captured enemies' bodies as slaves. The different motivations in each colony led to nuances in how the republic of Indians formed and operated in each of them—and whether such a system could endure.

Colonizers did not have the last say on what the system meant and Indigenous peoples influenced the political system in each colony.[26] For, on the other hand, the republic of Indians stands for the multiple ways the Indigenous peoples involved understood their relationship with European colonizers. Native leaders who became vassals, subjects, or tributaries carved out their liberties under a shared law that they influenced in order to protect their own interests. Depending on a number of factors, from varying populations to their different forms of internal governance, the republic of Indians looked different to different Native nations—even in the same colonies. From the perspective of Timucuas, it was one thing, from Apalachees another; it was different yet again, whether seen from the vantages of Pamunkeys or Chickahominies.

The republic of Indians differs as well from other historical models of interactions between Indigenous peoples and colonizers, notably the "Indians' new world" and the "middle ground."[27] While the republic of Indians in the South was a product of the process James Merrell called the "Indians' new world," it is primarily one of its political manifestations, the outcome of one Indigenous strategy for survival amid the chaos of the era. The republic of Indians resembled a "middle ground" in that it was a co-creation of a shared political space for Indigenous peoples and Europeans but it did not arise out of misunderstandings, whether of the "creative" or the more violent kind.[28] These systems emerged through decades of trial and error in which Native leaders gained ample experience with colonial expectations and ideas as together they built these regimes, even if their understanding was partly the result of what Adrian Masters calls "subtle forms of intellectual coercion."[29]

The Indigenous leaders who fashioned the republic of Indians had no trouble understanding the colonizers' demands—for their labor, for their land, for their wealth, for their allegiance. Nor did they find the colonizers' legal and political concepts beyond their grasp. Molding such concepts as "stranger" or "subject" in ways that suited their needs, Indigenous leaders at times successfully employed the techniques of early modern politics such as petitioning. In the pages ahead, you will meet more than a few Native people who understood colonial law better than the colonists.[30] Yet, their experiences as "subjects" and "vassals" of European empires sharpened their sense of independence and inspired their greatest legacy. The Native petitioners of the seventeenth and eighteenth centuries, addressing Europeans from a supposedly subordinate pose, conjured some of the most eloquent descriptions of sovereignty ever written—all without ever using the term. Their story is both Native American history and the history of empires, for they were active players in both.

In the early American South, the establishment of a republic of Indians led to a kind of merger of Native and European law that governed the Spanish and English empires on the ground. Native law was part of imperial law, even if only by the grudging admission of colonizers. From the highest vantage point, the republic of Indians in the South was one part of a multiethnic, regional Indigenous polity with a European paramount at its head and a colonial town as its center.[31] Together, Native and European laws served as a kind of constitution, codified in treaties, statutes, collective memory, and custom that governed relations between the republic of Indians and the colonial state.[32] In Florida, the constitution of the republic was a bundle of understandings and mutual obligations, which the historian Amy Turner Bushnell has called the "colonial compact."[33] In Virginia, the treaties of 1646 and 1677 codified the liberties, privileges, immunities—and restrictions—of tributary Natives and served collectively as the fundamental law.[34] In the Carolinas, treaties, "articles of peace," and trade agreements with individual Indigenous nations served as the basis for their political participation.[35] The political economy of the republic of Indians combined "staple finance" and "wealth finance," meaning that Indigenous subjects and vassals paying tribute in the form of commodities such as peltries and labor such as burdening.[36] Southeastern paramount chiefdoms were historically unstable past a certain size. Colonial polities that included a republic of Indians were able to overcome what the anthropologist Robin Beck calls the "inherent scalar limitation" of the old chiefdoms by imposing spatial order on its subjects.[37] Any perceived cession or compromise of Native sovereignty in consenting to such an arrangement—if there was a compromise at all—was conditional and potentially temporary, particularly when the party dubbed the stronger failed in its obligations to the weaker.[38] Throughout the seventeenth and early eighteenth centuries, plenty of Native people walked away when the deal soured on them.

The promise of the republic of Indians, despite its numerous failings, was substantial and Natives within it used their legal status to win political victories against colonizers. However "flexible" or precarious their status was in practice, Native tributaries in places like Virginia and North Carolina, much like Native vassals in Florida, were subjects of the Crown with a collection of liberties, including title to land, internal self-government, and channels for the redress of grievances.[39] Even if it was compatible with or even helpful to the ultimate goals of settler colonialism, Natives did not help forge such a system with the understanding that it would dispossess them, peacefully or no. Indigenous leaders constructed these systems so they could survive and to prevent dispossession. In the South, the Spanish and English empires came to resemble one another precisely because they depended to surprising degree on maintaining Indigenous political consent and their foundations rested in part on Indigenous law. Over time, Southern Native leaders inscribed the principles of protection, equality, reciprocity, and self-government into the legal codes of both empires.[40]

Until recently, the significance of Native Americans in the politics of European empires was not so easy to discern. From the very beginning, Spanish and English writers made strict distinctions between their two colonial projects, a process that notably accelerated in the eighteenth century and, with a few exceptions, has continued ever since.[41] The differences tended to depend on the role of Native Americans within each empire. James Adair, the noted chronicler of Chickasaw and Choctaw life in the eighteenth century, was typically dismissive of the seventeenth century's record of Native politicians. "The Spaniards," he observed, "have given us many fine polished Indian orations, but they were certainly fabricated at Madrid."[42] Adair vouched from his first-hand experience, that "the Indians have no such ideas, or methods of speech, as they pretend to have copied from a faithful interpreter on the spot."[43] Early English reports of the thundering orations of Powhatan or Opechancanough were fables "raised to that prodigious pitch of power and grandeur, to rival the Spanish accounts."[44] Scholars, sharing none of Adair's prejudices, have continued to draw sharp contrasts between Spanish imperialism and English settler colonialism, the one incorporating Natives as vassals and the other excluding them altogether.[45] The Spanish had an elaborate imperial legal code; the English had distinct codes for each colony.[46] The Spanish "and only the Spanish" agonized over the legal status of Natives and built an intricate system to protect their persons, goods, and lands; the English supposedly could not even "picture Natives as wards of any Crown."[47] Sweeping comparisons between places as different as Virginia and the Valley of Mexico accentuated these differences and overlook important similarities.[48] Shifting the focus to the early American South, where similar Native polities faced Spaniards and the English at roughly the same time, offers a much better measure for evaluating the differences and similarities between empires and the place of Indigenous peoples within them.

The Native petitioners who built the republic of Indians from the "bottom-up" at once legitimated and undermined the expansive claims of European empires.[49] Adapting preinvasion practices to colonial challenges, Native petitioners sought favors and rewards, exemptions from labor, protection for

lands, to install preferred leaders, avoid enslavement, ally with distant monarchs against colonists, ease harsh colonial laws, and even to amend the terms
of treaties and compacts that established the republic of Indians in the first
place. In a world defined and perhaps even held together by violence, these
petitioners sought order, justice, and peace with the invaders through law.[50]
Southeastern Native petitioners appealed to a shared law with colonizers, and
they left behind alternative Indigenous histories of colonialism in the heart of
the colonial archive—despite violent efforts to erase them.[51]

    This book watches the process of mutual creation unfold as Pamunkeys
and Apalachees, Chickahominies and Guales, Timucuas and Tuscaroras,
Chowans, and, occasionally, "Chichimecos," forged an American political
tradition that is far older and has lasted longer than the entire history of
the United States.[52] The first four chapters narrate the consolidation of the
republic of Indians in Florida and the rise of a republic of Indians in Virginia
during the first half of the seventeenth century. Chapter 1 offers a tale of two
presidios (fortified outposts for projecting colonial power)—San Agustín and
Jamestown—as they employed similar strategies to create political systems
that included Indigenous polities as distinct if subordinate republics. Chapter 2 explores the sudden and contemporaneous growth of the republic of
Indians in Florida and the beginning of the republic of Indians in Virginia.
Both developments eventually opened the way for Indigenous petitioners to
participate in politics and lawmaking in the 1650s and '60s. By the 1670s, the
republic of Indians in Florida and in Virginia had both reached their greatest
extent. Chapter 3 recounts the rebellions that tested and nearly overturned
the republic of Indians—the Chacato Revolt and the ensuing Apalachee-
Chisca War in western Florida and Bacon's Rebellion in Virginia. Instead of
destroying the principles of the republic of Indians, a cadre of Indigenous
leaders in Florida and Virginia emerged from these upheavals to rewrite the
covenants binding them with colonizers, so that the law codes in both colonies had never been so alike in their professed aims.

    In the second half of the book, the story begins to change, as English influ-
ence worked to transform the region according to different principles from
the Hispano-Indigenous ones that prevailed before the establishment of the
Carolina colony in 1670. The last three chapters turn to the world outside the
republic of Indians in Florida and Virginia, a world where Natives refused
to be vassals or subjects to anyone. Chapter 4 examines the pressures on
the republic of Indians as Native leaders outside it built networks of towns
to oppose colonial ambitions for empire, whether San Agustín's or Charles

TSENACOMACOH
1 Accomac
2 Appamattuck
3 Arrohateck
4 Chicacoan
5 Cuttatawomen
6 Kecoughtan
7 Kiskiack
8 Mattaponi
9 Moraughtacund
10 Nansemond
11 Nantaughtacund

FALL LINE

Rappahannock

Piscataway Creek

Potomac

Chesapeake Bay

NORTH

Rickahock

Bacon's Quarter

Mattaponi

Pamunkey

CHICKAHOMINY

Werowocomoco

Middle Plantation (Williamsburg)

Fort Henry
Curles Neck
Jordan's Point

York

James

Jamestown

Atlantic Ocean

Fort Christanna

Meherrin

Nottoway

[CHESAPEAKE]

Great Dismal Swamp

Bennett's Creek

FALL LINE

TUSCARORA

Roanoke

CHOWAN

Chowan

Edenton

Albemarle Sound

25 MILES
40 KILOMETERS

12 Occohannock
13 Onawmanient
14 Opiscopank
15 Pamunkey
16 Paspahegh   20 Powhatan
17 Patawomeck   21 Quiyoughcohannock
18 Piankatank   22 Rappahannock   25 Weyanock
19 Pissaseck   23 Warraskoyack   26 Wighcomoco
                   24 Werowocomoco   27 Youghtanund

BLACKMER MAPS

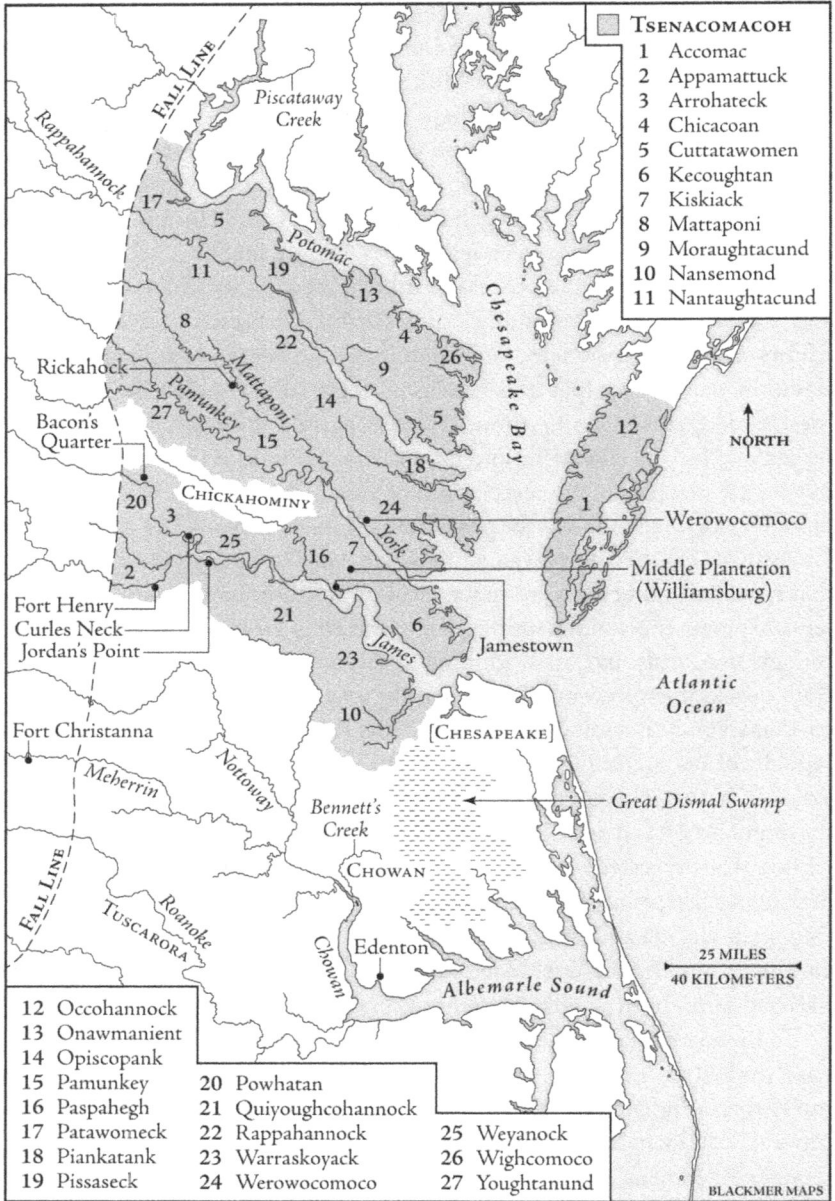

Figure 1. Virginia and North Carolina. Seventeenth through the early eighteenth century. Blackmer Maps.

Town's. From its beginnings as a town among other Indigenous towns, the Carolina colony gradually projected its influence into the council-houses of the South through trade in animal pelts and enslaved people. Some of the peoples Carolina drew into its rising "chieftaincy" or loose, regional network of Indigenous towns, were former Spanish vassals like the Apalachees, forcibly removed from Florida.[53] The Apalachees brought political expectations from the republic of Indians with them and helped trigger a fateful transformation in Carolina's imperial plans. Chapter 5 argues that Carolina's quest to convert the chieftaincy it had created into a massive if perverse semblance of a republic of Indians, partly in response to Apalachee demands, triggered the Yamasee War, the largest uprising of Indigenous people in the history of the early South. Still, tributary Natives carried on the principles of the republic of Indians long after the overthrow of Florida's missions and the revolutionary Yamasee War seemed to have discredited them. Southern Natives in Carolina, Florida, and Virginia remained committed throughout the eighteenth century to making the vision of equal commonwealths of Natives and Europeans possible. The story has many twists and turns but its beginnings, at least, are clear.

To understand the foundations of the republic of Indians we must go back to the early years of the seventeenth century, as the preparations for the Virginia colony advanced in England and while Florida was on trial for its life.[54] As early as the 1590s, the "many ducats" the king had spent on Florida seemed a losing proposition for the Crown. In 1602, a lengthy investigation by Fernando Valdés revealed a colony wholly dependent upon the surrounding Natives for its support, and its entire reason for existing. San Agustín looked less like a colony and more like the capital of a multiethnic Indigenous polity. A report from 1606 was typical of the many evaluations of Florida from that uncertain era. There was no gold or silver to be found as yet, but there were Indigenous converts to consider.[55] Then, in May 1607, just as the wheels of the imperial bureaucracy turned toward a final decision in Florida's favor, 104 English men and boys landed in the heart of Ajacán, as the Spaniards called the Chesapeake region, laying claim to a marshy island that the Paspaheghs used as a summer hunting spot. There the English raised a crude fort—and the foundations for the colony of Virginia—while the Powhatans carefully observed and tested them.[56]

This is where our tale begins, with two *presidios*, San Agustín and Jamestown, standing at either end of greater La Florida, eager to draw more Native polities into their allegiance as subordinate but protected commonwealths. Their moves were hardly the most important. Native leaders in both places

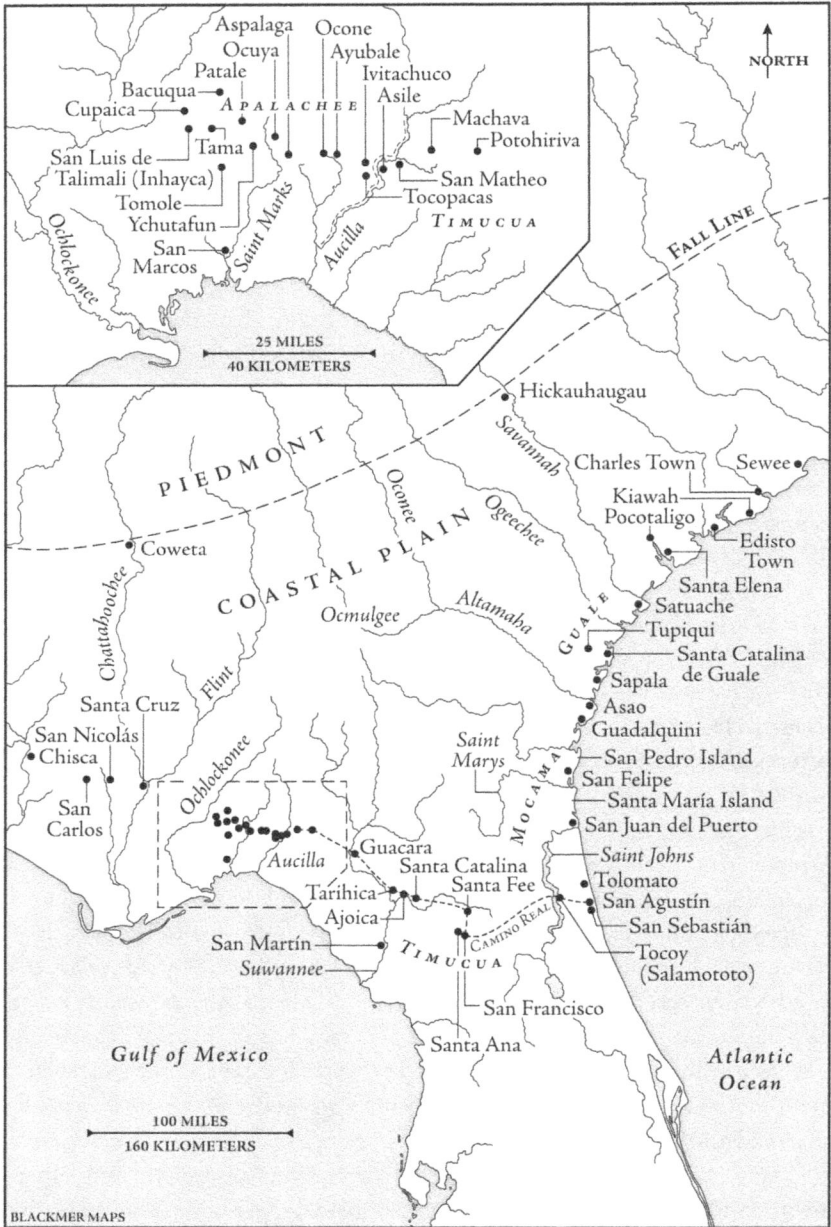

Figure 2. Florida and the Carolinas. Seventeenth century and early eighteenth century. Blackmer Maps.

would strive over the next century to tame those European outposts, and mold them into systems that protected and even benefited their interests. They did not succeed but they left an important legacy nonetheless. What follows is the story of how that process played out and why Tidewater Virginia, not Florida, is one of the few places north of Mexico where the principles of the republic of Indians live on today.

CHAPTER 1

_____

Caciques and Kings, 1608–1632

As the English swarmed Ajacán (Virginia), the king of Spain formalized his decision to keep San Agustín. The city he saved was poor, so poor that most of the year the lamps in the parish church burned bear's grease instead of consecrated oil.[1] The soldiers in the *presidio* knew the pains of hunger better than the fatigues of war. When the ship carrying the *situado* (the subsidy for the colony's support from the treasury of New Spain) was wrecked or became the prize of pirates, the men had one last resort. Once, years ago when there was "much need and hunger" because the *situado* was late, the soldiers looked just over the river to the town of San Sebastián. Andrés López de Simancas "was one of them."[2] The forty-year veteran remembered with gratitude the "more than eight months" the people of San Sebastián succored the soldiers.[3] In June 1606, López returned the favor. Although he "did not know how to write," the old soldier testified to the king of Spain on behalf of the family whose food and hospitality had saved his life, and he praised the family's scion, a man, he said, who had "always welcomed the Spaniards in his land and gave them everything he could": Don Gaspar Marqués, *cacique principal* (head chief) of the Timucuan towns of San Sebastián and Tocoy.[4]

Don Gaspar's petition to King Felipe III in late 1607 told of his family's loyalty through three generations, beginning with his parents Pedro Marqués and Catalina Marquesa, who were some "of the first Christians" in Florida and among the first "to give obedience to His Majesty."[5] To the end of his days, Don Pedro supported the friars, kept up the church, and did what the governor asked. Now Don Gaspar did the same, though his people were "poor and suffer want."[6] Don Juan de las Cabezas Altamirano, Cuba's then-visiting bishop, argued that the king should grant Don Gaspar's request for "a soldier's plaza without being obliged to the ordinary watches"—essentially a pension— "so that the rest of the caciques will be encouraged" to follow his example.[7]

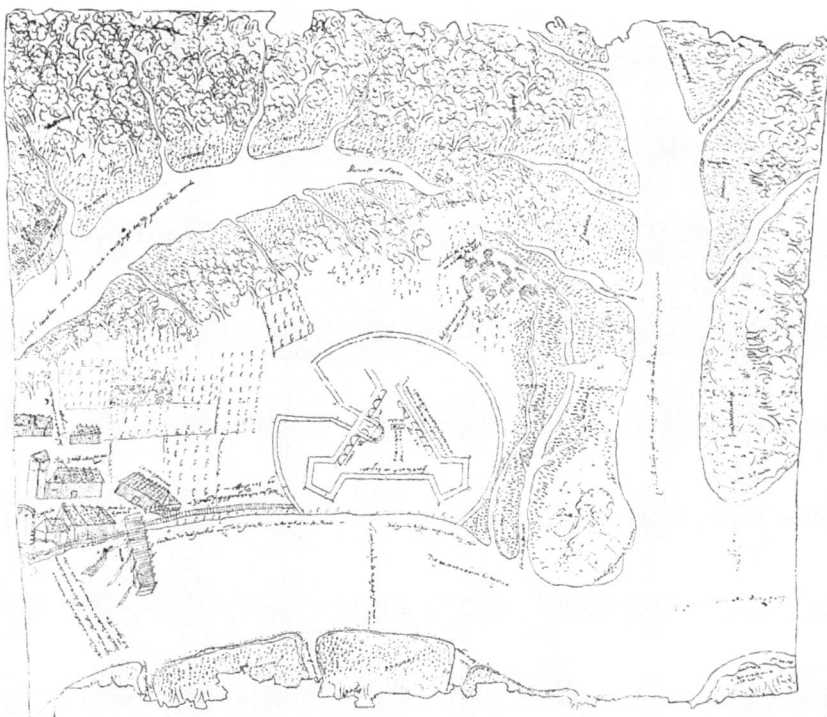

Figure 3. A late sixteenth-century view of the city of San Agustín and the Indigenous towns surrounding it. Nombre de Dios is on the right. Don Gaspar Marques's town of San Sebastián is on the left across what is now the San Sebastián River. "Plan of San Augustin de la Florida, circa 1595, Traced from the original, especially for this work, by D. Pedro Torres Lanzas, Chief of the Archives, from the hitherto unpublished original in the Archives of the Indies, Seville," in *The History of North America*, by Peter Joseph Hamilton, vol. 3: *The Colonization of the South* (Philadelphia, PA: George Barrie & Sons, 1904), inserted illustration between pages 12 and 13. From a scan provided by the P. K. Yonge Library of Florida History, Special and Area Studies Collections, George A. Smathers Libraries, University of Florida.

Don Gaspar Marqués was precisely the kind of Native leader—a friendly, helpful *cacique*—that the Virginia Company dreamed of meeting among the Powhatans. In 1608, it looked to the Spaniards as if they had already found him. On a visit to London, the Powhatan man Namontack, an emissary from Ajacán, was said to have been "coached" to approach the throne of King James without doffing his hat, a sign of his noble birth and of the support the country's Native rulers had for Virginia.[8] Don Pedro de Zuñiga, Felipe III's ambassador at the Stuart court, dismissed Namontack as "a very ordinary person" and scoffed at his planned display before the throne.[9] Although Zuñiga played off as farce Namontack's debut at the English court, the ambassador posted a secret map back to his sovereign in September that unfolded a familiar and threatening strategic picture.[10] Spread out on the map were the rivers of Ajacán, all of them studded with circles standing in for the numerous towns of Powhatans, and setting in alarming relief a triangular fort with a standard flying from its northern bastion. This was Jamestown. Florida began its life as a colony during the sixteenth century in much the same way, a fortified outpost amid scores of Native towns, all connected by waterways. What Zuñiga's map implied was correct. The triangular fort, built on Paspahegh land and soon filled with veteran soldiers, was basically a *presidio* trying to project its power into the Indigenous world surrounding it. The Spanish-inspired tendencies of Jamestown's early years have earned the Virginia Company's project the name "Protestant Mexico."[11] The name "Anglo San Agustín" is closer to the mark.

In the early years of the seventeenth century, the *presidio* at Jamestown experimented with the same techniques for pacification as the *presidio* at San Agustín, alternately opening trade relations with Natives and demanding tribute from them, all to win their allegiance. Sometimes it doled out gifts to pliant leaders and, at others, meted out brutal punishments to those who resisted. The English tried to harness Native labor, swapped hostages with the Powhatans to learn their languages, and planned to build a residential "Indian College," something that had been available to Florida's youth only in Havana and for a short time.[12] Without the services of an army of mendicants, Virginia relied on doughty laymen like George Thorpe who used many of the same tactics and suffered from many of the same delusions as their Catholic competitors.[13] Granted, in the years after 1614, the English rapidly took over Indigenous lands in a way the Spaniards had not—although the failure to plant more colonists in Florida was not for lack of desire, as we will see. Even with tobacco plantations cropping up on expropriated Indigenous land, the English colonizers and the Powhatans might still have grown to live side by side in two republics under the same king, just as metropolitan boosters in London were urging by 1612. As it happened, it would take another twenty-five years before something like the republic of Indians formed in Virginia. When Jamestown seemingly departed from Spanish precedents in 1622, it

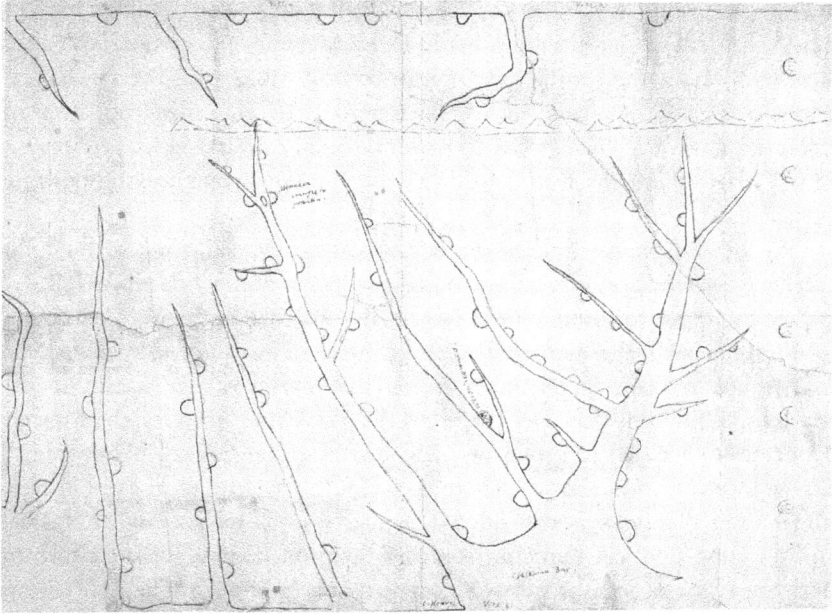

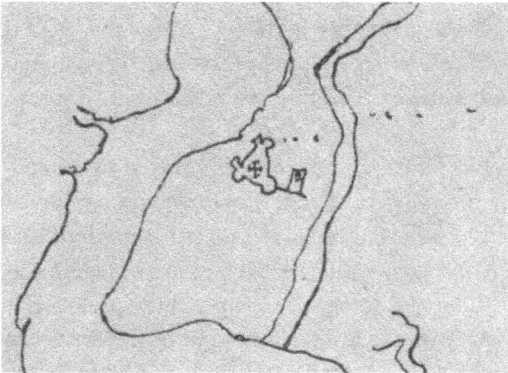

Figure 4. Bottom: Jamestown, as a triangular *presidio* in the midst of Tsena-comacoh, a world of Powhatan towns and rivers. The depiction of Jamestown comes from Zuñiga's map. "Chart of Virginia," in *The Genesis of the United States*, by Alexander M. Brown, vol. 1 (Cambridge, MA: The Riverside Press, 1890), inserted illustration between pages 184 and 185. Above: The surrounding Powhatan world and Werowocomoco come from an anonymous map of Virginia. Werowocomoco, "the place of the Antler-Wearers," Wahunsenacawh's capital, is the semi-circle visible near the center. Virginia, ca. 1610, Kraus Map Collection, Harry Ransom Center, The University of Texas at Austin.

was still following the strategy of the *presidio* but on a path forbidden even to San Agustín's founder, the Adelantado Pedro Menéndez de Avilés, no matter how badly he wished to take it. The war of 1622–1632 with the Powhatans was such a great departure from Spanish practice because it was not a war of conquest, seeking to bring Natives under colonial rule, but "a war of fire and blood" that killed, enslaved, and drove out the Powhatans leaving nothing but the land.[14]

To the Indigenous leaders whose lands they invaded, the two *presidios* must have seemed rather similar, too. The chiefs in both lands plotted strategies of their own to contain the strangers and to profit by them if they could. Wahunsenacawh, the *mamanatowick* (paramount chief) of the Powhatans, and his brother, Opechancanough, treated the English as *their* vassals, investing John Smith as a *weroance* (tellingly, this Powhatan word for chief meant a person with much to give away) and insisting that he lead his people to a new location, "Capahosic," where they would pay tribute in axes, knives, and hoes.[15] Wahunsenacawh offered regular lessons to his English vassals in Powhatan political thought, lecturing them on their obligations to him and his to them, in a process one scholar calls "mutual civilizing."[16] From Wahunsenacawh's perspective, it was the English who should comport themselves as the junior members of a larger polity with the Powhatans. And it was the English who repeatedly failed to live up to expectations. The Powhatan leaders let them know—sometimes violently—when the English disappointed them.[17]

In Florida, however, leaders like Don Gaspar Marqués enjoyed better success taming the intruders. Even haughty royal governors deigned to shower them with the largesse reciprocity demanded, even if it meant emptying their own household stores to do so. Don Gaspar, for one, tried to live out an Indigenous ideal of perfect union with the newcomers, a version of the philosophy of "a dish and one spoon" familiar from the political thought of Northeastern North America—only the Spanish took most of food from the bowl.[18] Don Gaspar's hopes for the union—protection from his enemies, heightened status, comfortable lives for his children—did not come to pass.[19] Successful as they were in training the *presidio* in the duties of a munificent paramount, Don Gaspar and his contemporaries could not wall off the dangers of colonialism. The collapse of their fortunes was staggering. Don Gaspar and the town of San Sebastián vanished from the records by the mid-1610s, victims most likely of the scourges of disease and overwork.[20] They were not alone. Death took its toll from Guales and, especially, the Timucuas throughout the early seventeenth century, remaking internal Native politics, and obliging Spaniards to look farther afield for Native vassals.[21]

And so, in the middle of July 1608, Fray Martín Prieto walked in his worn sandals and rough gray robe into the plaza of the town of Ivitachuco, the greatest of all the towns in the land of Apalachee. Even in their quest to grow the republic of Indians, the Spaniards depended entirely upon Indigenous people, in this case the Timucua leaders who brokered the deal while Prieto looked on.[22] A delegation of 150 people from Potano and Timucua brought the friar along on their mission of peace to their Apalachee enemies. In the town's plaza, the Timucuan party met a gathering of "seventy caciques" and their people, who, according to Prieto's likely exaggerated account, numbered as high as "thirty thousand," all eager, so he thought, to become vassals of King Felipe III.[23] The decision the Apalachee *caciques* made was momentous, but what they sought were allies and Spanish goods to strengthen their own positions. Florida's survival, no less than Virginia's, still depended on winning Indigenous support. Hence the displays by Namontack at the English court and the fears they aroused in Spaniards like Ambassador Zuñiga.

That October, Namontack's lord gave in to the impertinence of the *tassantasses*, as the Powhatans called the "strangers" from England, and agreed to host them at his capital, Werowocomoco, on the York River. He had refused a summons to Jamestown. The English planned to make Wahunsenacawh, the *mamanatowick* of Tsenacomacoh, whom the English sometimes called a "cacique," and who most people today know as Powhatan, a vassal of King James I.[24] For the leaders of the Virginia *presidio*, the visit was a test of their strategy to win the allegiance of the country's "natural lord." But instead of finding a loyal *cacique* in the mold of Don Gaspar Marqués, the English at Werowocomoco came face-to-face with a king who would have them for vassals.

Natural Lords

The two great events of 1608—the Timucuan-led embassy to Ivitachuco and Wahunsenacawh's reception of the English at Werowocomoco—happening as they did almost simultaneously, offer a starting point for comparing the processes that gave rise to hybrid polities in Florida and Virginia during the next half-century. Before joining the story of the South's politics during the seventeenth century, we must briefly account for its roots in the history of the preceding era. The paths that the players—Indigenous, Spanish, and English—took to the meetings at Ivitachuco and Werowocomoco were long and winding, but the stage they entered was ancient and of Native construction. The republic of Indians rested on a venerable political tradition established over centuries by the Indigenous chiefs whom the Spaniards called *señores naturales*, or "natural lords."[25]

The tradition's foundations in the Southeast go back a thousand years to Cahokia, the Indigenous city of some ten thousand people that grew in the American Bottom in the eleventh century.[26] Cahokia's Mississippian culture spread through trade—and sometimes through warfare and colonization—until it penetrated much of the interior Southeast. Far from timeless "prehistoric" utopias, Mississippian polities were ever-changing, and the people in large sites like Etowah in what is now northern Georgia, remade their social arrangements many times over, in "cycles of abandonment and reoccupation" that long antedated European colonization.[27] There were cycles of political and social arrangements, too, sometimes toward more egalitarian forms but generally toward polities with ranking chiefs at their head. The precepts of the rulers of this lost world have partially survived in the accounts of Hernando de Soto's Spanish invasion in the sixteenth century.

The 1540 speech by the female leader or *mica* of Cofitachequi, a polity in modern-day, upcountry South Carolina, welcoming Soto encapsulates Mississippian political ideals and suggests why they proved compatible with late medieval and early modern political theory: "I offer you my person, my lands, my vassals, and this poor service."[28] To the Spaniards listening to her speech, the words were those of a gracious noblewoman in firm command of her estates and people. To the *mica*, the speech was the epitome of her political convictions. The Mississippian way of life entrusted the care of the people and the land into the hands of semi-divine leaders with far-reaching authority. As the bridge between This World and the Sky World, the *mica*'s person was sacred and her rituals brought the rains that nourished the land and the crops.[29] She stood for the community in relations with outsiders, whether friendly or hostile and traded in exotic items, prestige goods, that enhanced her power. Her lands were clearly marked off in the patchwork of polities that made the Ancient South, a "bordered land," where buffer zones separated enemies and the stature of leaders was measured in the number of their tributaries.[30] Tribute flowed upward from the commoners to the nobles of a town, and from lesser towns to the lords of greater polities, in a hierarchy of obligations and duties reminiscent of European feudalism.[31] In exchange for the protection that she provided from outsiders and her intercession with the gods, the *mica*'s "vassals" performed various services at her request. They carried loads from town to town, labored in the communal fields, and moved baskets of earth to build the public works, including the earthen mounds, that still stand as monuments to the Mississippian legacy. But her "vassals" were also her extended kin, bound to the *mica* and her ruling lineage by reciprocal social and political ties.[32] The loyalties they felt toward their kin made Mississippians of all ranks tenacious defenders of their polities and their liberties, "each one of them," as a Spaniard later put it, willing to sacrifice themselves like "Mucio Scévola, the Roman" who calmly burned his own hand rather than betray his country.[33] The bonds of kinship and loyalty were strong. Indeed, it is worth remembering that vassalage developed in early medieval Europe in part as a substitute for reciprocal kinship ties, and this similarity proved of lasting significance to Natives who eventually accepted that condition in European empires.[34]

The peoples who later formed the Southern republics of Indians lived on the edges of the Mississippian world, but their polities shared many of that world's characteristics because in such a world a "polity was constrained to be organized into a chiefdom."[35] As the chiefdoms of the interior transformed after 1600 under the combined pressures of the Indigenous slave trade, the wider distribution of goods, changing norms of exchange, the spread of disease, and the creation of new networks of information, the ranked polities on the fringes of what became the "Mississippian shatter zone" survived.[36] Around the "shatter zone" a crescent of hybrid polities formed, where Spanish and English colonizers alike buttressed the old chiefly forms of politics, accepting tribute, governing through hereditary rulers, and incorporating Indigenous law into their own legal systems.

On those foundations the Spanish established the first republic of Indians in the South after successfully colonizing coastal Florida in 1565. While Hernando de Soto and his army seemed like the roving court of a Mississippian lord, Natives took to calling Florida's latest Adelantado, Pedro Menéndez de Avilés, the "*mico* Santa María," emphasizing the source of his spiritual power and his insistence that they accept *doctrineros* (missionaries)—first Jesuits, then Franciscans—into their towns.[37] The Jesuits penetrated as far north as Ajacán on *Bahía de la Madre de Dios* (Chesapeake Bay), though their mission there was short-lived owing to the resistance of a Powhatan man, Paquiquineo, better known as Don Luis.[38] Establishing bases in San

Agustín and to the north at Santa Elena on modern-day Parris Island in South Carolina, the *mico* Santa María proposed to be an "elder brother," both kinsman and lord to neighboring Indigenous polities, under their mutual father-king in Spain. Assuming the role of the "elder brother," he established a paramount chieftainship of unprecedented size and scope, encompassing multiple other chiefdoms, and used "Spanish governmental and judicial processes" to settle differences among its Native members, many of whom were historic enemies.[39] This "*Pax Hispanica*," really the product of making kin out of enemies in an expanding hybrid polity, endured after Menéndez but routinely broke out in violence against the demands and the constraints the new Spanish paramount imposed.[40] Guale rose twice, in 1576 and again in 1597–1600, only to return to the fold after renegotiating their compact with the Spanish paramount chief.

After a vicious punitive war concluded with the submission of dozens of Guale's *micos*, the melding of Indigenous and Spanish political and legal forms, such as written agreements and petitions, solidified the emergent republic of Indians there. The Guale *micos* who sought pardons after the 1597 revolt excused themselves by saying they did not know where or how to complain against one particularly overbearing friar, and even "if they had said anything, that they would have to be whipped."[41] Indigenous leaders were sending petitions over the Atlantic as early as the 1590s. With the pacification of Guale ongoing, Don Juan, *mico* of San Pedro, a town the rebels attacked for its loyalty to the Spaniards in 1597, petitioned the king to be installed as *mico mayor*—paramount chief under the Crown—of the whole province, a bid that ultimately failed.[42] Tellingly, San Pedro's Catholic *mico* also requested "a good amount of financial assistance in order to provide better gifts to the other *caciques* so that they will come to obey Your Majesty" and in turn to raise his own influence.[43]

Indigenous nobles' letters to the Crown usually contained requests to keep the attentiveness, favor, and largesse flowing to the local nobles within the republic of Indians. Like the *mica* of Cofitachequi sixty years earlier, the chiefs in the republic of Indians desired objects of power. Since 1593, Indigenous nobles received presents of clothes and tools from the fund for *gastos de Indios*, "Indian expenses," part of Florida's royal subsidy.[44] Such gifts solidified their relationship to the Spaniards and had a strong impact on Florida's colonial character. By the early seventeenth century, Natives had, in the words of Joseph M. Hall Jr., thoroughly "reshaped an outpost of empire to resemble a paramount chiefdom" to their political purposes.[45]

The terms of the foundational compact for this polity come through clearly in the agreement Guale *micos* made with Governor Gonzalo Méndez Canzo on 18 May 1600, concluding the 1597 revolt. Many of the same features would later appear in the "articles of peace" that English colonizers signed with Native leaders.[46] After they threw themselves on the ground and kissed the governor's hands, the *micos* agreed to his terms: they would be obedient vassals to the king; they would welcome and succor the infantrymen and friars who would go among them; they would grant safe conduct to Spaniards authorized to travel through their lands; and they would send as many laborers to the *presidio* as the governor should direct. If "some abuse is done to them, they should come and give him account" of it, and the Spanish paramount would punish the offenders.[47]

The Spanish paramount, much as an Indigenous paramount, had responsibilities to visit his people and to see they lived harmoniously with each other and with the Spanish soldiers and friars posted in their towns. Governor Pedro de Ibarra visited the provinces in 1604 "to maintain them all in justice."[48] The new governor showered Native leaders with gifts, bringing "some clothes, iron tools," to these "good Christians."[49] The king, the governor proclaimed, sought nothing but the welfare of their souls with money he spent on Florida.[50] Blending European and Indigenous forms, including the techniques of written law and gift-giving, Spaniards had laid the groundwork for this peculiar kind of paramountcy where Native leaders retained their own jurisdictions and held considerable sway over their aspiring overlords.

The sixteenth-century English *entradas* in the South tried to do the same. In Ossomocomuck (what is now northeastern North Carolina), the commanders of the Roanoke expedition stood witness as the lord of the Weapemeocs swore homage to Elizabeth I, the "great Weronza of England," in 1585 and later they dubbed a faithful ally, Manteo, Lord of Dasemunkepeuc.[51] In spite of the idealism of Sir Walter Raleigh or the carefully drafted ordinances for the soldiers that "no Indian be forced to labor unwillingly," the commanders at Roanoke found it impossible, as Ralph Lane put it, to restrain the "wild men of mine own nation."[52] The English failed at Roanoke in part by acting more like Soto than Menéndez. They ruined beyond repair most of their relationships with local Indigenous peoples. English projectors who planned a settlement in the Chesapeake at the turn of the century evinced a far better grasp of Spain's imperial history and the lessons it offered. That the English who colonized Virginia rummaged through Spanish-American history looking for techniques to conquer and exploit Natives is well known, but their careful knowledge of Spanish imperial governing institutions and techniques for dispensing justice to Native vassals goes mostly unremarked.[53]

On the eve of Jamestown's founding, Englishmen had formulated a working model of the Spanish Empire quite distinct from the Black Legend, a view that took into account the changes in imperial policy during the sixteenth century and one with potential applications for their planned commonwealth in the Chesapeake. The English borrowed from Spanish models of governance and creatively adapted them to novel circumstances on the ground in Virginia and their later colonies. After the Spanish conquests of Mexico and Peru— said Richard Eden, the brazen Hispanophile—Englishmen initially pictured Natives in both kingdoms as "Bondmen and tributaries," that is, as little more than slaves or serfs.[54] But Spanish "bondage," Eden explained, was merely the restraint of the law and therefore better "than their former liberty" that was "rather a horrible licentiousness than a liberty."[55] Nor were Indigenous tributaries legally "Bondmen," in the sense Eden's contemporaries supposed. Sebastian Münster's book on the early history of the Spanish Empire, which Eden translated and published in 1553, explained how Taínos on Española told the Spaniards they preferred to "pay tribute, than to be thus daily vexed with incursions, and never to be at quiet."[56] From writings like Münster's, the English came to view tribute less as an imposition and more as something of a relief to Natives, who as tributaries came under the protection of law.

English travelers in the later sixteenth century saw up close how the law stood as a shield between Natives and Spaniards and these experiences colored their own plans for eastern North America. In the 1560s, Henry Hawks found Mexico City in constant fear of insurrection and flooding, for the Nahuas, he said, "love not the Spaniards."[57] Hawks was convinced that only one thing explained why the city still stood. "The Indians are much favored by the Justices of the Country," he explained, "and they call them their orphans."[58] Whatever the offense, the Native vassal "holdeth his peace, until he finds an opportunity, and then taketh a neighbor with him, and goeth to Mexico, although it be 20 leagues off, and maketh his complaint. This his complaint is immediately heard, and although it be a knight, or a right good gentleman, he," the offending Spaniard, "is forthwith sent for, and punished both by his goods, and also his person is imprisoned, at the pleasure of the Justice," wrote Hawks.[59] "This is the occasion that the Indians are so tame and civil, as they are."[60] Under royal protection, after the emperor Charles V proclaimed them "free and out of bondage," Natives prospered, or so Hawks and his contemporaries believed.[61] Of Peru in the 1590s, John Ellis reported that "Lords or *Caciques* of the Naturals" on the route between "*Cusco* and *Potosi*" would "entertain you in the way, feed you in Silver vessel, and give you very good lodging, and if they like you, they will guide you with three or four hundred Indians."[62] Whatever their basis in reality, these impressions of the Spanish empire and of the republic of Indians proved influential on the minds of some leading lights of the Virginia Company. Figures ranging from John Smith to William Strachey to the younger Richard Hakluyt, had Spain's empire in mind as they contemplated their plans for a future English American empire. If the eighteenth-century British Empire was, as David Armitage argues, "Protestant, commercial, maritime, and free," the empire the English aspired to establish in the seventeenth century was "evangelizing, tributary, territorial, and, just"—at least by early modern European standards.[63]

By the time they arrived in the town squares of Ivitachuco and Werowocomoco, then, Spaniards and Englishmen could draw from a common stock of colonial precedents and held similar ideas about the obligations between empires and Indians. The societies of the Indigenous peoples they sought to colonize had key elements in common and important differences, too. The Apalachees in western Florida were the closest of the two peoples to Mississippian culture, while the Powhatans lived on its fringes. The Apalachees' ancestors built platform mounds near the Lake Jackson site above Tallahassee and well into the seventeenth century Apalachee towns had a strong chiefly class.[64] At the start of the century, the land of Apalachee was a patchwork of numerous towns, more or less autonomous. Some Apalachee towns were more influential than others, notably Ivitachuco and Inhayca, and the two towns, the former on the border with Timucua, strove to control relations with the Spaniards in the early days.[65] Perhaps they were acting as a bulwark at first against the intruders, but other towns eventually resented their preeminence in external affairs. In what is now Tidewater Virginia, the Powhatans were at first glance more centralized. Wahunsenacawh, who began his life as leader of the Pamunkeys, was gathering together a multiethnic chiefdom starting in the mid-sixteenth century in part to stave off external enemies.[66] In time, his domain of Tsenacomacoh would embrace some thirty individual polities and twenty thousand people, who paid tribute to him as *mamanatowick*, the paramount chief whose office was sacred.[67] Wahunsenacawh nevertheless was no absolute lord even if he did command some coercive power.[68] As often, he held his polity together by wheedling and cajoling and threatening much as would any other political leader. Nor was every nation within Tsenacomacoh pleased with his rise to power—none less so than the tenaciously

independent "coarse-pounded corn people," the Chickahominies—and the
discontented made common cause with the English for a time.[69] Varying
in language, culture, and political organization, Apalachees and Powhatans
nevertheless were both maize agriculturalists, lived in ranked societies with
hereditary leaders of varying authority, and possessed a cohesive sense of
identity, however diverse and fractious their politics could sometimes be.[70]
And to both of these Indigenous societies, Europeans were outsiders who
could be managed—in the case of Apalachee, distant and somewhat unim-
portant ones—at least at the beginning.[71]

Making Indigenous Vassals in Florida and Virginia

The long political history of the South and its political culture since Mississippian times informed Spanish and English colonizers as they pursued
the same objective on their missions to Ivitachuco and Werowocomoco in
1608—to make vassals and subjects out of Indigenous peoples. They came
to their tasks with a great deal of knowledge, even if little of it helped them
to understand their true situations as players in a larger Indigenous drama.
Both had learned from the lessons of the Iberian conquest in the Americas,
and both of them drew (in the English case, selectively) on the philosophy
that had curbed the excesses of the conquest era and reformed the Spanish
empire into an empire of law by the mid-sixteenth century.[72] At the outset,
they disclaimed violence—if only in principle rather than practice—and,
instead, sought to make Natives into vassals and converts by means of trade,
gifts, persuasion, and displays of spiritual power. The tactics of Franciscan
friars and of Jamestown's soldier-adventurers pursued one aim: winning
the support of the Indigenous leadership class, the country's "natural lords,"
whose consent was the surest legitimate basis for empire in the seventeenth
century.

In Florida, the work of making vassals went forward, as the Franciscan
friars Francisco Pareja and Alonso de Peñaranda wrote, "by means of poor
little friars (who go on foot through swamps and water up to their belts, bare-
foot and wounded)," so that "God Our Lord gives so many souls into his
Church."[73] Martín Prieto was one of those servants of God, although by no
means was he meek. In 1605, three years before his mission to the Apalachee
town of Ivitachuco, Prieto escaped the cloistered life of a monastery in Spain
and sailed for Florida.[74] Prieto was part of a massive spiritual and political

offensive that increased the number of friars in Florida almost tenfold in the early seventeenth century.[75] On reaching San Agustín, Prieto entered the vanguard of the missionary campaign in Potano, a land of Timucua-speaking towns west of San Agustín.

Political life for the Timucuas, as it did for the Apalachees, took place in towns. Above that level, Timucuan people gathered in "simple" chiefdoms, usually comprising around six towns.[76] The leaders of towns dictated the pace of conversion and dogged chiefs could make the friars' lives miserable.[77] Alone in his first posting in the new *doctrina* (missionary outpost with a church and resident friar) of San Miguel de Potano, Fray Martín lived on a diet of corn gruel, and led the teaching of the catechism by himself since there was no one else who "knew anything about it."[78] His pushiness with the town's old *holata* (chief) earned him the ribbing that decent Indigenous townspeople gave to anyone who flouted the standards of good conduct. The *holata* was just a boy when Hernando de Soto swept through the country and took him prisoner. He would never be a Christian, he said, because "he suffered a great deal" at their hands.[79] The priests of the ancient religion warned the friar off. He did not listen.

Martín Prieto was stubborn, proud, and a touch vainglorious, hardly one of the "poor little friars" of Franciscan propaganda. One day, he marched straight for the chief's house. The violation disgusted the old man. His attendants dragged Fray Martín out of the *holata*'s house while he recited the rudiments of the faith. Then, all of a sudden, the wind rose until it howled through the town. Thunder shook the roof of the chief's house. The people in terror "fell to the ground."[80] When the storm blew over and the clouds broke, only the mission church and the cross next to the plaza still stood. The fear of the Lord struck Santa Ana de Potano. (Or so Prieto said.) "I baptized there four hundred persons, including children and adults," he later recounted.[81] Another four hundred followed in San Miguel and San Francisco. In San Martín, a little boy on the verge of death accepted baptism and spoke miraculously: "Do not cry for me, rather sing, because I am the first one of this village who is going to see God and find peace. Cry for the unfortunate people who died without seeing this moment and are now suffering" in Hell.[82]

Although seeking the same end, the contrast between Prieto's attitudes and English thinking at the time is striking. Englishmen gave up believing such tales as Prieto's long ago—or so *they* said. It was folly "for preachers to run unto them rashly without some such preparation for their safety," said Richard Hakluyt, for "that were nothing else but to run to their apparent and

certain destruction, as it happened unto those Spanish friars that before any
planting without strength and company landed in Florida, where they were
miserably massacred by the Savages."[83] The adventurers of the Virginia Company were even blunter when they published their guiding principles a few
years later. The "wonders from heaven" that one could read about in Spanish
missionaries' accounts were all rubbish. It was impossible "to preach Apostolically," since the "commission of the Apostles is expired."[84]

Events in 1608, however, seemed in Spanish eyes to vindicate Fray Martín
Prieto's faith in miracles. When the *gran cacique* of Timucua, purportedly
the lord of twenty towns, told Prieto of the troubles he had with his vassals
and their war with Apalachee, the friar vowed to go and negotiate an end
to the conflict. He misunderstood the invitation. To the Indigenous leaders,
Prieto was to be a witness and a living connection to San Agustín, the source
of goods and prestige they were hoping to tap as part of a larger alliance.
The *cacique* sent runners ahead to Ivitachuco to prepare for the real negotiations. Women swept the roads clean. The council of *caciques* sat for days and
brokered a peace between the Apalachees and Timucuas. The council then
named the *cacique* of Inhayca, as envoy to the *presidio* at San Agustín, where
he would swear allegiance to the king of Spain. Soldiers stopped the party on
the road, escorting the honored guest into the city. Governor Pedro de Ibarra
would finish the work, Prieto fumed, and "claim the reward for which he had
not labored."[85]

The friar in his zeal refused to see the reality. The Franciscan was merely
the vessel for what the assembled lords of Apalachee and Timucua really
wanted and only the governor could provide. The English were right. The
days of preaching apostolically were over. So were the days of dramatic conquests, whether by the sword or with the catechism. The reform of the Spanish Empire in the sixteenth century transformed the process of colonization
everywhere. By the time Prieto started haranguing and bullying his way
around Potano, the governor, with his garrison, and with the gifts for *caciques*
from the royal fund set aside for "Indian expenses," had cleared the fields of
the Lord for the friars. Prieto seems never to have understood this, though
some of his brethren did. Fray Martín salved his pride with the assurance that
God would not leave his servant's deeds unnoticed. "But we are poor Franciscan friars," he sighed, "who only hope for reward in heaven."[86]

English colonial projectors understood the shift in Spanish imperial strategy that had taken place better than Prieto. Voracious consumers of Spanish imperial history, many of the Virginia Company's promoters embraced

Spain's hard-won lessons of the previous century about how to win the allegiance of Native vassals. The pacification and conversion of Tsenacomacoh would go forward "mixtly," they said, "by discovery, and trade of merchants; where all temporal means are used for defense, and security, but none for offense, or cruelty."[87] Conversion would come in time, they argued. To Werowocomoco in October 1608 the English carried gifts for the Great Powhatan and put their theory into practice. But there was nothing the English could bring, least of all the copper crown in Christopher Newport's care, to make a vassal out of Wahunsenacawh, *mamanatowick* of the Powhatans.

The town where the ceremony took place had been a sacred center for at least four hundred years before the English arrived. And for Wahunsenacawh, his residence in Werowocomoco was the fulfillment of prophecy. From the "hill of divination," the town of Powhatan on the Falls of the James River where his powers first met acclaim, Wahunsenacawh took up residence as *mamanatowick* in Werowocomoco, "place of the antler-wearers," antlers being symbols of sacred power.[88] Werowocomoco's architecture, its very layout, expressed Powhatan ideals about the proper relationship between the *mamanatowick* and his subjects. From the banks of the river, the English delegation would have passed through houses and on up the hill to another clearing, then crossed a series of trenches and berms, before reaching the *mamanatowick*'s residence, itself a maze of corridors and rooms.[89] The built environment mirrored the way Powhatans conceived of the status and relationships of the peoples within Tsenacomacoh. In a ceremony about a year earlier, Pamunkey priests ritually inducted John Smith into the sacred part of his duties as a *weroance* of Tsenacomacoh. The most important element of the ceremony was the ritual fire, representing the center of Powhatan life, surrounded by concentric rings of refined cornmeal, corn kernels, and sticks.[90] The ritual elements together comprised a cosmogram—a compact representation of the universe—mapping where people fit, from the most refined inner circle of civilized peoples at the core of the Wahunsenacawh's polity, outward all the way to the rough newcomers, the English, living symbolically on the outskirts.[91] Walking through Werowocomoco toward the center place was like walking through a larger version of this model of the universe. No one in Christopher Newport's party seems to have understood the symbolism and that every step into the town was supposed to take them closer to their own subjection, not Wahunsenacawh's.

For Wahunsenacawh's English visitors, the tension that day made Werowocomoco feel as if it might end up as their Cajamarca, the plaza where

Francisco Pizarro and his men first met and fought the Inca Atahualpa in 1532. The crowd milled about ill at ease. The matches of their guns smoked in readiness for the volley that would salute Wahunsenacawh after his coronation. The head that was to wear the copper crown was gray, long hairs dangling to the shoulders, framing a round face, plump but worn from "many cold stormy winters."[92] Over his long life, he had known wars and he had cherished the times of peace. "I have seen the death of all my people thrice," he once told John Smith, "and not one living of those 3 generations, but myself, I know the difference of peace and war, better than any in my Country."[93] There were grins from the crowd, a few chuckles perhaps when Wahunsenacawh refused to kneel. John Smith, who was there, thought Wahunsenacawh did not understand "the majesty, nor meaning of a Crown, nor bending of the knee, [and] endured so many persuasions, examples, and instructions, as tired" everyone until he grudgingly accepted.[94] When a pistol shot signaled the beginning of a musketry salute, the old man jumped, but soon recovered, "remembering himself."[95] The volley rang out from the barges in the river below, a salute to King James's greatest Native vassal. The transaction complete, the *mamanatowick* or paramount chief of Tsenacomacoh, natural lord of the country, had joined his dominions with the realm of England, or so the English thought.

The precedents and comparisons for Wahunsenacawh's coronation are various: English, Anglo-Irish, but above all, Spanish.[96] Indeed, in Florida, *caciques* regularly visited the *presidio*, received gifts, and paid homage as vassals to the king, reinforcing and expanding the republic of Indians. Wahunsenacawh, however, still expected to incorporate the English as subordinates within *his* empire and was under no illusions about what it meant to bend the knee. He proceeded to give the English their first full lesson on the meaning of Indigenous sovereignty. "If your king have sent me presents, I am also a king, and this my land," he said.[97] John Smith, who recorded Wahunsenacawh's speech, had a habit of borrowing from Spanish sources.[98] What the *mamanatowick* said echoed what the *holata* of the Timucua town of Acuera in Florida said when Hernando de Soto asked him to kneel and become a vassal of Charles V: "To what they said about giving obedience to the king of Spain, he replied that he himself was king in his own country and there was no necessity for becoming the vassal of another who had as many as he."[99] The Apalachees who welcomed Fray Martín Prieto and his Timucuan masters must have felt the same way about their sovereignty and they were in a better position to keep it that way.

Unluckily for Wahunsenacawh, the Powhatans did not have the luxury of distance from the English *presidio* that the Apalachees enjoyed from the Spanish. While the *caciques* of Inhayca and Ivitachuco garnered the prestige and power that came with gifts from San Agustín, they knew the Spaniards were up to a hundred leagues away through Timucua country. Wahunsenacawh used the gifts he received to shore up his authority so he could withstand the trials to come from the all-too-near English. One report a year or so later said Wahunsenacawh wore the copper crown in a ceremony for blessing his corn fields while showering gifts of fine beads on those he favored—a confirmation of his authority, not James I's.[100] In time, Wahunsenacawh received more presents from Jamestown: bedsteads, basins, pitchers, even a cat. To the Powhatan people who witnessed the boats that carried them to Werowocomoco, the piles of exotic goods looked like tribute from his English vassals.[101] For now, as the crown rested uneasily on his head, he handed over his old mantle and shoes to Christopher Newport. But he would never yield up his sovereign rights in exchange. Wahunsenacawh was a king. The Virginia Company would soon brand him a tyrant, shifting the Jamestown *presidio*'s strategy and taking it on another path, and one that, once again, was well-worn in Florida.

From Tyrant to Tributary

Wahunsenacawh's resounding refusal took little time traveling across the Atlantic. After Wahunsenacawh's surly response that he was a king, Richard Hakluyt the younger warned the English public of the sophistication and craftiness of Native leaders, finding examples in Florida's history.[102] True, the Indigenous peoples of Florida—"the richest Country in the world"— possessed "great valor and resolution," as Hakluyt explained in in his translation of the Gentleman of Elvas's account of Hernando de Soto's expedition. And the masterful address of one *cacique*, wrote Hakluyt, had so impressed his Spanish audience that one witness concluded "that no Orator could utter the same more eloquently."[103] The *caciques*' "fair and cunning speeches," Hakluyt warned, masked hearts ever ready to commit "bloody treasons" as the Spanish accounts "do evidently prove."[104] Signaling a turn from the peaceful intentions of the Viriginia Company touted, the Anglican parson warned that it was likely time to use force on the Powhatans, to mold them into shape, "to square and prepare them to our Preachers hands."[105] Rather than govern through the paramount chief, the English thereafter resolved to undermine Wahunsenacawh's "tyrannous" rule. The Virginia Company took Hakluyt's advice to heart and began the turn toward making the Powhatans into tributaries.

Florida's governors had done this, raising a corn tribute from Indian vassals until the end of the sixteenth century, and drafting laborers to support the *presidio* thereafter. Critics in Florida said the only reason the governor there imposed the corn tribute was to impress Natives inland with the size and strength of the combined Spanish-Indigenous polity since they "judge others according to the level of tribute" that a chief levied.[106] But a tribute's uses were more than symbolic. Although the prospect of Powhatan tributaries feeding Jamestown seems to be another far-fetched colonial scheme today—at least, when we judge the plan against the Mexican and Peruvian models said to have inspired it—Spanish Florida's success in harnessing tribute and labor from similar Native societies shows how serious the proposals were. Tribute was a viable option for supporting a colony in the South if Europeans could persuade Indigenous lords to yield it. There was the trouble. Most Native chiefs thought tribute should flow their way. The political implications of tribute were just as important—probably more important—than its practical uses.

The English desperately needed to get the tribute moving in the right direction, namely from Werowocomoco to Jamestown. For Spaniards, Indigenous peoples, and the English alike, tribute was a way of ranking political leaders and polities from superior to dependent. Those who paid tribute expected protection in the bargain. In European minds, protection was often a limited obligation to defend tributaries from attack or see justice done when a colonist injured a Native. To Natives, however, protection meant more than defense from human enemies but also from drought, withered crops, hunger, and plague. For them, the tribute they sent to a *weroance* or *mico* was a hedge against disasters, human-made and supernatural. Then, the tributary relationship had even subtler shades of meaning.

That tribute ran upward on an imaginary incline from the barbarous payers to the civil collectors is one of the unspoken assumptions that both colonizers and Natives made. Ironically, one consequence of the tributary gradient was that tribute became a way for Natives under colonial rule to hold onto their cultures and a measure of self-government. Once they paid, tributaries expected colonizers to leave them alone, free to obey their own laws and lords. Still, tribute could serve a disciplinary purpose, teaching tributaries obedience to new masters and offering those masters a way to show their beneficence by lowering or even dispensing with their vassals' obligations to pay. Wahunsenacawh's offer to John Smith that he pay tribute to him was as much about training subjects in proper behavior as the Virginia Company's plan to turn the Powhatans into tributaries was. With such an adaptable political weapon, Virginia sought either to overmaster Wahunsenacawh, turning the tyrant into a tributary, or overthrow him and take his kingdom by enticing his subordinate *weroances* to pay tribute to Jamestown.

Imposing tribute on the Powhatans was never far from the minds of the English adventurers, steeped as they were in the lore of the Spanish conquest. John Smith had already done so on his own initiative during his presidency of the colony in 1607–1608. Smith punished the "insolencies" of people like the Chickahominies, and forced them "with presents to purchase peace."[107] Instead of furrowing their brows in disapproval, Smith said his critics back in England ought to "peruse the Spanish Decades, the relations of Master Hakluyt, and tell me how many ever with such small means . . . did ever . . . subject so many several kings, people, and nations, to obedience, and contribution with so little bloodshed."[108] In early modern English, "contribution" meant to pay tribute. To the company's minds, imposing a regular tribute would ease the Powhatans' burdens, relieving them of the irregular and violent exactions of captains like Smith. Michael Lok's 1612 translation of Peter Martyr, appearing at the height of English tributary fantasies, noted how the Spanish monarchs decreed that the Taínos "should be used like tributary subjects, and ditionaries, and not in a servile manner."[109] Yet, calling Natives "ditionaries" still implied subservience—*in dicione*, that is, living at a conqueror's "absolute discretion."[110] Obedience to the English, the company said, would be freedom for the Powhatans.

In May, Virginia's governor, Sir Thomas Gates, sailed with instructions either to capture Wahunsenacawh or "make him your tributary" as well as "all other his weroances about him."[111] For the English, the term *tributary* smacked more of the older idea of a vassal as a pledged lord. Tributaries were the leaders of subordinate polities and tribute itself was a collective obligation, even though it was the responsibility of a Native lord to see it paid. Imagining a ceremony like the ones held every time a new governor arrived in San Agustín, the Virginia Company's instructions said that Indigenous leaders must come into Jamestown and "first acknowledge no other Lord but King James."[112] Thereby "we shall free them all from the Tyranny of Powhatan."[113] After swearing allegiance to the king, all the *weroances* and *weroansquas* would pay their tribute on a scale according to their "greatness of Territory and men."[114] Soon, the *presidio* at Jamestown would "quietly draw to your selves an annual revenue of every Commodity growing in that Country."[115] On the backs of Powhatan burdeners filing into the fort would come "so many measures of Corn at every Harvest," dyestuffs, animal pelts, and, most ambitious of all, the instructions demanded a quota of each *weroance*'s "people to work weekly," a ramped-up English version of the Spanish *repartimiento* labor draft.[116] Skins and hides, specifically beaver pelts, along with a trade in enslaved Indians of enemy nations, eventually became the tribute the Natives of the Tidewater paid beginning at midcentury. But Florida's experience makes the Virginia Company's plans for collecting tribute in foodstuffs appear feasible.

Until 1598, every married man in Florida's Native provinces owed an *arroba* of maize—about twenty-five pounds—annually to Florida's governor.[117] That year, Governor Gonzalo Méndez Canzo inspected the provinces and the "poverty and misery" he found there moved him to reduce the province's tribute to a token of obedience: "only six ears" of maize per married man.[118] Unlike the English notion of a tributary, Spanish Indigenous vassals had individual responsibilities, including tribute payments. By the turn of the century, the primary tribute Native vassals paid the Spaniards was in the form of *repartimiento* labor at the *presidio*. Burdensome as it was, the work was not by the week as the English envisioned it, but for a few weeks—though longer as the century wore on—each year.

Commoners in Florida still owed tribute and labor to their chiefs and throughout the century there were periodic complaints about chiefs levying excessive tributes on their vassals. The complaints usually reached San Agustín from a town's resident friar, who posed as the keeper the *cacique*'s conscience. In the 1613 Timucuan *Confessionario* that Fray Francisco Pareja compiled with the help of Timucua informants, priests found a handy set of questions to ask about how well their noble penitents observed the tenth commandment against covetousness. Prominent on the list: "Have you taken more tribute or something else from your vassals more than what you used to lay upon them or to take?"[119] In fact, the friars saw to it that labor was not abused by *caciques* so that it could be better exploited by themselves and the *presidio*.

Indigenous lordship had its limits in Virginia, too, and the English singled out the same "tyrannous" excesses as the Franciscans, when they discussed a future of tribute-paying Powhatans. When the *weroances* and *weroansquas* of Tsenacomacoh were tributaries to Jamestown, "you shall deliver them from the exactions of Powhatan."[120] One Virginia official estimated that "they pay eight parts of ten tribute of all the commodities which their country yieldeth" to the *mamanatowick*.[121] The fact that Wahunsenacawh redistributed what he collected, handing it out to the needy and deserving did not register in English propaganda. For years, it suited the Virginia Company to call Wahunsenacawh a tyrant. "It is strange to see with what great fear and adoration all these people do obey this Powhatan," wrote John Smith. "For at his feet they present whatsoever he commandeth, and at the least frown of his brow, their greatest spirits will tremble with fear: and no marvel, for he is very terrible and tyrannous in punishing such as offend him."[122] The Franciscans painted a similar picture of the sinful *cacique* and his wicked *principales* (councilors or headmen). Another question passing from confessor to *cacique* through the screen of the confession box in Pareja's *Confessionario* was whether he had taken his vassals' wages.[123] To lesser Native officials, the friar might ask if, in a fit of anger and for no other reason, they had ever punished a commoner.

Whether the tyranny of Powhatan or the covetousness of a Timucua chief, the myth of Native misrule justified colonial exploitation. Friars and adventurers alike convinced themselves that their rule would be mild by comparison. Natives, especially the lesser lords and the common people, they believed, would surely see the difference. The discipline of paying tribute would instruct them in proper obedience. If Natives did not come with a good will and become subjects and tributaries, if they persisted in their blindness, there was another course. "The country, they say," said the English preacher William Symonds, "is possessed by owners, that rule, and govern it in their own right: then with what conscience, and equity can we offer to thrust them, by violence, out of their inheritance."[124] Lest readers of his printed sermon miss his point, Symonds added a marginal note that made it plain: "Answer. Conquest lawful."[125] But Symonds's argument against a nameless "objector" reveals something else—that not everyone in England was so sure that Powhatan was a tyrant or that conquest was "lawful" after all.

Let the Divines of Salamanca Discuss that Question: English Debates over Native Rights

Even as Wahunsenacawh went from pliant *cacique* to tyrant and, finally, tributary in the Company's propaganda, the change in strategy sparked a debate in England about the Jamestown *presidio*'s strategy with the Powhatans. Not everyone in England approved of the company's new course, which sought to alienate a legitimate Indigenous king from his birthright and by force if necessary. Because the Virginia Company's defenders started with assumptions about "just" colonialism that were, in fact, conclusions that took Spain decades to reach, the debate over Indigenous rights in England hardly registers in most histories.[126] Moreover, the opposition comes through the historical record largely as an echo in company propaganda. The colony's detractors were the "filthy," the "vulgar," the "scum and dregs of the people."[127] These nameless objectors were persistent, for the company's preachers and pamphleteers frequently tried to refute them. These often-unnamed opponents, echoing the Spanish Dominican Bartolomé de las Casas, questioned by what right the English could force the Powhatans into submission.

Unfavorable opinion back in England was strong enough that sometimes it checked even Captain John Smith, the would-be conquistador. The Powhatans became "so insolent," Smith later wrote, because "the command from England was so straight not to offend them as our authority bearers (keeping their houses) would rather be anything than peace breakers."[128] To his companions in arms in a fight with the Pamunkey *weroance* Opechancanough, Smith affirmed that "our malicious council with their open mouthed minions, will make me such a peacebreaker (in their opinions) in England, as will break my neck."[129] Of himself in those hard early days, Smith wrote tellingly: "The Spaniard never more greedily desired gold than he victual."[130]

Victual must not become for Virginia what gold had been to the Spaniards in the pages of Bartolomé de Las Casas. "Let no man adore his gold as his God, nor his Mammon as his Maker," the Company proclaimed in 1610.[131] Nor would the English permit a bloody conquest only to "set their souls at liberty, when we have brought their bodies to slavery." "Let the divines of *Salamanca*, discuss that question," they sneered, "how the possessor of the west Indies, first destroyed, and then instructed."[132] No, Virginia must stick by the "mixt course," the policy of the *presidio*. By no means was it "unlawful, that we possess part of their land, and dwell with them, and defend ourselves from them," the company said, "Partly because there is no other, moderate, and mixt course, to bring them to conversion, but by daily conversation, where they may see the life, and learn the language of the other."[133] To elevate such "daily conversation," Virginia must have laws published so that "every common eye may take survey of their duties."[134]

In response to the misdeeds of Smith and other malefactors in Virginia, the company empowered Sir Thomas Gates and Sir Thomas Dale to impose martial law. The law code they issued reads like an English version of Felipe II's *Ordenanzas* of 1573, the great reforms of Spanish colonizing procedure. William Strachey, who studied law at Gray's Inn, prepared the code for publication back in England as *Lawes Divine, Moral and Martial*, no doubt to reassure Virginia's critics.[135] "Dale's Laws" prohibited offenses against the persons and property of Natives "upon pain of death."[136] Not only did Dale's laws aim to protect Native goods, homes, and bodies, but they even forbade pillaging any Powhatan "temple."[137] With just laws and upright lives to guide them, it was only a matter of time before the Powhatans exclaimed: "Blessed be the King and Prince of England, and blessed be the English nation, and blessed forever be the most high God, possessor of heaven and earth, that sent them amongst us."[138] The English would have a long time to wait. The reason is clear when we look south to Florida during the same time.

In San Agustín, the "mixt" course seemed to be working and Natives were eager to maintain their relationship with the *presidio* because tribute or gifts (call it what you will) flowed in the right direction—into the hands of *caciques*. In the Lenten season of 1609, "the Great *Cacique* of the province of Timucua" arrived with his heir and fifty men seeking, he said, the "water of baptism."[139] On Palm Sunday, Governor Pedro de Ibarra stood as "godfather of the great *cacique* and his heir" (thereafter known as Don Pedro and Don Sebastián), in Florida's oldest mission church, Nombre de Dios, while Fray Alonso Serrano baptized the whole Timucua delegation. Standing as godfathers to the rest were the officers of the Florida garrison. The *cacique* and his heir lingered to witness the processions and pageantry of Holy Week in the city and feasted at the governor's table.[140] On the king's account, the Timucua nobles were clothed but the governor also "gave them other garments from his house" before sending them on the journey homeward with a friar and "all the means that were needed to found there a new *doctrina*."[141] The *cacique*, wearing a cross round his neck, a gift from the governor, departed with his company, "all of them grateful for the will with which they were given presents."[142] The gifts enhanced their prestige, while baptism—setting aside its religious meanings—solidified fictive kinship relations with the governor, their titular paramount chief. From leaders regaled in San Agustín, other Natives in the interior, including the "cacique of Apalachee," would learn of the liberality of the Spanish paramount and come to pledge obedience too.[143]

Despite their words, Virginia's colonial leaders failed to perform the deeds to win the like cooperation from leaders in Tsenacomacoh. The stinginess of the English drove Wahunsenacawh to take what he wanted by stealth. The rumor at Jamestown was that Wahunsenacawh had amassed a king's ransom in tools and weapons and "an infinite treasure of copper," either secreted into his storehouses or taken from the bodies of slain *tassantasses*. When two messengers from "the great *weroance*, the lord governor," Sir Thomas Gates, confronted Wahunsenacawh they reminded him of the ceremony that took place outside his very doors in 1608, making him a vassal of King James. How dare the messengers lecture him about duties, he replied, when the *tassantasses* had failed in all of theirs. They might have lived in peace at Capahosic, he said, the place near Werowocomoco that he once promised to John Smith, sending him tribute in the very goods they now denied him. "You should depart his country," he said, "or confine yourselves to James Town only." Do not come back to me again, he added, unless you bring me "a coach and three horses, for he had understood by the Indians which were in England how such was the state of great werowances and lords in England to ride and visit other great men."[144] The English neither won his support nor had they won the allegiance of his people. Instead, the colony stumbled into full-scale war. Florida and Virginia were soon mirror images of one another—the one dependent on Native consent to grow, the other only able to expand without it.

The Colonial Mirror, 1612

By 1612, the challenges in Florida and Virginia were acute. Pausing on that difficult, if unheralded year, is important. Each colony's predicament was, in effect, a mirror image of the other's.[145] Florida was, at heart, a small military base with a string of outlying missions in the surrounding country manned by lone friars, a place unappealing to Spanish colonists, and totally dependent on the good will of Indigenous peoples for corn, muscle power, and knowledge of the interior. Virginia, meanwhile, was a budding settler colony with a growing population, but locked in a war with the Powhatans whose loyalty, or at least acquiescence, the colony could not earn. To escape the trap, Spaniards and Englishmen each promoted strategies we now think to be characteristic of the other. Florida's Franciscans urged settlement with sturdy, honest *pobladores* (planters), while the Virginia Company's penmen urged Spanish models of imperial governance that would shield Natives from grasping settlers. Yet, the cause of all the colonizers' difficulties were the actions—or rather inaction—of Indigenous leaders. In these colonies, little could be done peacefully without their consent.

Four years after Fray Martín Prieto's embassy to Ivitachuco, the Franciscans of Florida camped "on the frontier" of Apalachee but dared not enter. They hovered along the border "to learn and to know that Language," readying themselves against the day when they could at last cross over.[146] The friars assured King Felipe III in 1612 that the moment was not far off. Veterans of eighteen or twenty years, men who had spent their youth "reclaiming and taming Indians with so little hope of seeing this" moment, whose patient instruction of the Natives only "seemed to turn them to hate and abhorrence," men whose brothers gained the crown of martyrdom while they grew old in God's service, these men were now confident that the "hour of God" had arrived.[147] What held them at the border, they said, were the commands of the governor in San Agustín, Juan Fernández de Olivera.

Despite the continued success of the *presidio*'s basic strategy, Governor Olivera confessed that the task before him was more than San Agustín's overtaxed garrison could bear. "I have left off of naming some [missions] in Apalachee and other faraway parts that they have asked me for them," he said, fearing "some disorder" that might result if he did so without providing military protection.[148] The friars did not think soldiers useful for mending anything. The way the governor entertained them with food and clothes and spectacles and sent them home again "to be criers of his grand friendship" to all the peoples of the interior country—that was the best course with Native peoples.[149] "Everything that he gives them in peace," the friars explained, "is nothing in comparison to what would have to be spent on wars with them (more would have to be spent just on matches for the harquebuses) besides which war is of no effect with them, because they do not have in their towns buildings nor estates to lose."[150]

In the compounds on the banks of the James River in Virginia, where the colonists lived under a rigid martial regime and in dread of the Powhatans, the lesson was not lost either. "Weapons of war are needful, I grant," Robert Johnson, lectured them from London, that same year, "but for defense only, and not in this case. If you seek to gain this victory upon them by stratagems of war, you shall utterly lose it, and never come near it, but shall make your names odious to all their posterity. Instead of iron and steel you must have patience and humanity to manage their crooked nature to your form of civility."[151] Johnson's tune had changed. He once likened the Powhatans to "herds of Deer in a Forest."[152] Now, in that very same year, so did the Franciscans in Florida as they urged the king to see the futility of sending soldiers to do the work of priests. Free and in a "country wooded," in a war the Natives "would have done more damage to us than we to them," the friars said, and "besides which they are like Deer [*Venados*], they could have killed the people on all the paths."[153]

Neither Powhatans nor Apalachees were anything of the sort. They farmed, lived in towns, and followed leaders. In the Powhatan case, they exceeded early modern European expectations. "Although the country people be very barbarous, yet have they amongst them such government," said John Smith that year, "as that their Magistrates for good commanding, and their people for due subjection, and obeying, excel many places that would be counted very civil."[154] In Tsenacomacoh, there was a "rude kind of Commonwealth, and rough government," wrote Alexander Whitaker, and everyone followed the commandments of "their Kings, Parents, and Governors, both greater and less."[155]

But leaders could be quite responsive to the demands of their followers. In fact, what stalled the friars' hopes in Apalachee was not the governor's command but the will of Apalachee's common people. Some Apalachee leaders were ready to admit the missionaries and accept Spanish largesse and aid but "some of their Indians obey their caciques poorly."[156] In other words, the majority of the people were against the friars, their religion, and what it would mean for them: more work and less control over their own lives. "The caciques would like, with the favor and protection of Your Majesty," the friars said, "to subject their Indians."[157] The Virginia Company's problem was just the opposite. Four years after the ceremony at Werowocomoco, where the English still boasted that Wahunsenacawh made "a full acknowledgement of duty and submission," a true accord between the country's natural lords and the colonizing elite did not exist.[158] Spanish intelligence had it that the English could not venture outside their forts because of the "warlike" Indians who "pursue them continually."[159]

The Virginia Company blamed the war that erupted in 1609–1610 on "irregular persons": disorderly colonists and soldiers playacting as conquistadors. As the men in command at Jamestown "did nothing but bitterly contend who should be first to command the rest, the common sort, as is ever seen in such cases, grew factious and disordered out of measure," and "the poor Indians by wrongs and injuries were made our enemies."[160] Don Alonso de Velasco, the new Spanish ambassador in London, thought that the only option left for Virginia was to send more (and presumably better-managed) colonists. "It does not appear that they will be able to maintain themselves," he said, "unless they bring over so large a number of people that they can make themselves Lords of the Country, as the Indians now are."[161] Velasco could have said the same about Florida.

Even the friars in Florida thought it was long overdue for Spain to send out "pobladores," or planters to strengthen Spain's hold on the land and on the Natives. Friendly *caciques*, they claimed, "are desiring that Your Majesty send planters to their land so they can teach themselves how to farm and the rest of the things that are convenient."[162] In the early days of the missions, the Guales had attacked "the cattle that we were trying to introduce into the land, killing and extinguishing them as if they were pests," the friars said, "and the same they did to the trees and seeds, attempting not to leave either a Trace nor the smell of us."[163] The very landscape the Natives made and had tried to defend, the friars now praised as the work of nature. The prospects for Florida were as bright as the sun shining through the branches of the "clear forests of oak groves and elm groves, so clear that horses can run under them."[164] There were mulberry trees to raise silk, "good lands for bread," and swift rivers for the mills to grind the flour. In time, and with enough *pobladores*, Florida perhaps would be the breadbasket of the Indies, safe and secure from all enemies—and less dependent on Natives. Other than the closing appeal for the "exaltation of our Holy Catholic Faith," much in the petition from the Franciscans read like a promotional pamphlet from the Virginia Company, extolling the richness of the land.[165]

Curiously, at the same moment, Virginia's promoters dispensed advice that might have come from the Council of the Indies to Florida. The Virginia Company, Robert Johnson wrote, must consider their "threefold labor to be done upon your selves, upon your English, and upon the poor Indians."[166] In dividing up the duties of government between "your English" and the "poor Indians," Johnson echoed the description of the two republics, of Spaniards and Indians, from Pedro Ordonnes de Cevallos, later printed in the work of Samuel Purchas. "There is a two-fold government of Indies," he wrote, "one of *Spaniards*, which is the same with that of *Spain*; the other of *Indians*."[167] To the republic of Englishmen, or the "Colony (the common sort of English)," the Virginia Company "must let them live as free English men, under the government of just and equal laws, and not as slaves after the will and lust of any superior."[168] The republic of Indians, comprising the Powhatans, he said, you must treat as "equal with your English in case of protection wealth and habitation, doing justice on such as shall do them wrong."[169] Johnson closed with a recitation of the Spaniards' accomplishments in the Americas to make the English shrug off their "sluggish contentment." Now was the time "to make good that common speech, that English men are best at imitation, and do soon excel their teachers."[170]

William Strachey had this in mind when he compared the *weroances* of Tsenacomacoh to Andean *curacas* (chiefs). Equating the "Caciques or Commanders of Indian Towns in Peru" with *weroances*, Strachey supported the Company's justifications for tribute.[171] For "although they pay unto the king of Spain great Tribute, yet because they make exchange with the Spaniards for what remains, they do not only keep great Hospitality and are rich in their furniture horses and cattle, but as Captain Ellis vows, who lived amongst them some few years, their diet is served to them in silver vessels, and many of them have natural [native] Spaniards that attend them in their houses."[172] In the same manner, in Tsenacomacoh "the tribute which they shall pay unto his majesty shall be far less than that which Powhatan exacts from them."[173] Strachey sketched out a vision for an orderly colonial society, at once Native and English, much like Johnson's. "The English will take of their poorest into their families as their better sort shall by patents and Proclamations hold their lands as free burgers and Citizens with the English and Subjects to king James," he said, "who will give them Justice and defend them against all their enemies."[174] Strachey's Peruvian Virginia hinted at an urban world complete perhaps with Powhatan-run *cabildos* or town councils. To early modern thinkers, citizens and subjects were distinct, if overlapping, categories. One English guide defined citizens as "free-men, and do dwell in Cities."[175] They "live under the same laws" and, in England, even had "voices" in the kingdom's parliament.[176] As it happened, there were to be no Powhatan Burgesses but eventually there were many Powhatan tributaries in Virginia—though not anytime soon. As 1613 began, Virginia and Florida remained mirror images of failure waiting for the moment to resolve the dilemma.

Experimentation, Consolidation, and Divergence in Florida and Virginia

The two *presidios* broke the impasse of 1612 in very different ways. Jamestown's leaders overcame their challenges by forging new alliances with Natives in

Tsenacomacoh, while friars and soldiers in San Agustín opted to regroup and build upon their earlier gains in Guale and Timucua. In Florida, the Franciscans, still unable to advance into Apalachee, settled for institutional consolidation, formally organizing their provincial chapter in 1616. At the same time, the friars exerted relentless pressure on the Crown to invest even more in Florida's republic of Indians. Not even the promise of a heavenly crown of glory moved the king of Spain to spend much more on Florida than he already did. But in Virginia, colonial boosters had better luck with their schemes. The suddenness with which Virginians resolved the colonial predicament they faced in 1612 resulted from two breakthroughs, one notorious, the other lesser known. First came the 1613 capture of Wahunsenacawh's daughter and envoy, Matoaka (Pocahontas), her conversion to Anglicanism as Lady Rebecca (biblical mother to "two nations"), and her marriage to the tobacco planter John Rolfe in 1614.[177] The ensuing peace made way for the second breakthrough, the formation of an experimental republic of Indians and a hybrid polity encompassing the English and the Chickahominies. The effects of both events proved illusory, but the Chickahominy treaty is significant for what it suggested about the possibility of a "meeting of the minds" between Indigenous and English leaders even during Virginia's boom years of 1614–1622.[178] Within a few years, Virginia's experimentation with Native relations flagged and its leaders opted to consolidate their own institutions of governance, much as Florida's Franciscans had. The meeting of the first Virginia General Assembly in July 1619, notably absent of any Indigenous members—in contrast to the assemblies during Florida's gubernatorial visitations—marked the ascendancy of the colony's planters. The assembly's work pointed to the onset of an underlying pessimism about the future of forging a single commonwealth or even dual commonwealths with the Powhatans. Over the next decade, the two *presidios* of Jamestown and San Agustín traveled increasingly on separate courses.

Pocahontas's marriage to John Rolfe in April 1614 may seem like the fulcrum that lifted Virginia's fortunes, but another ceremony that year told the most about what kind of future Indigenous leaders and colonizers might make in Tsenacomacoh.[179] Just as the Spaniards in Florida had, the English in Virginia experimented with ways to combine Indigenous and European polities. With the Chickahominies, the English negotiated an agreement like the "colonial compact" familiar in Florida. Not long after word of the peace between Wahunsenacawh and the English had been "bruited abroad," two messengers from the Chickahominies, "a lusty and daring people," came into

Jamestown bearing "two fat Bucks for present" to the *tassantasses' werow-ance*, Sir Thomas Dale.[180] In 1614, a council of eight elders known as *man-guys* governed the nation "free from Powhatan's subjection, having laws and governors within themselves."[181] Wahunsenacawh, the Chickahominies said, was an "ill Weroaules," or *weroance* "full of cruelty, and injustice, covetous of those things they had and implacable if they denied him whatsoever he demanded."[182] Their decision arose from self-interest, an effort to avoid domi-nation at the hands of the Powhatan *mamanatowick*.

The six articles of the agreement that the Chickahominies negotiated with the English spelled out terms like those found in the submissions that *caciques* made in San Agustín. First, the Chickahominies became vassals of the king of England, vowing to serve the governor who ruled in the king's stead.[183] The Chickahominies promised to "take upon them . . . the name of *Tassantasses* or English men," thereby becoming "one people with us."[184] Here, most clearly was an example of how what Europeans termed vassalage and subjecthood were merely extended forms of kinship, at least in Native eyes. In addition to establishing boundaries and pledging to fight for the English, the most important article for the Chickahominies was the fifth, whereby they agreed to pay tribute in "obedience to his Majesty," assessed at a rate of "two bushels of corn a man." The rate of tribute was roughly equivalent to the two *arrobas* (fifty pounds) per married man that the governor of Florida used to collect from the province of Guale. Like the Guales, the Chickahominies valued this provision because it gave them European-made metal tools in return, in this case, for "Iron Tomahawks or small hatchets."[185]

Leaving for last what would have been the first in Florida, the English promised to lavish the eight *manguys* of the Chickahominies with gifts, including clothes much as the Timucuas accepted during Holy Week in 1609. The Chickahominy *manguys* would each have "a red coat, or livery from our King yearly," and instead of a cross around the neck, each would receive a "picture of his Majesty, engraved in Copper, with a chain of Copper to hang it about his neck."[186] The *manguys* were now "King JAMES his noble Men" and could be punished along with commoners who broke the pact, "because they stand engaged for them." The representatives of the English king, who was to assume the role of a paramount over the Chickahominies, declared that they "would permit them to enjoy their own liberties, freedoms, and laws, and to be governed as formerly, by eight of their chiefest men."[187]

For the English, the agreement amounted to what in Florida has been called "conquest by contract," and it left the Chickahominies' republic, their

Figure 5. Depiction of the Chickahominies ratifying their treaty with the English in 1614, from Theodor de Bry, *America*, part 10 (Oppenheim: Theodor de Bry and Hieronymus Galler, 1619). Courtesy of the John Carter Brown Library, Providence, RI.

self-government, firmly intact.[188] For the Chickahominies, the articles represented an attempt to form a mutual polity with the European invaders, one with a shared law that operated on two levels: managing relations with the new paramount chief, Virginia's governor, and maintaining their right to internal self-government. In return for "tribute," the Chickahominies gained something that was for them, as it was for the Native peoples of Florida, more valuable than corn—plentiful access to European goods. The agreement, however important as a model for future covenants, lasted just two years, with the English failing utterly to uphold the terms.[189]

While the Chickahominies and the English experimented with a model shared polity, in Florida the Franciscans seemed to have accepted the colony's dependence on Native cooperation, and they moved to consolidate their own positions with a grand symbolic gesture. Late in 1616, Fray Luis Jerónimo de Oré arrived, seasick and exhausted after twenty-five days' sailing, to the city of San Agustín, where a crowd of cheering soldiers and friars met him at the landing, heartening the weary traveler.[190] Oré was born in Peru, raised among Natives, and he turned his astonishing aptitude for languages to learning theirs, spending much of his early career as a priest translating the tenets of the faith into Aymaru and Quechua. As easy in the councils of *caciques* as he was in the courts of Europe, Oré rose steadily in the ranks of the Order of Friars Minor.[191] Oré's official task that fall was an inspection tour of the Franciscan missions in the provinces of Florida. But he also planned to convene the first formal chapter meeting of the Franciscan province of Santa Elena.

To Spaniards, the election of officers and the adoption of formal statutes meant that the missions there had attained maturity and staying power—not to mention a solid base from which to carry the banner of the faith into the interior country at last. His inspection tour was grueling for Oré, then just past sixty years old. The governor gave him a horse, but even as "a soldier brought it," Oré turned him away.[192] Mounts were for *hidalgos*, not humble men of God, and "he preferred to walk in the company of the religious."[193] Impressed by the devotion of the Native converts, he found their paths and the narrow logs that served for bridges less reassuring. "In my case," Oré said, "I confessed first and then crossed."[194] The difficulties of travel had already convinced Oré to spare the Indians the labor of carrying all the friars' "books and bundles of provisions" to San Agustín, and to instead hold the chapter meeting in the town of Guadalquini in Guale, a place easily reached "by water in canoes."[195] After saying mass and settling inside the church, the chapter heard a sermon from Fray Lorenzo Martínez, the tenor of which might be indicated by his earlier promise that a "crown of glory" in Heaven awaited the Spanish king for his care of the missions despite Florida's lack of earthly rewards.[196] The brothers elected Fray Francisco Pareja *padre provincial* (head of the chapter) along with four *definidores* (members of the chapter council) to advise and assist him. The chapter left in a candlelight procession, all of them singing the *Te deum* as they entered Guadalquini's mission church.[197] Oré preached a sermon on the Book of Kings, reminding the chapter's leaders to welcome to his table "the good and the worthy, but also to have the courage to punish the unworthy."[198] The convocation of the province of Santa Elena concluded in just four days, its officers, statutes, and ceremonies a demonstration of order and hierarchy in a land now fully pacified, *pobladores* or no.

The same year in which the Franciscans formally organized their chapter at Guadalquini saw a declaration of success from the Virginia Company: "We are now by the Natives liking and consent, in actual possession of a great part of the Country."[199] To prove it, the company invited a delegation of Powhatan dignitaries to visit King James's court in England. Rebecca Rolfe led the mission to herald Tsenacomacoh's successful pacification. But her father, the "Emperor of Virginia," Wahunsenacawh, was not pacified by any means. "I am now old, and would gladly end my days in peace," he told yet another impertinent set of *tassantasses* who pestered him, "so as if the English offer me injury, my country is large enough, I will remove myself farther from you."[200] Wahunsenacawh's councilor Uttamatomakin joined the delegation to England to gauge the invaders' strength. In Plymouth, he confronted their sheer numbers, and, in theological dispute with Reverend Samuel Purchas, their intransigence.[201] As for Rebecca Rolfe's view of the statement the Virginia Company made with her visit, her sharp rebuke of John Smith suffices: "Your Countrymen will lie much."[202] She took ill on the ship for home and died in Gravesend in 1617. Sometime in 1618, Wahunsenacawh, retired but still unbowed, followed her in death. His brothers, Opitchapam and Opechancanough, succeeded the old *mamanatowick* but it was Opechancanough, with his "noble Presence, and extraordinary Parts," who dominated the politics of the Tidewater.[203] As Opechancanough secured his position, the Virginia Company's shareholders ushered in a new treasurer and a raft of reforms to strengthen their hoped-for commonwealth, including the furtherance of plans for an "Indian College" upriver from Jamestown at Henrico City. Yet, the real signal about the future came in the late summer of 1619 when the planters met in a General Assembly, effectively consolidating their political and economic gains in this new institution.

The General Assembly that opened on 30 July 1619, in the "choir" of the church in "James City," with all its members seated according to their ranks, signaled a shift in the colonial project toward, at best, two very unequal commonwealths of Natives and English. Much as the Franciscan chapter meeting did for Florida just a few years before, the assembly's sitting was supposed to demonstrate Virginia's maturity. The days of martial law were over and civil government was firmly established. Yet, the whole project remained unfinished. No Powhatan "free burgers and Citizens" took their seats in the pews that Friday, disappointing the sanguine prophesies of William Strachey. Instead of a unified Anglo-Native Christian commonwealth, the colony in Tsenacomacoh was sliding into a model of two distinct commonwealths, and one far different from what English leaders contemplated in 1612.[204] The laws that the assembly agreed to, though offering protection to Powhatans injured by colonists, were decidedly unequal. The penalties were less for offenses against Natives. Still, the Powhatans found a voice in the assembly. Opechancanough was, in fact, a petitioner before the assembly—the first Native petitioner of many in the century ahead. Like Don Gaspar Marqués did years before in San Agustín, Opechancanough first approached the governor with his request "to procure . . . justice" on behalf of Accomacs from the Eastern Shore who had been robbed by a pinnace of English colonists on Chesapeake Bay.[205] Quite apart from the friendly, subordinate *cacique* of English fantasies, Opechancanough's petition was part of a bid to solidify the Powhatan political position in opposition to the invaders.[206] The General Assembly, meanwhile, reinforced the power of the planters in Virginia, much as the Franciscan chapter meeting signaled the priority of religious missions in Florida over dreams of further European colonization.[207]

Both the chapter meeting and the convocation of the Virginia Assembly, in fact, underscored the distinct shortcomings of their respective colonial projects. In Virginia, the chance of integrating Natives into a mutual polity seemed to be slipping away. While in Florida, there was little else than Native labor and Native souls to justify that colony's existence. At the start of the new decade, the *presidio* at San Agustín was still poor. In 1621, the "poverty" of the parish church where the people worshiped was "the greatest of all there is in the Indies."[208] The church had no "Rent, nor works, nor alms," read a petition from the church to the king, "because the *vecinos* [the city's residents] each day go into greater poverty and misery, for being soldiers and their salary is very short and badly paid."[209] Worse was the lot of the soldiers' wives and children, like the family of Captain Juan Rodríguez de Cartaya. After he drowned in a ill-starred attempt to rescue a comrade while in battle with Natives on Florida's southern Atlantic coast, his widow Francisca and their "seven children, five of them females [*hembras*]," unable to pay "the third part of her debts," lamented to the king how they had joined the ranks of San Agustín's destitute.[210] Florida's growth depended on winning more Native vassals like the "thirty Christian Indians" who had accompanied her husband on his fight.[211] But to do that required more expense to regale the *caciques* from far inland who were seeking missions after learning of the generosity of the Spanish paramount chief through their "communication and commerce" with its Native members.[212] After decades of projects and plans, Florida thus remained in the view of the Council of the Indies as a far-flung military outpost, waiting on sporadic royal patronage, and dependent on the regular contributions of the Natives surrounding it.

That same year, the *presidio* at Jamestown at least looked to be a success, having "pacified" the people of Tsenacomacoh seemingly as San Agustín had done with the peoples of Guale and Timucua. That image was likewise an illusion. Only George Thorpe, acting as a missionary among the Powhatans, urged the company to commit seriously to winning over Indigenous elites with gifts. Though "virtuous," Thorpe argued, the Powhatans were "a little craving" and "will be much allured" to subjection to the English if the company would "send something in matter of apparel and household stuff" for the leaders, especially Opechancanough, whom the lay missionary had befriended.[213] Later instructions to the governor urged him to use "the best means" to attract "better disposed" Powhatans to "Converse" and work among the English, crucially promising them "Convenient reward," presumably in trade goods—but spelled out no large-scale gift-giving campaign on the order of Florida's.[214]

Still, the Virginia colony had succeeded where the Spanish had notably failed. Hundreds of immigrants arrived yearly to the docks at Jamestown. As yet, a host of good and honest Castilian farmers had not arrived in Florida. Ironically, Florida's seeming success with Native leaders and its dependence upon them for food, for labor, for added defense, stymied all the plans to bring more Spaniards to farm their lands. To do so might have made the colony stronger against its European rivals, but would have weakened relations with the *caciques*. Friars, after all, were intrusive enough. Settlers—even kind, honest Castilians—might leave them alone at first, but their cattle would not, and the sight of lush Native corn fields might soon teach them to covet. Perhaps for that reason, Spanish proposals for immigration were always limited—a few Castilian or Indigenous settlers to instruct the Natives in husbandry and cultivation, and little else. Yet, reports from Virginia made it clear that the English believed that they could easily have it both ways, ruling (beneficently) over the Powhatans while filling their lands with hundreds of colonists.

A War of Fire and Blood in Virginia:
From Making Vassals to Conquering Land

What jarred Virginia almost irrevocably from its Spanish-inspired course was the Powhatan uprising of 1622. The blow fell on 22 March 1622 and killed

347 colonists, a third of the population, including George Thorpe. More should have died, the English believed, but the timely warnings from a smattering of Powhatan converts to Christianity gave Jamestown and a few other outlying plantations time to prepare. In the end, more did die as plague and hunger ravaged the colony. But the suddenness of the attack and the numbers of the slain do not explain the path Virginia followed thereafter. After years of devising their own strategies based upon Spanish models, English colonizers tore up all the precedents and pursued a course practically unthinkable for Spaniards in 1622: territorial conquest and Native extermination—in short, "a war of fire and blood."

The war they fought was not an embrace of then-current Spanish tactics but a rejection of them, and a radical departure from the path of the *presidio* of San Agustín. "Mark but the *Spaniard* who is in the same Continent with VIRGINIA, and has now perfected his work," said the Company's official response to the attack. "Mark and tell me, if he has not had more counterbluffs far than we, as out of their own histories at large may be proved."[215] Carry on "with constancy and courage," wrote Edward Waterhouse, and the true wealth of the Indies would be Virginia's.[216] Gold and silver were not Spain's greatest treasure: "Were it not for other rich Commodities . . . those of the Contractation house [the Casa de Contratación in Seville] were never able to subsist."[217] The real wealth was the "Commodities" that the Spaniards planted "in the *West Indies*."[218] Tsenacomacoh's rich lands held the same possibility. The historian Jorge Cañizares-Esguerra sees in Waterhouse an Englishman with a clear-eyed and up-to-date picture of the Spanish empire, an empire "organized around the pursuit of trade, agriculture, and commerce."[219] But when it came to the matter at hand in 1622—what to do about relations with the Powhatans—Waterhouse was far behind the times, turning back to the early, violent days of the Spanish conquest. The war he invoked recalled the worst excesses in Española, Mexico, and Peru, a time before Felipe II's *Ordenanzas*, even before the New Laws with which, as the English told the story, Charles V "by his Edict" set the "Naturals" free.[220] After a single "counterbluff," Waterhouse and the Virginia Company were ready to wage the kind of war that it took no fewer than three breaches of the peace for San Agustín's founder, Pedro Menéndez de Avilés, even to consider.

Menéndez, the man notorious for slaughtering Huguenot prisoners in 1565, recounted for officials in Madrid how he had overlooked "without coming to an open breach, many cases of Christians slain by them," that is, the Native peoples of the peninsular coast.[221] No matter how many "gifts and demonstrations of friendship" he gave them, no matter how many times they visited Havana and returned home safely again, they "have broken the peace many times, slaying Christians, and they have been forgiven."[222] One witness recounted how the *caciques* from all over the land came often to render obedience, a sight that reassured the soldiers there until "they understood the great cunning" the Natives had, for they still killed Spaniards with impunity.[223] His patience worn out with the mixed course, the *Adelantado* had asked the Council of the Indies to let him wage "a war of fire and blood" on Ais, Calusa, Tequesta, and the Natives of the Mosquitos.[224] Afterward, he said, the land there "will remain clear and unobstructed" of Natives.[225] "Those taken alive shall be sold as slaves, removing them from the country," he said, "and taking them to the neighboring islands, Cuba, Santo Domingo, Puerto Rico."[226]

The Virginia Company rehearsed a similar tale of Indigenous perfidy to justify its war of fire and blood against the Powhatans. Before that "fatal" Friday morning of the attack, the colony's "affairs were full of success, and such intercourse of familiarity, as if the *Indians* and themselves had been of one Nation."[227] A peace "stamped in Brass," which Opechancanough said would last till the sky fell, reigned over the land.[228] "But the Savages," he wrote, "though never Nation used so kindly upon so small desert, have instead of that Harvest which our pains merited, returned nothing but Briars and thorns, pricking even to death many of their Benefactors."[229] Opechancanough's coup, said Waterhouse, freed the English to brandish the sword, take up the torch, and let the mastiff slip from its leash.[230] The English, too, sought to clear the land of people, to "destroy them who sought to destroy us: whereby we shall enjoy their cultivated places, turning the laborious Mattock into the victorious Sword (wherein there is more both ease, benefit, and glory) and possessing the fruits of others' labors."[231] Any Powhatan taken alive, the English could "most justly" force to work, they claimed.[232] Much as Menéndez proposed, the Virginians would ship the Powhatans out of the country, too, "for the service of the *Somers Islands* (Bermuda)."[233]

Neither of these wars, Menéndez's nor Waterhouse's were true wars of conquest in the sense that Spaniards understood them by the early seventeenth century—they were wars of deportation and extermination. Another difference was that Menéndez thought the land his war would clear was worthless; Waterhouse and the Virginia Company prized the land in Tsenacomacoh above all else. The most important difference was that the Council of the Indies scotched Menéndez's war while the Council of Virginia had no qualms about waging theirs. The council rejected Menéndez's petition on the grounds that his was illegal and immoral. Wars of conquest, however brutal, vicious, and destructive they might be were waged to bring enemy peoples "into the jurisdiction" of the colonial state and the monarch, not to exterminate or remove them. Sometime around 1619, Fray Luis Jerónimo de Oré published his *Account of the Martyrs in the Province of La Florida*. The book offers a useful counterpoint, setting the war proposed in Edward Waterhouse's *Declaration* in relief. Spanish soldiers waged the campaign to quell the 1597 Guale uprising, for instance, not to exterminate but to "punish" Spain's rebel vassals until "the Indians made an effort to come back into the jurisdiction of His Majesty by appealing to the governor."[234]

The war raging in Virginia throughout the 1620s was instead a war to conquer territory, without regard to the people who possessed it. While some voices offered alternatives in Virginia, the clamor for revenge drowned them out. In May 1623, the English resorted to poisoning *weroances*, including Opechancanough, at what was supposed to be a peace parley.[235] The gambit failed and Opechancanough survived to outlive most of his enemies. In 1624, the Pamunkeys fought the English in pitched battle for two days straight.[236] The English militia staged campaigns of destruction, burning and pillaging houses, hacking up crops in the fields near Powhatan towns.[237] No longer needing the Natives, no longer trusting them, the English abandoned for a time the path officials in San Agustín walked.

Conclusion: Two Failed Presidios?

By the late 1620s, Florida and Virginia appeared to be going in entirely different directions, but they shared one thing in common—both had failed in their original aims. From its beginnings as a strategically located *presidio*, using a variety of means—economic, political, and military—to exert its influence over an Indigenous population, Jamestown in 1628 was instead the hub in a riverine network of fortified plantations struggling to seize and hold the Powhatans' territory rather than win their allegiance. In 1628–1629, there was a lull in the endless war in Tsenacomacoh, long enough for William Perse, "an ancient planter of twenty years standing," to take stock of the colony's wartime growth.[238] The Powhatans had not succeeded in drawing the English into their polity nor would they agree to be subordinates in Virginia's. "As for the natives, Sasapen [Opitchapam] is the chief over all those people inhabiting upon the rivers next unto us," he said, "who hath been the prime mover of all them, that since the massacre have made war upon us." The Powhatans faced armed plantations "with a convenient number of Musketeers, to the number of two thousand shot and upwards."[239] Perse's Virginia was free of the Natives because it was in thrall to tobacco, though he hoped that the colonists in time "may fall upon more stable commodities."[240] For their part, the Powhatans sought freedom from the English to save their very lives. They refused to become pliant *caciques* in the sense the English wished, remaining sovereign kings and queens. In this respect, Virginia's colonial project badly failed. In Florida, the problem was reversed.

Starting its days as a military outpost, guarding the route of Spain's treasure fleets against European interlopers, what we call Spanish Florida was, at the end of that decade, not exactly Spanish nor entirely a colony. Rather, the city of San Agustín was capital of a multiethnic hybrid polity dependent upon the labor and agricultural production of scores of towns of Timucuas and Guales.[241] Florida was a success but in all the wrong ways, from the colonizers' point of view. There was no commodity like tobacco to turn a profit or draw eager *pobladores*. There were no "*encomenderos*, workshops, nor mines"—in other words, no wealth, "which are the things that for the most part squeeze the Indians in work and consumes and finishes them," wrote Governor Andrés Rodríguez Villegas to King Felipe IV in 1630.[242] Native workers were Florida's only true wealth and the demand for them made the natural lords of the land wealthier and more secure—at least in the short run.

Many of Apalachee's leaders remained—because of the tenacious refusal of the people—unable to reach such an accord. Ordinary Apalachees well knew that admitting the friars and pledging fealty to the king in Madrid was the only devil's bargain their neighbors in Guale and Timucua ever made. Eager to relieve the king's conscience about the "good treatment and conservation of the Indians," Governor Rodríguez wrote that Florida's poverty had an upside: "The natives of this district are the best treated in all the Indies."[243] Showered with gifts from the king's hands, there were no Indians anywhere who were "less worked."[244] The skeletons of the dead buried in mission cemeteries beg to differ. The bones of ordinary Native men and women grew harder and arthritis withered their joints, all from carrying heavy loads over long distances.[245] In the same year as the governor's letter, the friars begged the Crown for horses to relieve Native burdeners from their loads. Natives outside the republic of Indians, the friars said, refused to become part of it "so as not to subject themselves to such heavy burdens."[246] Crowded conditions in missions made their towns cesspools of disease. Dental caries ruined the teeth of Natives now utterly dependent on the maize they grew in ever-greater quantities for the *presidio*. In short, the quality of life in Timucua, Guale, and later, Apalachee, fell steadily over the course of the seventeenth century.[247] And so did the power and independence of Native chiefs, whose efforts to counter the slide downward cried out in petition after petition to governors and the Crown.[248]

Remarkably, by the middle of the seventeenth century, the paths of Virginia and Florida began to converge again. More remarkable still was that Indigenous leaders made it possible. A handful of exasperated Apalachee political leaders, eager to curb the egalitarian tendencies of their followers and to solidify their position against foreign Native rivals, invited Franciscan friars—and Spanish largesse—into their towns. These Apalachee leaders found a governor eager to oblige them, permitting the republic of Indians in Florida to expand suddenly and rapidly to the west after 1633. The move marked a new era in the history of Florida's hybrid polity as the center of political gravity shifted west toward Apalachee province. In Tsenacomacoh, the turn came when a new generation of Powhatan leaders, desperate to end yet another total war with the English, forged a treaty that drew the colonists into a new polity, a kind of republic of Indians, that rose from the ruins of Wahunsenacawh's and Opechancanough's kingdom.

CHAPTER 2

"Poor Indians," 1633–1673

Three strange men shuffled into the city of San Agustín in the custody of the *mico* of Satuache in 1633. They came more than seventy leagues by canoe and on foot from Satuache, a Guale town far to the north on the Savannah River, but to the eyes of the city's curious residents, these gaunt strangers looked to have journeyed even farther. The month was November, with winter approaching, reason enough to bring the men down to the *presidio*. Even with the granaries full, their presence "among Indians so newly converted" would have put the governor ill at ease lest the men teach them their schismatic religion.[1] A career soldier, Governor Luís Horruytiner had tasted his share of hardship in thirty-seven years fighting the king's enemies on three continents, but he had known nothing quite as miserable as what he heard now.[2] The castaways were Englishmen who sailed from London "going in relief with supplies and ammunition to Ajacán"—Virginia—three years before.[3] The ship began to take on water and, off the coast of Florida, she sank. Forty men fled for their lives in the ship's boat only to face their doom on the land. Hunger, thirst, and disease whittled the forty down to thirteen. Native warriors attacked the knot of survivors, killing eight with their arrows, as the last five ran for the woods. Two other castaways refused to leave the woods and the *mico* of Satuache doubted whether he could "bring them to this presidio."[4] Then came a glimmer of good news: one of the shipwrecked Englishmen was "a blacksmith by trade," rare in San Agustín.[5] The news may have stoked in Governor Horruytiner, after his stints in the wealthy ports of Cartagena and Havana, the nagging suspicion that the king had somehow managed to promote him downward. Florida was short of everything, whether it be supplies or blacksmiths. On the governor's orders, the castaway blacksmith joined another English exile in San Agustín, a cooper by trade who, with a companion, had "wrecked on these shores" seven years before.[6]

Horruytiner shipped the rest of the men to Havana, every one of them now still farther from "Ajacán"—from Virginia—than when they started.

If by some chance the governor, discarding a lifetime of careful obedience to orders, had decided instead to send them northward to Virginia, the English castaways might have found it little more promising than the provinces of Florida. Whatever the pretensions to greater territory of its English rulers, Virginia in 1633 was, in fact, a corridor of rude tobacco plantations on both sides of the James River, cutting through Tsenacomacoh to the Fall Line, along with a smattering of settlements on the Eastern Shore of Chesapeake Bay—and a few creeping north toward the York River.[7] As in Florida where expansion followed water routes for ease of travel, Virginia's growth tracked Indigenous patterns and grew along deep, tidal waterways all the more convenient for rolling hogsheads of tobacco from barns to the shore and onto the waiting ships bound for England.[8] The cooper and the blacksmith of San Agustín would have found ample work in Virginia. Tobacco was in such demand there that the assembly passed a law forbidding tradesmen from leaving their professions to plant the esteemed weed.[9] The James River corridor, dotted with acres of plantations, was the earliest and best established along the "tobacco coast."[10]

On the Virginia corridor's edges, north and south, were independent Indigenous polities, survivors of ten years of war. While the *mico* of Satuache dutifully performed the requests of the governor in San Agustín, the *mamanatowick* of Powhatan, Opechancanough, strove to recoup his people's losses to the invaders. A bitter peace settled over the land after a treaty in 1632. Most of that treaty's terms are lost or unclear, save one: an injunction to the English not to parley with "or trust them," that is the Powhatans.[11] The feeling was mutual. Opechancanough wanted the English to keep their distance. In February 1633, Luis Horruytiner's English counterpart, Sir John Harvey mixed hope with wariness, reporting to the Privy Council that "we yet are upon good terms with the Indian, but stand at all times upon our guard."[12] Keeping the king's subjects on their guard required vigilance and a heavy hand. In June, Harvey passed sentence upon two men who broke the ban and dared to trade with the Powhatans.[13] (Just as, in San Agustín, labor was a valuable commodity along the James River. The delinquents each served the governor a month and the informers who ratted them out had them for a day each.) Nothing, not even the palisade wall Harvey had built across the Peninsula, could stop people from "parleying" and trading, however, in incidents large and small across the porous boundaries between Tsenacomacoh and Virginia. Nevertheless, Florida and Virginia still suffered under the same limitations as at the end of the 1620s but Native and colonial leaders in both places would soon achieve breakthroughs.

The year 1633, as Florida languished and Virginians sullenly kept the peace, marked the beginning of a new era that witnessed the sudden growth of the hybrid polity centered on San Agustín and the creation of an entirely new regime in Tsenacomacoh. The events of the next four decades redrew the jurisdictional boundaries in both places, dragging Natives, Spaniards, and Englishmen closer together, whether they wanted to be or not. Famine, drought, plague, rebellion, and war staggered all parties at midcentury, and forced them to reconsider their most fundamental political principles. Powhatans feared being taken as slaves or, what was unthinkable before, having their labor drafted and harnessed as vassals by victorious English colonists who were convinced they now had the power to do so. Burgesses, merchants, and clerics all busied their pens sketching plans and debating just what sort of empire England now possessed. Their fantasies soon met the reality of a new generation of determined Indigenous leadership. Together, colonists and Powhatan leaders would strike a covenant lasting another generation. In the provinces of Florida, the unrest of the 1640s led *caciques*, friars, royal officials, and hard-pressed royal governors in the opposite direction. A colonial society that survived on Indigenous labor faced the reality that overburdened Apalachees, Timucuas, and Guales were likely to destroy it unless they had relief—and speedily. Never before or after was the phrase "poor Indians" used quite as often or earnestly as in Florida and Virginia at midcentury.

In both places, the turbulence of the 1630s, the uprisings of the 1640s, and the experiments of the 1650s yielded finally to a new, Indian-driven politics by the 1660s. Florida's governor in 1643 once complained how the friars "are killing me with petitions."[14] His successors had cause to say as much about the Indians. Taking advantage of the Crown's duty to its lowliest vassals, commoners like Juan Orata and Agustín López pointed the way, pleading successfully with the king to free them from the prison cell to which Florida's governor had condemned them. Over the next decades, Native chiefs like Santiago, the *mico* of Tolomato and Don Benito, rightful heir to the Timucuan town of Machava, won royal decrees in their favor and rewrote the law in Florida to suit Indigenous interests. While still relying on networks of secular and religious allies, Spain's Native vassals in the provinces of Florida were unafraid to go over the heads of colonial officials entirely and take their cases directly to the king. In Virginia, the 1660s ushered in the politics of petitioning as these "poor Indians," now tributaries and subjects of the Crown, sought to build a kind of Tidewater republic of Indians. The Pamunkey chiefs, Totopotomoy and Cockacoeske, the Chickahominy *manguy* (councilor), Harquip, and other leaders used their influence to establish a place for Native commonwealths and Native law inside Virginia. Across the South, an Indigenous royalism developed among tributaries and vassals who looked to their respective Crowns as the guarantors of their rights and appealed to them over the heads of colonists and colonial officials.[15] But if the Crown protected the Indians, colonists wondered who would support them. Even as the republic of Indians enlarged, the cracks showed in its foundations. By the 1670s, the hybrid polities of the Southeast reached their greatest extent yet—in land area, population, and their Native members' status—only to contract in outbreaks of shocking violence.

Indigenous Insiders and Outsiders in the English and Spanish Empires

In 1633, the status of Indigenous people in Florida and Virginia still contrasted sharply. Florida's Indigenous leaders, whether in Guale and Timucua, for all the distinctiveness of their internal forms of government, were in many ways political insiders, part of the republic of Indians and vassals of the Crown.[16] The republic of Indians grew in Florida only when the governor and the Franciscans could persuade other Natives chiefs outside its bounds, like the *caciques* of Apalachee, to join. In Virginia, with few exceptions, Natives remained outsiders to the colonial political system, living on the other side of steep legal barriers. Peace there seemed to depend on the ability of Opechancanough and his English equivalent, Sir John Harvey, to restrain and separate their respective populations, rather than unite them.

Two transatlantic campaigns against the alleged excesses of colonial governors in the 1630s underscore the different positions of Natives in Virginia and Florida before the rapid political changes of the next decade. Sir John Harvey's defense of the peace with the Powhatans and his efforts to restrain Virginians' land hunger led to his ousting in 1635 and an appeal all the way to England's King Charles I, pitting the king's viceroy against his colonial subjects. The other campaign started in Cuba, where two Florida Natives, Agustín López and Juan Orata, prisoners in Havana's El Morro fortress, petitioned King Felipe IV of Spain to nullify the orders of the former colonial

governor who put them there. Although they were imprisoned, López and
Orata behaved like imperial insiders able to muster the support of the Franciscans and win the attention of the Crown. Their position was a sharp contrast to the circumstances of even the most powerful Powhatans who faced
exclusion and open hostility from Virginia colonists who were willing to stage
a rebellion if it would help to dispossess them. In the end, Charles I restored
Governor Harvey and Felipe IV granted López and Orata royal favor. Neither
judgment put the debates about the status of Indians to rest as Florida and
Virginia expanded. The outcomes in each case point to contemporary perceptions of a disturbing link between imperial authoritarianism and Native
American liberty, a contradiction at the heart of all their covenants and the
source of lasting tensions between Indigenous peoples and colonizers until
the end of the century.

San Agustín's dependence on Indigenous support and the republic of
Indians' efforts to grow westward help explain why the pleas of two Native
commoners from Florida would receive the careful attention of the Crown.
Confirming the rights of Native vassals was one way the king and his officers
in Florida could make joining the republic of Indians attractive. Throughout the 1630s, Florida's *presidio* tottered on the shoulders of the Indigenous
laborers from Guale and Timucua. Its position was never secure and survival
required growth. After twenty years, the leaders of at least a few Apalachee
towns far to the west of the *presidio* seemed ready, and their grip on their
followers appeared strong enough, to become a part of San Agustín's hybrid
polity. With the instincts of a veteran soldier, not to mention the importunity
of the friars and the insistence of far-off *caciques*, Governor Luís Horruytiner
revived the mission to Apalachee, officially dormant since 1612. Horruytiner
reminded the king about Apalachee, where "there are more than fifteen or
sixteen thousand very brave and agile Indians" inhabiting a "land of great
abundance and fertility."[17] The "valorous breasts and Christian spirits" of
the Franciscans impressed Horruytiner enough to send two of them—Fray
Pedro Muñoz and Fray Francisco Martínez—with everything needed for a
mission on 16 October 1633. Within four days, another friar arrived and told
the governor yet again how much the Apalachees "desired to see a Religious
in their land."[18]

For the Apalachee leaders who welcomed them, fears of Native outsiders,
including Amacanos and Chacatos, a desire for valuable trade goods, and
the unyielding assertiveness of their followers drove the decision to permit
friars into their towns. Governor Horruytiner later told the king how the

Apalachees welcomed them "with much display of joy."[19] Far from religious ecstasy, such exuberance likely had earthly origins. In the 1630s, waves of outsiders migrated to Apalachee and their presence threatened political stability. By one later account, unfriendly nations at war with the Apalachees surrounded the province—Amacanos, Apalachicolas, and Chacatos—the latter of whom "never have peace with anybody."[20] The lords of at least two Apalachee towns, Inhayca and Ivitachuco, consented to missions, explaining the number of friars who made the trek in October 1633. Once again, these two towns on either end of Apalachee stepped forward to manage relations with the Spaniards. Apalachee was still a land of towns—some forty in all— and Inhayca and Ivitachuco sought an advantage over the others. The alliance between the two towns and the *presidio* of San Agustín sowed distrust and fears in the hearts of *caciques* whom Inhayca and Ivitachuco shut out of the bargain.[21] For the lords of the two great towns, the benefits of the missions in shoring up the authority of their chiefs and swelling the influence of their towns outweighed the risks of conflict in Apalachee. The *caciques* of Inhayca and Ivitachuco had managed to spare their people the onerous duty of carrying the friars' supplies overland from San Agustín. Bread and wine for the friars and goods for trade instead came aboard a frigate from the *presidio* and weighed on Natives' backs for a much shorter time.[22] In tribute to his role in its founding, the mission established in Inhayca received the name "San Luís" in honor of the governor's patron saint.[23]

Such respectful approaches to the country's natural lords made quite a contrast with affairs in Tsenacomacoh, where only the forbearance of the *mamanatowick* Opechancanough and the hard justice of Sir John Harvey preserved the peace, although to no one's satisfaction. As small incidents of illegal trading and occasional violence mounted, Virginia's colonial grandees pressured the governor to end such "a dangerous peace made by him with the Indians against the Council's and Country's advice."[24] For his part, Opechancanough's forbearance is all the more astonishing since "above 2,000 persons" arrived in the colony that year when Powhatan corn cribs must have been near-empty after weevils ruined the crops.[25] Among Virginia colonists, discontent swelled with the Indian peace, the governor's high-handedness, and worst of all, his tightfisted control over grants of Indigenous land.[26] Great numbers of ordinary planters soon gathered to meet "in an unlawful manner."[27] Their defenders denied that the gatherings had any "bad intent, only desires to exhibit their complaints." Shackled in irons, the supposed ringleaders of the sedition, "desired the cause of their Commitment."[28] They would have it "at the Gallows," came Sir John's (purported) response.[29] When the council convened and George Menefie told Harvey the "chiefest cause" of the discontent was his "detaining of the Letters to his Majesty and the Lords"—in other words, restraining their right to petition against the governor's imprudent acts—Harvey tried to arrest him "on suspicion of Treason to his Majesty."[30] Instead, his councilors arrested Harvey. Virginia's leaders took revenge not on Opechancanough's people but on their governor. The fallen viceroy, who styled himself "His Majesties substitute," took his case to the king.[31]

While Virginians overthrew one governor, within the vast fortress of El Morro in Havana, two Mocama men from San Juan del Puerto plotted how they would overturn the orders of another. Agustín López and Juan Orata had languished in a dank cell for the better part of seven years. When a troop of Spanish soldiers marched through their town with handcuffed relatives of the ruling *cacica* in tow, she commanded her vassals—including Agustín and Juan—to stop the soldiers and free the prisoners. López and Orata chose loyalty to their *cacica* over obedience to the colonial governor's commands. For obeying their natural lord, her faithful vassals paid with their ears. To mutilation, Governor Luis Rojas y Borja added banishment for life.[32] In exile, Juan left behind a wife and "two little daughters."[33] Now, the men were the last of the prisoners banished to the Morro from their town. The others found release only in death. With the help of sympathetic Franciscans, they petitioned King Felipe IV on 2 July 1636. "We beseech Your Majesty would pardon us and order us to be Restored to our land," they pleaded, "as a most Christian King always does for the miserable and afflicted."[34]

The pleas of the "poor Indians" López and Orata, and of the faithful viceroy, Sir John Harvey, met with favor in their respective imperial capitals. In London, King Charles I, who had sent away his last parliament in 1629, was in the sixth year of his "personal rule" and disinclined to ignore an affront to his prerogative, least of all in a colony. Captain John West, who had taken over for Harvey, was now branded "the Usurper of the Government."[35] The protective detail of soldiers assigned for Sir John's safety from angry colonists became "30 Armed men" who had "beset Sir John Harvey's house."[36] By royal order, Harvey returned to his post, once again the authoritarian bulwark between the rabble and the Natives. As for Agustín and Juan, still trapped in El Morro, their plea found support in the Council of the Indies as its members deliberated in October 1637. In their *consulta*, or formal recommendation to the king, the council recounted the prisoners' sufferings, particularly the toll on their families "who go helpless and in great need."[37] Weighing the circumstances, the council hedged. Without the opinion of Florida's current governor or friars on the matter, they could not yet recommend returning the two men to their homes. But "considering how greatly they have suffered," the councilors said the king might pardon them, "giving them freedom in the city of Havana, where the governor could entertain them, and they could support themselves."[38]

The result of the two campaigns for royal vindication places the position of Indigenous people in the Spanish and English empires in striking relief, suggesting an interrelationship between imperial authoritarianism and Native liberty. By describing the politics of empire in terms of clashes between metropolitan governments and colonists, historians put Natives in the middle of the squabble. If only effective metropolitan control of the "frontier" and its unruly inhabitants had been possible, then Indians could have lived in liberty as royal subjects.[39] The assumption is that strong government—authoritarian rule—of the kind seventeenth-century Englishmen associated with Spain, was the only way to govern fractious colonists and protect Native subjects. The status of Indigenous people within the empires and the powers of absolutist monarchies, whether aspiring as in England or accomplished as in Spain, were joined. This is why López and Orata appealed to the "Planet King," Felipe IV, whose authority could rectify the mistakes even of his own governors, and whose lofty constitutional position made him seem their disinterested protector.

In Virginia, the apparent ties between absolutism and Indigenous liberty bred resentments, distrust, and fears among the English planters who worried that the colony's self-government would succumb to the schemes of the Hispanophile advisers surrounding the king.[40] Virginia's colonial oligarchy believed that any restriction on their expansion in favor of the Natives was, in fact, an attack on their budding commonwealth. The planters who made up the council in Virginia insisted on having an outsize say in their own government, and subjected instructions from England to their own judgment, suspending their execution for a time in an English version of *obedezco pero no cumplo*: I obey but do not comply.[41] Sir John Harvey, the stubborn viceroy, became a symbol of the union of Native American interests and the interests of the Crown.[42] To Virginia's planters, metropolitan aims were anything but benevolent. Stuart absolutism and Indian liberties were in their minds one and the same. Both came at the expense of colonial interests. Only a governor who had adapted to the demands of life in the colony, who had won the planters' trust by placing the heaviest hand of all upon the Powhatans, could hope to make the idea of Indigenous subjects imaginable if not entirely palatable. He had yet to arrive. For now, the Crown sent Harvey back in triumph and the peace with the Powhatans held another decade. Unlike the upstart Virginians who ousted Sir John Harvey, Agustín López and Juan Orata had gained a measure of royal favor even if it was to them a half-measure, a testament to the claims on the monarch that even the humblest Indian vassals possessed. At the bottom of the council's *consulta*, in a distinct hand, were two words expressing the "Royal Will": *está bien*, "it is well."[43]

The king of Spain and his councilors must also have approved what they heard from Apalachee, where cultivating good will with its Native lords was of utmost importance. The Spanish infiltration of Apalachee and the transformation of the province's leaders into imperial insiders depended on numerous concessions to prevent the kind of unrest that roiled San Juan del Puerto and sent Agustín and Juan to El Morro. "Having attention to the great labor that the Indians were suffering in carrying on their backs more than one hundred leagues from this city to the said province of Apalachee the supplies to the religious," Governor Luis Horruytiner ordered two pilots to reconnoiter a water route.[44] Forcing the Indians to the bitter labor of pack-carrying would hinder the conversion, "the roads being very rough" in Florida.[45] This concession represented a victory for the few Apalachee *caciques* who had so far brought their people to an alliance with the Spaniards. In a petition calling for improved transportation, including better roads and a stock of horses, Fray Juan Gómez de Palma told the king how travelers' tales of finding Indigenous burdeners "dead from hunger and fatigue" beside the *camino real* deterred conversions.[46] Although the privileged position of Inhayca and Ivitachuco, with the power that Spanish goods and friars brought, stoked the resentments of the other towns, most Apalachees who were not drawing the benefits also understood the costs of the alliance. They could see how the people from San Agustín were steadily building their own power too. As much as any rivalry among towns, the sight of Native men bearing heavy packs of supplies to the friars surely met the scorn and derision—if not a little fear—from the majority of Apalachees, strengthening their resolve to remain unbowed to the Spaniards' paramount chief. Thus a glimpse of the first ship bearing supplies from Havana overjoyed the Apalachees who watched it arrive "and so many sought the Holy Baptism," if only because the holy waters were also the symbol of the earthly alliance with the Spaniards.[47] Governor Horruytiner, preparing to leave office in 1638, felt bold enough to tell the king that the opening of Apalachee was "one of the most extraordinary services that I have made in the more than forty-two years that I have served."[48]

Despite the efforts to expand the republic of Indians westward and draw the Apalachees in, there was little progress from the Spanish vantage point until the 1640s. "I have not found more than two religious" in the whole province, wrote Governor Damián Vega Castro y Pardo in 1639, "who write to me that for lack of them, there has not been a greater increase of the Catholic religion."[49] Still, with only the two Franciscans "there [were] more than a thousand converts baptized" out of the population of 15,000 to 16,000 Governor Horruytiner estimated when the missions began, making the promise of labor from those thousands that much more alluring.[50] The most consequential breakthrough in Apalachee, however, was not religious but geopolitical. Outsiders still plagued Apalachee with violence, while inside its towns chiefs still appeared to have little authority over their subjects. To relieve the pressure on the Catholic *caciques*, Vega Castro y Pardo, working with the lords of Inhayca and Ivitachuco, helped compose a peace "in the name of Your Majesty" with the Chacatos, Apalachicolas, and Amacanos, "seeing that they conform themselves and are quiet and in friendship."[51] Promoting peace and harmony between the few Catholic Apalachees and the surrounding "infidels" may have given them some breathing space. Yet, the difficulty of unruly subjects remained. Burials at the early Apalachee mission in Patale suggest the persistence of egalitarianism and the weakness of chiefs, conditions that likely prevailed in many other towns.[52] The other step Vega Castro y Pardo took during his administration was potentially revolutionary and must have proved right all the doubters who mistrusted Spanish intentions. In a reversal from the decision taken in 1612, in around 1638 Governor Vega Castro y Pardo dispatched a small detachment of soldiers to protect the Franciscans in Apalachee, monitor trade with Havana, and to strengthen the power of the few chiefs in the republic of Indians whose provinces, he declared "were Annexed to the Jurisdiction of this government."[53] If such were his intentions in sending a detachment of soldiers, they would backfire spectacularly within just four years.

As the 1640s began, Florida still relied on Native foodstuffs and labor, while Virginians continued their quest to seize ever more acres of Native land for tobacco. Both colonies had grown in the previous decade and ultimate success seemed within their leaders' grasps. The trials of the 1630s and early '40s warned of the dangers ahead. What looked to Spaniards like a sudden leap into Apalachee, was, in fact, just a few steps made under the watchful eyes of shrewd *caciques* in the same two towns, Inhayca and Ivitachuco, who had handled dealings with the Spaniards since at least 1608. For a small footing, the friars and the governor unwittingly stirred up the jealousy and suspicion of most of the rest of Apalachee's towns. And the presidio's plan to use the riches of Apalachee's leading towns to free itself from dearth and dependence played into the hands of Inhayca's and Ivitachuco's *caciques*. They rescued San Agustín only to make the Spaniards more dependent on them for survival, thus concentrating regional power in their own council-houses.[54] Much as the Powhatans had tried to do with Jamestown in its early years, the leaders of Inhayca and Ivitachuco strove to tame the Spaniards and turn them into their clients in order to draw tribute from them in valuable European goods.[55] In Virginia, the peace between the colony and the Powhatans, meanwhile, was brittle and would not hold unless the settlers showed restraint—which they seldom did. When a planter murdered a Weanoke man on the path, mistaking him for another Native man who allegedly robbed him, Virginia's council, fearing reprisals, punished the Englishman with a fine and an order to abandon his home, likely because it was too deep in Powhatan territory.[56] Opechancanough once again forbore to make war and joined a petition with his "great men" to remit the Englishman's penalty.[57] The colony's governor, still acting as partner in the peace, obliged in the name of the English king.

More and more, the distant Crowns of Spain and England looked like Indigenous peoples' best potential European ally—powerful enough to punish colonists, but far enough away not to impose themselves on Indians. The case of the prisoners, López and Orata, shows the reach of the Spanish king's justice and what posing as his loyal vassal could mean for an Indigenous petitioner. Charles I's decision to uphold Sir John Harvey—and Harvey's peace with the Powhatans—hinted at the prospect of a meaningful alliance between English king and Powhatan *weroance*. For now, they were mainly just possibilities. In the mid-1640s, war returned to Florida and to Virginia. The result was the growth of the republic of Indians and the rise of new generation of Native political insiders in both colonies.

Holy Violence: The Third Anglo-Powhatan War and the Apalachee Revolt

By 1644, the English had little faith in their efforts at converting Native peoples, especially in Virginia. So far, the labors of English evangelists had "been to small purpose" in America.[58] Some of the hotter sort of Protestants believed they could break the impasse by force. Echoing the Book of Luke's parable of the banquet, the preacher William Castell doubted the godly would convert such "hardened infidels, unless they were better able to give them Law, and by a holy violence compel them as it were to come in."[59] Castell's fantasy was the nightmare of every Powhatan, indeed every Native family anywhere on the continent. A conquest would give the English "greater power and means to take away their young children, whereby they might become ours, and so be brought to the knowledge of Christianity."[60] The stymied English took some comfort from reports of Florida where, Castell said, the Indians "hate the *Spaniard* extremely" so that they never "obtained any strong footing there."[61] In fact, at that very moment, Spaniards in Florida, despite drought, poor soil, failed harvests, and missing *situado* shipments, boasted to their king about the number of Native souls they had reaped. Florida was at peace in August 1644, and the Franciscan *doctrineros* avowed that the conversion in Apalachee "is much increasing each day."[62] That the hybrid polity functioned at all was a miracle. Without supplies from the *situado*, the "Infantry was forced to go to the woods and lakes to find and take out Roots for their bread."[63] The Natives were "so very poor" but the governor behaved as a proper paramount chief, providing the needy "with seed corn, so that they may sustain themselves, and with some iron tools" from his own stocks.[64] A good soldier was ever ready to perish in the Crown's service but Castro Vega y Pardo preferred to face an enemy he could shoot at rather than famine.[65] Englishmen and Spaniards looking for war would soon get their wish as Natives from Tsenacomacoh to Apalachee rose up against the theft of land, the abuse of their labor, the gradual encroachment of Christianity on their religions, and against other Indigenous people they saw as colonial collaborators. The sudden spate of "holy violence" in the 1640s ended with Spaniards and Englishmen seemingly in just the role William Castell hoped—as conquerors holding the power to remake Indigenous societies. Just as abruptly, their illusions vanished.

Virginia's war began just "a little before break of day" on 18 April 1644, a date ever after "yearly celebrated with thanksgiving" for the colony's deliverance.[66] At dawn, the Powhatan *mamanatowick* Opechancanough launched a massive attack killing five hundred colonists along the James River.[67] While their kingdom was in the midst of civil war, English interpretations of Opechancanough's motives varied, with some arguing he took advantage of chaos in England and others contending that his actions were the instrument of a god outraged at Virginians' impiety.[68] Only later did one writer come close to fathoming Opechancanough's motivations, claiming his warriors "assaulted, no persons, nor invaded any man's possessions or goods, that they knew had bought their lands of them, and covenanted with them, for them and made good their covenant."[69] Most English had never kept their faith nor lived as decent neighbors—much less as the pliant subjects Opechancanough and his long-dead brother Wahunsenacawh had wished for long ago. The loss of land to the English colonizers threatened Powhatan subsistence and much more. For the Powhatans, this was a holy war, too. Old towns, sacred places, and the graves of their ancestors were now trod over by arrogant strangers who would have met the humblest Indigenous pilgrim with a shotgun. Opechancanough fought to restore those hallowed sites to his people.[70]

Virginians ignored the message of the attacks and took the war to the very seat of Powhatan power, "burning their towns, even their king's own house and their treasure house."[71] By May 1645, there were plans to build forts at the heads of Virginia's rivers to overawe the Powhatans and to control them and the Indian trade after the war.[72] Virginia's wartime policies and the plans for a future of regulated exchanges were the innovations of the colony's new governor and captain-general. Sir William Berkeley—courtier, cavalier, playwright—won the appointment as governor of Virginia in 1642 after fierce lobbying at Charles I's embattled court.[73] In the sudden onslaught of 1644, he took charge, first organizing the war effort and then setting off to England for arms and supplies. The war dragged into 1646, when Berkeley returned from a mission to England to obtain supplies and arms. In the woodlands to the west of Henrico County, Berkeley's cavalry seized the venerable Opechancanough, while he fled the battlefield on the backs of the men who carried him in his old age.[74] This stunning victory, wrote Thomas Ludwell, twenty years later, had "Secured that Country from those fears that had oppressed them from their first seating."[75] In what his staunch friend Ludwell thought was a stroke worthy of the Spanish *conquistadores*, Berkeley "rendered the Indians so Subjected to this Government that I may confidently affirm the Like Conquest hath been made by no other English Government in the West Indies."[76] A later map of the Chesapeake commemorated the spot where the deed was done: "*Here about* Sir Will Barkley, *Conquered and took Prisoner the Great Indian Emperor* Abatschakin [Opechancanough], *after the Massacre in* Virginia."[77] To others in the years ahead, the capture of Opechancanough was the climactic act of "holy violence" that would at last compel the Powhatans to come in.

In 1647, just a year after Sir William Berkeley captured Opechancanough at the head of a thundering "Party of Horse," the province of Apalachee in Florida was, for the moment, quiet.[78] At San Luís de Inhayca, the governor's lieutenant and his family dwelled with the small detachment of soldiers stationed there.[79] The soldiers lived close to the town in a crude, wooden blockhouse. When the invitation arrived for a feast in the town of San Antonio de Bacuqua, the provincial lieutenant Captain Claudio de Florencia accepted gladly.[80] The Spanish infiltration of Apalachee was moving but at the pace set by its natural lords: slowly. Of forty *caciques* in the Apalachee towns standing between the Aucilla and the Ocklockonee rivers, only eight had ordered their vassals to dig a field of corn to feed a Franciscan *doctrinero* by 1647.[81] The invitation to Bacuqua, therefore, appeared providential to the Spaniards, a divinely appointed moment to carry on the conversion of Apalachee in the latest town to welcome friars and the one farthest north.[82]

The provincial lieutenant took his entire family to Bacuqua as a show of good faith, but the gruesome events that followed never faded in the memories of the Spaniards or of "the old Indians of the province" of Apalachee, not even after the passage of more than sixty years.[83] In the middle of the feast, Apalachee insurgents killed the whole Florencia family and "dragged away the bodies and threw them into a lake."[84] Most of towns of Apalachee joined Bacuqua in the coup against the Spaniards, all except the leading towns of Inhayca and Ivitachuco and their satellites and allies, whose power the insurgents were just as keen to demolish.[85] Turning on the Spaniards as the source of their rivals' power, the rebels "burned some Churches and Convents" and killed three friars.[86] The friars who escaped did so "with the favor of some Christian Indians." Rumor in San Agustín had it "that the Infidels of the said Province were joined with others of the nation that are called Chiscas, who live without known habitation in the woods and that threaten the Christians" to "leave behind the law of God or they would kill them."[87]

From San Agustín, the royal officials plotted to suppress the revolt much as the Virginians had done after Opechancanough's uprising in 1644. To put down the Apalachees and Chisca insurgents, they dispatched Captain Don Martín de Cueva "with a Troop of Infantry" to take "in hand the Heads of this uprising."[88] But this immediate military action would not be enough for "reducing this Province to the obedience of Your Majesty," Florida's royal officials wrote. To do that required another invasion and a fort "with thirty or forty soldiers . . . for reducing these Indians."[89] Fortunately for the *presidio*, what Aubrey Lauersdorf has called the Apalachee-Chisca coup against

Inhayca and Ivitachuco, drew into the conflict the Timucuas who had brokered the original alliance with the Spaniards.[90] That July, after Timucuan
militia pacified their rebel neighbors, Florida's royal officials proclaimed victory in a war they could never have won on their own.[91] Yet, winning the war
left Spain's ambitions even more dependent on the republic of Indians than
before.

The Powhatan coup of 1644 and the Apalachee-Chisca coup of 1647 were
bold and well-coordinated political strokes in service of Indigenous political
principles, rather than the desperate struggles to drive out Europeans they
once seemed. Opechancanough never gave up the goal of making Tsenacomacoh safe for Powhatans by turning the *tassantassess* into compliant neighbors. From his vantage in the heart of Pamunkey country, the English were
anarchic, creeping like a poisonous vine onto Powhatan land, little by little.
Once they cleared a field and put up a dirt-floor house, they lived as a law
unto themselves. With a blow of enough force, perhaps the English would
change their ways at last and agree to confine themselves to one place.[92]
Opechancanough's coup again failed in its aims, but the English could only
pose as swaggering victors afterward. The decision to gamble on the capture
of Opechancanough was taken to force Tsenacomacoh's leadership to bargain
for terms, revealing Virginia's weakness.

Apalachee's insurgents and their Chisca allies were fighting to reach
terms, too, in their case a "realignment" of the whole region's politics from
what they saw as the Hispano-Timucuan east to an independent Apalachee-
Chisca west.[93] They attacked Spanish friars and soldiers as the agents of
Inhayca's and Ivitachuco's power. The internal—and independent—political
dynamics among Apalachee towns were important and they transform the
meaning of the events of 1647. But they should not simply overshadow what
else was at stake in the fight. In aligning with the Timucuas and the Spaniards, those two towns had introduced more than copper kettles or fine suits
of clothes; they let corruption seep in and, with it, the looming threat of
colonial tyranny. The Chiscas, for one, would never shake the fear of being
swallowed whole in the sprawling hybrid polity to the east and would join in
another coup—this time on the side of Chacatos—later in the century.

The character of early modern warfare also played a role in tempering
the colonial victories both in Virginia and Florida. War to the death was a
battle cry to rouse spirits, not a viable or even a desirable strategy.[94] Neither the English nor the Spanish could wipe out their Indigenous enemies,
nor subdue them forcibly, certainly not without substantial help. All the

belligerents—Indigenous and European—fought with an eye on the peace parleys to come, where they would press their advantages while framing the new political settlement. The wars were over. The debates about what came next were only just beginning.

New Covenants: Establishing the Terms
of the Republic of Indians

The wars in Tsenacomacoh and Apalachee ended with new covenants that radically altered the status of all the parties, whether Native, Spanish, or English. Apalachees who resisted the Spaniards and their Timucuan allies saw their leaders either hanged or sent to San Agustín as *forzados*, prisoners sentenced to hard labor.[95] Before long many more Apalachee men felt the weight of packs on their backs while they trudged the royal road as cargo-carriers and *repartimiento* workers at the command of their chiefs. The Spaniards thought they had annexed Apalachee to San Agustín's jurisdiction at last. But with every laborer who slogged to the *presidio* from Apalachee, the Spaniards felt the strength of the *caciques* of that rich land. The rulers of Apalachee's towns would become a political force in the years ahead—a force that could upbraid friars, check governors, and win the favor of the king. In Tsenacomacoh, after Opechancanough passed from the scene, Virginia's governor, in his capacity as the English king's viceroy, gradually usurped the powers, without accepting the traditional duties, of the office of *mamanato-wick* or paramount chief. Rather than breaking apart, the Powhatan chiefdom was reformed into a republic of Indians and the treaty negotiated in October 1646 served as its constitution.

Seeming to win the upper hand in so startling and sudden a manner, Spaniards and Englishmen believed they possessed unprecedented power to remake Apalachee and Powhatan society. Victory deluded them. Neither of the wars of the 1640s was the Indians' "last stand."[96] The end of the fighting marked the beginning of a new phase in the Indigenous effort to transform the colonies who "conquered" them into a system responsive to Indigenous expectations and interests. Skilled Native leaders with considerable negotiating power stepped forward to hammer out new covenants with the colonizers. In Florida, the Apalachees helped to expand and eventually pushed to reform the republic of Indians, but in Virginia, the Powhatans were creating a whole new regime—and it is worth dwelling on what they built.

Opechancanough spent his last days a captive brooding in a James-town jail. The "emperor" had once fought hand-to-hand with John Smith, supposedly, wrote a later commentator, seized briefly "as *Atabalipa* was by *Piçarra*."[97] Now, Virginia's Atahualpa at last waited in confinement but not, like the Inca, to fill his cell with a ransom of gold. Opechancanough himself was the prize. The story handed down through the generations was that the "Indian Emperor" was destined for the royalist capital in Oxford, to ride in a triumphal parade for the harried King Charles I. The "Fatigues of War" and extreme old age had winnowed the flesh on the old *mamanatowick* down to the bone.[98] That "ancient Prince" who grappled with John Smith a genera-tion before now sat, eyes closed—his "heavy" lids drooped with age so that he needed an attendant to raise them—listening to the "great Noise of the Treading of People about him."[99] When he heard the sounds of the gawk-ing crowd, Opechancanough upbraided Sir William Berkeley in words that recalled Wahunsenacawh's retort at his coronation in 1608 that if the English king had sent him gifts, then he, too, was a king. If it had been my "Fortune to take Sir William Berkeley Prisoner," Opechancanough said, I "should not meanly have exposed him as a Show to [my] People."[100] Before the governor could have Opechancanough loaded aboard a ship for England, one of the great man's guards, "basely shot him thro' the Back."[101]

Necotowance, Opechancanough's successor and presumably his nephew, came to the ensuing peace talks with the goals of saving his people and pre-serving his office as paramount chief.[102] A man too often treated as a hapless victim—or worse, a nonentity—it was Necotowance who laid the foundation for the republic of Indians in Virginia. Two years of war had already sundered the allegiance of several of his subject nations, including the Rappahannocks.[103] Any compact with the English would have to recognize his title and authority. On the other side, Sir William Berkeley, feeling flush with victory, nevertheless understood its limits. The governor believed that Necotowance's consent was the surest basis of a lasting settlement between Englishmen and the formida-ble Powhatans.[104] According to Roman law, as Jeffrey Glover explains, treaties between putative unequals might still be the result of true "*consensus ad idem*, a 'meeting of the minds' or voluntary agreement between parties."[105] Virgin-ians were tired of war, whether at home or in England. Powhatans were still daunting foes who would never be subdued by force. There was room, then, if only a little, to negotiate.[106] Berkeley and Necotowance met on a small patch of common ground. Together, the governor and the *mamanatowick* wrote the constitution for what would become Virginia's republic of Indians.

In the treaty's very first article, Necotowance took the extraordinary step, a choice Wahunsenacawh flatly rejected throughout his life, of becoming a vassal of the king of England.[107] The *mamanatowick*, now styled "King of the Indians," held "his Kingdom from the King's Majesty of England."[108] In the course of their negotiations, Necotowance and Berkeley settled on terms that could satisfy both parties. Necotowance's successors, therefore, were to "be appointed *or* confirmed" by the king of England's governors in Virginia.[109] The equivocal wording was deliberate and satisfied English pretensions to sovereignty while recognizing Powhatan autonomy and custom. In the years ahead, Virginia's governors left the matter of succession to Indigenous custom much as their Spanish counterparts did, while reserving a "right to discern what the customary law of succession" demanded.[110] With the exception of the executions of the *caciques* involved in the coup of 1647, Apalachee's leaders never lost control of chiefly succession. Nor were the Indigenous towns of Florida reorganized with *cabildos*, Spanish-style town councils, as in much of the rest of the Spanish Empire.[111] Thus, chiefly power in Florida and Virginia fared better than elsewhere in the Americas. Florida's governor mostly interceded on the occasions when Natives' choices threatened colonial interests or when leaders committed gross misconduct, as in the case of the *mico* of the Guale town of Sapala in 1650, who stood accused of "oppressing" his vassals "with excessive charges and tributes and other wrongs."[112] But such exceptions proved the rule that, in Florida, custom was the guide in matters touching the succession of chiefs. This seems to have been the rule in Virginia. While claiming power over the choice of Necotowance's successors, the Virginia colony pledged "to protect him or them against any rebels or other enemies whatsoever."[113] Necotowance may have asked for this clause to shore up his own position much as Indigenous leaders in Apalachee had done with the Spaniards. Paying tribute was part of the bargain. For the Apalachees, the tribute they paid came in the form of *repartimiento* labor on public works in San Agustín.[114] For the Powhatans, the tribute was peltry, specifically beaver furs.

The treaty made the Powhatans tributaries of the English at last, a move with precedents in Algonquian law, the works of European philosophers from Machiavelli to Grotius, and in Spanish imperial institutions and legal concepts.[115] Necotowance swore to "pay unto the King's Governor the number of twenty beaver skins at the going away of Geese yearly" to seal the covenant and as "an acknowledgement" in exchange for royal "protection."[116] In contemporary Spanish political thought, Native tribute was similarly an acknowledgement of vassalage and a token paid in exchange for the king's protection. Tribute, wrote the jurist Juan Solórzano y Pereira in 1648, "ought to be paid to the King our Lord, in recognition of vassalage."[117] Solórzano thought "it is just and necessary that the same Indians should contribute something" to the king for, among other benefits, "protecting them in peace, and war."[118] Tributes were the lifeblood of a commonwealth and vassals should happily and willingly pay them. Citing the sixth-century Roman writer Cassiodorus, Solórzano argued "that these tributes ought to be paid with delight from everyone, for they redound in common utility, and secure the establishment and firmness of the Republic."[119] In Virginia, too, tribute became the bond between Indigenous subjects and the English monarch that ensured his loving care.[120]

The promise of colonial protection was costly, arguably costlier for the Powhatans than for the Apalachees who faced few settlers on their lands until the last quarter of the century.[121] Besides submission to the Crown and pledging to pay tribute to the English, Necotowance assented to a staggering colonial land grab, and agreed to keep his people to lands north of the York River on pain of death. Giving up the land on the south side of the York River was a major concession that pulled the ground out from under some of Opechancanough's original allies in the war. By the terms of the treaty, the Chickahominies lost all of their homeland in the Chickahominy River basin.[122] The treaty meant that armed colonists would keep any Indian from even visiting their former towns and burials, although archaeological evidence suggests they continued to do so.[123] The remaining articles regulated the exchange of messengers across the boundary between the colony and the "King of the Indians," and banned Englishmen from "entertaining," that is, hiring Indians under any circumstances.[124] Virginia's Assembly recorded the covenant as the first act of the October 1646 session. The Powhatans engraved the document in their memories. So "that they may distinctly remember what is proposed to them" Powhatan leaders assigned to one person "one article, and another a second, and another a third, and to divide them amongst them."[125] The Powhatans remembered the bad parts of the treaty but concentrated on the good, as they strove to transform the brusque document of their supposed defeat into the constitution for a polity where Natives and English colonists were equals.

Within just a few years, the ideal of harmonious republics, English and Native, under the same king, came to life in a ceremony at Jamestown in March 1649. Necotowance entered Jamestown with five *weroances* "attending him."[126]

Behind them, came burdeners with the twenty beaver pelts in tribute.[127] Sir
William Berkeley, flanked by his ten-member bodyguard, greeted the dignitaries with a speech recalling the reciprocal duties Powhatans and Englishmen
owed one another. Necotowance replied with a "long Oration," on the meaning
of the treaty of 1646, closing with a promise of fidelity to the covenant with
the English. "*That the Sun and Moon should first lose their glorious lights and
shining,*" he said, "*before* [I] *or* [my] *People should evermore hereafter wrong the
English in any kind, but they would ever hold love and friendship together.*"[128]
The concession he purportedly made that day, allowing Englishmen "*to pass at
all times when and where they please throughout His Dominions,*" was likely his
undoing.[129] The "five petty Kings" who joined him in Jamestown that day later
withdrew their support. The chiefdom broke apart not long after that, although
scholars debate why and who exactly was responsible. Most historians have
argued that the chiefdom broke apart under the strain of war and loss if not
outright colonial pressure, although Dylan Ruediger has made the intriguing
suggestion that individual *weroances* deliberately dismantled the chiefdom not
in anguish but as a strategy to confound colonial control.[130] In any case, the
Powhatans after Necotowance agreed to the treaty of 1646, as Robin Beck has
astutely observed, became collectively "vassals of a foreign *Mamanatowick,*
England's Charles I."[131] Necotowance's successors, the *weroances* and *weroansquas* of distinct nations, having exchanged the "house of Pamunkey" for the
house of Stuart, would truly forge the new system into being.[132]

After Necotowance's demise, Ascomowett, *weroance* of the Weanokes,
Ossakican, *weroance* of the Chiskiaks, and Totopotomoy, the *weroance* of
the Pamunkeys joined the republic of Indians after "their several Petitions"
to the Grand Assembly pledging "themselves tributaries to his Sacred Majesty" and demanding secure land title.[133] A brave warrior, member of a high-
ranking lineage, Totopotomoy at one time might have expected to succeed
to the office of *mamanatowick* himself. Instead, he carried the title "Commander, and Leader over" the Pamunkeys.[134] Like the other *weroances* who
lodged their petitions with the assembly, Totopotomoy conceded "that the
Sovereignty of the land whereon they live" was the English Crown's.[135] But
Totopotomoy retained much of his power, his people's customary law, and
a preeminent place in the new regime. The land patents that each *weroance*
received in 1649 resembled a *composición de tierras* in the Spanish Empire,
whereby they received clear title to their land in exchange for a hefty fee.
In this case, the charge came as thousands and thousands of acres over and
above the five thousand they requested.[136]

Nevertheless, the petitioners won concessions that came as stipulations on their patents and were in effect amendments to the articles of the treaty of 1646. Ascomowett's petition asked for two special favors to be "Inserted into his Patent," including title to land on the James River outside the "Bounds Limited by the treaty" and the "Privilege to hunt upon all Waste land there-unto adjacent without the bounds" of his land.[137] The assembly granted the petitions of Ascomowett, Ossakican, and Totopotomoy in hopes, they said, of the *weroances*' "Reducement [reduction] to Civility, and a hopeful progress there to their Conversion to Christianity."[138] The demands of the Indigenous petitioners, however, were what prevailed in the long run. In the following year, 1650, the assembly suspended land grants to Englishmen and invited other *weroances* and *weroansquas* to petition individually for patents at the rate "of fifty Acres of land for Each Bowman."[139] The terms Ascomowett "Inserted" into his patent became the standard, with future grants to include "liberty of all Waste and unfenced Land for Hunting for the Indians."[140]

The petitions from the three *weroances* set the pattern for the republic of Indians in Virginia, a pattern that they gradually wrote into the statute books, and that built on the treaty—rather, the constitution—of 1646. That constitution established a broad category of Native subjects with a host of duties and protections and stands to this day as the foundation of Virginia Indians' sovereignty. For the English, the most important obligation the treaty imposed on tributaries was to serve as guides, porters, and warriors who would help expand Virginia beyond the Fall Line.[141] For the Indigenous leaders who became tributaries, the treaty was an opening, too, a chance to wield continued influence on colonial politics.[142]

The beaver pelts Native subjects paid in recognition of their obedience to the king entitled them to certain rights, among them the right to petition the governor, the assembly (for a time, at least), and theoretically the monarch. Native petitioners would ward off grasping settlers and win special favors, immunities, and liberties, which colonial authorities then codified in written statutes and orders. We should not exaggerate what tributary status meant, but nor should we deny that it offered real protection and lasting political influence, not only in Virginia but in other English colonies including Mary-land and New York.[143] Indigenous tributary subjects were key players who made their laws and values part of the "Stuart imperial project."[144] In addition to the privileges and liberties its *weroance* and people possessed as royal sub-jects, each tributary nation had its own specific body of privileges and liber-ties or, to put it into Spanish legal terms, its own separate *fuero*.[145] A tributary nation's *fuero* included privileges both ancient, such as the right to choose its leaders according to custom, and modern, such as the stipulations about hunting on "Waste land" that Ascomowett asked to be included in his land patent. What the system in Virginia most resembled after midcentury was the *república de Indios* in Florida. As the harshest terms of the treaty of 1646 gradually eroded under the outpouring of Native petitions, the resemblance would only grow over time.

As Natives seized on new political possibilities, a few Spanish and English colonizers softened their harsh stances toward them, making appeals for mercy and to the rule of law, rather than violence. Despite the wreckage in the missions, where Apalachee and Chisca insurgents had taken "the Ornaments, chalices, and other things that were dedicated to the divine cult," before burning mission churches to the ground, Franciscans urged leniency.[146] In July 1648, Fray Pedro Moreno Ponce de León, Procurator General of the Franciscan Order in the provinces of Florida, begged the king to condemn only the worst offenders in the revolt and to "lift the punishments and impositions on the rest of the Indians."[147] Moreno's motives were not entirely disinterested. If the king forgave the rebel Apalachees then they would be under obligation to the Franciscans, whose pleas for mercy would "attract others to the union of the Church."[148] Even among the English, some writers shared Fray Moreno's concerns. In 1649, William Bullock weighed the best course to take with the Powhatans after the murder of Opechancanough. The war years convinced Bullock that force "hath been fatal to the Indians, there having been great numbers of the slain."[149] Like the Franciscans, he believed further bloodshed was unjust and too costly either in treasure or lives. Natives could not be "wholly vanquished" without an extirpation.[150]

While they agreed on substituting law for violence, by midcentury Spaniards and Englishmen had different views about the use of Indigenous labor in the republic of Indians. After the Apalachee Revolt, Florida's *repartimiento* was under attack from clerics, *caciques*, and the Crown. Don Diego de Villalva, the governor of Cuba, at Fray Pedro Moreno's request, asked the king to send fifty friars at royal expense.[151] For the sake of the conversion and no doubt the benefit of Cuban merchants, the governor urged that the alms to support the friars—vestments, wine, oil—should go by ship from Havana directly to Apalachee, sparing Natives from burdening.[152] "Until now it was brought from Mexico to the *presidio* of San Agustín," Villalva explained, "and from there it is carried by land to Apalachee (more than one hundred leagues) with great costs and risks to the Indians."[153] A royal *cédula* (decree) the same year ordered Villalva to embark two hundred "draft-horses" to carry the friar's supplies "without loading the Indians."[154] Under pressure from Franciscan lobbyists at court, the king issued yet another royal *cédula* in August 1648 that struck directly at the abuses of Florida's *repartimiento*. The king was dismayed to learn how the governor, "other Ministers, and soldiers take married Indian men from the Doctrinas and busy them in digging the earth" for the Spaniards' support.[155] The poor Native men forcibly "detained all the year," were "sickening and dying and not making a Life with their wives."[156]

At the same time in Virginia, Native labor appeared open to exploitation—at least in the fantasies of colonial promoters in England. While the enslavement of Native peoples has received much-deserved attention, English colonizers envisioned other means of harnessing Indigenous labor, especially after Opechancanough's death.[157] William Bullock suggested that English colonists approach their neighboring Indigenous leader with the proposition "that if he send thirty or forty men to help in your Harvest, he shall have a Cloak, or Breeches and Doublet, or the like, and his men should have every one something."[158] The proposal was something unheard-of since the days of the Virginia Company, an English *repartimiento*, a public draft of low-wage Indian labor. Other Englishmen criticized such worldly thinking. Thomas Thorowgood argued that some Natives "are unsubdued by the Spaniards to this day, not so much because they are a warlike people in their kind, but especially by reason of their poverty and indigence."[159] The English should not succumb to the same motives. Hamon L'Estrange, Thorowgood's opponent in a controversy over the origins of Native Americans, at least on this point agreed with him, writing that "the sacred hunger of Gold (which the Americans call the *Christians God*) and too much *meum* and *tuum* [mine and yours] have overleavened the whole lump, and been the prime authors and actors in our plantations."[160] Even so, by the middle of the seventeenth century, Englishmen believed their power in America was growing and, with it, the potential to further exploit Indigenous people, while always measuring their own achievements against Spain's.

The inclusion of Indigenous tributaries as subjects with legal protections was an important part of how Englishmen thought about their burgeoning empire, much as rule over its innumerable Native vassals was for Spain's sense of imperial mission. In 1651, George Gardyner published a "geographical description" of the Americas that placed England's empire on the same stage as Spain's.[161] With its astounding breadth of territory, immense wealth, and myriad "civil" Native vassals—where in the Valley of Mexico alone there were "reckoned to be six hundred thousand tributary Indians"—it was Spain's empire that Gardyner looked to emulate and, ultimately, surpass.[162] The English, he pointed out, ruled tributary Indians too. In Maryland, Virginia, and what Gardyner called "Old Virginia"—soon to be Carolina—Indians paid "contribution" to the English.[163] Although Virginia was "without any Mineral, save Iron, Stone," Gardyner reported that the Indians subject to the English paid the governor "great tributes of skins."[164] Gardyner, in imitation of the Spanish Jesuit José de Acosta, proposed a tripartite classification of the Americas' original inhabitants. For Acosta, what distinguished Natives in his typology was their internal form of government—whether "Monarchies," "Commonalities," or those *indios de behetría*, who lived without king or law or fixed settlements.[165] For Gardyner, the differences among his three types of Native societies were the result of the kind of government *Europeans coloniz- ers* claimed to exercise over them. Between the Natives who "live within the government of the *Spaniards* after the same manner that they do, in apparel, building, trades and Religion" and the Chichimecas and Caribs beyond all colonial control, were the Natives, as Gardyner put it, who "live under the contribution of the English."[166]

Without knowing it, Gardyner landed on the truth about the "conquest" of the Powhatans and what tributary status meant to Indigenous leaders like the Pamunkey *weroance* Totopotomoy who accepted it. What distinguished them, notably in Virginia, Gardyner argued, was that Indigenous tributaries preserved "their ancient Customs, Religions, and Manners," and retained their "several Governors, or Kings."[167] Their cultural attainments may not have seemed as spectacular to English colonizers as the temples and palaces of the "civilized" Natives in New Spain or Peru. Southern Natives' houses rested on "frames of Arbor works" and were "covered with the bark of trees," Gar- dyner noted.[168] But these hardy warriors and sage councilors had kept a large measure of their liberty. For the tribute they paid, England's Indian subjects enjoyed "good privileges over the English."[169] Gardyner missed other import- ant facts as well. Had he known much about Florida, he would probably have placed the Apalachees or Timucuas in a similar category with the Powhatans. Indigenous peoples in Florida also kept their customs, their leaders, if not always their traditional religions. And the Apalachees, Guales, and Timucuas held what Gardyner would also have called "good privileges," though they were not simply granted at colonial hands. The privileges the Natives pos- sessed were hard-won. Through the trials of the next decades, Indigenous subjects and vassals would seek to win more.

The relative freedom Indian tributaries enjoyed under their covenants with the English was a point for national self-congratulation and, ironically, a justification for more American conquests. By the 1650s, English writers lamented the "narrow hearted" Tudor king Henry VII who turned away Christopher Columbus, and gave up the riches of the Indies while condemning Indigenous peoples to Spanish cruelty.[170] The *"Poor Spirits of our English Kings"* made them *"almost guilty of the Blood shed in those parts, through their neglect."*[171] With their new empire of Native tributaries, Gardyner and others believed the English could rectify those mistakes. Besides, England in 1656, after the Parliamentarian victory in the Civil Wars, was kingless and with a Lord Protector eager to free the Americas from what he saw as Spanish bondage. Oliver Cromwell's "Western Design," a massive assault against Spanish America, did not liberate the "poor Indians" but an amphibious expedition under William Penn and Robert Venables managed to annex Jamaica to the English Protectorate.[172] News of the fall of Jamaica caused the governor and captain-general of Florida to call up the Indigenous militia, fearing San Agustín was next. In Virginia, there were troubles closer to home. A great movement of Native peoples from the north brought hundreds of Native refugees to the Fall Line and threatened colonial gains. Both events in the same year would put the republic of Indians in Florida and Virginia to the test.

Western Designs: War, Crisis, and Reform in the Republic of Indians

Although the nervous planters of Virginia had no inkling of the truth, the hundreds of unknown Indians who arrived in the spring of 1656 were refugees from the north, Eries who had fled disastrous Haudenosaunee (Five Nations Iroquois) raids.[173] The English called them Richahecrians. History knows them better as the Westos.[174] The assembly resolved on a stern course with these "new come Indians."[175] The colony won the territory at the Falls in what it called "a just war," securing title to it "at the last conclusion of peace with the Indians."[176] Invoking the terms of the very same treaty, the assembly next called up the "neighboring Indians to aid them."[177] Messengers rode to meet the Pamunkey *weroance* Totopotomoy and the Chickahominy *manguys* (councilors) to muster their men for an expedition against the invaders.[178] Totopotomoy came at their call. The Pamunkey *weroances*'s significance in the colony's politics made him the only Indigenous leader whom the legislative act authorizing the expedition summoned by name, and he soon gathered his bowmen and left his town. Totopotomoy left behind a wife. Cockacoeske was an heir of the *mamanatowick* Opechancanough and to his ancient office in her own right. Totopotomoy's departure at the head of his bowmen was the last time she saw her husband alive. When Totopotomoy reached the encampment at the Falls of the James River, the colonial commander Colonel Edward Hill invited the Richahecrians' leaders to a friendly parley. The Richahecrians were amicable and had "brought much Beaver with them" as gifts and as enticements to "the intercourse of commerce."[179] Once the parties met and the discussions had begun, Hill's men repaid the Richahecrians' trust by killing five of their envoys.[180] The battle that followed—the Battle of the Bloody Run—was a rout. Hill's men broke before the guns of the Richahecrians. In the smoke and confusion, Totopotomoy's bowmen stood their ground. The great *werowance*, by one account, so "desirous to shew his fidelity to the English," led his men "in the pursuit of those other Indians, and thereby lost his life."[181]

In April, around the time that the assembly mustered Totopotomoy and the Pamunkeys, Florida's governor, Don Diego de Rebolledo, commanded the Indigenous militia to hurry to San Agustín. News of the fall of Jamaica to English forces in 1655 led Rebolledo to fear San Agustín was a target.[182] Over the past year, life for the hungry soldiers and their families in the *presidio* grew desperate. For the Natives in the provinces, it was even worse. When Rebolledo sent Captain Francisco Garcia de la Vera to collect the men from Apalachee and Timucua "for the sowing and labor of the fields for the infantry," news came back from the provincial lieutenant and the friars with news that appeared to seal "the total Ruin" of the *presidio*.[183] The provinces were in the grips of a "Great contagion," with mass death and "a great number of Indians and others very sick, for which cause, the People cannot come" to work.[184] Ruthless in his determination to round up labor to feed the *presidio*, Rebolledo sent Captain Antonio de Argüelles into Ybiniyutti, a province of "Infidel Indians" who harbored fugitive Apalachees who had fled to avoid the *repartimiento*.[185] The governor commanded Argüelles to go from town to town and snatch whomever he could find.[186] With the same ruthlessness, Rebolledo readied for the imminent English invasion, and in his haste, ignored the customary laws of the republic of Indians. In his order calling up the militia, the governor did not exempt the Indigenous nobles from a requirement to carry the supplies for the journey to the *presidio* on their backs. Burdening was the work of commoners. *Caciques* directed the labor but never performed it themselves. Although it was a long time in coming, Rebolledo's order was the catalyst that broke the compact between provincial nobles and the paramount in San Agustín that held the two republics of Indians and Spaniards together.[187] The Timucuas revolted in the name of the king. The Timucua nobles expressed the prevailing attitude in 1656 when they boasted "that they had not been conquered but with the word of God."[188]

The Battle of the Bloody Run in Virginia and the tumult that would be known as the Timucuan Rebellion in Florida rattled the republic of Indians in both colonies and led to frank reappraisals of what it meant for Indigenous people to be vassals or subjects of European empires. Totopotomoy's death had multiple meanings. He died in order "to secure his people's place in the empire" and the Pamunkeys' preeminence among the other tributary nations, a prominence that spelled influence over the colonial government.[189] His death stood also for an ideal of equality between Indians and English under the same sovereign. Finally, Totopotomoy's death marked the beginning of another chapter of the Indigenous struggle to transform Virginia into a polity that worked for them, foreshadowing a time when Native petitioners strode the halls of colonial power in James City. In Florida, Timucuan *holatas* rose against the governor in San Agustin in defense of the covenant they had established with the king of Spain, which like the Powhatans' 1646 treaty, guaranteed their place within the Spanish Empire. Their values were much the same as Totopotomoy's. The *holatas* fought to preserve their people— suffering as they were under the colonial labor draft—and just as importantly the respect due their high stations as Indigenous nobles. A few colonizers, most of them clerics, seconded the Indigenous complaints in the two colonies. The campaigns that followed the events of 1656 would eventually rewrite colonial laws in ways that reflected the views of Indigenous leaders.

As the Timucua Rebellion exploded in Florida, in Virginia, the disaster at the Falls of the James aroused righteous indignation in the colonial assembly. After a trial and debate over his guilt, the Grand Assembly stripped Edward Hill of his offices and held him responsible for the costs of the gifts needed to make peace with the Richahecrians again.[190] In the burgesses' view, Hill's conduct proved how little Virginians cared about "shedding Indians' blood, though never so innocent."[191] Stung by the loss of Totopotomoy and his warriors, the assembly repealed the act allowing colonists to shoot Indians on sight for trespass. Now, only a felony and that on the word of two witnesses, could justify killing any "Indians that are in our protection," a striking (if wholly inadequate) amendment to the constitution of Virginia's republic of Indians, written in Totopotomoy's blood.[192] The changes did not go far enough for his widow and heir.

Cockacoeske never forgot her husband's death—and she never forgave the English their incompetence nor "the very unchristianly" way they repaid his service.[193] Born perhaps in the 1630s, Cockacoeske possessed a solid claim to the title of *mamanatowick*, one which she would make good in the years ahead.[194] In 1656, Cockacoeske succeeded Totopotomoy as *weroansqua* of Pamunkey. From his death to hers, Cockacoeske devoted her prodigious political talents to recovering the strength of Tsenacomacoh.[195] When she spoke, burgesses and councilors listened. When she sent letters to English allies, her words carried weight. Laws sometimes changed under her influence. The day even came when the Pamunkey *weroansqua* wrote a whole new treaty with the English. She became the foremost Indigenous leader in Virginia and never missed the chance to remind the English of the Pamunkeys' importance or of their supreme sacrifice at the Bloody Run. A generation would pass and still, whenever colonial officials asked Cockacoeske for Pamunkey men to fight in their wars, she would cut them short with the reminder that Totopotomoy was dead. According to the Reverend Lionel Gatford, who lent his voice to the cause of reform in Indian affairs, Totopotomoy wanted the English to respect and protect Cockacoeske, writing that she "ought to have been taken into their special care."[196] She made her own way instead, forging alliances with English colonizers within a moral climate that seemed to be shifting just a little in favor of Native peoples.

In both empires, religious ministers spoke out against violations of the covenants binding Europeans and Natives together, although the English clerics who did so, like Lionel Gatford, are seldom remembered today. With the verve and moral certitude of an English Las Casas, Gatford penned a remonstrance to the lord protector, Oliver Cromwell, against the conduct of Virginia's planters toward the "poor Indians." Whenever "Indians do chance to come into any of their Plantations, and are taken," Gatford alleged, "the English oftentimes tie them alive to trees and burn them to ashes, or else otherwise murder them, without showing any cause, farther than the pretending that the Indians are not to be trusted."[197] The planters took "the Indians' goods from them by force."[198] And they had "turned some of the Indians out of their places of abode and subsistence," Gatford said, even "after that the Indians have submitted to the Colony, and to their Government, and have taken up their own lands after the custom used by the Colony."[199] What good, then, was becoming a Christian if becoming a tributary and subject afforded them "no security or protection to them or theirs"?[200] Gatford's was but one voice and it carried little weight in England. In the Spanish Empire, the voices of the Franciscans echoed farther and the friars proved stronger allies to Florida's Native vassals. But the root of the matter was the same: what good was the republic of Indians when colonists or governors flouted the laws protecting the liberties and privileges of its members?

For nearly half a century, Fray Juan Gómez in Florida had witnessed "the travails and persecutions of the poor Indians" and "how they have been such faithful vassals of His Majesty and obedient to the royal crown."[201] The revolt of the Timucuas, he implied in an April 1657 letter, was justified. Rebolledo's breach of custom with the Native nobility, "obliging them to come . . . one hundred leagues to the *presidio* of San Agustin, loaded as if they were mules and horses" was unconscionable.[202] Governor Rebolledo, made a mockery of the king's promise to keep his noble Indigenous vassals in the same high rank they had enjoyed before their conquest by the Gospel.[203] The Timucua leaders balked, "for seeing themselves as natural lords in their lands," wrote the Franciscan chapter that fall, "and that they would be forced to carry, a thing they were never accustomed to do, and that was only done by the lowliest of their vassals."[204] In Florida, the Timucuan Rebellion also threw into question whether subjection to the Spanish king, let alone conversion to the Spanish god, was worth the costs.

Even as Gómez wrote the king of Spain and Gatford published his remonstrance to the Lord Protector of England, Indigenous vassals and subjects drafted petitions and laid plans. In those dark days, Native petitioners recited histories to illustrate how far the ideal of the republic of Indians had fallen. "For in the past anciently according to what we hear from our Fathers and grandfathers and what we have experienced some years," the *micos* of Guale wrote King Felipe IV in 1657, "the governors of these Provinces and the rest of the Spaniards loved us, consoled us, favored us . . . like fathers they treated us, speaking to us as sons."[205] But now, they said, "all has been turned to the contrary."[206] For the Guale *micos*, the fight was about restoring the republic of Indians to what it once was. For Cockacoeske, now *weroansqua* of Pamunkey after Totopotomoy's death, the task ahead was to lay the groundwork to strengthen her position in colonial politics and forestall the same sort of downward slide in status that the Guales had witnessed. She began an intimate relationship with Captain John West, a prominent English landowner—descended from nobility and two Virginia governors—who had also once accompanied Totopotomoy home after official business in James

City in the early 1650s.[207] Her son by Captain West took his father's name
and became Cockacoeske's designated heir while she lived, with the plan that
he would be fully fluent in the English language, manners, and laws when
he took over.[208] In the next decade, Native leaders like Cockacoeske and the
Guale *micos* plied every avenue for justice, to courts, assemblies, councils,
even to the king. Far from defeated in the 1640s and '50s, Indigenous leaders
in Florida and Virginia intensified their political efforts, rewriting the laws of
both colonies and defining in their own terms what it meant to be vassals and
subjects of the Crown.

Native Petitioners Rewrite the Law

The *cédula* from the king landed like a thunderbolt from the sky. Dated
26 February 1660, Felipe IV's decree exempted the people of the small
Mocama town of Nuestra Señora de Guadalupe de Tolomato from the
"chores" that Florida's governors ordinarily forced them to do. No more
could the governor summon Tolomato's men "for the unloading of the Ships
that arrive to the Presidio . . . and other services."[209] No longer would they be
"taken away from their labors when they are occupied in the sowing of Maize
that is their common sustenance," leaving their wives and children in "great
hunger and need."[210] Two years before, Santiago the *mico* of Tolomato and his
principales, had written to King Felipe IV. Tolomato's leaders hearkened back
to the founding of their town on its present site just "three leagues distant
from the *presidio* of San Agustín."[211] Once the seat of a paramount chiefdom,
until the 1620s Tolomato stood far to the north on the mainland across from
St. Catherine's Island. Perhaps to punish them for their part in the very rebellion that sent Agustín López and Juan Orata to the Morro in Havana, Governor Luís Rojas y Borja moved the entire town of Tolomato southward to a
spot just above San Agustín.[212] In those days, there were plenty of men in the
village to carry the loads the twelve leagues to San Juan del Puerto, the next
town in the chain that moved supplies northward to relieve the soldiers and
friars stationed in Mocama and Guale.[213] By midcentury, a little more than
a generation after its refounding near the Spanish *presidio*, Tolomato now
"could not turn up thirty men, counting *caciques* and *principales*, to continue
the work."[214] The king heard the pleas of his "faithful and loyal Vassals" in
Tolomato.[215] He commanded his governor and captain general in the provinces of Florida "not to occupy the residents of the said Town in your own

and private conveniences and that you will procure their conservation and relief by all means possible."[216]

In March 1661, as Tolomato's new law made its way across the Atlantic, Virginia's Grand Assembly met in James City, where a crush of petitioners swarmed lawmakers, packed the few houses and ordinaries in town, and pressed their cases.[217] Petitions were one way for Virginia colonists to influence the law much as they were in England, and the right to petition was far more important to most people than the franchise.[218] Everyone from the richest planter to the poorest servant cherished the liberty to petition, and efforts to hinder it met with condemnation.[219] That spring, Nicholas Boot was there to renew his patent of denization, which the assembly had granted him in 1658.[220] John Harlow, who a jury had found guilty of planting a small quantity of tobacco "after the day appointed by act," haunted the burgesses in hopes that they would overturn his conviction or at least waive the fine.[221] Another petitioner—a man of importance and influence—joined the crowd in James City. He sought a patent for his large landholdings near the head of Mattaponi River. His name was Harquip, and he was the most important of the *manguys*, or councilors, of the Chickahominies. The sight of an Indian amid the usual crowd of favor-seekers was nothing out of the ordinary. In October 1660, the assembly heard the petition of the Accomacks "that the English seat so near them, that they receive very much damage in their corn."[222] A commission soon went out to survey boundaries for land "sufficient for their maintenance" that could never be sold "to the *English*."[223] Harquip's petition succeeded too. The Chickahominies won a legal promise that "no Englishman shall upon any pretense disturb them in their said bounds."[224] He received his patent and in it a clause forbidding the sale of any part of the Chickahominies land "unless the major part of the great men shall freely and voluntarily declare their consent in the quarter court or assembly."[225]

By the 1660s, Natives like Santiago and Harquip were leaders in an Indigenous-driven politics that helped rewrite colonial law in Florida and Virginia. Santiago's path and Harquip's were different. Santiago pitched his appeal over the head of the governor and straight to the Spanish king. Harquip had to ply his petition through local institutions under the control of the very people who, not long ago, had waged a brutal war against him. Still, the results were similar. Native vassals and subjects forged a mutual law with Spaniards and Englishmen, at a pace that picked up substantially after midcentury. In time, the English Crown would have the same importance for Native subjects in Virginia as the Spanish Crown did for Native vassals in Florida. The underlying commonalities between Florida's *república de Indios* and the Virginia tributary regime were thus as much the product of Indigenous agency as of any shared intellectual currents among Spanish and English colonizers.

Whether Spanish or English, colonists and colonial officials were usually shocked at Natives' political savvy and their ability to rewrite the law with their petitions. In San Agustín that autumn, the news of how the poor Indians of Tolomato had won a royal decree left Governor Alonso de Aranguíz y Cotes flabbergasted. The Natives, he told the king in November 1661, could not be responsible as there were only "very few" who were capable of writing—overlooking how the "few" who could compose letters would readily have done so.[226] Most Virginia colonists would have shared the Florida governor's disbelief. English Virginians tended to see Natives as stumbling blocks in the way of law rather than as its authors. In their minds, the subjection of the Powhatans delivered Virginia from what John Hammond had called "the Country's minority," a time when "fear of the Indian" prevailed.[227] Where Opechancanough once held sway, now justice is "duly and daily administered" in the counties where every "two miles" a colonist could "find a Justice."[228] Francis Moryson, compiler of the colony's 1662 law code, directly connected Opechancanough's capture in 1646 to the triumph of English law and justice. To Sir William Berkeley, whom he hailed as Opechancanough's conqueror, "we owe both the Laws we Govern by, and the Country it self now Govern'd by those Laws."[229] Though colonists believed that Natives were an obstacle to the rule of law, in fact their petitions were essential to its establishment. While the significance of petitioning for Natives in the Spanish Empire is well known, in English colonies like Virginia, petitioning was fundamental to the pursuit of Native rights. With each successful plea—no matter how specific to the individual petitioner's circumstances—Natives established enduring legal precedents.

The "poor *Indians*" used their power to inscribe the principles of protection, equality, reciprocity, and self-government into the legal codes of both empires. The principle of protection meant that the law had to guard Native lands, property, and lives. Native complaints inspired several statutes in colonial Virginia designed to preserve all three. The *weroance* of the Weanokes, victim of "many disadvantageous bargains," petitioned the assembly for relief from his creditors who had "imprisoned" him in 1660.[230] An order followed to set the *weroance* free "according to his petition."[231] The *weroance*'s petition contributed to establishing the principle—later written into statute and a treaty—that Indigenous leaders were privileged from arrest except on an order of the governor and council.[232] What prompted lawmaking in other cases were what we might call "shadow" petitions—that is, petitions where only an indirect record survives rather than the plea itself.[233] An early law confirming Indian land titles came about due to the "many complaints [which] have been brought to this Assembly touching wrong done to the Indians."[234] For years, Native tributaries in general complained how English planters forbid them "to hunt in those woods, or to fish in those rivers, wherein they challenge a right."[235] After the complaints of tributary Natives, "believed by divers sober and discreet men of the Colony to have a right as well as themselves" to hunt, gather, and fish on the land, Virginia law codified their customary rights to collect all sorts of "Wild-Fruits" with a county court's order.[236]

As Native petitioners defined it, the protection of law should secure not just their rights to property but their liberty—whether freedom of movement or freedom from enslavement—and that of their children. Anonymous Native petitioners in Virginia who gave "divers informations . . . to the Assembly" won a law banning the buying and selling of Indigenous children.[237] The text of the statute suggests that tributary Natives of all ranks may have petitioned about this matter, citing "their parents" and "some of their great men" as victims of violence and fraud.[238] With their petitions, Indigenous leaders unwittingly brought the laws of Virginia into greater conformity with those of Florida—and with the Spanish laws of the Indies more generally.[239] In numerous *cédulas*, based on the "great truths" of classical and patristic sources, wrote Solórzano y Pereira, Spain's monarchs had ordained "that the Indians ought to be conserved, and maintained in their entire liberty, and full, and free administration of their goods, as the rest of their vassals in other Kingdoms."[240] In Virginia, under the pressure of Indigenous petitioners, the law said that "Indian's [*sic*] Properties in their Goods" were "assured and confirmed to them" and made "their Persons" inviolable as those of any English subject.[241]

The principle of equality between Native subjects and European subjects was fundamental to the republic of Indians as Natives understood it. Virginia law professed to treat Native tributaries as equals of English colonizers. When English colonists stole from Natives or harmed them, they were to be punished as "if the same had been done to any *English* man."[242] In 1663, Virginia law declared that Natives "shall have equal Justice with our own Nation, as the Laws already made have provided."[243] The law sometimes overrode equal treatment for the sake of protection, limiting Natives' ability to sell land, for instance, making them commensurate with orphans whose guardians could not sell during their minority.[244]

Equality also meant keeping up buffers between Indigenous peoples and colonizers. Natives and colonists erected protective boundaries between themselves, though at the beginning in Virginia, near-total separation—a kind of "racial apartheid"—prevailed for a time.[245] Such measures were ostensibly for the Natives' protection as much as for the protection of the colonists. One pious reformer wrote in 1662 about how Native tributaries often complained that the Sabbath day "was the worst of the seven to them," because Sunday was when "the servants of the Christians Plantations nearest to them, being then left at liberty, oft spend that day in visiting their *Indian* Towns."[246] In the 1660s, the colony issued "Badges . . . with the name of the Town graved upon them" to all *weroances* and *weroansquas* "within our Protection," a measure with roots in the beginning of Iberian colonization of the Americas.[247] Maintaining boundaries did not mean they would never cross over them. So long as one of them had a badge, a whole party of Indigenous people could leave their town on an errand. The law's enforcement was uneven, with punishments—in the Natives' case a "ransom" of "one hundred Arm's length of Roanoke"—falling on them more often than on English colonists.[248] Tributaries on the "South-side of the James" petitioned about the inequitable enforcement and had the law changed so that English offenders "shall be liable to the same Censure and Penalty as the law imposeth upon an Indian."[249] No less an authority than the "acute *Acosta*" had averred that "the gracious lives of Christians" was the surest aid to converting Natives.[250] But short of reducing Englishmen to political life in towns and reforming *their* manners, keeping them out of Native towns was the alternative in Virginia, just as it was in Florida.

The principle of reciprocity also became part of the foundation of the republic of Indians in the early South. In framing laws to protect the Natives "Tributary to the English," Virginia legislators believed that "Assistance and Reciprocal care, will make them and us have an equal Interest in the others preservation."[251] Native petitioners in Virginia had been cultivating the same idea for decades. In this, they again resembled Native peoples to the south. In Florida, Guale *micos* told the king that they would fight and "die with all of our vassals on the side of the Spaniards" if need be, displaying their commitment to the ideal of reciprocity.[252] By their services to the colonies and their increasing professions of loyalty to the Crown, Indigenous leaders tried to show how their survival was essential to the survival of the colonies.

For such a system of reciprocal duties to work, its laws had to be mutually comprehensible to all its members, Native and European. *Visítas* or the periodic inspections of the provinces of Florida were occasions for Natives and

Spaniards to discuss the law and to publish new regulations. Like the Spanish *visíta*, English colonial officials sent out special commissioners to look into the causes of disputes between Native and English tributary subjects. Commissioners in Virginia led parties on horseback into tributary Indian towns each year to "proclaim" the law and "the . . . Articles of Peace between Us and the *Indians*."[253] Native subjects and vassals were conversant in the law by midcentury. A Powhatan *weroance* once reportedly refused to accept "Indian custom" of compensation after the English murdered twelve of his people, saying "he expected such justice to be done and such punishment to be inflicted upon those murderers, as the English used to inflict upon the like amongst themselves."[254] More often, Indigenous leaders insisted on their customary law holding sway, especially in their internal affairs.

Most important of all to Native petitioners, nearly all of whom were leaders of their communities, was the principle of self-government. In Virginia and Florida, Indigenous custom usually governed the succession of chiefs. Native claimants to office used petitions, whether directly to the governor as regional paramount or in the course of regular provincial visitations, to notify officials of a vacancy.[255] Although the English, unlike the Spanish, claimed the power to appoint Native leaders and defend their appointees—a power Virginia's assembly dramatically restated in 1663—throughout the century, the governor settled for confirming the candidate "upon whom the right of Government of that Indian nation does devolve."[256]

Indigenous customary law thus became a part of imperial law because of leaders' tenacious defense of self-government. In thorny political matters, *weroances* and *caciques* could draw on what might be called a *mnemocracy*, the elders and leaders who possessed the collective memory of the customs, precedents, and written laws that comprised the constitution of the republic of Indians. When a Spanish visitor-general met a knotty problem of the succession of *caciques* in one of the towns on his inspection tour, he submitted the question to the *mnemocracy* in the village and, in some cases, to the collective wisdom of the whole province in a general assembly. When a Timucuan man called Benito stepped forward to claim his right as *cacique* of the town of Santa Elena de Machava during a *visíta* in 1670, the visitor-general first consulted with "many other *caciques*, *principales*, and ancient Indians from different Towns of that Province" who confirmed the claim's legitimacy based on matrilineal descent.[257] Although his successful invocation of Native custom is significant, Benito went a step further, petitioning the king of Spain in 1676 to shore up his new position, insisting that he and his heirs receive a hearing in the Council of the Indies before they could be deprived of the office.[258] But his expectation, no doubt, was that the matrilineal customs of Machava would receive primary consideration in the council's deliberations. A similar (if grudging) respect for Indigenous customary law held in Virginia. As Thomas Ludwell put it in the mid-1660s, disputes inside Native towns were "still left to the Decision of their own Customs."[259] Both the Spanish and English empires recognized and respected Indigenous law— its authority was written into colonial statute books and the decrees of kings.

The symbolic presence of the European monarch in the lives of Indigenous vassals and subjects grew as Native leaders increasingly identified their principles of protection, equality, reciprocity, and self-government with the respective Crowns of Spain and England. Native leaders associated their cause with the monarchs in the hope of placing their rights out of the reach of grasping colonists. Tolomato's *mico* Santiago spoke the minds of many other Indigenous leaders when he told the king that "our relief consists only in the patronage of Your Majesty as such a great Lord and Catholic Prince."[260] The pageantry and symbolism present even in the colonial outposts of Florida and Virginia reinforced the idea that the monarch's word commanded everyone in his domains. When they walked into a courthouse or visited the capital to petition or to pay tribute, Native subjects in Virginia would have seen the royal arms, and heard officials invoke the name of the king.[261] When a new *cacique* or *cacica* took office, Florida officials charged them to uphold "the service of God Our Lord and that of His Majesty, which as Christians they should uphold, and as loyal vassals obey."[262] In 1666, San Agustín mourned the demise of Felipe IV with all "the honors and obsequies" possible despite the "dearth of this government."[263] Tears turned to joy afterward as the *presidio* celebrated the accession of the new king, Carlos II, then just four years old. Across the city, "banners were Raised for Your Majesty, proclaiming you as our King and natural lord."[264] Surely, the mourning and the joyous acclamations took place "the same in all the *doctrinas* that are in these provinces," as on other state occasions.[265] During Carlos II's improbable thirty-five-year reign, Native vassals, never caring about the king's infirmities, proclaimed him the head of their republic and appealed to him as the guarantor of their liberties.[266] England's Charles II took on a similar role in his dominions, spectacularly so in the aftermath of Bacon's Rebellion in the mid-1670s, contributing to the growth of an Indigenous royalism.

Both crowns, Spanish and English, were spacious enough to encompass all kinds of Natives, Christian and "heathen," in their protection and could afford to honor their laws to boot. The strength and durability of Native status in Florida and in Virginia, however, depended on their usefulness to the empire. The work Natives did in Florida, whether in the fields raising the corn to feed the infantry, carrying loads across the peninsula, manning ferries at river crossings, cutting wood, unloading ships at the docks, or building forts, made the "conservation of the Indians" and the survival of the Spanish *presidio* one and the same. In Virginia, land was the most valuable thing any Indian possessed. Next to land, in the colonist's esteem, was the trade in goods for beaver pelts, deerskins, and slaves. Native subjects did other work too. They hunted wolves for bounties, fished and fowled for planters for a wage, and (something unthinkable to Florida Natives forced to do so) some even hired themselves out to colonists "as Carriers or Porters."[267]

The difference was in who benefited from Natives' work. In Florida, a wide swath of the Spanish population, ill-clad and hungry in the stints when the *situado* failed, depended on Indigenous labor for food. In Virginia, the tributes Natives paid and the profits from the trade in peltry, went to a small clique surrounding the governor that, in turn, was aligned with leaders like Cockacoeske of Pamunkey. A planter could not even hire a tributary Native "unless by a License obtained from the Governor himself," and then not "without leave of the King, or Great-man."[268] The thinness of their local political support did not stop Native leaders from establishing a body of liberties, privileges, and immunities under law. Virginia's Indigenous nobles could count on powerful allies but shuddered to think what might happen if the multitude of colonists proved too difficult for their high-placed friends to control. When the crisis came, Cockacoeske, the *weroansqua* of Pamunkey, and the rest of the "Indian kings and queens" looked above the governor's head and joined their cause to King Charles II's, solidifying the bond between Indian liberty and Stuart absolutism in a treaty that read like a Native subject's charter of rights.

Conclusion: The Liberties of Her People

In 1633, most Native people in Florida and Virginia were outsiders with little formal standing in either colonial political system. Forty years later, after a series of wars, uprisings, and upheavals many Native leaders—whether Pamunkeys or Apalachees—had become political insiders working skillfully within the Spanish and English empires. We must not overstate their success.

What rights Indigenous chiefs won, especially in Virginia, were contingent on maintaining their alliances with other colonial power players, proving their value to the colony's larger security and prosperity, and in occasionally making a well-timed threat to remind their European neighbors of their continued power. But the gains Indigenous petitioners won were real, forming a body of law that colonizers had to respect or find a way around.

Even as the imbalance of power between them and colonizers seemed to grow, Indigenous leaders did not give up on trying to bring the colonies of Florida and Virginia into line with their expectations. In Florida, demographic collapse and the burdens of the labor draft could not stop Indigenous leaders' drive to reshape San Agustín and Florida into a system that worked for them. The petitions of numerous Indigenous leaders in Florida and the complaints they made in formal visitations, were part of this ongoing effort. In Virginia, historians have exaggerated the extent of Powhatan defeat in 1646. The English could never win a war with the Powhatans outright and had to come to terms—however harsh they seemed on the Indigenous side. The treaty of 1646, ending the war in Virginia, opened avenues to Indigenous political participation—especially in the form of petitioning. By the later seventeenth-century contemporary Native leaders in both places like the Mocama *mico* Santiago of Tolomato and the Pamunkey *weroansqua* Cockacoeske used petitions and the lobbying of colonial and imperial officials to protect their power and their people.

At the end of the century, the then *weroansqua* of Pamunkey informed the Virginia council "that several English have Encroached upon the Liberties of her people, Contrary to the Articles of Peace, and Several Orders of the General Court," not to mention numerous acts of the assembly.[269] By the "Liberties of her people," the queen meant the body of rights, the equivalent of a *fuero* in Spanish law, that her predecessors Totopotomoy and Cockacoeske built with their petitions and lobbying. These liberties under law that tributary *weroances* and *weroansquas* had managed to establish for themselves were a thorny issue in Virginia by the 1670s. The surviving nobles of old Tsenacomacoh had managed to keep both a portion of their lands and their religion. A growing faction of colonists believed that elite tributary Indians like the king of the Weanokes and the queen of Pamunkey used their undue influence to win excessive privileges under law.

In Florida, the threat to the "republic of Indians" came not from Spaniards but from Natives who refused to live under what they believed was an alien and unworthy system of government. For Chacatos and Chiscas, the republic of Indians meant little more than foreign tyranny. Their leaders waged war rather than submit to a vassalage that brought them few benefits and many burdens. In Virginia, the "poor Indians" seemed too powerful for poor Englishmen to stand. At midcentury, George Gardyner warned that the Powhatans enjoyed "good privileges over the English, which in time may prove a third Massacre."[270] The massacre that Gardyner foretold would come to pass—but it would be a massacre of tributary Natives by the English.

CHAPTER 3

"Emboldened Indians," 1674–1678

The world of Native Southerners had not yet tipped wholly out of balance when the summer of 1674 began. On clean-swept plazas throngs still cheered on the players of the ballgame as they swerved and collided in their quest for the sacred poles.[1] Under the roofs of bustling council-houses the leading men talked business and drank *cacina*, the caffeinated beverage brewed from yaupon holly leaves, each day till noon.[2] In the fields of maize near quiet villages, children kept watch for birds as they always had.[3] And on the farm plots where servants and slaves twisted the suckers off tobacco plants in sight of ramshackle plantations, the days went on as before.[4] Across the land, some Indigenous leaders anxiously felt their power slipping away, even as Spaniards and Englishmen grew haughtier by the day. Times were hard but the times were predictable, at least for now.

Most Native elites sought to keep what they still possessed, though a few dreamed of recovering what they had lost. Sometime in the that year of 1674, as she left her town on the mainland of what is now Georgia for the island of Sapala, Ana Estasia, *mica* of Santa Clara de Tupiqui, longed for the power to make things be as they once were. Fleeing gun-toting "Chichimeca" raiders from the north, the *mica* vowed to uphold the dignity of her office if only for the sake of her nephew and heir Alonso.[5] In Virginia, twenty years had passed for Cockacoeske since Totopotomoy fell with his Pamunkey warriors fighting the very Westos now driving Ana Estasia into exile. Although she cultivated friendships among the English, including the alliance with Colonel John West that produced her son and heir, Cockacoeske saw colonial rule with clear eyes. With their common allegiance to the Crown, the scattered Powhatan nations seemed far weaker than they would be if united again. Within just three years, Cockacoeske would arise unexpectedly with the power to change all of it. In Apalachee, after the tumults of midcentury, a new generation of warriors and scholars such as Matheo Chuba and Juan Mendoza of San Luís de Talimali, were taking elevated seats in their council-houses. The Apalachee nobles' expansive vision, drawing on the power of the republic of Indians' alliance with Spaniards, encompassed plans for growth into the north and west, toward the towns of the Apalachicolas and Chacatos.[6] Eighty years old that summer, the Chacato leader Diocsale was one neighbor who feared their growing power and influence and bristled at the thought of joining the republic of Indians. On the summer solstice, as he watched his town's *cacique* kneel before the Apalachee's Franciscan priests and take baptism, Diocsale dreamed of returning to the life the Chacatos knew before the European invasion upended it.[7]

Ahead of them all were years of omens, wonders, and puzzling contrasts. None of the signs were visible yet that summer. The plagues of flies rising from the ground, the flocks of birds so thick they broke tree branches, the comet that almost cut the sky in two above the Chesapeake were a year away.[8] When they appeared, so too would a man the governor of Virginia deemed a rebel for doing what few Englishmen thought was a crime: fighting Indians without a commission. Fewer still would have guessed how this rebellion against the "Darling Indians," the tributaries the governor "favored and Emboldened," would end: with the rebel Englishman dead and the bold Indians writing the terms of the peace.[9] Neither did anyone in Florida foresee how a wily Chacato man more than a hundred leagues from San Agustín would, with Chisca help, crumple the colony's flank and halt the friars' progress—and Apalachee's—into the west and north. Nor could they have imagined the war that followed Diocsale's rebellion and the miraculous light—some said it was the Virgin Mary—that shone in the heavens, urging on to victory a troop of Catholic Natives who had not so much as stirred against the heathen enemy without their governor's blessing.

The upheavals that rocked the South after 1674 shook the republic of Indians in Florida and Virginia, and changed how Native Americans and colonists tried to live together from San Luís de Talimali to the Falls of the James. On the edges of the provinces of Florida, the Chacatos, Chiscas, and Apalachicolas rejected the trappings of the *república de Indios*, putting a firm period to the further spread of Florida's preferred theory of Native commonwealth. Even in the heartlands of the missions—in Guale, Timucua, and Apalachee—the ideal of the Native commonwealth showed dangerous signs of strain, even decay. In Virginia, the colonial uprising known as "Bacon's Rebellion" threatened the tributary regime, specifically its promise of Native political participation, and nearly destroyed it. Yet, in Virginia as in Florida, the crises of the next four years "emboldened" Indigenous leaders to reclaim lost power, to restore balance, and to rewrite the covenants that bound them to Spaniards and Englishmen. Native leaders, no less than colonial authorities, sought greater control over their own people and lands, the better to survive in uncertain times. On the other side of those turbulent years, the legal codes of Virginia and Florida, with rules that Native leaders inscribed into treaties, statutes, and regulations, had never before looked so alike in their aims.

Wholly a Thing in the Clouds: The Crisis of Native Status in Florida and Virginia

In September 1674, the octogenarian traditionalist Diocsale bitterly complained of how the Chacatos' thirty-year-old *doctrinero* (missionary) was forcing prominent holdouts like him to convert to Catholicism. Fray Rodrigo de la Barrera wasted no time in discussion. The friar called for military aid.[10] Twenty-five Apalachee "gun men," made up the bulk of the task force under the command of Captain Juan Fernández de Florencia that occupied the Chacato towns for more than a week.[11] Diocsale needed no further proof that the conversion of their towns earlier that summer brought the Chacatos under Apalachee dominion. Here were the Chacatos' true overlords dictating terms down the barrels of their arquebuses. The troops cast out the Chiscas, unconquered peoples living to the west, who rejected Spanish overtures and regularly supped with Diocsale and menaced the friars. But the astonishing feat that Apalachee guns achieved next the friars credited to Florencia's "great prudence."[12] Diocsale, along with his two confederates, kneeled before the whole village as Fray Rodrigo baptized them. Arising, resigned enough perhaps to seem penitent, was a new man, Juan Fernández de Diocsale. Captain Juan Fernández de Florencia, Diocsale's godfather and namesake, shortly wrapped up his business but not before "another fifty" Chacato waverers accepted baptism to the "glory of God our Lord and of his majesty" King Carlos II.[13]

The sight of armed Apalachee soldiers apparently accomplished what the friars' exhortations to Christian unity and peace had not. The ideal of the harmonious Christian community might have accorded well with the consensus-based politics in most Southeastern towns. But colonizers in the

1670s wanted far more. Fray Juan de Paiva's tireless campaign to abolish the traditional ballgame in Apalachee and western Timucua exemplified their rising authoritarianism.[14] When supporters of the game said "it was good policy that some places should be at odds with others," their understanding came from deep-seated Indigenous ideals of community and of the game as a source of greater cohesion within that fundamental political unit, the town. Paiva denounced the idea as "Luciferian."[15] Attacks on Native customs were a short step from attacks on customary law and they augured a coming crisis in the status of Indigenous vassals and subjects.

Across the South, imperial politics were taking an authoritarian turn in the 1670s. Force was always an important element of colonialism but in the provinces of Florida and in Virginia after the upheavals at midcentury, violence was a latent but potent threat that deterred outsiders from joining the republic of Indians.[16] Together, Native subjects and colonists tried to sublimate conflict into the forms and processes of law. Mounting pressures both inside and outside the republic of Indians led Native and colonial leaders to use those legal channels to seek greater authority for themselves. The instability within the republic of Indians, and the seeming chaos outside it, put Indigenous leaders and colonial officials on a collision course as the latter usually resorted to a heavier hand to deal with the challenges they faced. Sometimes, their interests coincided, but often colonial demands for greater control met Indigenous pushback from leaders defending their status.

The internal pressures on the system were almost entirely the result of decades of colonial exploitation. Inside the republic of Indians, populations were falling, either as peopled died or they fled to avoid onerous work and seek greater safety. Guale, Mocama, and Timucua suffered the worst of it in Florida, while Apalachee's numbers held steady.[17] The latest census of the tributaries in Virginia, meanwhile, put the number of fighting men at 725.[18] Despite their dwindling ranks, Spain's Native vassals and England's Native subjects still had work to do and tribute to pay at rates established when they were much more numerous.[19] On top of the labor these Natives performed on public works or in killing wolves and hunting beaver, there were threats from myriad foreign enemies bearing down on the edges of their lands.

In the north, above Virginia, were the Susquehannocks, Doegs, and Haudenosaunee. The Susquehannocks were traders and renowned soldiers and statesmen who built a powerful nation, Gandostogue, straddling the crossroads of empires and Indigenous peoples above Chesapeake Bay.[20] In the early part of the seventeenth century, they even set themselves up as protectors over the tiny outpost of New Sweden in the Delaware Valley.[21] The Susquehannocks' remarkable abilities to adapt to circumstances, using far-flung networks of kin to draw more powerful nations to their service, made them geopolitical players—despite their relatively small population— throughout the next decade.[22] At Maryland's invitation, a group of the Susquehannocks took refuge on the Potomac in a fort near Piscataway Creek. Like everyone else, including the Natives of Virginia's tributary regime, the Susquehannocks feared the might of the Haudenosaunee, especially "Senecas," a term colonists used to mean not just the actual "Keepers of the Western Door," but a variety of allied Natives who raided deep into the Southeast.[23]

To the south, near the provinces of Florida, the most dangerous foreigners were the Chiscas with whom the Chacato Diocsale kept up kin ties, and the slave-raiding Westos. Gabriel Diaz Vara Calderón, the Salamanca-educated bishop of Cuba who visited Florida in 1674–1675, must have thought Florida's frontiers, with their fearsome "barbarians" to the north and west, resembled those of the Roman Empire.[24] Because he had to "pass by the frontier of the country" of the Chiscas and Westos, the bishop kept a personal guard of three whole companies of soldiers and warriors, one "of Spanish Infantry from that *presidio*" and two companies of Native warriors, that included "*arcabuceros*" armed with guns and "*flecheros*," bowmen.[25] The Chiscas menaced Apalachee's frontier, living "in little hamlets without fixed populations" and who "feed themselves from the chase, nuts, and tree roots."[26] The terror the Chacato Diocsale later sowed with his threats to call in the Chiscas to enforce his will make sense after reading the bishop's estimate of the Chiscas strength: over four thousand![27] The Chiscas were not the most fearsome outsiders of all. From Guale to Apalachee, marauding over the whole of Florida's "northern frontier" were the Westos, whom Spanish documents often called "Chichimecos," and who had been raiding the missions since 1659. The Westos were, according to Bishop Calderón, "Gentiles, so barbaric and cruel that their whole end is to pounce on the Towns of both Christians as well as Gentiles, taking from them their Lives, without excusing age, gender, nor rank, roasting them and eating them."[28]

In 1674, the Westos allied with the English at "San Jorge," as the Spaniards called the recently founded Charles Town, to attack Spain's Native vassals.[29] In the Westo capital, Hickauhaugau on what is now the Savannah River, English traders were instructing warriors to handle firearms for the purpose.[30] As it armed the Westos, San Jorge itself grew in numbers of men, arms, and other supplies "from Virginia and Bermuda," but worst of all the English were gathering to themselves "different towns of Indians" as allies, and thus adding to the threats menacing Florida.[31] Florida's governor, Don Pablo de Hita Salazar, opted for drastic measures in response. He consolidated mission towns and, fatefully, urged the settlement of a "Body" of Spanish families in the heart of Apalachee, convinced that only with Spaniards settled amongst them could the Natives effectively "make opposition to any Invasion of enemies."[32]

By the summer of 1675, colonial and Indigenous leaders in Virginia and Florida were uneasy about the future just as the status of Native vassals and subjects came under open attack. In his seventieth year, Sir William Berkeley was beginning to feel how feeble his grasp on the colony might be. The troubles started in June in northerly Stafford County on the Potomac, when neighbors found a plantation overseer named Hen lying across his own doorstep. The dying man's words sparked an uncontrollable cycle of vengeance: "Doegs Doegs."[33] The local militia set off after the offending Doegs, but wound up in a firefight, to their shock, with a party of Susquehannocks. The Susquehannocks soon launched strikes across Virginia's western frontier. With the countryside convinced "that all the Indians were conspired against us," even the tributaries were targets for settlers' vengeance.[34] By the fall, a duel of letters began between the governor and a newcomer to the colony who waged a private campaign against the tributary Appamattucks for allegedly stealing his corn. Nathaniel Bacon translated the gripes of the backcountry into eloquent manifestos. "To me," he wrote, "this story of siding with or protecting any Indians is wholly a thing in the Clouds."[35]

The two governors, Salazar and Berkeley, and the polities they presided over were in dangerous predicaments. Within a year's time Berkeley sighed, "How miserable that man is that Governs a People where six parts of seven at least are Poor Indebted Discontented and Armed."[36] Those angry, armed men now threatened the Crown's Native subjects. Governor Hita Salazar could well have commiserated with his Virginian counterpart. A career soldier, Hita Salazar's last posting took him, his wife Doña Juana, and their six children to the busy port of Vera Cruz, where he served as *corregidor*.[37] He arrived in San Agustín in time to take over the construction of the Castillo de San Marcos, a massive coquina-shellstone fort just north of the city. His labors strained "a man poor such as I," he later wrote to Spain's regent, Queen Mariana.[38] He, too, confronted a surly, armed populace. Fresh disturbances from Diocsale and his Chisca allies in the Chacato missions threatened Apalachee and the whole of Florida. To the queen, he confided his fears for the provinces. "For if our hold on them," meaning the Chacatos and Chiscas, "should falter, it would be possible for new disturbances to occur," Hita Salazar wrote, "especially [now] that they have become acquainted with firearms."[39] With guns and determination, a few more rebels could topple the republic of Indians in either colony.

The response to Diocsale's grumblings about the priests was indicative of a growing authoritarianism that threatened Indigenous status across the South. From Florida to Virginia, colonial officials responded to the challenges of the decade with a heavier hand, often clashing with the aspirations of Native leaders to preserve their status and the legal protections that had given them a say in how the overall system was governed. But for some leaders, the idea that they needed "protection" in the first place was the real problem.

The Revolt of the Chacatos: Diocsale Rejects the Republic of Indians

That summer, the rains came late to Apalachee. Everyone in San Luís de Talimali was still working in the maize fields at the end of July 1675, when yet another letter from Fray Rodrigo de la Barrera arrived for the provincial lieutenant Andrés Perés.[40] On 26 July, Fray Rodrigo feverishly scratched off his plea for help. "The devil sleeps not," he warned, "nor with his craftiness leaves off urging these natives to their doom."[41] Fray Rodrigo did not sleep much, either, least of all now. Outside the thatched roof of the convent in San Carlos de los Chacatos, the political winds blew in Diocsale's favor. The pro-Chisca party had risen again under Diocsale's leadership. With his firm confederate Ubabesa, he waged a covert campaign targeting other key figures in village life, asking them to contribute deerskins each as a pledge of loyalty and as gifts to win the non-interference (if not the direct support) of Tawasas and Apalachicolas, powerful potential allies to the north and west.[42] Feeling his strength growing, Diocsale asked Carlos the *cacique*, Felipe the *usinulo* (beloved man), and Cutca Martín, the *inija* (second-in-command) of the town of San Carlos, to join him for dinner. Later testimony claimed that all three were aghast when they heard Diocsale's proposal. Drive out the priest? Only his superior could do that.[43] To anyone who doubted the wisdom of his plans, Diocsale's threats were allegedly blunt: he would have them killed by the Chiscas.[44]

On surmising the truth about what Diocsale was up to, the Franciscan told a lie, saying he desired to go to the neighboring town of Santa Cruz de

Sabacola for confession.[45] Fray Rodrigo's ruse suited the conspirators, who now planned to trap and slay him on the road to Santa Cruz. After a week stuck in the convent, his Chacato escorts arrived around midnight on 29 July for the journey. A "little stretch" down the road they asked if he had a light. Fray Rodrigo bent down to pick up the tinder. The pair already wanted to sit down for a rest and smoke their pipes by the road.[46] As the friar rose back up with the light, one of them "gave him a knock upon the head with a hatchet" that forced him to the ground.[47] Before he could catch his breath, another blow from the hatchet slashed the priest's face, leaving him bloodied.[48] Stumbling to his feet, the friar, who little more than a year ago led a quiet life of contemplation in a convent in Seville, took his *escopeta*, the musket "that he carried and discharging it," he shot dead the "Indian who had struck him."[49] The other assailant ran off into the woods before Fray Rodrigo could reload.

What Spaniards called the "revolt" of the Chacatos—without the Chiscas—might have been a minor affair, little more than a case of a few disgruntled Native men throwing out their priest in defense of their old customs. No Spaniard died in the event. Barrera, who seemed bent on martyrdom, lived another twenty years.[50] (Indeed, Barrera lived long enough to advocate a very different policy in Apalachicola a decade later, arguing that chiefs there "will not be deprived of their right as natural lords.")[51] A decisive show of force, some tearful confessions from the ringleaders, and promises of amnesty for all who would return to their proper obedience, might have crushed the revolt in yet another "secondary war," annexing the Chacatos permanently—at least in the Spaniards' minds—to the provinces of Florida.[52] But Diocsale, with his kinship ties to the Chiscas, his unique role as their advocate in Chacato councils—a kind of *fanni minko* or adopted advocate— had enlisted them in the fight for Chacato independence from the Apalachees and Spaniards. The provincial lieutenant immediately tried to counter Diocsale's diplomatic moves, sending the Chisca-language interpreter to talk with their *caciques* "requiring them not to give the Chacatos favor."[53] The danger was great "because the Chiscas are many."[54] Nothing better illustrates the Chisca connection than Diocsale's statement on the morning of the attack on Fray Rodrigo. When his daughter-in-law, Elena, told him the priest still lived, Diocsale shook his head. "I am old," he said, but still "if I got down to it, I would have cracked him like a pumpkin."[55] And then "he started hollering like a Chisca."[56] That war cry struck fear in towns all around. Balthasar, the *cacique* of Santa Cruz, made plans to abandon the mission there unless the provincial lieutenant sent three soldiers to guard the town, fearing the

Chiscas would kill them if they stayed.[57] Diocsale's war cry signaled that no easy "secondary war" was possible with the Chiscas involved. Nor were the motives of the Chacato rebels as simple as the Spaniards believed.

The Chacatos and Chiscas who joined them in the "coup"—much like the coup the Chiscas launched alongside disgruntled Apalachees back in 1647 as Aubrey Lauersdorf has shown—fought for higher political ideals than historians have usually acknowledged.[58] It is true that Fray Rodrigo obliged Diocsale to give up three of his four wives after his baptism in September 1674. Ubabesa and Juaquín, too, chafed under the friar's harsh alien morals. Certainly, the Chacato Revolt was partly a defense of endangered "marriages, sexual practices, and family life" and partly "a culture clash over sexual mores," as two noted historians have variously described it.[59] And Chacato women, especially Diocsale's three wives, who as the owners of the household where he lived had much to lose under the new Franciscan regime, must have played even larger roles in the tumult than the Spanish record affords them.[60]

Just as important to the rebels were politics and political philosophy. The Chacatos were a small people caught between large, rival nations. The driving issue was about with which of those nations they would align themselves. In 1674, their leaders put them under the thumb of the Apalachees and knew it.[61] Nevertheless, it was "from dread of the Apalachees" that Miguel, the *cacique* of San Nicolás who had welcomed the Franciscans, abandoned his town following the attack on Fray Rodrigo.[62] The Spaniards counted for less in Chacatos' minds, except as the source for exotic goods and a strange but potent (and intrusive) religion.[63] In 1675, Diocsale committed the Chacatos to the Chisca alliance. The Chacato "revolt" was the latest move in the heated Native geopolitics of the Southeast—but it also uncovered something else.

The revolt of the Chacatos also exposed how far from the ideal the *república de Indios* had fallen. Even if the Chacatos perceived them as the Apalachees' servants, the Spaniards contributed their part to the uprising in the person of Fray Rodrigo de la Barrera and the political ideas he preached. Spanish law, since the sixteenth century, said that *caciques* would keep their high rank after becoming Catholics and vassals of the king. "Some naturals of the Indies were in time of their infidelity Caciques," Felipe II decreed in 1557, "and Lords of Peoples, and because after their conversion to our Holy Catholic Faith, it is just, that they shall conserve their rights, and having come to our obedience, not be made of worse condition."[64] Yet, Diocsale understood that even if Chacato leaders were the ones who agreed to allow a missionary into their towns, afterward, power was no longer entirely theirs. Fray

Rodrigo's behavior "made them of worse condition."[65] He posed as one of them, a high-ranking figure with a field of maize to support him. He treated their granaries as his own, writing to the provincial lieutenant that there was food enough to feed his soldiers when they arrived.[66] He dared to berate elite men in public—and flog women.[67] He demanded obedience without earning the peoples' loyalty. And when obedience was not to be had, he called in the Apalachees to compel the people to do his bidding. If Diocsale really did threaten to have the Chiscas murder anyone who opposed him, he could have pointed to Fray Rodrigo's own tactics as an excuse. The uses of force in politics may have been the only lasting lesson the friar taught his "children." Although it was not yet apparent to the governor or the Franciscans, the significance of Diocsale's achievement was that he had halted the growth of the missions for good. Fray Rodrigo was not an exception in a system that otherwise worked. The friar never suffered disciplinary action. The Spanish authorities, with their forceful response to the revolt, in effect sanctioned the friar's earlier deeds, never even questioning them.

After two inquiries in October 1675, one at San Carlos and the other held in San Luís de Talimali, fittingly in the heart of Apalachee and the real source of Diocsale's fears, three Chacatos were tried and convicted for that summer's rebellion. No ordinary magistrate, said Spanish law, could "deprive the Caciques of their Caciqueships by any criminal cause or suit."[68] (Similarly, in Virginia "no Person of what quality soever" could "presume to Imprison any Indian King without a special Warrant from the Governor, and two from the Council.")[69] The condemned were only the men the Spanish could catch. The rest of the alleged ringleaders—Luis Ubabesa, Bacta Diego, Coquita Luis, and the man who provided Fray Rodrigo's deadly escort, Cutca Martín—were still at large, refugees living in Tawasa as planned. Diocsale was banished to San Agustín.[70] His rebellion was finished. The war of the Chiscas on the "republic of Indians" was just beginning.

Diocsale's rebellion was no simple uprising in defense of plural marriage but a wholesale rejection of the republic of Indians and everything for which it seemed to stand for as of 1675. For the old rebel, the republic of Indians represented Apalachee domination, priestly rule, and outsiders trampling on Chacato customs and customary law. In Florida, the resistance to the republic of Indians was Indigenous-led and challenged the disturbing authoritarian implications of European "protection." To the north, however, the rebellion brewing in Virginia challenged the republic of Indians on other grounds—that it offered any protection to Natives at all.

The Return of the *Mamanatowick*:
Cockacoeske's Victory in Bacon's Rebellion

In Virginia's Henrico County along the James, at a place the locals dubbed "the Curles," Junn, an enslaved Indigenous woman "about 40 y[ea]rs old," toiled in the fields pulling weeds from the ground between the hills of tobacco. Junn was the living embodiment of her master's political principles.[71] From time to time, Junn caught glimpses of this peculiar man when he came out of the house, in the few moments he spared from his "solitude and mystic employments."[72] Spending most of her workday outdoors, some afternoons she might have heard the sound of heated, boisterous talk and a sprinkling of laughter from the main house as her master entertained his guests. Like Juan Fernández de Diocsale had done before his rebellion, Nathaniel Bacon began courting a following not long after he arrived. A Virginia councilor since March 1675, Bacon, with his Cambridge master's degree and legal studies at Gray's Inn, dazzled his visitors with his erudition.[73]

After dinner, while deep in their cups and "making the Sadness of the times their discourse," Bacon probably rehearsed his brief against Virginia's republic of Indians.[74] Downriver from the Curles were the Appamattucks, tributaries and subjects to the English Crown. Their *weroance* paid the king's viceroy, Sir William Berkeley, an annual tribute of beaver skins as did all the tributary nations, including the powerful and prominent Pamunkeys. In exchange, as one of Sir William's cronies put it—making an "Assertion" that Junn's master loathed—"the Governor and Council" were "bound to defend the Queen [of Pamunkey] and the Appamattucks with their blood."[75] Junn's master denied this. No Native person, not even a king or queen, had any claim to the "benefit and Protection of the Law."[76] What it came down to, was the very meaning of the law itself. "For that the Law does reciprocally protect and punish," Bacon would later explain. Whether in their "Person or estate" every offender must "make equivalent satisfaction or Restitution."[77] But Natives "cannot according to any form of any Law to us known be prosecuted, served or complained against."[78] Their persons were too difficult to tell apart, their many languages too garbled to understand, and they were too poor to "make us Restitution or satisfaction."[79] Slavery, such as Junn suffered, was the only fit condition for a Native person within Virginia.

For all the attention historians have paid to Nathaniel Bacon, his rebellion was but one side of a larger debate about the status of Indigenous subjects in Virginia.[80] The rebellion opened a political opportunity for Cockacoeske and other tributary Native leaders to strengthen their positions through a direct appeal to the Crown and its servants.[81] Cockacoeske, for one, as Hayley Negrin put it, "staged her own rebellion."[82] The celebrated Pamunkey *weroansqua* seized the moment to restore the paramount chief's office, becoming *mamanatowick* with royal backing. From her position she fought against enslavement, dispossession, and in favor of a stronger alliance with the English that guaranteed not just protections for the empire's Indigenous subjects but a recovery of landscapes and waterways and, above all, of sacred power.[83] The events of 1676–1677 in Virginia also marked what we might call England's Valladolid moment, but with Bacon versus Cockacoeske, a settler and Indigenous leader locked in a great debate over the place of Native peoples within the growing Stuart empire.[84] Bacon had the first word but Cockacoeske had the last and most important.

Starting with seditious table talk, Bacon's ideas soon slipped out of doors. Hearing how his polished words lent authority to their deepest-held views, Bacon's regular dinner companions, aspiring frontier bigwigs all—William Byrd, Henry Isham, James Crews—decided one day in April 1676 to put their tribune in front of the people.[85] Ending their revels, they rowed over the James River into Charles City County to visit the militiamen who mustered there—really an extralegal force of backwoodsmen.[86] Crews made sure "to take a quantity of Rum with them" to ladle out to the thirsty camp on Jordan's Point.[87] When the multitude of armed men saw the short and "slender" form of Bacon, the long black hair framing his "ominous, pensive, melancholy" face, hats flew up, gunshots rang out, and the men cheered: "a Bacon! a Bacon! a Bacon!"[88] There was a maxim of politics then current in Virginia, "That the Wise and the Rich were prone to Faction and Sedition but the fools and poor were easy to be Governed."[89] Only the first part of the saying, the part about the rich, was true that year. In 1676, the common people were utterly irrepressible.

The men in the crowd, drunk on rum and delirious with joy at the sight of "a Bacon," were not merely the bumptious, racist ciphers we tend to conjure today from the royal commissioners' reports following the rebellion. These men—and women—had a simple grievance and the governor's refusal to relieve it perplexed and angered them. The times demanded that an army of the people go out and take the fight to the enemy, they thought. When would Sir William Berkeley let them go? When the country was "again overrun and ruin'd by these Heathens"?[90] The Susquehannocks who still raided throughout the countryside, after all, were "numerous enough (though they yet appear but in parties) to Endanger the loss of this Colony," the men told the king in one of a flurry of memorials that descended on Whitehall that year.[91] When the drink wore off and they were again "dispers'd from each other," the truth was that these men "of the Frontier Plantations" were terrified.[92] Their "Importunity" made a rebel of "his only son," said Thomas Bacon, Nathaniel's "sad father," petitioning the king.[93] My "son hath by his Compassion and assistance," Thomas wrote, "become obnoxious to the Letter of the Law by adventuring upon so public a good without the Allowance of the Governor."[94] Or at least so said the man who less than two years before had sent his "only son" to Virginia hoping never to hear from him again.[95]

After a deadly march at the head of his army against Virginia's allies the Occaneechis, pillaging their fort on an island in Roanoke River, Bacon's place at the head of the Indian-hating mob was assured.[96] That May, the people of Henrico County elected the twenty-nine-year-old Bacon a burgess in the first elections in Virginia since 1662. For him, the trip to James City brought fresh excitement. For the other burgesses, the tasks of military preparations consumed their attention. As the assembly readied for war, "Settling the Quotas of men Arms and Ammunition [and] Provisions" from each county, they included the anticipated contribution of one person in particular.[97] A special messenger rode to the head of the York River with an invitation for the queen of Pamunkey to appear before the joint committee on Indian affairs.

Cockacoeske surely received the summons to James City in silence. The caprice of the English was too much for words. Sir William Berkeley had not long ago cut off the sale of arms and ammunition to the tributaries, but now he needed their soldiers to fight the Susquehannocks.[98] Once again, the English came in their "great Exigency," making demands when they were in truth "Supplicants to her for a favor."[99] The memories of Totopotomoy and so many Pamunkey warriors who fell at the Battle of the Bloody Run in 1656 came back. So did a keen sense of the present troubles. Scattered, their numbers and their lands seemingly melting away, the Powhatans inside the tributary regime lacked coordination. The queen resolved to make an impression. She succeeded.

Thirty years later, a burgess who witnessed Cockacoeske's entrance into the council chamber still remembered everything about it—her fringed mantle, her black-and-white beaded crown that reflected the spiritual and earthly authority of her office, her respectful escorts who kept silent unless she deigned to let them speak.[100] The effect of her appearance kindled recollections of "Opechancanough a former Emperor of Virginia."[101] As soon as she had entered and, "after a few Entreaties" sat down with the committee looking down on her, the chairman asked her how many "men she would Lend us for Guides in the Wilderness and to assist us against our Enemy Indians."[102] At her right hand, Cornelius Dabney, the queen's interpreter and scribe, leaned toward her and dutifully translated the question in a hushed tone. *Ask my son*, she said, quietly. Dabney related her answer. All eyes in the hall turned to the man at her left, John West, "her Son a Stripling of Twenty Years of Age," no doubt resembling his famous father.[103] The young man demurred and "referred all to his Mother."[104] Now arrived the height of the planned demonstration. Cockacoeske addressed the committee for "about a quarter of an hour."[105] Although details about her comportment have survived, witnesses were apparently too awestruck to record her speech.

From documents she sent in her name we can imagine the contents of Cockacoeske's address. Cockacoeske likely schooled the committee on her history of loyalty to the Crown, of her assurance of the king's protection, of her own high station, the obligations the Virginians owed her people by treaty, and the little thanks she had received for her pains. She punctuated each part of her speech with the words "*Tatapatamoi Chepiack*," which Edward Hill, the son of the very commander who led the Pamunkey king to his doom, translated as "Totopotomoy [is] dead," a reminder of the Pamunkeys' sacrifices and that she was *weroansqua* now.[106] Asked three times how many men she would send, Cockacoeske answered "*Comotinch*."[107] "Six," Dabney translated. Asked a fourth time, she answered after a long pause and the clerk wrote down the answer: "Twelve." With the business concluded, she "rose up and gravely Walked away, as not pleased with her Treatment."[108] Cockacoeske entered the room a *weroansqua*, an ordinary chief at the summons of the English but she left with the bearing of the *mamanatowick*, the paramount chief of Tsenacomacoh.

Cockacoeske stormed out of James City just in time. Not long into the assembly's session, Henrico County Burgess Nathaniel Bacon got a jump on his enemies and slipped upriver before they could arrest him on fresh charges of plotting rebellion. From his base near the falls of the James, Bacon rallied his supporters into an army. On 23 June 1676, they took Virginia's capital and received his army's commissions at long last. After desultory marches near the heads of the rivers, at the end of July, Bacon rallied his followers for a convention of the people at the Middle Plantation, modern-day Williamsburg, Virginia.[109]

The Virginia Company of London once quipped about the "divines of Salamanca" and their academic debates over Native rights.[110] In Virginia in 1676, the argument over the legal status of Native Americans was anything but idle disputation. The woods surrounding Middle Plantation where Bacon gathered his supporters that summer were an English stand-in for the arcades of the Collegio de San Gregorio in Valladolid where Juan Ginés de Sepúlveda and Bartolomé de Las Casas argued over the status of Indigenous peoples, with Bacon in the role of the former. When his opponents said Bacon planned "to Level all," they should have included the estates and dignities of the Native kings and queens, who were in his mind an Indigenous adjunct to the parasitic Anglo-Virginian elite.[111] Nearly twenty years before Bacon, the Anglican clergyman Lionel Gatford wrote how some Virginians claimed that they could seize Natives' "lands and estates" on the principle of "dominium fundatur in gratiae"—that dominion is founded in grace.[112] Heathens, they claimed, had no rights to property or to anything else under law. In Bacon, the defenders of this principle found their champion. Berkeley, he said, had "Bartered and Sold his Majesty's Country and the Lives of his Loyal Subjects to the Barbarous Heathen."[113] In a colony where, after 1667, baptism did not confer freedom on enslaved people, the idea that tributaries as "hereditary heathens" enjoyed not only a modicum of liberty, but rank, dignity, influence—power even— was outrageous to Bacon and his supporters.[114] Bacon flattened the status of Indigenous people into a single category of aliens, without commonwealths or nations of their own, whom settlers could enslave at their pleasure.[115]

The status of Indigenous rulers as kings and queens under English colonial law especially galled Bacon and contrasts with their titles in Florida. Although an early Spanish-English dictionary published in London in the 1590s defined *cacique* as "King among the Indians," Spaniards seldom used the term *rey* or *reina* to describe Indigenous leaders, sticking to the Taíno-derived *cacique* or some equivalent.[116] Spanish decrees forbade *caciques* from styling themselves too grandly lest it threaten "Royal preeminence."[117] Some tributary Native leaders in Virginia retained Indigenous titles the government recognized, such as *manguy* or *weroance*, usually translated as "Commander" or "Great Man." Still, the commonest terms in official utterances and documents were king and queen.[118] But if the titles differed from Florida, what mattered most was that the influence Native leaders wielded in Virginia was much the same as in the Spanish colony.

What Bacon truly detested was the power Native leaders like the Pamunkey *weroansqua* Cockacoeske or Harquip the Chickahominy *manguy* wielded, the favors they received, the laws they changed.[119] Bacon arraigned Sir William Berkeley's regime "For having protected favored and Emboldened the Indians against his Majesty's most Loyal Subjects."[120] Bacon jested how, instead, his supporters "find them all alike, neither can we distinguish this fatal undistinguishable distinction of the Governor."[121] Never mind the messengers' striped coats, the badges, the laws against entertaining Natives, the boundaries that separated Indigenous from English spaces, which began with the treaty of 1646. Open war was the only logical recourse under the circumstances, Bacon argued.[122] When a poor Englishman had no relief from oppressive government, the petitions of the "Darling Indians" won favor from the governor, his council, and even the assembly.[123] As one observer at the time summarized Bacon's sense of the matter, Bacon "Upbraids the Governor for maintaining their [the Native tributaries'] quarrel (though never so unjust) against the Christians rights and interest."[124] The reality was surely worse from Bacon's perspective. The tributary kings and queens were not above the law in Virginia—they helped write it. That summer of 1676, Nathaniel Bacon made his brief in the debate over Native rights. The Native kings and queens would have the last word on the very same field at Middle Plantation. No one knew that then, of course, least of all Cockacoeske, who now awaited the rebels. Having rendered his judgment on her and the rest of the Native nobility of old Tsenacomacoh that summer, Bacon led his forces to execute sentence on the Pamunkeys.

Learning of Bacon's approach, Cockacoeske was in a legal quandary.[125] One hundred and fifty men stood at her command, eager to strike the invading colonial rabble.[126] But if she resisted Bacon, Virginians could wind up twisting her actions into a justification for his invasion of her land. Rebel that he was, there was no guarantee that the Virginia Assembly might not ratify some of his acts afterward. Subsequent events proved this fear to be well-founded. Then there was another problem. Tributary kings and queens held title to their communal lands only as long as they occupied them. As recently as 1674, an English colonist petitioned the governor's council successfully against the tributary Nanziatticos who allegedly "Deserted the Lands Laid out for them by Public Authority and have not Lived on it this Two years Last past."[127] The June assembly, under Bacon, declared any and all abandoned Native lands "vested on the country."[128] If Cockacoeske and her people fled, even if Bacon's corpse wound up in a gibbet, "loyal" and land-hungry Virginians could finish what he started by declaring the Pamunkey reservation forfeit. This feature of the law points to the tributary system's compatibility with the objectives of English settler colonialism. But deserted Native lands were forfeit in Florida too. Natives who fled into *el monte*, the woods, whether to escape the friars or avoid work, were outlaws and rebels as far as the Spaniards were concerned.[129] By refusing to fight Bacon, Cockacoeske could at least keep her reputation for having "never at any time betray'd, or injured the English," a fact "well known to the whole Country."[130] So, the "Good Queen of Pamunkey" fled into the waterscape she knew so well, composing in her mind the petitions she would file when it was all over.[131]

After two weeks in vain pursuit of Cockacoeske, Bacon's army, sated with plunder and prisoners, turned toward James City. In September, they besieged Virginia's capital, parading their Pamunkey prisoners, along with loyalists' captured wives, on the siegeworks—"Bacon's trench"—in view of Berkeley's forces, who promptly withdrew. Bacon then entered the capital and burned it to the ground.[132] In a month, the arch-rebel was ill and his cause languished. By October, Bacon found himself "besieged by sickness, and now not able to hold out any longer, all his strength, and provisions being spent."[133] At last, around 26 October 1676, Bacon "surrendered up that Fort he was no longer able to keep," his own louse-ridden body, "into the hands of that grim and all conquering Captain, Death."[134] The rebellion in his name was hardly over but its leader's great argument—that Indians deserved no protection in law—would soon face a decisive rebuke by the king of England himself at the queen of Pamunkey's behest.

Just as Nathaniel Bacon lay dead of the bloody flux—his corpse "where deposited till the General day, not known"—a new trial convened in San Agustín where the imprisoned Juan Fernández de Diocsale stood accused of plotting war on the provinces of Florida from his cell.[135] Don Pablo de Hita Salazar pronounced sentence at last on 3 January 1677, upholding, on account of his great age, Diocsale's banishment for life in the *presidio*.[136] The individual fate of the two arch-rebels, Diocsale and Bacon, one now dead, the other seemingly contained, mattered less than the events they set in motion. Bacon's death and the collapse of his rebellion could not stop the return of the *mamanatowick*, Cockacoeske, nor the forging at Middle Plantation of a new covenant for the republic of Indians in the spring of 1677. Nor could the governor of Florida avoid the war that Diocsale's diplomatic maneuvers with the Chiscas brought to pass. As the Spaniards raised a stone fortress to watch over San Agustín, from a wooden fort far to the west the Chiscas waged ceaseless war against the most important part of Florida's republic of Indians—the province of Apalachee.

The War of the Chiscas: Saving the
Republic of Indians in Florida

The harvest was in the granaries. Shucked ears of maize by the hundreds lay snug behind the wattle gates—"a few boughs," huffed one friar—that the townspeople used to cover the entrances to the corncribs.[137] In every house, the cooking fires smoldered. Mothers hushed their children to sleep. Old men already snored, up to their chins under heavy pelts even though it was the end of August 1677.[138] Yet, in the council-house, the leading men of San Luís de Talimali were still far from rest. Ringing the hearth, while the council fire crackled and started to roar again, Juan Mendoza, Matheo Chuba, and the town's *inija* Bentura sipped *cacina* "with other principal men," keeping watch with them that night.[139] Like Nathaniel Bacon's dinner companions had done just a year ago, the *principales* (headmen) of San Luís made the sadness of the times their discourse.

Every night for the last two years, the men of San Luís kept watch for the Chiscas. The raiders plundered and killed travelers on the "Royal Roads," struck towns in the middle of the night, enslaving "men and women and the little children."[140] Try as they might, the watchmen of San Luís "never could nab" the marauders, "for their incursions being by night" it was near impossible.[141] Twice, the Apalachees managed to free some women captives from the Chiscas but could achieve nothing more.[142] The constant, fruitless vigilance took its toll. Bitter about the Franciscans' attacks on their traditional ballgame, commoners were now muttering about their leaders, the same leaders who agreed to tear down the sacred goalposts from the plazas, and who were powerless to stop the Chiscas.[143]

When Spaniards refused to act, the Apalachee leaders of San Luis de Talimali took up the defense of the republic of Indians on their own. The men resolved to lead their own war against the Chiscas in 1677 and they presented a long account of their exploits to the king, through the provincial lieutenant and the governor. More than a narrative of events or petition of merit, the document presented an implicit critique of Spanish failures to contain the Chiscas—not to mention the refusal of some Apalachee towns to help—and a justification for the actions of the *junta de guerra* that convened in San Luís. Within the framework of petitioning, requiring a pose of subservience, Native leaders could make subversive points. Their actions in the war of the Chiscas in 1677 gave them added leverage with colonial and imperial authorities and eventually enabled them to make changes to the

Figure 6. Visitors to a council-house like the Apalachee Council House reconstructed at Mission San Luís in Tallahassee, Florida would have ducked low as
they entered the spacious chamber. Photographs by the author.

compact binding the republic of Indians and the republic of Spaniards in
Florida.

Even when Florida's governor acted, what he did seemed ineffective. Just
the month before, on 3 July, during a summer when the Apalachees "endured
many alarms and outbursts" from the Chiscas, the governor finally shipped
off the Chacato rebel, Diocsale, into permanent exile in New Spain.[144] Old as
he was, the Chacato rebel had simply refused to die quietly in San Agustín
watching the Castillo de San Marcos rise stone by stone. Even as the Spaniards
poured tens of thousands of pesos into the unfinished Castillo, the Chiscas
at little cost built a *palenque* (fort) of their own.[145] The Chiscas' fort stood two
days march past the Chacato towns, well away from the Apalachees and the
Spaniards. The palisade enclosed shelters for the warriors' families in case of

siege.[146] Diocsale, the "idol of the Chiscas," had committed to the most effective strategy for hobbling Florida.[147] While Hita Salazar and the Crown piled on defenses in San Agustín, the mission towns remained convenient targets for raids.[148] This fact of the vulnerability of the provincial towns, so obvious to Diocsale and the Chiscas—as it was to numerous other Native strategists, not least among the men in the council-house at San Luís—was not yet apparent to the Spaniards.

The junta in the council-house of San Luís on that August night—for that is what the knot of men "reasoning" together became, a formal *junta de guerra* or council of war—resolved upon stronger measures.[149] One of their number said what they were all feeling and "proposed going out to hunt for the enemy."[150] There were nods of agreement from the members, but not all of them. The council, knowing what must be done but doubting if they could do it, fell into debate. "And some said we will not be given license" to wage a war, they said.[151] A few stout hearts among them, no doubt, were prepared to go without Spanish permission and made their readiness known. But this course seemed dangerous. For to go without the governor's leave would be to take the rebel's path—the very road Nathaniel Bacon took. Although not a man among them knew the name of Bacon, the leaders of San Luís understood implicitly his mistake and were not about to commit the same crime.[152] Besides, the Apalachees had suffered too long for the Spaniards not to let them go. "They will not deny us this, for each day" the Chiscas "are killing us, our relatives, and what is most to be sorry for," the men said, "are the slaves that they carry off."[153] Yes, we will have a commission, they said. "We are Christians and vassals of the King our Lord," the council declared heartily, and "may God save him for many years"![154] With "everyone unanimous and agreed," they walked out of the council-house to find the provincial lieutenant and "to ask for permission."[155]

When the delegation from the council-house told "our lieutenant and War-Captain and head in this province," what they wanted, Juan Fernández de Florencia was delighted and he granted them permission without hesitation and promised to help.[156] The men cheered.[157] The war was on. At dawn, the troop returned to the council-house "very pleased and joyous" and began preparations for the expedition against the Chiscas.[158] Eighty-five men mustered from San Luís alone, most of them longbowmen. The town's contingent was actually even bigger, with eight Chines and ten Chacato refugees from nearby towns under the jurisdiction of San Luís joining the expedition as scouts.[159] Their bows and fifteen "armas de fuego"—firelock muskets—were soon stacked in the council-house.[160] To the men who wielded them, Florencia gave powder and a "pouch of bullets."[161]

A swift runner tore out of town, "dispatched to the rest of the places" to invite the leaders in all the Apalachee towns "if they should like to go with" the bold men of San Luís.[162] On 2 September, after prayers and a speech from the provincial "War-Captain," Florencia, "exhorting" the men to "comport themselves as brothers, unanimous and agreed," the army marched out under the command of its "four principal commanders": Captain Juan Mendoza; Field-Master Matheo Chuba; Don Bernardo, *cacique* of San Damián de Cupaica, who brought seventy men; and Bentura, *inija* of San Luís.[163] Two leagues from San Luís, by the yellow waters of the Ochlockonee River, the army rested and the captains counted their men.[164] One hundred and ninety all told, harquebusiers and archers, hailing from seven towns, comprised the Apalachee army.[165] Only certain towns, most of them near San Luís, rallied to the junta's call. None came from Ivitachuco, the other great town that for so long had steered relations with the Spaniards, a noticeable gap in the army's muster roll that has led to speculation about the reasons why. The leaders there withheld their support for the expedition perhaps because they had caught the Chiscas who committed "the murders" in their town, satisfying the demands of justice.[166] Or maybe it was pique, a flare up of the rivalry between towns. Ivitachuco was the highest-ranking town in Apalachee and its leaders may have begrudged Talimali's boldness. Perhaps Ivitachuco's leaders encouraged the towns under their direct influence to withhold support. If rivalry was at stake, San Luís had the better of it. The expedition and the leaders' account of it added luster to the reputation of the town's leaders, all the way to the court in Madrid.[167]

On the banks of the Ochlockonee River, the western border of Apalachee, with the enemy's lands before them, the captains rallied their troops for the trials ahead. For if "we come to fulfill the desires of seeing our enemies," that "as Christians, God shall favor us," said the captains, and then looking to the banner they carried, with Our Lady of the Rosary on one side, "and so shall His Mother Most Blessed."[168] Twelve men went ahead of the army as "spies" to explore "the country in front of them and twelve . . . remain[ed] behind each troop with some arquebusiers."[169] The march into Chisca country had begun.

The journey was hard. The men slept in gullies and next to creeks and behind thick canebrakes, and at every stop, the soldiers kept a strict watch. At the "River of Santa Cruz," the Apalachicola River, Balthasar, *cacique* of

Santa Cruz, "waited with Canoes so that they might cross."[170] When the Chacatos revolted back in 1675, Balthasar nearly bolted from his town, fearing Diocsale's wrath and Chisca raids. Meeting the Apalachee force, Balthasar vowed to lead six of his own men to track down the Chisca fort, proudly declaring why he would fight. "He was a vassal of his Majesty," the *cacique* told the Apalachee captains, "and that even though he was a new Christian, he had the Heart in God and in his Most Blessed Mother, and that he was going from a very good wish to die for God our Lord and for his King and for his country."[171] As they passed through the deserted Chacato towns, supplies were already running low, with the men "taking only a fistful . . . of toasted corn" each morning.[172]

Then came one of several miracles: the scouts came across more tracks, many more, all clustered together. It was buffalo, enough the captains hoped, "to make Shields and to Relieve the hunger that was all around."[173] One of the men suffered "with a fever and pain in his side."[174] The others debated whether to send him back home. No, the man said, do not send me back. For "he wished to go to die and see their enemies."[175] The ill man spoke for them all. When the Chacatos began to grumble, calling the Apalachees "boys" who "did not know how to fight," the captains rebuked them on behalf of the whole army.[176] "Sons, we are Christians, and we bear every one of these travails with much patience, and so have you," they said, but "if you wish to return," then "we will have to carry you by force until you place us where the fort of the Chiscas is."[177] Take us there and then you can decide to fight or "you can move aside."[178]

Eighteen days out of Apalachee Province in the middle of the night on the "eve of the Apostle Saint Matthew," 20–21 September 1677, the army reached the massive Chisca fort, some three hundred paces in length.[179] At three o'clock in the morning, the captains and their contingents of soldiers, still under cover and undetected, stood at their posts for the assault. On the eastern flank, "where the sun comes out," Don Bernardo of Cupaica stood ready "with his drum and Fife" silent for now.[180] Captain Juan Mendoza and his men were on the western side. In the center, Matheo Chuba and his company crouched beneath the army's banner "on which was set a Crucifix, and on the Other side Our Lady of the Rosary."[181] The plan was simple but audacious. Following tactics learned from their enemies, the Apalachee army would focus its strength, charge against the weakest wall, and force their way through.[182] At the very moment when they were rising to charge, there was another miracle. "We saw a great Light that had the height of a man, that went up behind us."[183] As the light "expended itself," the awestruck witnesses, some thirty in all who could swear to it, said that "in the middle we saw that it had a spot of blue," the color of the Virgin Mary's robes.[184] The sign from the heavens alerted the Chiscas. An enemy Chacato lookout caught sight of them and "began to give cries that we were coming."[185]

"We charged," the Apalachees remembered afterward, "all of us, in an instant."[186] They hit the Chiscas with a "Load of harquebus fire and arrows" and "hurled themselves" inside the fort.[187] The Chiscas were barricaded inside "three large houses."[188] From slits in the walls of the houses, the defenders hit the Apalachees with "so many arrows, that it seemed like a very thick smoke" covered them.[189] The Apalachees tore into the houses, ripping down board after board. The Chisca soldiers tried to hold them off with arrow fire, while behind them a mass of desperate people began to pull back toward the river next to the fort. A tree "caught fire and burned many houses."[190] The Apalachees looked on in wonder as its "leaves burned as if they were tinder."[191] Under the glow of the burning tree, the Chiscas "were throwing themselves" from the bluff into the river, "men as well as women with their babies at their breasts," and drowning "even though," as the Apalachees said later, "we wished to capture them and would favor them and bring them back Alive."[192] The dead were found everywhere: eighteen men and a little boy in the houses, countless women and children who hid in "shelters" and burned alive.[193]

At daybreak, the Apalachee captains (blood-soaked, they said, "from top to bottom"), were "the owners of the Field."[194] From the charred boards of the ruined Chisca fort, the victors "made a small stockade" to shield themselves from the Chiscas' arrows, still flying at them from the bows of the warriors across the river.[195] To keep up their spirits and drown out the Chiscas' "many war-cries and howls," the men played their "drums of war" morning and afternoon.[196] After three days, the officers ordered the men into formation to march out in twos, "carrying our wounded loaded in the middle," and shooting dead two Chiscas who dared block their path home.[197]

In a clearing about half a league from the battlefield, the Chacato scouts stumbled on some seashells and cooking pots with herbs. It was a Chisca charm, the Chacatos said, placed in the army's way "so that we will not find how to go back to our lands."[198] Undaunted, the captains ordered the soldiers to march on. Heathen spells were vain next to the "help of God and of the Virgin."[199] On 5 October 1677, cheerfully bearing the wounded on stretchers, the captains of Apalachee returned triumphant to San Luís. All readied themselves for the winter and the honors and rewards that would be theirs with the coming provincial visitation by the Spaniards. The men of San Luis, not the Spaniards, had saved Florida and the "republic of Indians," much as Cockacoeske had saved it in Virginia.

The Congress at Middle Plantation:
Restoring the Republic of Indians in Virginia

On 29 May 1677, "being the day of His Majesties Birth and Happy Restauration," "at the New Guard-House" at Middle Plantation, the Native kings and queens of the Tidewater had buried the principles of Nathaniel Bacon and restored the republic of Indians in Virginia.[200] During the "Congress at Middle Plantation,"[201] like the visitations of Florida's Native provinces that would take place that winter, Indigenous leaders gathered to resolve differences with colonizers, restore harmony among themselves, and to enact significant changes in the law that bound them all together. With Cockacoeske's leadership, the English Crown reaffirmed its commitment to the legal protection of Natives in a treaty that more than any other embodied principles in common with the *república de indios* in Florida. The treaty was Cockacoeske's definitive refutation of Bacon's legal arguments and a diplomatic feat as daunting as any warrior's exploit.

The path to Middle Plantation was hard for Cockacoeske. When a new assembly, full of triumphant loyalists, opened at Sir William Berkeley's Green Spring mansion back in February, Cockacoeske was a humble petitioner.[202] Understandably, she asked "to have her lands restored," explaining that her decision to flee "was occasioned through her fear of the Rebel Bacon and his Accomplices" and not from any disobedience on her part.[203] The assembly restored Pamunkey lands but only so long as she followed the laws passed in March 1676 and any other commands from the assembly.[204] The queen lodged altogether ten petitions that session, sketching a rough draft for the new treaty she planned to make with the English. She petitioned that "her Indians" not be "employed by the English" as hunters or laborers without her consent.[205] She wanted a limit on how many men could "be required on service" for the colony as warriors, gaining a promise that "not above a third" would serve at once.[206] Those who fought in the country's service should keep the plunder, she said. She wanted hunting and fishing rights, the "liberty to gather bark from trees"—and got them, so long as nearby English settlers gave their permission first.[207] "To her petition praying that her Indians may not be abused by the English," the assembly gave a rather unsatisfying answer, telling her to complain to "a Justice of the peace" who would compel the offending colonist "to appear at the County Court," a decision tantamount to making the accused the judge of his own case.[208] Fortunately, the queen of Pamunkey had powerful friends.

To quell Bacon's Rebellion, King Charles II sent three commissioners, Sir John Berry, Herbert Jeffreys, and Francis Moryson, along with their clerk, Samuel Wiseman, and more than a thousand redcoats who soon swarmed "the Camp at Middle Plantation."[209] All three commissioners were metropolitan-minded imperialists with military or naval careers.[210] By the time they arrived in early 1677, the rebellion was over. The commissioners' task thus shifted from suppression to investigation. Proceeding county-by-county, the petitions and grievances poured in to the commissioners' sessions detailing what caused the troubles in Virginia.[211]

The deluge of settlers' complaints did not keep the commissioners from attending to the matter "of Renewing a Peace with the Neighbor Indians."[212] Commissioner Francis Moryson, the compiler of Virginia's Restoration legal code, knew the colony and Cockacoeske well. Moryson had "always been my friend," she said.[213] Like any politician of the day, Cockacoeske worried about her standing at court, telling her "Netop," her friend, Moryson, "I have none to confide in in England Save yourself."[214] The commissioners singled out Cockacoeske for the king's favor. "We could not but Present her case," they told the king, from whom a small gift would "oblige and Gratify this poor Indian Queen."[215] Of the gifts, only one remains: a metal gorget with Charles's royal arms to wear around her neck.[216] But the new covenant the Pamunkey queen forged with the royal commissioners and signed in the ceremony in May 1677 was far more important.

In front of the camp's guardhouse, Cockacoeske and "several Indian Kings and Queens" stood to hear the terms of the treaty they had made.[217] With "Silence Proclaimed," the articles were read one paragraph at a time as the interpreters explained the meaning of each one. Cockacoeske stepped forward "to sign."[218] She kneeled "with the rest" who together were "Publicly acknowledging to hold their Crowns and Lands of the Great King of England."[219] Herbert Jeffreys signed on King Charles's behalf. This "Paper (under the Seal of this Colony)," he said, "was to bind this Peace strongly betwixt us."[220] Cockacoeske and the rest of the *weroances* and *weroansquas* present, "all Kneeling again," kissed the document, passing it "from hand to hand."[221] With that act, the colony's original aristocracy was restored to its liberties and rights and Virginia's Native commonwealth reconstituted.[222] The Congress at Middle Plantation closed with booming "Field Pieces" and the clatter from "Volleys of Small Shot, and general acclamations of Joy" from the soldiers, the commissioners, and the Crown's tributary Native subjects.[223]

The articles of peace, known today as the Treaty of Middle Plantation— *"Founded upon the strong Pillars of Reciprocal Justice"*—guaranteed the Natives' *"Just Rights"* and provided means for *"Redress of their Wrongs and Injuries."*[224] The tributaries accepted "Subjection to the Great King of *England*" and in return they held their lands and property "in as free and firm manner as others His Majesties Subjects."[225] Redress would be open to them before the colony's governor who would act in the king's name "as if such hurt or injury had been done to any *Englishman*."[226] Equal justice for tributary Natives was "but just and reasonable," the new covenant declared, "they owning themselves to be under the Allegiance of His most Sacred Majesty."[227] In a sign of how far-reaching were the treaty-makers' intentions, the eighteenth article required that conflicts "between any of the *Indians* in Amity with the *English*" come before the governor, to "whose final Determination the said *Indians* shall submit and conform themselves."[228] The treaty outlawed the enslavement of tributaries.[229] And it recognized Cockacoeske's authority as a paramount chief under the governor, signaling a commitment to rule through Native chiefly lineages and the reconstitution of a united Powhatan polity under her leadership.[230]

Cockacoeske was not the only leader who ratified the treaty's terms. There was her son, Captain John West, "a good brave young man" who had "been very active in the Service of the English"; the queen of the Weanoakes who "had taken to herself the name of Queen Catherine [of Braganza]" to mark the occasion; the king of the Nansemonds, "a very friendly Indian and much conversant among the English"; and last, the ancient king of the Nottoways who "Governs his people with prudence and good Discipline."[231] Three years later, at least five more nations were signatories to Cockacoeske's treaty.[232] The leaders who signed—some of them from far outside the traditional bounds of Tsenacommacah—continued the trend of Indigenous royalism, calling on the Crown as the guarantor of their liberties.

The commissioners asked for clothes and adornments symbolic of royal protection and that suited these Native nobles, who regarded gifts to be a "Sacred Pledge of friendship."[233] The commissioners also requested "Silver

Badges to the number of Twenty with the names of your Majesty and the Tributary Princes inscribed."[234] Once, such badges were simply a way to tell friend from foe—without one, a Native person was liable to be shot until the legal reforms of the 1650s. Now, the badges, along with robes and crowns, signified the respect due to the kings and queens. With these tokens, King Charles II could "beget a reverence to them from their own people as well as your Majesty's Subjects in Virginia, when they shall see hereby that they are in your Royal Esteem as well as Protection."[235] As the commissioners gushed in their report back to Whitehall, the Native kings and queens "expressly own to have their immediate dependence on, to owe all Subjection and allegiance, and to hold their Crowns of and from your Majesty to whom they most justly give the name and Title of great King."[236] This admission, claimed the commissioners, "more than ever was Stipulated of, or owned by them in any former Treaty had or made by them."[237] Most colonists in Virginia had their doubts about the treaty and especially about the elevation—at English expense—of Tsenacomacoh's old aristocracy.[238]

On 18 October 1677, the Committee of the Privy Council for Trade and Plantations reviewed the treaty before ratification and met colonist's objections head-on. Coming to the article that kept the English from settling within three miles of the tributaries' towns, Major Robert Bristow, a merchant who had earned the commissioners' good opinion, objected to the provision "as a thing very inconvenient and prejudiced to the English planters."[239] Bristow's objection foreshadowed struggles ahead between tributary Natives and colonists. Then, near of the end of their sitting, Thomas Lord Culpeper, the next governor of Virginia, asked in "what manner the Indians are to be treated, as well in Civil as in Criminal causes."[240] After a debate, the committee made a decision. The officials in Whitehall resolved that the tributary Natives "ought to receive the same measure of Justice from the English, as the English, by law, expect from them."[241]

There were Indigenous leaders who questioned the treaty's terms too. The Rappahannocks and Chickahominies suddenly found themselves again under Pamunkey domination, subject to the authority of the restored *mamanatowick*, Cockacoeske. Judging by Cockacoeske's own complaints to Virginia's governor in June of 1678, the Chickahominies were surly and uncooperative, bitter about the subjection that Article XII imposed, fearful of what seemed to be Cockacoeske's plans to absorb them, and eager to do what they could to escape. Cockacoeske's dignity was on her mind and she complained to the governor of how the Chickahominies had "promised to keep three of their

Great Men to Wait upon the Queen to receive her Orders."[242] The *manguys* of the Chickahominies also had their dignity to consider. When Cockacoeske sent for them to parley on the terms of their incorporation with the Pamunkeys, they argued with her about what they owed her in obedience. She, in turn, "did . . . urge to them The Articles of peace."[243] Cockacoeske "provided a Cabin purposely for their entertainment that night, but the next morning the Said Indians were gone, and the Mats they lay upon, was found burnt."[244] The disturbances were serious but they should not overshadow the treaty's significance.

"Cockacoeske's treaty," the Treaty of Middle Plantation, made Virginia's tributary regime—on paper at least—into a republic of Indians under the care of the English Crown. What the *weroances* and *weroansquas* created in their deliberations during the Congress at Middle Plantation endures as the epitome of what Virginia owes to the Native nations on whose land it stands, and the document is foundational to their sovereignty in modern times.[245] For all its achievements, however, the treaty was a dead letter without the support of English colonists and of the Indigenous people, notably the Chickahominies, who now found themselves bound to its terms whether they liked it or not. In the coming years, Pamunkeys, Chickahominies, and English officials would put the treaty to the test. During the winter of 1677–1678, as Virginia's grand treaty was went into force, the Native lords of Florida gathered in their assemblies, received Spanish inspectors on an official visitation of their towns, and wrote new laws to govern the republic of Indians. There, too, the consent of the country's natural lords was required before any great changes could be made.

The Native Assemblies of Florida: Governing the Republic of Indians

The provincial visitations of 1677–1678 offer a glimpse into the minds of Indigenous leaders in Florida that year, revealing concerns in common with their counterparts who gathered for the Congress at Middle Plantation in Virginia. In these meetings between Native leaders and colonial officials, Indigenous customary law was most in evidence as a vital part of imperial law. Although Anglo-Americans boast how Jamestown hosted the first legislative assembly in North America, the provinces of Florida had held general assemblies during periodic *visítas* (inspection tours) long before 1619.[246] The assemblies in the council-houses of Florida, however, included the whole of the leadership class—the entire Native commonwealth—sitting together to hash out the great issues of the day. In November 1677, each of Florida's four Indian provinces—Guale, Mocama, Timucua, and Apalachee—had their own political and administrative structure, with the governor's handpicked lieutenant ostensibly overseeing its affairs. Akin to the local grandees who sat as justices of the peace in Virginia's counties were the *holatas*, *micos* and *micas*, *caciques* and *cacicas*, along with the corps of Indigenous officials, including *inijas*, *mandadores*, and *fiscales*, who handled day-to-day town business from the labor draft to public works. During the visitation, the Spanish provincial lieutenant was suspended, Indigenous nobles were fair game for the complaints of their vassals, and "questions about the possession" of hereditary offices lay open for investigation and settlement.[247] This extraordinary circumstance reflected the extraordinary nature of a provincial visitation and its objective to promote the "good republic."[248]

The visitors of 1677, like Virginia's royal commissioners, were all veteran soldiers: Antonio de Argüelles for Guale and Mocama and Domingo de Leturiondo for Timucua and Apalachee.[249] Unlike the English royal commissioners, who needed a writ of oyer and terminer to exercise their judicial powers, Argüelles and Leturiondo possessed sweeping authority to hear grievances, prosecute crimes, and to "apply redress" in the governor's name.[250] In the visitors' trains came interpreters: Diego Camuñas for Guale and Juan Martín for the Timucuan speakers in Mocama; Juan Baptista de la Cruz for Timucuan and Diego Salvador for Apalachee. Keeping track of every official act were the ever-present *escribanos* (notaries), so essential to Spanish judicial and political proceedings. A notary's role was expansive and his oath even more elaborate than the one Secretary Samuel Wiseman swore before the English royal commissioners.[251]

Everyone whom this party met on the road and in the towns that they inspected were to offer them aid in the performance of their duties. While the English royal commissioners came with the king's command to Virginia's colonial officials "to be in all things helpful" to them, the Spanish crown set limits on what the provincial visitors could expect from Native vassals.[252] In a royal *cédula* from 31 May 1676, King Carlos II commanded visitors not to take supplies or use Natives to carry "baggage" unless it was paid for and "voluntary."[253] This order was especially important in Florida where the visitors and their parties would have traveled with a train of Native burdeners who carried the baggage on their backs.

On 23 December 1677, Ana Estasia, the *mica* of Tupiqui, waited for them in San Joseph de Sapala to set everything to rights. After fleeing her town three years before, the *mica* of Tupiqui had not received the respect in Sapala that she felt she deserved. That year, there was no general assembly of the province of Guale where Ana Estasia could have learned about the plights of her fellow leaders. Across the provinces, there was a rash of chiefly resignations, notably by women, in Guale and Mocama—and Timucua—at a time when women like Cockacoeske of Pamunkey and Catherine of the Weanokes in Virginia were politically ascendant. One suggestive resignation was that of María, the *cacica* of the Timucuan town of San Francisco de Potano, who petitioned the visitor to let her transfer her office to her legitimate heir Miguel.[254] Perceptions of gender roles was an explicit influence on her decision. Miguel, she claimed, "had sufficient age and experience to be able to govern" and he "would do it better than her" for she was a "woman and could not look after the cares and duties" of office.[255] Following standard procedure but perhaps fearing the whole matter was a coup by the men of her council, the visitor confirmed that María resigned of her own volition.[256] Even so, the pressure from the leading men of the town likely played a part in the *cacica*'s decision. In any event, Ana Estasia, the *mica* of Tupiqui, was determined not to give up her privileges let alone her office and she intended for her heir, Alonso, to inherit them intact.

On arrival in Sapala, Antonio de Argüelles gathered everyone inside Sapala's council-house on Christmas Eve. Ana Estasia took her seat on the raised benches with the rest of the *caciques* and *principales*. The notary read the *auto*, the governor's order for the inspection of the provinces, and the visitation of San Joseph de Sapala began. Diego Camuñas stepped forward when the notary finished. The translator for the Gualean tongue announced that Captain Argüelles "will hear all of the controversies they have between themselves."[257] Ana Estasia listened as the interpreter continued: ". . . or about rights to *cacicados* [chiefly successions]."[258] When Camuñas was through, Ana Estasia spoke first. Ever since I came to Sapala, she said, the leading men of this place refused to sow a field for my support. They are my vassals and yet they do not help me.[259] Sapala's principal *mico*, Felipe, spoke next. Until now, I knew nothing about this, he said, "nor had he an instance for doing it."[260] Felipe balked, saying they could only be commanded to do it.[261] That last blow hit the mark. Argüelles hesitated, saying he would wait on the matter until the natural lords of the province "assembled to give their reason for better adjusting it."[262] Argüelles tried to calm the assembly and put them in mind of their duty to their king and their god.[263]

Ana Estasia's bid for power over the other *micos* in Sapala, like Cock-acoeske's plan to bring the "scattered Nations" of Virginia under her rule, depended on colonial backing. Cockacoeske won it but Ana Estasia did not. Cockacoeske, as head of the "house of Pamunkey," had a firm precedent for her claim to be a paramount chief. Ana Estasia, as Felipe pointed out, was on shaky ground. Tupiqui was once the center of a chiefdom that, after 1580, was itself subject to Tolomato.[264] Sapala had been in another chiefdom alto-gether. But the general assembly of Guale's *caciques* might still have ruled in Ana Estasia's favor had it met. Whether Sapala ever owed tribute to Tupiqui's chiefs may have been irrelevant. What mattered was that the *mico* or *mica* of Tupiqui was once a paramount with towns under their rule, and there-fore outranked Sapala's *caciques*, who had never been more than the leading men of a lesser town. When the two towns merged around 1674, the *mica* of Tupiqui expected the people of Sapala to respect her rank and support her in proper style, even if they never had any obligation to do so. Ana Estasia and Felipe could both be right. Sapala owed the *mica* a field of corn even if it was unprecedented.

Precedent was not the only consideration when Native and colonial offi-cials decided to bolster a chief's authority, whether in Florida or Virginia. The Chickahominies, with their long history of independence from the Pow-hatans, had as strong a precedent against Cockacoeske's claims as Felipe had against Ana Estasia's. The English royal commissioners put them under the queen of Pamunkey nevertheless. Other needs overrode the Chickahominies' objections. For one, the "Good Queen of Pamunkey" deserved royal favor, not just the gifts of clothes or the silver-plated gorget, but real backing to afford her befitting dignity and style, including Chickahominy great men to attend her.[265] The greater her power over the other tributaries, the easier it would be for the English to govern all of them—especially the Rappahan-nocks and the Chickahominies, such "a deceitful people" as Cockacoeske put it in one letter.[266] The English, weary from their own dealings with the independent-minded Chickahominies, were happy to subject them to her.[267] The return of the *mamanatowick* promised more tributary soldiers to defend Virginia, more beaver pelts in the governor's hands, more peace and quiet on the colony's boundaries, and an end to their wrangles with the Chicka-hominies. What would backing the *mica* of Tupiqui have given the Spanish?

The Spanish visitor-general could have tried at least to persuade Felipe and the other "leading men" in Sapala to honor Ana Estasia. But Argüelles dithered over Ana Estasia's request for the sake of keeping Sapala together.

There were legal arguments against it, not least the expectation from royal decrees of 1614 and 1628, leaving matters of chiefly succession and power to Native peoples' "ancient right and custom."[268] The population of Sapala was low—just fifty people, according to a 1675 census—and morale was much lower.[269] If the *mica* were a *mico* (a male chief) would Felipe have given a different answer? Part of what stirred up Indigenous opposition against Cockacoeske in Virginia was her gender. In the seventeenth century, a Native woman of rank could overcome the limitations of gender, even in the eyes of male colonial officials.[270] But masculinity had sunk into what one scholar called its "nadir" after the humiliation of Powhatan men at the hands of the English in 1646 and the Westos ten years later.[271] With male pursuits of war and hunting under server constraints, resentments may have deepened. In Florida, Sapala's men had suffered in their own war with the Westos. Perhaps digging a field with their own hands for what they saw as a presumptuous outsider was more than they could bear. If Argüelles ordered Felipe to have his men sow a patch of corn for Ana Estasia, would they fight when the Westos raided again or would they have abandoned the town for another site? Tupiqui and Sapala had to be as one if they were to withstand the enemy. Maybe that is why no record of the anticipated general assembly in Guale survives—Argüelles never called one together so he could avoid any more quarreling between the chiefs during such dangerous times.

Even while the visitation of Guale and Mocama was underway, Domingo de Leturiondo and his companions were passing through Timucua and Apalachee. The high point of the visitation in Apalachee came on 22 December when "all of the *caciques* and *principales* of this province" packed onto the benches of Tomole's council-house in a "junta general," or general assembly.[272] The decree calling them together bid the natural lords of Apalachee to say freely what was on their minds, above all to name what measures they thought best for the province's "good government."[273] Murmurs of discontent among the commoners about the ballgame's abolition set the assembly's agenda and, much like Ana Estasia's case in Sapala, the assembly's deliberations show the extent to which Indigenous consent was a necessary component of imperial law.

In the general assembly, Domingo de Leturiondo called on the natural lords of Apalachee to deliberate on the matter freely and make a binding decision. If the game "were bad, it shall be declared as such and be quashed for life."[274] But if "it does not bring inconveniences, let it be exercised freely."[275] All the gathered nobles spoke according to their ranks, from the leaders of

Ivitachuco down to the lord of the humblest village in the province.[276] None voted for the game to continue. The assembly declared that only dissenters were men "who played the game as their trade" while the rest of the people of Apalachee "had already gotten over it."[277] With that, the visitor, in the governor's name, "conforming himself with the opinion of them all" commanded that it be played no more.[278] Not every law that *caciques* and Spaniards made together was happily obeyed, certainly not in this case. Many ordinary spectators and the players, notably in Timucua, resented the campaign against the ballgame and defied attempts to ban it.[279] Native Southerners have kept the ballgame alive to the present day.[280]

In the crowd of dignitaries that day sat men who had risked their lives for the preservation of Apalachee and the republic of Indians: Matheo Chuba, Juan Mendoza, Bentura, Don Bernardo of Cupaica, and scores of other warriors who served in the war against the Chiscas that fall. Leturiondo praised their valor, but noting the absence of prisoners in the army's train on their return to San Luís, the visitor paused, "commanding them likewise that those who would surrender themselves, and women and children, they should not kill them," but rather "using with them pity and carrying them back for their slaves."[281] Leturiondo then proclaimed that all who fought in the campaign were now *norocos*, one of the highest ranks in the warrior class.[282] Honor was their only reward for the moment. Like the crowns and robes for the tributary kings and queens in Virginia, the clothes "printed with bright colors" that Governor Salazar wanted to bestow on the Apalachee captains "from the hand of their King," were years in arriving.[283] The imperial bureaucracy was still grinding on the request in September 1680.[284]

The Native assemblies of Florida in the winter of 1677–1678 show the power of Indigenous customary law and how much the empire depended on Indigenous political consent to function. The two examples from Sapala in Guale and from the Apalachee general assembly at Tomole, also show how the interests of *caciques* and colonial officials had to come together to make any meaningful legal or political decisions. By the late 1670s, the interests of Native elites in the provinces and the governor in San Agustín largely aligned. Both sought to buttress chiefly authority in order to hold towns together so they could serve the larger goal of preserving Spain's and its Indigenous vassals' hold on the region. When a leader's request did not appear to serve the larger goal, as in the case of Tupiqui's *mica* Ana Estasia, Spaniards joined with other Indigenous leaders to deny it. The power of Indigenous leaders varied from town to town and province to province, forming a sort of hierarchy with the Apalachees at the top in Florida, much as the Pamunkeys were pre-eminent in Virginia. While they courted the Apalachees on whose good will, labor, and foodstuffs the *presidio* depended, the Spaniards could afford to disappoint one Guale leader whose requests might have upset the delicate situation in her town in any case. The deliberations in Sapala and Tomole were but a small sampling from an extensive visitation that included assemblies in numerous towns who heard complaints, settled disputes, and left behind regulations for the good government of the republic of Indians. Collectively, the Native assemblies of Florida had the same effect as the congress held at Middle Plantation—they rewrote imperial law on the ground—and unwittingly drew two very different colonies closer together.

Reciprocal Justice: Legal Convergence in Florida and Virginia

A comparison of the Treaty of Middle Plantation and the rulings and regulations from the visitations of Guale-Mocama, Apalachee, and Timucua shows that, as 1678 began, the letter of the law in Virginia and Florida had never been so alike. The legal convergence was the result of a general merging of interests between Native and European leaders in both Virginia and Florida following the crises of the previous four years. From the crucibles of Bacon's Rebellion and the Chacato-Chisca troubles (not to mention the menace of the growing Indian slave trade), Native leaders achieved political settlements that increased their power over their towns and in relation to colonizers.

The similarities began with the relationship Native subjects and vassals had with the Crown. The tributaries owned "all Subjection to the Great King of *England*" (article I), held their lands if they "maintain their due Obedience and Subjection to His Majesty" (article III), and paid their tribute in person to the king's governor "in acknowledgement they hold their Crowns and Lands of the Great King of *England*" (article XVI).[285] Throughout the visitations of Florida's provinces, the visitors reaffirmed the ties between the king of Spain and his Native vassals. Each *cacique* the visitors installed entered office "in the name of his majesty."[286] At every stop, Leturiondo and Argüelles reminded the people of their duties to "both majesties"—to the king and to the Catholic faith.[287] In Apalachee Province, the visitor commanded the lieutenant to mark the towns that "are missing the royal arms in the churches" and to raise them in token of the royal patronage of the church and as vivid reminders of the peoples' duty as loyal vassals.[288]

The foremost duty of Indigenous vassals and subjects was to defend the colony in war. The Virginia tributaries, the treaty said, acted in the first instance as a kind of border patrol or customs service, always obliged to escort and "send a safe Conduct with the Foreigner, upon any Lawful occasion of his coming in," but never in disguise (article VIII).[289] No *weroance* could refuse a peaceful foreigner with a valid reason for travel from entering the colony. But should enemies come "near the *English* Quarters," the tributaries must inform the nearest militia officer, "and acquaint him of their Nation, number, and design, and which way they bend their course" (article IX).[290] In return, the "friendly *Indians*" could expect the colonial militia to "Aid, Strengthen and join" with them "against any Foreign Attempt, Incursion or Depredation upon the *Indian* Towns" (article X).[291] For the protection of their towns and for their service in defense of the colony, "every Indian fit to bear Arms" would receive "sufficient" ammunition and would receive pay for joining the colonial militia "upon any March against the Enemy" (article XI).[292] The treaty in Virginia set high expectations for mutual defense, exceeding the reality in Apalachee in 1677–1678. During the Chisca War, the provincial lieutenant provided powder and shot to the Apalachees but no Spanish soldiers accompanied them or did much in their defense. The Native militiamen conducted the campaign on their own with official sanction. As officers themselves, the Apalachee captains were uncomfortable having Spanish soldiers with them who had little inclination to follow Natives' orders.[293] But the reciprocal obligations of defense were important expectations in both places.

The two composite polities also placed restrictions on Natives' movements even while calling on their services as soldiers and laborers. The curbs on free movement were part of the colonial drive to fix Natives in place and make them more pliable to colonial goals, undoubtedly, but those rules also reflected the wishes of anxious Native elites everywhere who feared their populations would disappear. Before they could "keep any Neighboring *Indian* as Servant"—or even "entertain" a tributary Native for any purpose—colonists in Virginia needed the governor's permission (article XIII).[294] By implication, the Native servants or visitors involved needed their *weroance*'s permission. And a *weroance* or *weroansqua* could expect the governor to look to them first in any case concerning a person from their town. Any "Vagrant or Runaway *Indian*" must return "to his own Town" or the colonists who "harbor or entertain" them would be liable to pay a fine (article XIV).[295] As written, articles XIII and XIV seem to be about preventing Natives from doing mischief against colonists.[296] But they were also measures to strengthen the hand of Native leaders, as Cockacoeske's February 1677 petitions made plain, giving Indigenous leaders assurances that the English would not permit their populations to dry up from flight nor allow their jurisdiction over their own people to dissolve.

Flight was also a problem in all the provinces of Florida and *caciques* were as worried about the issue as any provincial lieutenant or visitor-general. In Guale, the regulations forbade people from "moving themselves with weak cause from one Council House to the other," to get out of the labor, whether in the fields or carrying loads, they had to perform for their leaders and for Spaniards.[297] In Apalachee Province, the regulations stipulated that "no person may move himself from his town to another without first obtaining special license from the lieutenant of these provinces and"—most importantly—"from his *cacique*."[298] The provincial lieutenant's duty was to make sure the motives Natives had for moving were not spurious ones such as "running away from work," in which case he would not give license.[299] "Nor shall vagrants be tolerated in the towns," the rules proclaimed.[300] The provincial lieutenant in this case assumed the role of enforcer for the chiefs who did not want to lose their vassals to flight. Two places were exempt from this order: the western Apalachee town of Bacuqua, since it was "frontier" town and faced possible "invasion from enemies," and the Timucuan service town of Hivitanayo, which needed workers.[301] Tellingly, the penalty for letting in stragglers from other towns, a fine of twelve deerskins, fell on *caciques* who were always eager to gain vassals.

While the law fixed them in place, it raised legal buffers around Native towns to keep out unwanted people and livestock. The Treaty of Middle Plantation blamed the "the Violent Intrusions of divers *English* into their Lands" for Natives' taking up arms in the past and ordered "That no *English* shall Seat or Plant nearer then Three miles of any *Indian* Town" (article IV).[302] If any colonists made "any Encroachment upon their Lands" the government would have them "removed from thence."[303] The formal law of the Spanish Empire, published as the *Recopilación de las Leyes de las Indias* in 1680, declared that "Spaniards, Negroes, Mestizos, and Mulattos shall not live in the Towns of Indians," nor even linger in one for more than a few days.[304] Even if they somehow bought land in a Native town, Spaniards and other outsiders were not allowed to live there because they taught the residents "bad customs."[305] The 1677 treaty blamed, among other problems, the intrusions of domestic livestock—"Cattle and Hogs"—on Native lands for their part in the late tumults, but their behavior produced friction across the Americas.[306] Under Spanish law, "large livestock ranches" were not to come "within a league and a half of the ancient Reductions" while "they of small livestock" could not come within a "half-league."[307] The remoteness from Spanish habitations of most of Florida's Native towns meant that there were, with some exceptions, fewer worries about the need for buffers.[308] Most squabbles over boundaries in Florida were between Native towns, like the one in Apalachee that resulted from Ocone townspeople poaching deer on the town of Ychutafun's land.[309]

Such quarrels between Natives were the formal responsibility of their paramount chiefs, the governors of Virginia and Florida. The treaty of 1677 established two levels of dispute resolution: by "Indian Kings and Queens" and by "His Majesties Governor." The treaty also implicitly validated indigenous laws and customs as suitable for resolving disputes among themselves by acknowledging a qualified Native right to self-government. All tributary *weroances* and *weroansquas* had "equal Power to Govern their own People, and none [were] to have greater Power then [any] other" (article XII).[310] There was, of course, one exception. Yet even the exception proved the rule that indigenous custom was a recognized part of Virginia law. Article XII restored the office of *mamanatowick* and returned it to Cockacoeske, placing "several scattered Nations," notably the Chickahominies and Rappahannocks, "under her Power and Government."[311] Even Cockacoeske's reach had limits. Should her power and government fail to satisfy (or restrain) "her Subjects," they could, in turn, "repair to His Majesties Governor, by whose Justice and Wisdom it is concluded such Difference shall be made up and decided" (article XVIII).[312] To better impart his "Justice and Wisdom," and to keep the English from lying to them, article XIX said there would "be one of each Nation of our Neighboring *Indians* that can already speak, or may become capable of speaking *English*, admitted together with those of the *English*, to be their own Interpreters."[313] In Apalachee and Timucua, the visitor ordered schools established "to teach reading and writing to the boys" and ordered every town to "plant a good field" to support each school.[314] Both the Spanish schools for boys and the requirement that Native interpreters be present during any business with the English sought to promote the mutual intelligibility of the law. In Virginia, the interpreters would have their work cut out for them.

The treaty of 1677 obliged Virginia's governor to settle every and "any Discord or Breach of Peace happening to arise between any of the *Indians*" who were tributary subjects of the Crown.[315] His rulings were final.[316] The governor acted as an appellate judge in Indigenous cases much like a provincial lieutenant in Florida. Article XVIII assigned to Virginia officials duties that in Apalachee and Timucua were nothing more than what Spaniards deemed "agreeable for the proper dispensation of justice."[317] Each provincial lieutenant in Florida had to "visit the towns in his jurisdiction every four months," resolving controversies among the Natives.[318] Much like a provincial lieutenant or a visitor-general, under article XVIII the governor of Virginia would presumably have to rely, at least to some extent, on Native law and the opinions of Native leaders to settle their disputes.

What the Spaniards had done in Florida for more than a century, the English in Virginia were complaining of in less than a year. The queen of Pamunkey and the Chickahominies came before the council to resolve their ongoing disputes. "We used our best endeavors to bring them to a temper," wrote Philip Ludwell, "but it is in their nature not to recede from their demands and that made our pains ineffectual."[319] The "temper" of the tributaries was as bold as ever. Better to let the Natives cut each other's throats, Ludwell thought, than to sit in judgment on all their petty quarrels. Too much weight has rested on Ludwell's opinion, who decried articles XII and XVIII as counterproductive innovations. The truth was just the opposite. Tributary Natives had petitioned colonial institutions, from the assembly to the governor, whenever they had a grievance or a request, ever since 1646. Opechancanough's death had not merely set "all the nations Tributary to that house at Liberty," but had joined them in a composite polity, a republic of Indians under the governor.[320] Article XVIII simply codified the governor's role as paramount over that polity in the largest possible terms.

Justice in Virginia had parallel tracks and the king had two categories of royal subjects, English and Indian. Cockacoeske, hoping "my examples will be a pattern" to all the Native tributaries, told Francis Moryson how she regarded "that Great King of England to be my very good friend, as also my real Defender, to whom I shall pay as much Loyalty as any of his English Subjects."[321] Virginia in 1678 was as close to having "two republics" as any place in English America in the seventeenth century.

Still, the ideal of two republics, of equal commonwealths, poorly describes the reality in either colony. The republic of Indians in Florida was itself many republics, Christian and "heathen," populous and small, strategic but weak (as in Guale), or strategic and strong (as in Apalachee). The smallest and the most important of these republics were the towns themselves, each with their officials, customs, and histories. The towns in turn nested within, and were part of nations that shared languages, cultures, and histories in common. Apalachee was the most coherent of the nations by the 1670s. The nations inhabited provinces, a Spanish administrative unit that became more and more important as the original Native population declined and new peoples moved into them.[322]

Various distinctions separated the provinces, the nations, and individual towns one from the other, determining how they fit into the larger hybrid polity and how the Spanish treated them. To Spanish officials, the most important distinction, judging by the documents they left behind, was between Christian and "heathen." In towns where the people were Catholics of long-standing, whatever the other circumstances, the Spanish were more deferential to the wishes of Native leaders, more respectful of local customs, leaving the resolution of disputes to them both. But the divide between Christian and heathen was not in fact the most important one distinguishing the many republics of Indians in Florida. New converts like the Chacatos and unconverted peoples like the Tocopacas or Yamasees, whom the Spanish invited into their frontiers for the same reasons the Romans welcomed the Germanic hordes into theirs, were alike treated with force or instructed in its use. Where the Natives were hard-pressed but small in number, the Spanish sometimes gave in to their demands—even if reluctantly and always reminding them of the consequences, such as in Guale's shrinking northern towns. The Spanish did so to keep the Natives together and in good spirits. In strong, populous, strategic Apalachee, the Spaniards had no choice but to follow the proper forms, yielding as much as possible to government by the Natives' natural lords. Even this would change with time.

The tributary nations of Virginia were unequal to each other in rank, too, as article XII proved. The Pamunkeys were decidedly more influential in imperial councils and seemed more useful to imperial goals than the Chickahominies. But as the events in the years ahead would show, the Chickahominies could use article XVIII, with the governor's authority to resolve disputes, quite effectively to get their way, however outnumbered and harried they often felt. *Weroances* and *weroansquas* (and Chickahominy *manguys*) in Virginia could use colonial political support as well as any *cacique* in Apalachee, Timucua, or Guale. Together with colonial officials, the Native leaders of the South built the "Strong Pillars of Reciprocal Justice" on which their composite political systems with their shared laws, mutual obligations, and promises of equal protection depended.

Conclusion: Rebellions Against the Republic of Indians

Juan Fernández de Diocsale and Nathaniel Bacon rebelled against this system, the republic of Indians, each for his own reasons. But the differences in their motives are telling and speak to the characteristics of each colony. In Virginia, the arch-rebel was an Englishman; in Florida, an Indigenous leader became the symbol and magnet for discontent. In Virginia, the issue was whether Indigenous people could be protected subjects; in Florida, the issue was whether Indigenous people might remain independent of such "protection." Their distinctiveness came from the divergent circumstances on the ground—in demographics, motives, and social structure—that were in turn the products of how the two composite polities developed over time in each colony. Yet in the long run their uprisings served the same historical ends. Diocsale revolted to free his people from exploitation, the friars' sham morality, and the lackluster promise of Christian commonwealth—just a thin disguise for Apalachee domination as he saw it. Bacon rebelled to exploit Natives more profitably by taking their goods, their lands, and their very lives. He tried to do away with the cover of tributary status that hid the danger of Native "kings and queens" who were so much "favored" in the colony's highest councils that they could write their own laws.

Neither rebel seemed a victor in 1678. In both places, the republic of Indians drew strength from a renewed alliance between Native leaders and colonial officials. On paper, the statuses of tributary Indians in Virginia and Native vassals in Florida were now of equal strength. In the end, however, over the next twenty years, the wake of Diocsale's and Bacon's movements rippled out—the one east and north, the other west and south—enveloping and nearly swallowing up the old ideal of equal republics forever. During those years of swirling changes, nations small and great called upon the decaying ideal in eloquent words and with equal fervor but not with equal success. Still others abandoned the republic of Indians altogether, looking to themselves and their own devices to cut another way forward, perilous though it was.

CHAPTER 4

"Neither Vassals nor Subjects," 1670–1700

In the latter half of the seventeenth century, some Native American nations cleared another path for themselves, one that led far from the republic of Indians. The road was hard but it beckoned with the elusive promise of freedom. The men who took this path had to pick up shotgun and shield, walk for league after league on narrow traces in darkness, had to be willing to hide for days waiting for the moment to strike. They had to be quick and quiet, running headlong into sleeping villages in the predawn murk, setting fire to all the houses before anyone inside was awake.[1] These warriors struck so fast that pursuit was fruitless. The people of many a devastated village had the same experience in tracking the raiders as one Spanish soldier who arrived too late to help save a sacked Timucuan town.[2] With the town a smoldering ruin around him, the soldier and his sixteen men followed the raiders' trail for two days and never found their quarry. Once out of reach of reprisal, the successful plunderers had to stop their ears against the cries of the women and children they bound with cords and told curtly to walk or die. A "grand reception" awaited them at the trail's end with celebrations and fresh clothes, the raiders always said, leaving off any mention of the market where the captives would be sold as slaves.[3] The guns they took in return from the merchants who supplied them meant at least that the men's own children could sleep soundly at night.

The nations that followed this path became what Robbie Ethridge has called militaristic slaving societies.[4] For guns, they traded hides and deerskins and enslaved human beings to colonial merchants, almost all of them Englishmen working on the outskirts of the law. Devoting their utmost efforts to war was a strategy for survival, a way to trounce ancient enemies and hold the new ones—European colonizers—at bay.[5] To their victims, these militarized Native nations were Chichimecos and man-eaters, infidels who pillaged and murdered Christians. Many who once took baptism now gladly torched churches after making off with all the plate. One typical raid on a Timucuan mission in central Florida left the "Chapel and the friars house" in ashes and the shredded remains of "a Manuscript of prayers written in Spanish and Latin" blowing in the wind as evidence of the outrage.[6] The geographic extent of their marauding was apparent as early as the 1660s when enslaved Indians with names like Francisco entered the records of Virginia.[7] The Westos and the Tomahitans turned to this way of life early. One of the Virginians who traded guns to these nations and whose servant went on raids with them said that such was "the course of their living to forage, rob, and spoil other nations."[8] Other people came to this way of life after they were persuaded by the alternatives. They stood for loftier aims.[9] The Yamasees, a nation forged out of displaced people who flooded Spanish missions in the 1660s, found life in the republic of Indians as unbearable as slavery and left it behind. Their warriors soon returned to the missions armed with guns declaring the overthrow of the priests, the labor draft, and the end of submission to any king. They were the spearhead of a political revolution. For such Native peoples, who transformed themselves in the chaos of the era, would be "neither vassals nor subjects" to anyone.[10]

What started with a few "Spanish Indians" enslaved in Virginia swelled into hundreds and thousands, shipped to New England and the West Indies to work until they died. Almost all of them passed through the same port. Two women who escaped a coffle in the dead of night recalled with terror where their captors said they were bound, "San Jorge," already a byword for Indian slavery by the 1670s.[11] San Jorge, or Saint George was what the Spanish called the small outpost whose welcoming Native neighbors must have known briefly as the town as Kiawah, after the land of the *mico* who took in the newcomers.[12] Expecting the strangers to protect them from Westo slavers, their Indigenous neighbors in Sewee assumed care of the fledgling settlement as a mother town might do for a daughter town, sending ample corn to tide them over as they sowed crops of their own and built a palisade for defense.[13] Such hopes proved fleeting as Charles Town, capital of the new Carolina colony, became the emporium of the slave trade. Charles Town's humble beginnings were partly to blame. With no profitable commodity ready to grow in the ground, the early colonists took to seizing and selling Native captives instead, usually mouthing arguments from just war theory and the law of nations.[14] Until the early 1680s, the Carolinians did so in alliance with the dreaded Westos themselves.[15] Bonds with the Savannahs and the Yamasees followed, as the English cast aside one ally for another in ruthless succession. By the early eighteenth century, the commerce had ensnared some 51,000 human beings.[16] Most of the victims came from Florida's mission towns but the impacts were felt far and wide, threatening the liberties of Indigenous peoples across the South.[17] The slave trade was to be the ultimate test of the republic of Indians.

Militaristic slaving societies like the Westos chose to blaze one path and they forced other Native towns to make a choice of their own. In 1670, the range of potential decisions open to Native leaders debating in their council-houses was still wide, even if the stakes never changed. The right choice meant survival and the wrong one meant enslavement and death. For some harried towns that remained independent, submission to the Spanish or the English was a possibility, affording a promise of legal protection from dispossession and enslavement. For others, especially in the towns of Escamaçu, on the coast of modern-day South Carolina, the Spanish alliance, with its demands for labor and religious conversion, was distasteful and they were looking for other allies just as the first Englishmen put down roots at Charles Town. For people already living in the republic of Indians—whether in Florida or Virginia—most chose to redouble their commitment to the alliance with colonizers despite mounting disappointments.

Above the din of war and the murmurs of ceaseless deliberations, arose some of the most eloquent expressions of what the republic of Indians meant to the Indigenous leaders in Florida and Virginia who tried to keep it alive. From the heat of so much struggle came Indigenous interpretations of colonial history, the meaning of the law, and the duties of monarchs to those they ruled—of whatever nation. Theirs was the answer to the Yamasee manifesto. The defense of the republic of Indians took place in council-houses and *juntas* as much as in combat against enemy warriors. Indigenous leaders waged their fight with volleys of petitions and well-timed speeches aimed to strike not the enemy but the hearts of their feckless protectors, English or Spanish. Victory depended on holding European empires to their obligations to protect loyal Indigenous vassals and subjects. All the while, Spaniards and Englishmen alike grew more brazen, disregarded established covenants, and sought to impose their own law on Indigenous vassals and subjects. Everywhere, including Florida, emboldened colonizers threatened Indigenous lands and Native leaders looked for new ways to protect them. Colonizers' actions endangered the positions of established leaders within the republic of Indians, threatening long-held rights over labor and tribute, and igniting a debate about what made for the best kind of political community. For every vassal or tributary who held fast to the republic of Indians, there were many more who voted with their feet, striking out for the interior or for the warmth of other council fires where Native voices were the decisive ones. This clash between political philosophies drove the rise of the large independent, egalitarian, Indigenous societies based on towns and committed to their own sovereignty that were to dominate the next century.

That the future belonged to large sovereign nations was becoming clear to some people by the end of the century, but they differed about the reasons why or what it meant. Spanish observers were certain that San Jorge's policies, though successful in routing San Agustín's influence, had sown the seeds of Carolina's own destruction. The "liberty" that Indian allies of the English—the Savannahs, Yamasees, and others—then enjoyed, including freedom from the call of the mission bells, the liturgy of the mass, the strictures of the Evangelical law, and the hardships of regular labor for colonizers to the Spaniards seemed little more than licentiousness. There lay the hidden danger to these *Luteranos*, "Lutherans," as some Spaniards still called the Protestant English. The Spanish could take some cold comfort in this. For surely the day of reckoning would come for the proud men of San Jorge when the gun-toting Native towns they had "liberated" would turn against them. Time would prove the rueful Spaniards right, but there would be no return to the old order they craved. For the Indigenous nations concerned, what the Spaniards called licentiousness and the English thought was a liberty granted from colonial hands was nothing less than a defiant charter of sovereignty— and it was nonnegotiable.

Strangers in the Council-House

The council-house rose from the earth, reaching for the Sky World where heroes and gods dwelled. Nothing so divine was on the minds of the English visitors that day at Edisto Town in Escamaçu in the summer of 1666. Though hard-nosed agents of English colonization, the party of strangers nevertheless gaped as they approached the towering council-house "through a spacious walk rowed with trees on both sides, tall and full branched."[18] Spaniards called these structures *bohíos*, a Taíno word they usually translated to mean huts.[19] Another Englishman in the 1660s compared the one he visited to a "Dove-house."[20] An enormous dove-house at that, measuring "two hundred foot at least, completely covered with *Palmetto*-leaves."[21] One later traveler remarked that the "State-House" where the Indians received him "was as dark as a Dungeon, and as hot as one of the *Dutch*-Stoves in *Holland*."[22] At the center, a fire burned night and day. On a clear day, such as that day, a shaft of light from the sun penetrated the gloom through the opening in the roof. On benches and on the clean-swept dirt floor sat all the commoners of the town— "the whole rabble of men, Women and children."[23] Within beat the pulse of the town's civic and ritual life. The great political events of the late seventeenth century unfolded around the fires of council-houses like the one in Edisto. The ambitions of all the players, Native, Spanish, and English were decided under such roofs.

The violence of the era sundered the older, larger polities and hastened the ascendance of individual towns like Edisto. In the late seventeenth-century Southeast, the harmonious, well-ordered town was the Indigenous political ideal and the "fundamental" unit on which ambitious leaders—Native and European—sought to build larger political forms, whether chieftaincies, nations, or empires.[24] The leading towns jostled for wealth, influence, power, and prestige, while the inhabitants of many were hoping only to survive.[25] Towns, not frontiers, not borderlands, nor the many-sided contest between empires, were the defining political fact of the Southeast in the late seventeenth century, an insight that often ends at the stockades of colonial settlements.[26] The *presidio* at San Agustín was one such township connected to others in its Indigenous "provinces." The future Charleston—in 1670, a village of 150 strangers living in the boundaries of the *mico* of Kiawah—was another. Hickauhaugau, the Westo capital near the falls of the Savannah River, still another—and certainly one of the most important.[27]

The rival appeals of outsiders, whether traders, friars, governors, or other Indigenous leaders, added to the pressure inside Native council-houses. Towns faced the blandishments of competing actors, all of them with their own motives. Deciding whether to let them in and agree to their demands, Native leaders balanced the rewards with the risks. Outsiders were conduits to spiritual, economic, and political power that could help a town survive the wars of the slave trade. But their gifts too often threatened to usurp chiefs' traditional authority and towns' autonomy. Paths radiated out of each town, joining it with its allies while avoiding its enemies. To understand the Southeast, then, we must picture it in the way that Native peoples did in their maps—as a collection of circles, representing nations, which were themselves collections of towns of varying influence, and all connected in intricate webs of paths, each route reflecting a deliberate political decision.[28]

There on a mission of reconnaissance for the Lords Proprietors of Carolina to lay the groundwork for a new colony, the English party under Robert Sanford would have to play by Indigenous rules as soon as they entered. With the ostensibly peaceful intentions of Carolina's distant European proprietors before them, the English visitors offered the Native chiefs they met gifts and a promise of alliance. Following Indigenous protocols, the Englishmen left behind one of their own to be the living embodiment of the agreement. In time, the man who stayed became a kinsman through marriage to Native leaders all over the region. Although his skills and connections were the result of adhering to Native rules of hospitality and friendship, he would be one of the first people who showed English colonizers a very different route to power and wealth by breaking those very same rules. No one watching then would have guessed such a turn of events as the strangers stepped inside. The men who governed Edisto and nearby Santa Elena were still the ones in the elevated seats, making the decisions. For Robert Sanford and his men, their bowed entry into the council-house at Edisto was their passage into the political realities of the Southeast.

Perched inside with his *principales* (headmen) on a raised bench, the *cacique* of Edisto, "an old man of a large stature and bone," looked down on the guests and in his mind's eye could have silently consulted a mental chart of the country surrounding his town.[29] The picture was grim.[30] A later observer would note that all the towns in that vicinity were "in a pound"—crammed uncomfortably between the Westos toward the interior and the southerly coastal missions where the Natives were dedicated "Spanish Comeraro[s]," or comrades.[31] Alliances and conglomerations, peoples coming together and exchanging knowledge and goods, made survival in this harsh reality possible. The English strangers now before him offered gifts of power that would help preserve the town, not to mention the *cacique*'s place in it. And Edisto's *cacique* could accomplish all of this without converting to the Spanish religion as the people to the south had done. With joy, he welcomed the strangers, placing their captains, Sanford and Cary, by his side on each hand.[32] Seated in places of honor, the guests received presents of deerskins, while the people performed "their Ceremonies of Welcome and friendship."[33] That evening, "after a few hours' stay," the strangers departed for their "Vessel with a great troop of Indians" following them, including "the old Cacique himself."[34]

At Santa Elena, near Port Royal, the *cacique* Niquisalla staged his own ceremony to solemnize the compact between his town and the one that the English strangers hoped soon to establish, vouchsafing the alliance with an exchange of emissaries. The *cacique* delivered "his Sister's son" (presumably his heir) to Sanford, charging the English captain to "clothe him" and bring the young man back in a few months.[35] For his part, Sanford offered a volunteer whom he was sure was steadfast in "his resolution to stay with the Indians" and there promote "the mutual learning [of] their language."[36] Little is known of the volunteer's life before that moment. But in time, he would grow into one of the most accomplished of the many men and women whom the Spaniards and Florida Natives called *atequis* and the English, "linguisters," the vital interpreters who made peaceful relationships possible between towns. He was the ship's "Chirurgeon," and his name was Henry Woodward.

Woodward's adoption in Santa Elena mixed Indigenous rituals and forms with an English ceremony of possession. The young Englishman immediately earned the place of privileged outsider with a *sábana* (field) of corn to feed him much as a Franciscan friar had for support.[37] With this field came the Indian labor to cultivate it. Much as Sanford had enjoyed a seat nearest him, the *cacique* "placed Woodward by him upon a Throne" before the people present.[38] To be seated, and especially to be carried on others' backs, signified high status in Native as well as English culture. To the people of the town, Woodward had become one of them, an honored captain with a field of corn to feed him. Woodward's enthronement to the approbation of the townspeople followed the taking of turf and twig as a final ceremony of possession.[39] With the seeming consent of the country's natural lords, Sanford left Woodward behind in "formal possession of the whole Country to hold as Tenant at Will" of the Lords Proprietors.[40] A high-status woman, the sister of the *cacique*'s heir no less, took charge of the doctor's welfare during his separation from the English.[41] Perhaps Sanford's report, telling the proprietors that "she should tend him and dress his victuals" discretely covered up the plain facts: the young woman was now Woodward's wife.[42] Theirs was a short honeymoon. Within a year, a detachment of Spanish soldiers picked up Woodward and hauled him south to San Agustín where he lived until 1668.

Before seeing and hearing of it for himself, most of what an educated Englishman like Henry Woodward might have read about Florida was old and fabulous, summed up as early as the 1620s in Samuel Purchas's pithy observation: "So fatal hath Florida been to Spain."[43] "The truth is," an English translator of Spanish books confessed, "there are not so many Relations extant of *Florida* (which is the name the *Spaniards* gave to all that part of *America*, that lies to the Northward of *Mexico* or *New-Spain*, before the *English* and other Nations settled Plantations there) as there is of Peru and New-Spain."[44] What little was known seemed ominous. The country south of Virginia seemed to be a vast waste, a land of war, the graveyard of *conquistadores*. Florida had yet to yield anything of value. Spain, wrote Peter Heylyn in 1652, in order "to keep some kind of possession, though not finding it in riches answerable to their greedy desires, fortified S. *Matthews* and S. *Augustines* on the East-side of the *Demy-Island*." Like "*Aesops Dog* in the Manger," the Spaniard, Heylyn quipped, "neither resolved to plant himself, nor willing that any others should."[45] That province, wrote another midcentury cosmographer, was "ennobled hitherto rather by the great pains which the Spaniards have taken, and the ill success which they have met with in their discovery and search of this Province, than by anything else they have discovered in it answerable to their desires."[46]

There were yet some things of value the Spanish found in Florida and had cultivated at great hazard: Native labor and Native souls. The missions were the source of what wealth could be found in Florida. While in San Agustín, then a military town of a few hundred people, the former ship's surgeon lived in the home of Francisco de Sotolongo, then the city's parish priest, who thought the Englishman ripe for conversion to the Catholic faith.[47] Prisoner that he was, Woodward must have made good use of his time in the *presidio*, no doubt exploiting the good father's missionary zeal for his own gain, by soaking up everything he could about the provinces of Florida, especially the Native missions. Woodward, in his discourses with the priest Sotolongo, must have learned of the chain of towns from Guale in the northeast to Timucua in the center and on to Apalachee in the far west. The *camino real* or royal road—such as it was—connected the towns and mission stations together, making it possible to succor the *presidio* with Native-produced food and labor. It was likely this intelligence, gleaned during his sojourn in the *presidio* that eventually trickled back in letters home to England from later colonists carefully plotting their insurgency against the Franciscans. While Woodward collected information about the capabilities of Florida's republic of Indians, his stay was interrupted by a forceful demonstration of Spanish weakness.

On 29 May 1668, Robert Searle, an English sea rover with a commission from the Governor of Jamaica, struck San Agustín, ransacking and "profaning" the images and the churches, embarrassing the governor—who allegedly abandoned the townsfolk for the relative safety of the *castillo*—and capturing "some Indians" who "were attending to the service of some of the residents" of the city.[48] Empowered by a "particular chapter of his instructions and patent from his Governor," Searle and his crew seized Natives and people of African descent, "not reserving any color," as Sotolongo later reported, "even though by their nature they are free."[49] The priest decried how the English enslaved Native peoples and urged the king to "provide a remedy to secure the Liberty of Your vassals."[50] Sotolongo's would be one of many such letters reaching the Spanish court in the years ahead.[51]

Among the prisoners Searle snatched up was one Henry Woodward. The attack on San Agustín eventually brought him all the way to the new settlement of Charles Town. Serving again as a privateer's surgeon, Woodward sailed about the Leeward Islands in the hopes of eventually making his way back to London and there to report to Carolina's eight Lords Proprietors. By then it was 17 August 1669, in the middle of hurricane season, and a storm drove his ship to wreck on the beach at Nevis.[52] There, cast ashore "whereby being disabled to perform his voyage," the expert Indian "linguister," the in-law of the *cacique* of Santa Elena with kin connections radiating across the region, and not least, the "Tenant at Will" of the Lords Proprietors of Carolina, despaired of ever making good any of his hard-earned experience.[53] He made arrangements to sail for England and was at the docks when a ship "happen[ed] to touch" at Nevis's quay.[54] It was part of a flotilla of three vessels late from England, fitted out at the Lords Proprietors' expense, and bound for Santa Elena. Learning of their destination, Henry Woodward "voluntarily deserted" his plan to sail for England "purposely to manifest his ready inclination to promote" at last the designs of the eight noblemen in whose name he possessed the country, the "True and Absolute Lords and Proprietors" of Carolina.[55]

What Woodward had learned over his long travels colored his ideas for promoting Carolina. Through his connections across the Native South, he saw just how vast the land was and how numerous its towns and peoples. From the Westos he learned what guns could do in that world of towns and what commodities were most valuable in that world. And from Robert Searle and the sack of San Agustín Woodward learned how determined Englishmen could expand their empire at Spanish and Indigenous expense, and do so rather easily, while profiting themselves at the same time.[56] Far from forwarding the designs of the Lords Proprietors, Woodward would eventually tear them up and pursue a different strategy, one that owed more to the Westos and Robert Searle than the philosophy of John Locke, putting the republic of Indians in jeopardy.

Searle's actions in San Agustín—enslaving free Native vassals and, indeed, without "reserving any color" from slavery—flew in the face of the plans that Woodward's masters, the Lords Proprietors of Carolina, were making at that very moment in their London headquarters at "little Exeter House in the Strand," the home of Anthony Ashley Cooper, then Lord Ashley.[57] Once a minor nobleman from the West Country, he was by 1669 the chancellor of the exchequer, and one of the foremost peers of the realm. Through his doors passed messengers and merchants and prospective colonists for Carolina. Within, Ashley's faithful scribe, physician, and amanuensis John Locke frequently sat toiling with a goose quill at his master's direction. Despite the attentions he lavished on "my Darling" Carolina, Lord Ashley was only one out of eight proprietors to whom King Charles II had granted the territory between Virginia and Spanish Florida as a reward for ushering him back on his throne.[58]

Like Ashley, each of the Lords Proprietors of Carolina had a circuitous route to the power they possessed.[59] First in rank and the king's (often-grudging) gratitude was Edward Hyde, earl of Clarendon and lord chancellor of England. Clarendon was the rock of Charles's exiled court, often the king's shrewdest advisor, and, to the young king's ears, the shrillest.[60] Next in eminence was George Monck, former general under the Commonwealth and Protectorate, now duke of Albemarle, whose late shift to the king's cause in 1660 made the Restoration possible.[61] William, Duke of Craven, had contributed tens of thousands of pounds to Charles I. For his pains, the Commonwealth proscribed him and sequestered his property in England.[62] Sir George Carteret and Sir John Colleton, the first who held Jersey for the Crown and the latter who tried to hold Barbados, received shares too.[63] Rounding out this congeries of royalist heroes was John Berkeley (later involved in the proprietorship of New Jersey) and his brother, Sir William Berkeley, governor of Virginia, who had earned his knighthood in service to the doomed cause of Charles I in the Bishops' Wars, and who during the Civil War held his colony in the royal allegiance longer than any other.[64]

The difficulties in melding together the talents of so many prickly nobles and gentry perhaps explain the baroque complexity of the colony's *Fundamental Constitutions*, with its conciliar form of government, and "court" for each of the eight proprietors. But the document's provisions on Natives were comparatively unambiguous and drew on its principal author's Hispanophilic tendencies. Lord Ashley, who once said of himself that he was "of all the English Nobility the most affectionate to the Spaniards," took the largest hand in framing the *Fundamental Constitutions*.[65] His Iberian-inspired attitudes suited the court of Charles II, where the queen was Portuguese and the government was negotiating a sweeping treaty with Spain. Ashley's Spanish predilections showed in his plans for a Carolinian aristocracy, his attitudes toward neighboring San Agustín, and his policies with respect to Native peoples.

For Indigenous peoples, styled in the document the "aboriginal inhabitants" of the land, there was no hint of their dispossession nor any sanction for their enslavement. The *Fundamental Constitutions of Carolina*, first drafted in 1669, held Natives' lands and their governments apart, protecting them from the English. The Lords Proprietors laid plans for their gradual integration into the polity. But the process was to be peaceful. As the Spanish in Florida had done, English metropolitans urged that the colonists proceed cautiously, observant of the rights of the country's natural lords. They deployed agents to gather intelligence and to negotiate with the local *caciques*, they claimed Natives as subjects, and even used language redolent of Spanish colonial theory in some of their earliest land transactions. The Lords Proprietors and their officials on the ground, nevertheless, waged a deliberate insurgent campaign to counter Spanish influence in the region. From Lord Ashley's vantage, the goal was to build a more perfect republic of Indians of their own.

The Lords Proprietors declared from the beginning that all Indians within a four-hundred-mile radius from Charles Town were "Subjects to the Monarchy of England."[66] The blanket coverage of legal protection included a prohibition on Native enslavement or, in the euphemism of the day, the colonial government was "not to Suffer any of them to be Sent away from Carolina" except in a just war between Indians and Englishmen.[67] The proprietors did not limit subjecthood to Natives who traded with their colony or to the towns that remained independent of any other European alliance. The order was provocative, especially coming from Shaftesbury, who professed such affection for the Spaniards. The proprietors' imaginary circle encompassed Guale, San Agustín, and a sizeable portion of Timucua province in Florida. But for the other regions encompassed within the order, the extension of legal subjecthood to Natives regardless of their religions squared with the English Crown's commitment and firm policy during the later seventeenth century. Soon, more of the proprietors' advance agents would arrive in the council-houses of the South, ready to urge the natural lords of the country to make a choice about their allegiances.

By the time the fleet of ships set out from Barbados carrying the first wave of colonists for southern Carolina, the stage was set for a clash between distinct political models. The colony's agents would soon abandon its owners' high ideals and the promises they had made to their Native neighbors in Escamaçu, trading their principles for the easier and more profitable strategies Henry Woodward had learned from Westos and the pirate Robert Searle. A curious mixture of weakness and strength moved them along that path—the weakness of Carolina's early prospects and the surprising strength of the republic of Indians in Florida.

A New Circle on the Map

Santa Catalina de Guale in the summer of 1670 was the northernmost part of Florida's *república de Indios*. Head of Guale province, braced against the worst of Westo and pirate raids, the settlement at Santa Catalina sometimes had the air of an armed camp. In a clearing on the island stood a town of hundreds of Guales and a resident Franciscan friar. The wattle-and-daub church, with its peaked thatched roof and extra covering of pine boards along the sides, was spacious and imposing, accommodating a large congregation.[68] Fields surrounded the townspeople's homes which, in turn, nestled around a well-swept plaza. On 15 May, *The Three Brothers*, a sloop out of Barbados, part of a small fleet on its way to fulfil the Lords Proprietor's plans and plant a new colony, "came to Anchor" near Santa Catalina, looking "to wood and water" after a long voyage by sea.[69] Before long that Saturday, the island's Guale inhabitants were crowding the beach and "very freely came aboard" ship to trade, offering the weary passengers and crew corn, peas, leeks, onions, deerskins, and clay pots in exchange "for beads and old Clothes."[70] The sloop's passengers soon learned of the mission system whence this bounty came. Native labor tending Native fields were the basis of Spanish strength. Several of the passengers stretched their legs on excursions to the town of Santa Catalina, stopping in at the Indians' homes, and returning with stories "of brave plantations with a 100 working Indians and that they want nothing in the world."[71] The very next day, a Guale man climbed aboard with a gift "of bread" to the sloop's master and "promised him Pork for truck."[72] To one of the ship's curious passengers, the man appeared to be "An Indian Semi Spaniard."[73] This encouraging reception from one of the region's Native towns did not last long.

On 18 May, the ship's master and some of the crew rowed to the town to trade but did not return by the "next tide" as promised. After passing the night with every hand aboard at "a strict watch," at ten o'clock the next morning the sound of a drum broke the silence.[74] From the trees near shore, came "Spaniards Armed with muskets and swords," and one man waving a white handkerchief, who urged the sloop's crew and passengers to "yield and submit to the sovereignty of Sant Domingo"—that is, the *Audiencia* of Santo Domingo which had jurisdiction over Florida—for their captain "was in chains."[75] With the master and a good portion of the crew imprisoned in the town, a band of the passengers took charge, including a young Barbadian named Maurice Mathews. To the file of Spanish soldiers on the beach, Mathews cried that if they returned the prisoners, the English "would depart in peace."[76] All he got in return was a hail of bullets and a "cloud of Arrows."[77] Mathews took the helm and, with a favorable breeze from shore, steered "out of their reach" while a sailor, John Hawks fired back with a musket, one of only three in the sloop's armory, and drove the Spaniards again into the trees.[78] At noon the next day, after a decent interval spent hoping the Spaniards would change their minds, the sloop's company "hoisted and away," sailing north before the wind.[79] They left behind at least a dozen prisoners, not least John Rivers, storekeeper for the Lords Proprietors, and Anthony Ashley Cooper, Lord Ashley's "Kinsman."[80] With that, the lost member of the Carolina fleet set out on the last leg of the journey to join the other colonists at Port Royal.

Their narrow escape from Santa Catalina taught the English lessons about their place in the region and about the strength of Florida's republic of Indians. To the Native peoples surrounding them, the English colonizing on the northern coast were part of a distinct town and nation, a new circle on the map of political and trading relationships and therefore comprehensible. Once they reached their destination, the colonists aboard *The Three Brothers* would be part of a town like Santa Catalina, and the many other towns up and down the coast and in the interior country. They would face the same problems of keeping the peace inside their walls and good relations with the people outside them. And they would be expected to follow the same rules of neighborly conduct.

The sloop's passengers—and indeed, all the colonists who went on to establish Charles Town—found themselves in a populous, complicated Indigenous world, one that Spaniards appeared to have mastered with the help of friendly *caciques*. In their joy at the fresh food and the chance to stretch their legs on shore, the people aboard *The Three Brothers* had not anticipated the combined power of Natives and Spaniards nor the sudden show of force. They could draw another lesson—and Maurice Mathews did—from the encounter. The Natives, even in the chief town of Guale, long a Spanish mission province, were friendly, civil, and eager to trade. Only the Spaniards with a few soldiers and the wily Franciscans kept the town on the island from welcoming the newcomers as allies. The realization that the English were entangled in a complex Indigenous world hit home again when two high-ranking Native men, Alush and Shadoo, met the sloop's passengers at Port Royal with word that the rest of the fleet was in Kiawah at the *mico*'s invitation and "further promised us on the morrow to carry us thither."[81] By then, word had spread and yet another canoe appeared alongside the sloop "but we sent them after a little stay away being all too numerous."[82] With Shadoo pointing out the course, *The Three Brothers* made way for Kiawah. A Bermudan sloop "going out A fishing" met them near the bar and "piloted us into Kiawah river" and the new town on its banks.[83]

What the passengers found on shambling down the gangplank was a small village on a neck of land that jutted out of the west bank of what was now called the Ashley River. Already, there would have been frenetic activity aimed at the future of the plantation, with colonists felling trees, making clearings, and running trials of foodstuffs and exotic commodities—ginger, sugar, cotton, indigo—that they hoped would grow in the Kiawah soil. But the real work of building community and establishing firm relations with their neighbors was just beginning.

Towns, whether Native or European, confronted a similar set of problems, internal and external. Internally, there was the problem of social cohesion and order. Externally, there were the problems brought on the path from other towns: war or peace, trade goods, new ideas, and the strangers who carried them. The two sets of concerns, internal and external, were not easy to separate into discrete problems but were often intertwined. Within towns, the challenge was to reach that elusive object, harmony. But differing opinions unsettled consensus. The younger generation was ever eager to challenge the older. The councilors of colonial Charles Town were no less restive under aging leadership than the eager young warriors in an Indigenous town like Edisto or in the mission of Santa Catalina de Guale farther south. Restraining young men, whether with law or religion, was a constant theme in the letters of colonists, the harangues of Native elders, and the prayers of Franciscan friars. Then there was subsistence. The agricultural calendar and agricultural concerns dominated town life, Native or European. Colonists who sought wealth had first to put corn in the ground. Even then, they were forced to rely on their neighbor towns for support. Native towns feared for their stocks and fields lest they be destroyed in an enemy raid. But if it could secure the necessities, a town could look confidently outward onto the various roads to wealth leading beyond their fields. Consensus about how to deal with these problems was difficult to find, as the values of the young clashed with those of their elders, and new ideas—often in the form of outsiders, including friars and traders and soldiers—circulated about what constituted, as one Guale leader put it, the "common voice" and the "common good."[84]

In the Native South, towns were not just physical locations but bodies of people who, together, strove for consensus and their collective well-being. A town could move from one site to another, could even combine with another town, and yet it would retain its separate and distinct character.[85] Town governance was generally in the hands of a council even if there were still some hereditary offices. Trade with Europeans over the course of the century made all kinds of once-rare, prestigious goods attainable to the meanest commoners who could sell a deerskin or a slave. In many towns, chiefs kept their titles but lost their coercive power.[86] Of all the information the English had before colonizing south of Virginia, what they knew of Native government, at least, was surprisingly close to the mark. The "Government of these Chiefs" had "somewhat of the *Parliamentary* way used with us in *Europe*." The genius of the Natives' "*Parliamentary* way" was that "in all matters of concernment those *Chiefs* advised with their *Council*, so if it were a business which concerned the *public*, their Priests and others of most note for gravity and wisdom, were admitted to the *Consultation*."[87]

To the Natives of Kiawah and roundabout, life in the English town—at least in the first few years—might have seemed familiar in other ways. Women were quite influential in Native towns, especially women who headed matrilines or extended kin groups, and they wielded considerable power.[88] Women often exerted political pressure over male-dominated councils on matters of peace and war and in disputes over justice. In Charles Town, women wielded influence of their own that spilled over into the records on more than one occasion. When two runaways, Richard Batten and William Loe, were sentenced to death, their "extraordinary penitency" was not enough to spare them. It was only after the "warmest solicitations" of "the Ladies and Gentlewomen of this Country" that the Grand Council suspended their sentence.[89] Such a demonstration was hardly uncommon in early Charles Town. Contentions and strife were rampant in the South's newest township.

Like any Southeastern town, the newest one at Kiawah strove to rise above contention and achieve consensus and, finally, peace. "I find," wrote Thomas Colleton of the townspeople at Kiawah, "they are in divisions amongst themselves through the pride and insolence of some and ignorance of others."[90] As was the practice in Native towns, the English town at Kiawah strove for tranquility through a variety of means. Some stressed the role of religion and ritual in soothing discord. The council asked for "an able minister by whose means corrupted youth might be very much reclaimed."[91] The unity of the town, they believed, depended upon godliness: "for where the Ark of God is, there is peace and tranquility."[92] Others proposed political solutions. The colonial surveyor Florence O'Sullivan, in a letter to Lord Ashley, prayed for an Anglican minister, yes, but also for "an able Counsellor to end controversies amongst us and put us in the right way of the management of your Colony."[93]

Complaints poured into the headquarters of Lord Ashley, now the leading Carolina proprietor, about the want of good, politic counsel to guide affairs toward harmony and prosperity. There were not more than five "men of the Council that have any reason" and even "those good honest men but knows nothing of planting."[94] The "very aged" governor, William Sayle, was out of his depth and "hath much lost himself in his Government."[95] Sick most of the time, some thought fevers had addled his brain.[96] Worse, he was pusillanimous before the Spanish threat, refusing to reply in kind to the alarm of August, when a Native and Spanish force threatened the town. In short, Sayle was "ancient and crazy."[97] What was lacking were "good men of reason fit for a Commonwealth."[98] Without sagacious counsel and the harmony it would bring, any Southeastern town was liable to fail.

Towns had, above all, to provide for security, subsistence, and population. For defense, the English at Kiawah had established the town palisaded and kept the people in constant readiness till they were "more like soldiers in a garrison than planters."[99] For subsistence or, having "provided for the Belly," they planted maize and accepted gifts from Sewee and other towns.[100] Most important of all was recruiting more people. This last requirement dogged Indigenous towns in the region, too, and led them to combine and merge in a process modern scholars call "coalescence."[101] Unlike the Natives, the English could call on vast reserves of the population to supply "more people which is," wrote one of them, "our greatest want."[102]

History showed plainly what became of European towns in America that failed in these objectives. Examples abounded from Sagadahoc to Jamestown to prove how "hunger starved infancy seldom produces strong maturity."[103] Yet, Charles Town's denizens did not have to rummage through the annals of colonization to find what the consequences of failure might be. They could find it in the recent histories of their Indigenous neighbors. What made the Westos so dreaded among local Native peoples was how they struck at the very essence of survival, coming "upon these Indians here in the time of their crop and destroy[ing] all by killing Carrying away their Corn and Children."[104]

To prevent the disasters that befell their neighbors, the new townsfolk lived in close proximity together, having only taken up "in A semicircle about the Towne ten acres" each for planting.[105] Following both the practice of Native people in time of conflict and the wisdom gained from hard experience, the townspeople lived relatively close together, refusing to "separate before there are more people come."[106] So far, the layout of the town was not entirely out of the ordinary when compared to its Indigenous neighbors at Edisto or Sewee. But they were soon expanding by fission into what, to Natives, must have seemed a separate town of its own. Soon, Joseph West reported that he had established Lord Ashley's plantation on "above 30 Acres of ground . . . and palisaded it so that we are able to defend ourselves against 1000 Indians."[107]

Viewed as its Native neighbors might have—as a town among other towns in the region—early Charles Town seemed rather ordinary. For a time, harmony prevailed at least between the English and the Indigenous towns in the surrounding area who welcomed them. Even the dispersed settlements that were gradually moving into the countryside might not have seemed alarming to the colony's Indigenous neighbors, who themselves preferred to spread out when it was safe.[108] The good feelings did not last long. Thinking of Charles Town in this way makes it possible to pinpoint when matters went astray and the English abandoned their neighborly tone. Within a year's time, the English circle on the Native map was growing—and it was forging new paths to power that put it on a collision course with Florida's republic of Indians.

An Englishman for Their Cacique

Peeking out of the palisades of the town at Kiawah, and looking beyond the immediate troubles at home, two aspiring leaders looked toward Florida and surveyed the strategic landscape. Together, they plotted an Indigenous insurgency against the Franciscan friars whose dreaded influence and subterfuge they saw behind every hamlet where a cross shaded the council-house.[109] Expansive and "ingenious," the colonist William Owen arrived aboard the *Carolina* with three servants in tow.[110] Joseph Dalton had gained the notice of the council with his penwork, and they soon made him their secretary and the colony's official register. Never mind the contention between political factions, what made Dalton's task truly difficult was that there was "very little paper in the whole Colony being most of it lost and damnified in the voyage." Nevertheless, Dalton acquitted himself well, making "the best shifts [he] could with a small quantity of [his] own."[111] The new secretary was resourceful and bold, rather impertinent in fact, a fault he graciously covered by begging Lord Ashley to "pardon a pen stupefied with zeal for the prosperity of Carolina."[112] Read side by side, the pair offered the Lords Proprietors differing but complementary advice. Dalton stressed the "several advantages" Charles Town had over San Agustín, Owen the strengths of the town's Spanish rivals.[113] They proposed a future where Charles Town would win preeminence among all the towns in the region and, as Lord Ashley later put it, give every Native town in the surrounding area an Englishman for their *cacique*.

Settled as Dalton famously put it "in the very chaps of the Spaniard" he and Owen agreed heartily about which sort of Spaniard most to fear.[114] The kind that came armed not with chain-shot but with a rosary. The "friars will never Cease to promote their Tragic ends by the Indians," Owen wrote to Lord Ashley, "whom they instruct only to admire the Spanish nation and pay them Adoration equal to a deity."[115] The steady indoctrination of the Franciscans taught their charges to fear no other European power, for the Spanish were "of an Angelical production" and "all other people are their slaves and vassals."[116] With their "advantage of the Indian tongue" the friars could "incline the Indian to do anything."[117] Demonstrations of English power had weakened their hold, casting doubt in the minds of "some of the most intelligible Indians on this side the Cape" about the "verity of the friars' Doctrine."[118] But there remained many Indians who were unconvinced. Even though, as Owen reported, "there are only four between us and St. Augustine" the friars presented a danger all the same.[119]

Learned Anglo-American opinion validated Owen's nightmares of scheming mendicants. The Catholic powers—notably Spain—had "little cause to glory" in their conversions of Indians in the Americas, the great Puritan divine Increase Mather snipped.[120] "For as for many of their *Converts*, inasmuch as they are become *Vassals*, not only to the Heresies, but to the Persons of those who have Proselyted them," Mather wrote, "they are as Christ said concerning the Proselytes of the Scribes and Pharisees, twofold *more the children of Hell*, than they were before; and many of them know little of Christianity besides the *Name*."[121] In what passed for a joke from his pen, Mather recounted the "celebrated Story of that Franciscan" who wrote his friend for a book that he had heard about, a work that would make the task of converting the Indians all the easier. The Franciscan "desired his Friend to send him a Book called the *Bible*, for he heard there was such a Book in *Europe*, which might be of some use to him."[122]

But for all his advantages, for all his vaunted ability to make Native people into vassals to false doctrine, the archetypal Franciscan had a weakness that Dalton might have picked up on the political winds blowing among Native peoples. The "Indians that are under him dare not trust [him] for his long continued tyranny among them has taught them how to desire liberty," Dalton observed, "and well he knows that they will be the chief Instruments to cut him off if ever an enemy comes against him."[123] Far from masters of the Indians, the friars were "so surrounded with false friends" that they could not hope to retain their influence much longer.[124] As it happened, the friars *were* surrounded by false friends in Florida, including at times the colony's governor. By the 1680s, the feud ran hot, with Governor Juan Marquez Cabrera accusing the Franciscans of tyrannizing over the inhabitants of the missions. The governor presented himself as the defender of the Natives against the oppressions of the friars that included whippings, refusing to pay for Native work, and carrying heavy burdens—charges the Franciscans rebutted.[125] Perhaps word of discontent with alleged Franciscan mistreatment was spreading up the paths to Carolina.

To their opponents, especially the very same Franciscan friars, San Jorge's agents brought nothing to Native towns but an invitation to lawlessness. From San Agustín, it looked as if the English intruders endangered not just the liberty of Native towns but the very souls of the people who resided within them, souls that the Spanish Crown spent millions to save from perdition—not to mention all the hands lost who could have labored to feed the *presidio*. Even as Owen and Dalton laid plans to foment an Indigenous rebellion against Franciscan tyranny, officials in the Spanish *presidio* were learning as much as they could about their English enemies. The Spanish watched for hopeful signs that Charles Town, not San Agustín, would succumb to a Native overthrow. An "infidel Indian" from Santa Elena named Diacan claimed he had

visited San Jorge and reported to the royal officials news of an unhealthy settlement of "about thirty small houses" of roughly a hundred men and a handful of women.[126] Already, there were hopeful signs of strain in the little town's
relations with its Native neighbors who "had been killing their cattle, cows,
and pigs."[127] Perhaps, instead of toppling the friars, the Carolinians would be
destroyed by the very Indians they hoped to make their subjects.

Rather than faltering, the English seized the initiative. From the reports
of Owen and Dalton arose a strategy for infiltrating and co-opting Indigenous authority in the region, establishing an Anglo-Native world with
Charles Town at its center. "I return my thanks for the Letter you sent me,"
wrote Lord Ashley in reply to William Owen, and "I think we may well take
our measures from thence."[128] Lord Ashley encouraged English colonists to
insinuate themselves into Indian communities in order to glean intelligence
on their politics and gain influence, knitting together a network of allied
towns.[129] The very choice of "Cassique" as the name for the second order
of nobility outlined in the *Fundamental Constitutions* advertised a strategy
for co-option of Indigenous power structures.[130] In theory, the new English
"Cassiques" were expected to blend into the ranks of the existing Indian
caciques of Carolina, and eventually succeed to their places. Two such aspiring English *caciques*—Maurice Mathews and Stephen Bull—received Lord
Ashley's special favor. His letters to both men reveal how he pictured Carolina's future ruling class and its relation to the Indigenous political structures
they were seeking to understand in greater detail. Quite unlike Captain
John Smith, who dodged Wahunsenacawh's offer to become a subordinate Powhatan *weroance* in Tsenacomacoh, English infiltrators in Kiawah
and the regions beyond it sought, and claimed to have accepted, offers of
indigenous titles.[131]

In a 1671 letter to Shaftesbury, Maurice Mathews compiled an astute
report on the political organization of the Indians around Charles Town. By
now, Mathews was earning a reputation as a shrewd operator. One contemporary later portrayed him as a combination of "Machiavelli Hobbes and
Lucifer in a Huge lump of Viperish mortality [with] a soul as big as a mos-
quito."[132] The local Indians, he wrote, "have 4 or 5 Cassekaes [caciques] more
or Less; Truly to define the power of those Cassikaes; I must say thus; it is no
more, (scarce as much,) as we own to the Topakin in England."[133] Matthews
may have meant that the *caciques* he met were no greater than "toparchs" or,
small-time potentates lording over the countryside back home in England.[134]
Later, promotional pamphlets thus highlighted the alleged weakness of

Native governments. "They are divided into many Divisions or Nations, Gov-ern'd by *Reguli*, or Petty Princes, which our *English* call *Cacicoes* [*caciques*]," wrote Thomas Amy a decade after Matthews.[135] "I find no tributaries among them," Mathews wrote.[136] The Indigenous world he described was instead largely egalitarian and peaceful. Among the Indians "intermarriages and poverty causes them to visit one Another; never quarrelling who is the better man," Mathews explained.[137] In 1672, Lord Ashley congratulated Mathews on his election as the "Cassica" of a group of local Indians.[138] He promised to make Mathews "a more considerable Cassique than any of the Indians."[139]

Captain Stephen Bull, an early member of Charles Town's Grand Council, was another colonist who heralded a pattern for future relations with Indig-enous peoples. In August of 1673, when other colonists complained about Bull's "acquaintance among and interest with the Indians," Lord Ashley, recently created first earl of Shaftesbury, privately encouraged his work as "very wisely done."[140] Bull's apparent election as a local *cacique*, he wrote, was perfectly in keeping with "our design which is to get and continue the friend-ship and assistance of the Indians and make them useful to us without force or Injury."[141] He closed his letter to Bull, declaring that he "could be very glad that all the Tribes of the Indians round about us had each of them an English-man for their Cassique."[142]

To the Native towns choosing them, these foreign "Cassiques" might have been the glue in a tightening alliance with Charles Town. Perhaps the Indige-nous peoples who elected an Englishman for their *cacique* thought they were taking part in the coalescence of a new nation, a nation that included the English, and in which the fear of common enemies—Westos and Spanish Indians—formed a common interest. Or these English "Cassiques" were not local headmen at all but rather beloved men chosen by Natives to represent their town's interests to the English, rather like the celebrated *fanni minkos* or "Squirrel Kings" of the Chickasaws and other nations.[143] Despite adoption into the community, despite (in some cases) marrying into a matrilineage, these new men never truly renounced their old allegiances nor the ambitions of their former lives. As events showed, these men held few scruples about running guns and starting wars in Indian country to get what they wanted. Many of the traders, starting with the famed Dr. Henry Woodward himself, were little better than pirates of the land. Whatever the case, the "neighbor Indians" and the English town at Kiawah were more and more involved in one another's lives.

The English town's Native neighbors regularly traded and worked alongside the newcomers, much as was the case in Spanish San Agustín. Prospective Carolina colonists, wrote one pamphleteer in the 1680s, could count
on friendly, neighboring Natives like the Sewees to offer "their services to
fish, and hunt their game for a Trifle; to fall Timber, to plant Corn, and to
gather in their Crop: as also to pilot, and convey them from one Settlement
to another."[144] The Indians performed all these good turns supposedly out of
love for the English, "as if their Souls lived only in the bosom of the *English*
by natural instinct."[145] The regular work Natives did in Charles Town was not
much different from the sorts of tasks they performed in Florida. In addition to the *repartimiento*, paddling canoes, and shouldering Spanish cargoes,
the people in Santa María de Guale, for example, brought meat, shellfish,
fish, firewood, cassina, and "twenty-six pounds" of ground maize per day to
the garrison of thirteen soldiers who were posted there to defend the town
against the Westos, Yamasees, and, of course, the Carolinians.[146] Both colonies relied on the services of Indigenous peoples.

Frequent contacts led to insults, trespasses, and misunderstandings that
required open paths to resolve disputes peacefully when their foreign *caciques* could not. As in colonies throughout the Southeast, Natives often took
their grievances to Charles Town, as in February 1674 when "certain neighboring Indians" complained of how three Englishmen stole their goods.[147]
The Grand Council ordered the offenders to make compensation in kind "for
their trespass."[148] By 1678, Indigenous informants from Santa Elena who regularly traded in "San Jorge" were reporting how the English now had a bustling
port where ships came and went, laden with "wine, sugar, and other goods,
and many people."[149] Outside the town, the English were sowing much wheat
and corn and other fruits," no doubt placing further strain on their Indigenous neighbors.[150] As the volume of Indigenous petitions increased, in 1680
the Lords Proprietors even established a special commission to inquire into
them and see that "due care be taken for the equal Administration of Justice
to them, and to preserve them from being wronged or oppressed by a due
punishment of those who shall presume do to do."[151] To keep a better account-
ing of the process, the commissioners were to write down all "the Petitions
and requests or the Substance of them to you made by Indians, whether it
be Grievances, Informations, or otherwise."[152] But by then, the severe strains
were beginning to tell and the "Grievances" were mounting. Charles Town
had long since begun to shake off the strictures of conduct that applied to

Native towns and was taking the region on an altogether different path than its neighbors had expected.

The Lands That God Gave to Them

Just as there were signs of steady integration between some Native towns and Charles Town, there were also fissures and a growing disagreement over the nature of their political relationship—the same as in Florida. Commerce and influence held this emerging Anglo-Native polity together, with traders and cultural brokers like Henry Woodward circulating through Native towns. Making matters worse, the slave trade exploded after the autumn of 1674 when Woodward himself, to the accompaniment of shotgun salutes, strode into the Westo capital, Hickauhaugau.[153] On the roof of the council-house, little children lifted the thatch and peeked into the proceedings as the Westo leaders gave long speeches professing their friendship for the English, sealing an alliance—and the fate of other little children far from there—with their words.[154] Carolinian agents like Woodward behaved much as did the influential Indigenous headmen of the time who pulled Native towns together in what Robin Beck has called "chieftaincies," or "loosely organized, regional polities," with the key difference that Carolina's agents expected rigid obedience to them.[155] A newcomer in Charles Town in the early 1680s, for example, told his father back in England "there are above 40 several Kingdoms" of Natives all well known to the colony's governor "who upon any occasion summons their Kings in."[156] This casual assertion of mastery must have galled the Native peoples like the Sewees who once nurtured the English in their colony's infancy.

What seemed like a chieftaincy, or loose grouping of towns, on first joining it, often came with demands Natives in such an arrangement did not expect to hear—a source of confusion that would eventually lead to a regional Native American uprising. Just as important, the English town in Kiawah was experiencing its own growing pains and its internal structure and ethos were changing in ways that surely made it seem less familiar to local Natives. Carolinians became more and more aggressive in their demands, seeking tribute from their neighbors, and taking their lands. In Florida, too, the 1680s witnessed a similar reckoning, in that case over what membership in the republic of Indians really meant. There, too, aggressive neighbors made designs on the lands and the prerogatives of Native leaders in towns near the *presidio*.

In both places, Native leaders stoutly defended "the lands that God gave to them" from dangerous encroachments.[157]

Even before its plunge into the slave trade, Charles Town, the English village in Kiawah territory, began to transgress the usual standards for neighborly behavior in Native eyes. While Native towns had supplied the English with food in the earliest days of settlement, the English turned hungry Natives away when drought stalked the land for much of 1671.[158] In response, "the Kussoe and other Southward Indians" repeatedly seized a "great quantity of corn . . . out of the plantations" in the dead of night, prompting the Grand Council to declare "an open War" on the Kussoes "and their co-adjutors."[159] Adding further injury, Stephen Bull arrested "two Kussoe Indians now in Towne" to prevent their escape lest they warn their compatriots.[160] That the pair were there at all suggests the Kussoes and the English enjoyed friendly relations, and that their nighttime raids were merely the response of aggrieved allies in need who were seeking to redistribute the food denied them. After the punitive war against the Kussoes, the Grand Council ordered them "to pay a deer skin monthly" as tribute "or else to lose our amity."[161]

The colonists at first imagined that the Indians sought out the English in order "to be protected from the Westos" and the Spaniards.[162] As time wore on, the would-be protectors viewed their erstwhile allies as subjects or worse. When word reached Charles Town in 1674 of a plot by the Stonos and their *cacique* "to confederate certain other Indians to murder some of the English nation," the colony declared it an act of "Rebellion against this Settlement."[163] To punish these rebel subjects, the Grand Council called up a detachment of nine men under Maurice Mathews' command to take the *cacique* alive and "him cause to be brought to Charlestown to answer to these things."[164] Should the *cacique* resist, Mathews' company should take stern measures "whether by killing and destroying the said Indian and his confederates or otherwise."[165] The English could sell obstreperous captives as slaves.

Tribute became another bone of contention between Natives and colonizers in Carolina and Florida as the slave trade threatened political relationships. From the very beginning of the Carolina enterprise, the Lords Proprietors and colonizers on the ground hoped to exploit Indigenous tributary networks for themselves. Lord Ashley asked his agents in the field "to send me word whether the Indian Cassiques your Neighbors be absolute supreme Lords, in their own Territories, or else be Tributary Princes and pay subjection and homage to any greater King who is their Emperor."[166] In 1676, the Lords Proprietors demanded from the governor of Albemarle County, in what would become North Carolina, "a true account of what tribute or payment are rendered by any of our people or officers from any of the Indians and upon what account such tribute or payment is demanded or prove due."[167] Lasting tributary relationships developed in the Albemarle region, notably with the Chowans after their defeat in what Lars Adams calls the "Chowan River War" of 1675–1677, part of the larger upheaval triggered by Bacon's Rebellion.[168] For the most part, Natives surrounding Charles Town had little interest in entering a tributary relationship, whatever the desires of Shaftesbury or colonizers on the ground. Maurice Mathews' disappointing reply was typical of what the English found near Charles Town. The Natives, he said, "are generally poor and Spanish."[169] Carolina was hardly alone in its increasingly high-handed treatment of Native leaders.

While the English searched for tributaries to exploit, the Spanish in Florida were actively disrupting Indigenous tributary relationships and the chiefly prerogatives that came with them, all under the cover of enhancing the colony's security. In 1680, the Crown barred *caciques* from "imposing tributes"—which had occurred with the "tolerance of the governors"—regarding the practice an affront to the "Royal Dominion."[170] One Native leader who suffered from such decisions was Merenciana, a Mocama *mica*, who had demanded tribute from still-friendly Yamasee migrants to the islands of Santa Maria and San Pedro, islands she claimed to be under her jurisdiction.[171] Merenciana's tributary arrangement with the Yamasees—"Poor strangers," as the governor termed them in a letter he sent her, who "were cast out of their lands by the enemy"—was similar to other compacts between a host town and newcomers seeking refuge, including one documented from Apalachee province.[172]

The agreement Merenciana made with the Yamasees stipulated that in exchange for room to plant a town, the refugees would hand over some part of the fruits of the land as tribute.[173] Instead of approving the deal as Spanish authorities did in the case of the influential and numerous Apalachees, the governor made arguments from Spanish law, specifically concerning hunting and gathering on purported wastelands, to diminish Merenciana's rights as a high-ranking chief within the republic.[174] Even though the Yamasees had settled on Merenciana's lands, the governor insisted that they were strictly the king's vassals and not hers. The inequality in treatment between different peoples within the same republic of Indians would not go unnoticed. Nor would the implication that attacks on Indigenous leaders' political jurisdictions were connected to attacks on their rights to land.

Throughout the era, threats to Native land increased across the region as encroachments and seizures by Englishmen and Spaniards became commonplace, even as metropolitan officials decried the practice. Defeated and hard-pressed by English expansion, the "Cassiques natural born Heirs and sole owners and Proprietors" of the Kussoes along with their "subjects and Vassals" deeded a vast tract of their coastal land to Carolina.[175] In Florida, well-connected officials, including the then royal accountant, and their families benefited from taking "pieces of land" from Natives living near San Agustín.[176] In 1681, the venerable Indigenous town of Nombre de Dios "a quarter of a league" from the *presidio*, won a royal decree restoring "the lands that God gave to them and they have inherited from their forefathers" and that unscrupulous Spanish officials had taken from them.[177] Without the protection of the government, the *caciques* would be "forced to desert their Town to go search in strange lands," a fate they dared not contemplate.[178] The problem was arguably worse in Carolina where English colonizers were "scattered about the country," claiming parcels of land for themselves.[179] Outlying farmsteads were not unheard-of in the Native South but the spread of English plantations outside Charles Town far exceeded the norm. Even as colonists established new towns, such as "James Town" home of a cohort from New York, they soon spilled outside their bounds.[180] Following up on Indigenous petitions, the Lords Proprietors scolded the colony's council "that the Indians have made Complaints that some of our People encroach upon them we hope you Adjusted that Business to their Satisfaction."[181] The Lords Proprietors, fearful that their colony was losing valuable allies who protected the borders and hunted down runaways, forbade "any person to take up land within two miles of the same Side of the River of an Indian Settlement."[182]

Human beings were not the only ones "Encroaching upon" the Natives and forcing them "to Remove from amongst us," as the proprietors put it.[183] Colonists' hogs roamed unfenced and unchecked on the lands surrounding Charles Town, rooting out crops from the fields, and devouring the browse that attracted deer. Herds of hogs plagued the country, eating "Acorns Hickory Nuts Berries and roots" and so multiplying "at very easy rates."[184] Left free for most of the time, English owners called them back home again "once in two or three days" by "blowing a horn and throwing A handful of Corn" in the dooryard.[185] As the colonists founded new towns and outlying plantations, the hog infestation grew worse. No wonder, then, "that divers Indians" were caught "lurking about James Town" and had "destroyed several hogs there."[186] If the English would not control their animals, their Native neighbors would have to do it for them. Regardless, squatters and stray hogs were the least of their worries.

The terror of the slave trade drove many Native towns off their God-given lands. Spanish vassals, the Guales and Mocamas on the coasts of modern-day Georgia and northern Florida, victims of raids since at least 1659, were at last forced to move close to the *presidio*, although not without insisting on making the decision themselves after consultation, as was their right as members of the republic of Indians. When daily "infested by the English enemy," Indigenous leaders still found time to deliberate with Spaniards on what course was best for "this Republic and Provinces."[187] In 1684, Governor Juan Marquez Cabrera held a *junta* in San Agustín to settle the question of whether and where the people of Guale should move. The records reveal a dispute with Guale leaders, the Franciscan friars, and royal officials all urging plans in their competing interests.[188] But they also demonstrate how Native leaders in Florida obliged Spaniards to win their consent before making important decisions—even in moments of extreme crisis. Undaunted before the raids of the "enemy corsairs," the Franciscans stood their ground and the governor accused them of hindering the move southward purportedly in hopes of founding more missions in the north.[189] Spanish officials, meanwhile, wanted the Guales to be reduced and congregated into a few towns close to the *presidio* in the "smallest district that can be."[190]

Yet, no move was possible without the consent of Guale's leaders, many of whom had committed themselves to remaining on the northerly isles of Sapala and Guadalquini. They held out from consenting to the move until their views, at least, were heard. In the end Guale's Indigenous leaders were willing to relocate to the islands of Santa Maria and San Juan but only on their own terms. The islands offered room enough to plant crops to support their population as well as plenty of fish, seafood, and an "abundance of cacina," the caffeinated leaves of the yaupon holly.[191] Moving closer to the *presidio* made it easier for infantry to reinforce the Guale and Mocama towns in case of attack but it also meant that Spanish officials could keep a closer watch on Indigenous leaders. The places where they lived now, spread out and surrounded by "dangerous sandbars," were difficult to reach by boat.[192] But the *caciques* wanted more than speedy infantry reinforcements—"being neighbors to this Presidio they expect to be Relieved in their necessities," likely including supplies if needed.[193] Even as they made their preparations for the move, another horde of pirates attacked Guale and Mocama towns shortly after the council met, turning an orderly retreat into a rout.[194]

In Carolina and Florida, the gulf between Natives and colonizers was widening over what their political relationship should be. After a century of life in the republic of Indians, Native leaders in Florida, like the *caciques* of Nombre de Dios and *Cacica* Merenciana, had grown used to having their customary laws and privileges respected. No longer, so it seemed. Now, from the Crown to the governor, Spaniards were imposing their laws oftener and with a heavier hand. In Carolina, some neighboring Natives may well have looked to the English at first as kinfolk and potential constituents in a larger nation of towns confederated for defense against the Westos and other common enemies. Instead, within a few years, many of them wound up enslaved by their erstwhile allies. If an equality of towns joined together in league was Natives' original objective, Charles Town began to assume airs of preeminence over the peoples it did not force into bondage. The heavy-handedness of officials—Spanish and English—made it harder for chiefs to keep their people from leaving the republic of Indians. The trade in Indigenous slaves would make it practically impossible. The subordinate, Indigenous commonwealths of the South were on the brink of destruction. But, as often happens, the most elegant statements of the ideal sounded at what appeared to be its demise.

Miserable Vassals and True Subjects

For many Native Southerners the ideal of equal commonwealths under the same king was still worth fighting for. In the 1680s and '90s, Indigenous leaders from Florida to Virginia penned forceful petitions in defense of their rights. Even in the midst of chaos and war, Natives saw to it that the forms of law were followed and their demands were heard. In petitions and in speeches during council sessions, they presented sophisticated histories of colonialism from Indigenous perspectives, expounded the meaning of the law as they saw it, and spelled out the ideal relationship between monarchs and their Indigenous subjects, vassals, and tributaries.

Theirs was a losing battle only in hindsight. The disintegration of the Florida missions was not foreordained. The retreat southward from Guale and Mocama lasted a generation. Although their destruction in the early eighteenth century was dramatic, Apalachee and Timucua had withstood the pressure on them for a long time before the end came. Nor did the Indigenous tributaries of Virginia—and, later, the Carolinas—quietly fade into

decline and irrelevance. All along the way, Native leaders argued and negotiated and insisted on living according to terms of their choosing. The words
of two petitions from 1688–1689, one from the Apalachees and one from the
Chickahominies, offer a glimpse into how Native leaders conceived of their
duties and privileges as vassals and subjects and what membership in the
republic of Indians meant to them.

The churn of inter-Native politics and worries about outsiders consumed most of the ink in both of their letters. From Florida, the Apalachee
leaders told the king of their hopes for growing trade with their neighbors,
the Apalachicolas, to the north. They shared their desire for protection from
the English and their Indigenous allies. And the Apalachees explained how
they had agreed to help build a blockhouse for defense and touted the efforts
to convert their "pagan" neighbors. In Virginia, the Treaty of Middle Plantation that rebuilt the tributary regime after Bacon's Rebellion nearly caused as
much trouble as it resolved.[195] The Chickahominies complained of Pamunkey highhandedness, Iroquois attacks, and sought a place of their own called
Rickahock to build a new town where they would be free from both. Although
the Haudenosaunee warriors who terrorized Virginia's Algonquian tributaries fought in the tradition of "mourning wars," taking captives and "requick-
ening" them as living replacements for lost kin, they still brought the same
destabilizing consequences as the militaristic slaving societies did in the deep
South.[196] Neither the Apalachees' petition nor the Chickahominies' got much
of what it asked.[197] But they left behind for us an important record of Indigenous political thought at a crucial time. These "miserable vassals" and "true
subjects," as they called themselves, dreamed of a future where law and justice
prevailed, a world far different from the swirling reality all around them.

The Apalachees' petition took form on 21 January 1688 in San Luís de Talimali (near modern-day Tallahassee), home to a garrison of Spanish soldiers.
Six Apalachee leaders put their names to a letter in their own language and a
Spanish translation. The letter's signers were all men of influence and power.
About half of them styled themselves "holahtas," a word for chief or headman
that "appears to be a loan from Apalachee into Timucua."[198] Now, in their supplication, the chiefs prostrated themselves figuratively before the distant and
diminutive King Carlos II of Spain, "smelling the soles of your noble feet."[199]
Sitting under the roof of the council-house, where the low doorway obliged
all visitors on entering to lower their heads before them, the Apalachee chiefs
recounted their people's beginning, their condition in this world, and their
resignation to the will of their creator. "God," the Apalachee *holahtas* declared,

"with his power, having raised us from nothing and misery, for it being his will, we live even though with toils and misfortunes."[200] This was more than a veiled complaint. The king, "Pin holahta chuba pin Rey"—"our great chief, our King"—should see their patient suffering and relieve it.[201] As pious Catholics and loyal vassals, the petitioners accepted their lot. "It is not important that even though we live so, with our little understanding, all the days without ceasing," they continued, "So, we say: 'Our maker desires it so."[202]

While the Apalachee leaders related a history of their faithful and long-suffering service alongside the Spaniards, the Chickahominies stressed their history of independence from Englishmen and other Native nations. The story they told of the past was more comforting than their present circumstances. Weaker than the *caciques* of Apalachee, the group of exiled Chickahominies huddled for shelter amongst the Pamunkeys, a people "maliciously disgusted" with them. The exiles feared Seneca raiders from the north and hoped to find strength in numbers. Three *manguys* (councilors), Herquapinck, Paucough, and Hearseeqs, drafted their petition for "Virginia's viceroy," the governor, Francis Howard, Baron Howard of Effingham.[203] The Chickahominies, the *manguys* declared, "in times past were a people numerous and of great Strength and Authority amongst themselves in this Country, and lived under the freedom of their own wills Lawes and order and had Large limits bounds and privileges in this Land."[204] In a word, the Chickahominies asserted their sovereignty. The Chickahominies had lost nearly everything "by the Disposition of Almighty Power and the prevalent forces of the High and mighty Kings of England."[205] Once sovereign, self-governing, and free on spacious territories of their own, by 1689, the Chickahominies had, they said, "lost those their large possessions and are Reduced to an Exiguous Body of people."[206]

But as "miserable vassals" of the Spanish king or "Subjects and Tributaries" of the English, the Apalachees and the Chickahominies counted upon liberties and privileges that they expected their European monarchs to honor. Many of these expectations were in writing and others were unwritten customs. The Apalachee petition captures the oral culture and the language of diplomacy that many Native peoples shared throughout the Southeast. The king's power and his words nourished the body politic. "And that just as the plants eat, live, and nourish themselves form the dew that comes to them with the night," the Apalachee leaders declared, "so we and all these your miserable vassals keep themselves and live with your noble and foremost word."[207]

While the Apalachees stressed the orality of law, law as word, the Chickahominies emphasized written documents, as their fellow tributaries often did

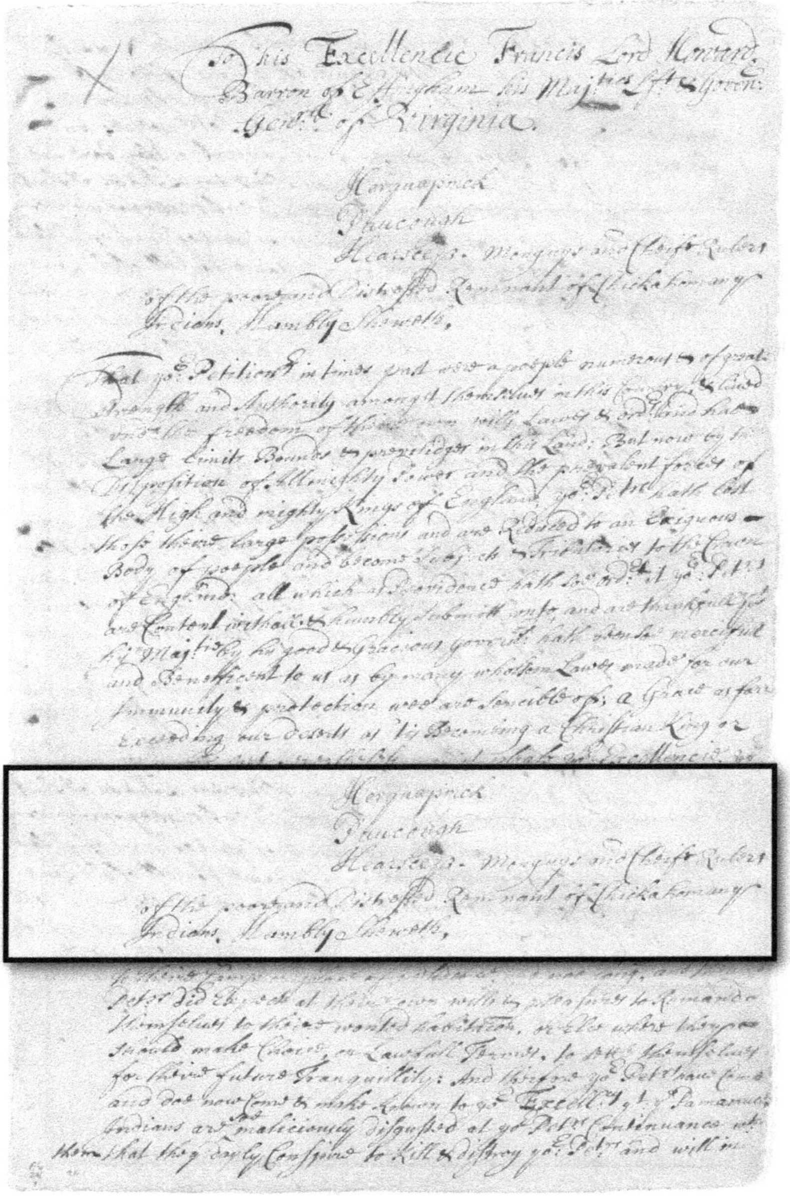

Figure 7. Petition of the Chiefs of the Chickahominy Indians (names appearing in the inset) in 1689, Library of Virginia, Colonial Papers, box 142, folder 6.

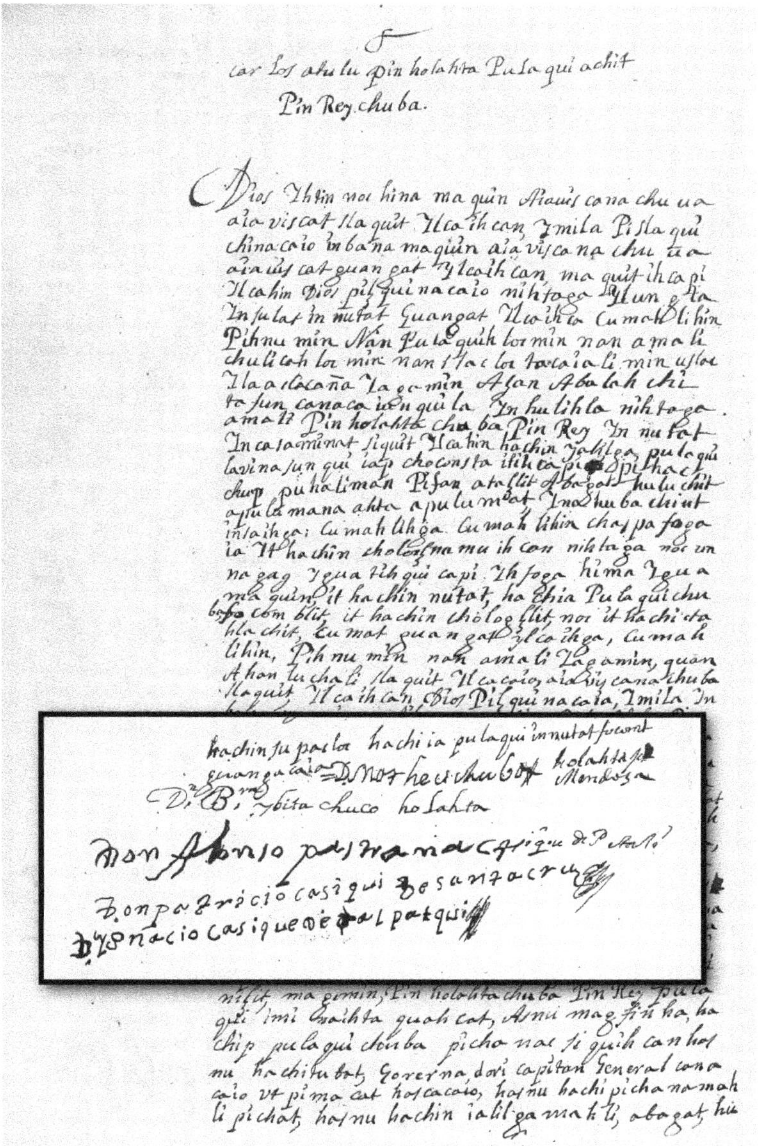

Figure 8. A nineteenth-century copy of the Apalachee-language version of the 1688 letter to Carlos II (the names of the signers appear in the inset). Buckingham Smith, "Documents in the Spanish and two of the early tongues of Florida (Apalachian and Timuquan)" [in Spanish], Codex Ind 38. Original in the John Carter Brown Library.

in Virginia.[208] Submitting to the decree of heaven that they should be subjects of the English Crown, the *manguys* were "thankful for his Majesty" who "by his good and Gracious Government hath been so merciful and Beneficent to us as by many wholesome Lawes made for our Immunity and protection we are Sensible of."[209] Attributing to the English monarch the authorship of all the "many wholesome Laws" for the "Immunity and protection" of the tributaries represented more than a posture of humility for Chickahominy great men. If the "Crown of England" was the fountainhead of the laws for the Chickahominies' protection, that fact lent those laws all the greater weight and the air of inviolability. This edifice of law was, the *manguys* believed, "a Grace as far Exceeding our deserts as 'tis Becoming a Christian King or Government."[210] But this conceit, designed to elicit favor from the aristocratic Virginia governor, excluded the contributions of Natives in fashioning and maintaining those "wholesome Lawes." The Chickahominies, as had all tributary Natives, of course, played a role in making and keeping the body of law they now claimed.

Both sets of petitioning leaders looked to a European monarch as the head of the larger body politic and as the source of justice against unruly colonists and protection from their Native enemies. While the soul "is from our creator," the king was, in Apalachee thought, their head, providing for "our body and its government," and responsible for "correcting it, training it, and chastising it."[211] The great men of the Chickahominies, for their part, addressed themselves to the governor in Virginia who stood in as the "king's living image," while always dutifully professing that the "High and mighty" king of England was the real source of their liberty.[212] Although in both cases, appointed royal governors acted in their kings' names in the colonies of Florida and Virginia, the Native leaders appealed above them and emphasized that their liberties, privileges, and immunities came from the highest possible earthly sources. They did so with good reason.

After generations of colonialism, the Native vassals and subjects shared vocabularies, ideas, and laws in common with the colonizers whose governors stood in for the new paramount chiefs, the kings of Spain and of England. Yet, the shared inheritance was dissolving. In this moment of flux, the two petitions capture an interesting distinction between English-Indigenous subjecthood and Spanish-Indigenous vassalage. For the Chickahominies, being a subject meant appealing to written charters of liberties, guaranteed by the monarch. For the Apalachees, being a vassal of Spain's king was a more personal relationship, meaning their rights did not rest merely on legal abstractions but on binding ties that had to be continuously renewed. The Apalachees' and Chickahominies' worries about the outside world, the world beyond the tributary regime or the *república de Indios*, reflected the growing influence of new powers in the region, powers who professed one set of principles and acted on another.

The Principles of the Bishop of Chiapas

In the late seventeenth century, metropolitan Englishmen cherished the views of the reforming Dominican, Bartolomé de Las Casas, as if his words were their own. Las Casas, in fact, was practically an honorary Englishman, for the "principles of the Bishop of Chiapa[s]" were so congenial "to the Genius and Constitution of this Island," as one of his London translators, Joseph Sennet, put it.[213] "To hear him in his dispute against Doctor Sepulveda, decry all methods of Violence for the propagation of Truth, as more suitable to the Maxims of Mahometism than the Principles of Christianity: To hear him assert the Natural Right of all Mankind to Liberty and Property, and inveigh against all Usurpation and Tyranny in the smartest Terms, is enough to move any one's Wonder."[214] The alliance between Charles Town and the Westos, then the Savannahs and, later, the independent Yamasees, heightened the Indigenous slave trade to a fever pitch, and belied English colonizers' own professed principles. The Spanish and their Native vassals sought to hold them to account.

After years of pressure from Indigenous leaders and an incessant back-and-forth between the governors of San Jorge and San Agustín, the attacks on the Crown's Catholic Indian vassals finally led to a remonstrance from Spanish officials. Souls that Spanish Franciscans with royal patronage had won at great expense and trouble were now toiling to their deaths in the English West Indies. In 1693, the imperial *Junta de Guerra* urged the king to lodge a complaint "about these matters with the King of England, through the Minister of Your Majesty that attends in London."[215] The council placed before the "Royal Notice" word that the English had made prisoners of "different Indians Christian and Infidel, from the Provinces of Guale, and Apalachicola, of the obedience of Your Majesty and sold them for slaves in the Windward Islands."[216] They deplored how the English of "San Jorge" had forced Catholic Indian vassals to "leave the Evangelical Law, and return to their errors, superstitions, and ancient Idolatries."[217] In 1694, amid heightened tensions, the

Quaker John Archdale received his commission as governor of Carolina.[218] On his arrival in 1695, the diplomatic wrangling intensified.

The troubles arose in Apalachicola, once nominally a "province" in the northwest of Spanish Florida, and from Carolina's faithful partners in the slave trade, the Yamasees. Florida's governor, Don Alonso Laureano de Torres y Ayala argued that "the Towns of Apalachicola which belong to this Government And have always Live[d] under our obeisance And . . . have Revolted from it and Live In their wickedness and Rebellion."[219] The Apalachicolas had resettled near Ochese Creek, a tributary of the Ocmulgee River, to be nearer to Charles Town after punitive Spanish attacks in the 1680s under Antonio Matheos.[220] Even so, they were, Florida's governor declared to Archdale, "neither vassals nor subjects of your Government."[221] Had he stopped there, the Apalachicolas themselves would have agreed. Instead, he continued by announcing that these Natives were vassals "of mine and as they Doe ill they must be Chastised."[222] Carolina's governor, meanwhile, claimed that the "Ogumulgees, who I suppose are the same you call Apalachicoloes" were his vassals and that he had "sent an express to them to command them that they do not Commit any acts of hostility on any of your Indians, and do expect that you give the like also to your Vassals."[223] Less than a decade before, one of Archdale's predecessors, James Colleton had done the opposite with the Yamasees and disclaimed any pretensions to rule them.[224] Either way, Indigenous independence belied either governor's assertions. Despite Archdale's "command," the violence continued.

A Yamasee attack on a Florida mission town brought matters to a head and inspired Archdale to strike a tiny blow against the Indigenous slave trade for the sake of furthering Carolina's neglected missionary goals. The Yamasees, the very refugees who had filled *Cacica* Merenciana's islands a decade before, were now firm allies of San Jorge, who had rejected Florida's republic of Indians.[225] During Archdale's term, the Yamasees went back to Florida to raid Santa Maria, bringing captives to Charles Town "designing to sell them for Slaves to *Barbados* or *Jamaica* as was usual."[226] Archdale learned of the arrival of "three Men and one Woman" and promptly ordered them in for an interview with the help of "a *Jew* for an Interpreter."[227] Under interrogation, Archdale learned that these Spanish-speaking Natives "professed the Christian religion as the Papists do."[228] Archdale then "thought in a most peculiar manner" and concluded that "they ought to be freed from Slavery."[229]

Archdale's "peculiar" decision sought to give Christian Indigenous converts the presumption of freedom in order to make conversion more attractive, especially to Native towns under the government of the English. "Peculiar" in those days may well have meant that Archdale decided the case of the Native captives like a casuist—that the circumstances were unique and demanded a special resolution. Or his word choice underscored that Archdale's decision defied the prevailing legal trends in the English colonies, which gave Christianity no such presumption of freedom, not for Africans or Indians. He hoped thereby to make allegiance to the English politically, and not just commercially, attractive to Natives. The Cape Fear Indians in North Carolina, for example, "desired to come under the *English* Government" after suffering in slave raids at the hands of other Indians who were subject to Carolina.[230] English traders encouraged the move, telling them "that if they came under the *English* Government the other *Indians* durst not touch them."[231] Archdale then accepted the Cape Fear Indians' allegiance on the condition that they offered "Civil Usage" to castaways on their coasts.[232] The agreement was typical of the English version of the "colonial compact." Archdale had ambitions to push another term into the deal—the right of missionaries peacefully to enter Native towns, concluding that persuasion was the key and that Natives "will never be won to the Gospel of Peace by the Banner of War."[233]

By the end of the seventeenth century, policies like Archdale's, based on the "principles of the bishop of Chiapa[s]," were too little, too late. Nor could Spanish hand-wringing and diplomatic remonstrances make much difference in the minds of Natives inside and outside the republic of Indians. In 1699, Diego Huste and Juan Chicasle, Guale *micos*, wrote Spain's king in behalf of the towns of San Felipe, Santa Maria, and Tupiqui—a people "abandoned and annihilated," they said. Huste and Chicasle petitioned the king to relieve their people of the "burdensome" duty of supporting those thirteen soldiers charged with protecting them from their Native and English enemies.[234] In their request, the *caciques* made a telling, if veiled, criticism about their status within the republic of Indians. Have the soldiers maintain themselves from what comes to them as pay from the annual royal subsidy, the pair argued, "in conformity" with the practice in Apalachee Province.[235] Years of unequal treatment, as they saw it, had taken a toll. The rulers of populous Apalachee, the breadbasket of the *presidio*, were spared the indignity of the sorts of chores that caused Guales "to neglect to take care of our children and towns."[236] Little did Huste and Chicasle know it but Apalachee leaders were writing the king with complaints of their own that were just as harrowing and just as familiar.[237] Across the South, the theft of the land, the daily trespasses and demands of colonists, the disrespect for leaders, the attacks on towns, and the losses of so many souls to the slave trade had discredited Christianity and tarnished the republic of Indians as a model for how Europeans and Natives could live together. Natives now looked more and more to their own resources and began forging larger polities to counter the sway of the empires of which many had once been part.

Conclusion: Liberty Without Law or Reason

By the century's end, Spain and England faced similar challenges of Native "governance." As Archdale put it to Laureano Torres y Ayala, "undoubtedly you must need know the Temper of the Indians as well as myself how hard a matter it is to keep them from taking revenge for Injuries or the death of any of their nation."[238] In other words, the tradition of independence in the council-houses of the South, a tradition that lived on even among Catholics in the *república de Indios*, was impossible to restrain.

Astute observers in San Agustín were far ahead of Charles Town in recognizing the problem. Alonso de Leturiondo, pastor of San Agustín's parish church, surveyed the difficulties confronting Florida as Spain's power everywhere seemed in decline. Contemplating the death of King Carlos II, Leturiondo looked with dread to the future, and saw little but war. The English, he wrote the ailing king, were "gaining vassals so they will have people for wartime" when it arrived.[239] One after another, Apalachicolas, Yamasees, Ocheses (Lower Creeks), and "many other Nations" were giving "obedience to the Governor of San Jorge."[240] Like housebreakers—*ladrones de casa*—English traders were stealing "the vassals that for so many years have been under the obedience of Your Majesty," Leturiondo protested.[241] More galling was how the Crown "spent so many millions for ... reducing those Souls to the Holy Gospel."[242] The Natives would learn "the bad customs, and the heresies of the English."[243] Natives would now have recourse to "the life of brutes, without law, and without reason."[244] All so that "the English" may "buy little Indians [*indiecitos*, i.e., children] for shotguns, carry them to their land, and sell them as Slaves."[245]

Whether he knew it or not, Leturiondo had diagnosed the contradiction at the heart of England's growing southern empire. The empire stood upon the relative freedom of the fortunate Native towns who were its allies and not its slaves. Yet, the English, also thought of the relationship in terms of Native subordination. Over time, English reformers would reach Leturiondo's conclusions. More troubling were the developments outside Leturiondo's—and most other Europeans'—ken. English traders and Spanish friars, archetypes of older histories of imperial competition, were not the only outsiders bidding for influence around the council fires of the Native South. Towns across the region kept the path open to envoys from their Indigenous neighbors, crossing ethnic, linguistic, and confessional lines to do so. These Native traders and emissaries were busy knitting together networks of towns into an alternative to colonial domination. This clash between independence and obedience was the essence of the dilemma that would trouble Carolina's leaders during the early eighteenth century when the war Leturiondo predicted finally came. Native leaders sitting around council fires in places like the Yamasee town Pocotaligo proposed a simple answer to the problem: complete independence. Together, they would lead a Native American revolution and forever remake the South.

CHAPTER 5

"As the Spaniards Always Have Done,"

1700–1715

In the crisp stillness of a January morning in 1704, the Apalachee town of Ayubale stood along Florida's *camino real*. Darkness covered the town and the road was empty, but had a party of friendly travelers come there in daylight they would have thought it indistinguishable from any other Native town in the South, save for the church and the cross that stood outside it.[1] Since the mid-seventeenth century, the people of Ayubale had dedicated themselves to Nuestra Señora de la Concepción. The village church, humble from the outside, may have glittered within. An inventory of church silver from that August suggests what the church in Ayubale might have contained—silver chalices, crosses, rich tapestries, and communion vessels.[2] After a mass of thanksgiving the travelers might have walked across the plaza to their lodgings on one of the hurdles inside the council-house. Or, had they kin in town, the visitors would have slept in one of the dwelling-houses along the plaza's rim. But no travelers were on the east-west road that morning. On the paths running from the north, an army of enemies, Apalachicolas and Englishmen, approached.

The invasion of Ayubale was long in coming, the response to an incident five years past and that had little to do with competition between England and Spain and everything to do with relations among Native peoples. The trouble started when a party of Chacatos killed and plundered some Apalachicola deer hunters and carried their spoils back to Ayubale, where the people welcomed them.[3] The Chacatos were refugees who contracted with the leaders of San Luis de Talimali to live on land surrounding that town about a decade before. The Apalachicolas may have held the Apalachees responsible for the Chacatos' actions in a variation of a law observed among other Southern Native peoples that when a band of refugees finds a nation "willing to adopt them, and is pursued thither by their enemies, this is in effect to declare war against the nation adopting."[4] Whatever the legal justification, by the afternoon, the town of Ayubale would be ashes but its memory would haunt English imperialists with a vision of the strength of the republic of Indians.

At the head of the avenging force—or so he thought—was Colonel James Moore. The plunder from Spanish churches and the bodies of Indigenous slaves built Moore's fortune and his manor near Goose Creek, a tributary flowing into the Cooper River.[5] Just past fifty years old in 1704, Moore had usurped the governorship of South Carolina in 1700, besieged the Castillo de San Marcos in 1702, and retreated from its walls in disgrace after only two months, when Spanish sails appeared at the harbor's bar.[6] Said to be fond of a tipple, his enemies accused him of drunkenness on the night those Spanish ships appeared. While in his cups, Moore resolved "to Fight thro' the Enemy" on the morrow, they said. "But the Pillow, which often lets out Heat to make way for Caution, changed this his Resolution."[7] A patron of Charles Town's first library, in San Agustín his army burned the Franciscan convent with all its volumes, "Worth above 600£," to the ground. Lost "were a Collection of the Greek and Latin Fathers" and even "the Holy Bible itself," which the soldiers torched on account "it was in Latin."[8] For one who knew him, Moore was "a very ingenious Gentleman sure enough, but I fear he will not make a good philosopher, being otherwise full of Employment, and besides his Genius does not lie that way."[9] Rather, his genius lay somewhere else entirely.

As early as the 1690s, Moore had formulated an astute—and typically ruthless—philosophy of the Native South's geopolitics and South Carolina's place at its center. The "English Safety," he believed, "Consists more in being Capable to Cause the Several nations of Indians to war upon one Another, than in reconciling their quarrels."[10] To control Indigenous nations, they must have no trade "but what they have from and by permission of this Government . . . And then when they have no Arms, by the terror of our Arms we Secure our own peace."[11] Through commercial monopoly and terror, the trader-planters of Charles Town would "become Arbiters of peace and war."[12] As Colonel Moore rode high in the saddle on the path to Ayubale, at the spearhead of a plundering expedition to recoup his honor and grow his fortune, the old slaver must have felt satisfaction to witness his philosophy in action. Not entirely ignorant about their place in this Apalachicola-led expedition, the Carolinians understood that they were following Native directions and exploiting Native quarrels to justify the war on Ayubale. When the Commons House urged South Carolina's new governor, Sir Nathaniel Johnson, to approve an incursion into Apalachee the previous September, they called it an "undertaking for the *assistance* of our Friendly Indians."[13]

Those "Friendly Indians"—Apalachicolas, Cowetas, Cussitas, the peoples later known as the Lower Creeks—quickly spread through the town of Ayubale "about Sun rising."[14] But their enemies were ready for them with improvised fortifications. Near the church, the army met stout Apalachee opposition. The townspeople, reportedly armed with bows and arrows, rallied inside the sanctuary, barricading the doors. Relentless, the invaders hacked the church doors down with their hatchets. The resident *doctrinero*, Fray Angel de Miranda, stood and suffered alongside the people of Ayubale, "with all valor, fighting from the morning until two in the afternoon."[15] Shoulder to shoulder with their priest, Apalachee warriors fired against wave after wave of enemy attacks until their ammunition ran out. Only then did they surrender. Amidst what Spaniards saw only as the gathering ruins of Apalachee, the friar's defiance nearly overshadowed the bravery of Ayubale's Apalachee defenders, earning him the praise of Florida's governor who commended his deeds to the king of Spain himself.[16] When their enemies tied Apalachee captives to stakes and tortured them, the victims praised God. That "in some Indians, recently converted, such deep faith would be found," left the governor in awe and even hopeful for the future of Florida.[17]

Fray Angel's deeds and the devotion of his Apalachee comrades-in-arms caught the outsized admiration of hostile observers, too, inadvertently helping to inspire a new phase of English imperialism in the South. After hacking their way into the heart of Ayubale's defenses, where "the Indians in it obstinately defended themselves," Moore reported that he and his men met with "a friar, the only white in it, [who] came forth and begged mercy."[18] Colonel Moore's understated dispatch did not do justice to the sense of wonder Ayubale's resistance and the sight of Fray Angel de Miranda had aroused in some who witnessed or heard about it. "What mighty influence," marveled Thomas Nairne, "the Spanish Friars had upon the Indians . . . of Apalachee."[19] A trader and planter in southerly Colleton County, by 1704 Nairne already had contacts among the neighboring Yamasee towns. By his own admission, he had been pestering the Society for the Propagation of the Gospel (SPG) to send able ministers into Indigenous towns. The exemplary life of Fray Angel de Miranda and of the other armed Franciscans he met with while "knifing all the Indian towns in Florida . . . subject to the Spaniards" only strengthened his conviction that not just missionaries but a general imperial reorientation was indispensable to Carolina's ambitions.[20]

For Nairne must have realized that Carolina was not the only winner in the overthrow of Florida's missions, that the victories against the Apalachees were really victories for the Creeks, and that as the colony grew stronger, so did the Native polities that fought its battles.[21] If their Native allies became too emboldened in triumph, Carolina's far-flung trading empire was doomed. Nairne began to conceive of a system based on a philosophy very different from James Moore's. What was needed, Nairne believed, were men "disinterested from all the wrangles of trade."[22] More than that, new institutions must be established, with new laws and new officers—preferably missionaries but others might take on the task—who would become for Natives "a Protector to represent their Greivances to."[23] Carolina must restrain violence, dispatching agents to settle Native disputes rather than enflame them. Then Carolina's "Indian Subjects" would prove of greater loyalty and usefulness—in short, the result would be greater colonial control. The answer burned as bright to Nairne as the fires that had consumed Ayubale and other towns in Apalachee. After torching its missions to the ground, South Carolina would have to become more like Florida to survive its Native allies' growing strength. Nairne's proposals are only half the story. Indeed, his plans were not even the most elaborate in the era that included John Lawson's grandiose vision for the "Regulation of the Savages" in North Carolina and Alexander Spotswood's thoroughgoing revamping of the tributary regime in Virginia. The sudden burst of interest in such Spanish-inspired strategies as religious missions and protectors of Indians that gripped the Southern colonies in the early eighteenth century had other, less visible sources. Indigenous leaders across the South, a cast including Nottoways in Tidewater Virginia, Yamasees near Port Royal, and refugee Apalachees on the Savannah River all contributed to the drive for imperial reform.

By far the most surprising and significant results came in South Carolina, a colony better known in those days for growing rich by capturing and selling thousands of Indigenous slaves. In an effort to buttress its frontier defenses, the colony forcibly resettled "free" Indigenous migrants from Florida and unwittingly created a determined lobby in favor of reforming the colonial system. The Indigenous refugees from war-ravaged Florida who came north by the hundreds brought with them the experiences and expectations of a century of Spanish colonialism.[24] The Yamasees, South Carolina's closest Native allies, already counted in their Upper Towns several towns of Guales who had spent time in the missions of the Georgia coast.[25] The Yamasees absorbed even more refugees from Guale after the invasion of Florida in 1702. From 1704 to 1706, hundreds of free Apalachees came north, too, whom the Creeks and their South Carolinian allies relocated on the Savannah River the better to control and exploit them. The plans to exploit the Apalachees failed as the refugee *holatas* (chiefs) pressed their case with the governor, English missionaries, and in the halls of the Commons House of Assembly, South Carolina's colonial legislature. Apalachees and Guale-Yamasees put to use their tested strategies—all honed in Spanish Florida's restless politics— to tame their would-be colonial masters. Through petitioning, lobbying, and what Denise Bossy calls "spiritual diplomacy," the Yamasees as well as the forced Apalachee migrants strove to make Charles Town more obedient to their demands, much as they had tried to manage San Agustín to their benefit.[26] Under Indigenous pressure, the English would, in the words of Thomas Nairne, do "as the Spaniards always have done" and build a republic of Indians of their own.[27]

To Us, Justice is Not Dispensed

Invading armies were only the proximate cause of the demise of the Florida missions. The long dissolution of the *república de Indios* in Florida was as much the achievement of Spaniards, Guales, Apalachees, and the Chacatos themselves as of their Apalachicola, Yamasee, or English enemies. Rather than honoring their obligations as they seemed to Thomas Nairne always to have done, by the turn of the eighteenth century, the Spaniards were imposing their law arbitrarily on Natives. Seeing little choice left to them, many Indigenous people simply slipped away. The republic of Indians was a shambles and the Natives from Guale to Apalachee fled their towns in disgust, so they "may not be bossed around as the said Spaniards ordinarily do."[28] There was still hope. The Crown repeated its promises to protect Spain's Native vassals. To their petition of 1699, the "miserable and afflicted" *caciques* of Guale Province, Diego Huste and Juan Chicasle, received a clear reply. The king ordered Florida's new governor, Joseph de Zuñiga y Cerda, to "punish with all rigor of law" the offenders, who were, in that case, the governor's own soldiers.[29] The king lectured Governor Zuñiga that one of "your foremost obligations is to attend to these Indians so that they will be maintained without the burden and oppression" of Spaniards and other non-Natives.[30] Within two years of the thundering royal decree, Guale was completely overrun. In Apalachee, the province's most prominent chiefs sent petition after petition—to sympathetic Spaniards, to the governor, even to the king—all foundered until that province was also destroyed. Don Patricio Hinachuba of Ivitachuco and Don Andrés of San Luís de Talimali, two of the most eminent leaders in Apalachee, told a dying Carlos II flatly that "to us, justice is not dispensed."[31]

Reputed equals with their own commonwealth, leaders, and laws, those who ruled the republic of Indians could justly complain of the decline in the standing of all three. Despite having the sympathy of the king, Indigenous leaders' usual strategies did not seem to work anymore. When a response to their complaints finally came from San Agustín, it became clear to Native leaders like Don Patricio that even the Apalachees—long numerous and influential in Florida councils—had been demoted in the eyes of the Spaniards.[32] Instead of honoring the authority of chiefs and of Native law and custom, the governor curtailed them in proclamations posted by the entrance to every council-house. Instead of offering with alacrity to lead counterattacks against their heathen enemies, the Spanish did their best to restrain aggrieved Native warriors crying out for vengeance. A Spanish postmortem on the fall of Apalachee concluded that the "Christian Indians, on seeing themselves harassed by the enemy on one side and the scant protection they received from here, rose up and went with the heathens and the English."[33] Yet, in the end, the Spanish did not simply fail to protect their Indian vassals but actively drove them away with their ceaseless demands. Apalachee and Guale refugees would never forget the disastrous decline of the republic of Indians in Florida, and the experience would guide their actions when they resettled in South Carolina.

The most glaring problem in the provinces of Florida in 1700 was the breakdown of the barriers between the two republics, notably in Apalachee's San Luís de Talimali where the Florencia family treated the town as their own informal and illegal *encomienda*. The troubles were in part the consequence of the long-ago decision of Governor Pablo de Hita Salazar to allow settlers into the province. With the connivance of Jacinto Roque Pérez, lieutenant of Apalachee, the Florencia family set up a cattle ranch nearby. They made incessant demands for personal service from the townspeople of San Luís— for fish on Friday, for women to grind their corn every single day, even for "an Indian who goes and comes every day with a jug of milk."[34] The Florencias fit into what was, in fact, a regional pattern of settlers who viewed their Native neighbors as a convenient pool of labor, as Apalachee exiles would learn during their time near the English in Carolina. The Florencias' cattle, hogs, and horses trampled on the Apalachees' fields and on their rights. To avoid the "continuous work," the Apalachees would not come into town, not "even to mass do they come, on feast days."[35] Many Apalachees were living in the woods a league away after the Spaniards kicked them out of their residences.[36]

The collapse of the buffers between republics was symptomatic of a general disintegration of traditional institutional safeguards, leading the Apalachees to seek out sympathetic colonists to be their patrons and defenders in hopes of countering influential Spaniards like the Florencias. Don Patricio remembered Antonio Ponce de León as a fair and courageous *visitador* who championed the Natives and punished errant Spaniards. In 1699, Ivitachuco's *cacique* wrote the "chaplain of the organ of the Parish of Florida" to enlist him in a lobbying campaign to win justice for the Apalachees.[37] I was "always named as their defender," Ponce explained to the king in 1702, "with which motive they seek me out with any injuries that had been done to them, soliciting by means of my littleness to take some relief in their pains."[38] The Apalachees recalled Don Antonio's father, Sergeant Major Nicolás Ponce, with fondness as one "who so cherished and protected us" and whose influence in San Agustín might persuade the current governor to remove the Florencias.[39] To deal with a family as well connected as the Florencias, the Apalachee *caciques* needed a rival patronage network of their own. The Apalachee leaders' network also included Alonso de Leturiondo, whose "printed memorial," the Council of the Indies cited in its resolution after reviewing Ponce's letter.[40] But the Apalachee leaders must have resented being obliged to make end runs around the governor or line up advocates to reinforce their case with a king who had over and over again promised Native leaders justice. The situation was so bad that already many Apalachees "were taking themselves off into the woods, others to San Jorge with the English."[41] The flight of their vassals diminished the status of Native leaders like Don Patricio. The lengths they had to go to for justice further eroded his status as a chief and the status of every Native vassal in the provinces of Florida.

High-ranking men saw their power curtailed and their persons abused more than ever before. After recounting the history of the Florencias' invasion of San Luís and the damages from their cattle ranch, Don Patricio's and Don Andrés's petition put at the top of the list of their "other greivances" how the matriarch of the Florencia clan "gave two smacks" to a *cacique* in San Luís for not "having brought her fish one Friday."[42] Worse was the response from the governor to their petitions. While enjoining his lieutenants in the provinces to redress their grievances in the future, there was no mention in his order of past offenses. When he came to the subject of cattle, Don Joseph de Zuñiga y la Cerda said nothing about keeping colonists' stocks out of Apalachee fields. Indeed, he singled out Apalachees for killing cattle without acknowledging they may have had good reason to strike at the offending beasts. Any Natives who killed Spanish cattle, stray or not, faced harsh punishment. More to the point, "if it is learned that some cacique or caciques shall consent to and cover up taking part in" killing cattle, "it will be punished and remedied."[43] Apalachee complaints against the would-be *encomenderos* of San Luis received no such diligent attention. The order placed *caciques* in an inferior position relative to the Spaniards in their midst and on an even more humiliating equality with their vassals.

Spaniards—from the governor to his lieutenants to the boisterous family of usurpers in San Luís—were trampling over the rights of Native leaders in matters of labor, self-governance, and trade while treating the same men's reasonable petitions as nothing but hysterics. Native vassals labored without pay and complained about it without redress.[44] Spaniards corrupted the Chacatos and the governor did nothing but take the power to govern them away from the Apalachees.[45] Although under the oversight of San Luís's *caciques* under the terms of a 1694 agreement, if the Chacatos disobeyed new orders from San Agustín they would "be punished with the uttermost Rigor" by the Spaniards, not the headmen of San Luís.[46] Anxious about the influences coming down the paths from the northwest, the *presidio* also tried to limit the Apalachees' friendly trade and intercourse with the Apalachicolas. Officials in San Agustín deemed the peace the Apalachees had agreed to with the Apalachicolas suspect, again threatening the prerogatives of the republic of Indians.[47] The occasional commerce in hides, horses, and guns that the Apalachees enjoyed with the Apalachicola towns could now only continue with the governor's say-so. And then, only for goods of Native manufacture but nothing "brought in by the English."[48] There was one commodity the Apalachicolas most coveted from Apalachee traders. Suffer them not, commanded Don Juan de Ayala Escobar, Apalachee's *visitador* in 1701, to give the Apalachicolas horses.[49] The Apalachicolas "did not desire anything," wrote the governor a year later, "except pack horses which the English ask of them for their traffic."[50]

Packhorses spelled an end to the one practice that, above all, exemplified for Natives the European drive to usurp the power of chiefs and humiliate common men—burdening. Not only did Apalachees carry goods for the Spaniards, they often went unpaid for their trouble. One visitor in 1694 handed down orders that "no person whatsoever" was "to have the Indians carry for him unless he pays him for his work."[51] Yet, Apalachee teemed with horses. None other than Thomas Nairne vouched for the province's reputation as a good horse country. "That Country is full of Cattle and horses," Nairne observed in 1708, "which before the war Belonged to the Spaniard and Apalachee Indians but are now wild."[52] Other postwar accounts testified to the Apalachees' rich stock of horses. A common complaint from the Apalachees was that the Florencias and the soldiers stationed in San Luís frequently stole the Natives' mounts.[53] Still, for all their growing stocks, their Apalachicola trading partners might have said, the Apalachees still carried burdens for the Spaniards.[54]

Worst of all, the Spaniards were threatening the age-old traditions of the Native leadership class at a time when their fighting ardor was needed most. After a Timucuan official carried out an unauthorized raid allegedly for trophies, Governor Zuñiga outlawed scalp-taking altogether, branding it "a fiendish custom, born and raised in their primitive heathenism."[55] Florida's Native vassals must find "other means and acknowledgment to signalize for *norocos* and *tascayas*"—the two orders of warriors among Apalachees and Timucuas—"who make some kills in a lawful war."[56] Enforcement of the order rested on the shoulders of "the caciques of the towns," the very people who should have been the staunchest defenders of custom.[57] Spanish foot-dragging in the wake of an Anglo-Apalachicola attack on Timucua in May 1702 strained the nerves of Native elites across Florida even further. When Don Patricio Hinachuba and other leaders demanded a massive retaliatory expedition, the governor dismissed their entreaties as "the clamorous importunity of the Indians."[58] If they were serious about preserving Florida, Spaniards should have heeded them instead of cutting them off.

Spanish officials in Florida often credited English success in Indian affairs to their willingness to flaunt the strictures of law. As Governor Zuñiga put it in 1702, the Apalachicolas, Ocheses, and Yamasees preferred to ally with the English "because they do not impose upon them the law that we do."[59] This new generation of Spanish leaders lacked the subtlety to see that their predecessors had not so much imposed law on the provinces as they had worked with Native leaders to establish a mutual law. Rather than respecting this shared law, Spaniards by the eighteenth century were handing down new laws that were a heavy burden on Natives but not on the Spaniards who most often transgressed them. With this kind of conduct, Spain's Native vassals could have well believed they had not a single Spanish friend left. Little surprise, then, that the rumor slipped into Charles Town that "the Apalachees" were "inclinable" to deserting Florida to join the Carolinians.[60]

When petitions to officials got them nowhere, when they had run out of friends to do them justice, the numbers of Apalachees who appealed to the trail or to the woods only swelled. They carried the weight of their political expectations along with their worldly possessions on their backs. In Carolina, four towns of free Apalachees would rise on the banks of the Savannah River after missions like San Luís de Talimali had burned to ash. But no matter how far they fled, the same problems, the same demands, confronted them at every turn, now from English colonists intoxicated with visions of empire. The Apalachees and their proud *holatas* were but one nation out of many who found themselves caught in an emergent polity with Charles Town as its paramount and head. In time, they would try to do the improbable and rebuild the republic of Indians there on new if stony ground.

The Greatest Quantity of Indians Subject
to This Government of Any in All America

At the end of the year 1700, word jogged up the Trading Path of the accession of a new governor in distant Charles Town. By the time John Lawson, the London naturalist, and his companions heard it from a Native war-captain above the Congarees, the message had already traveled up the path and back down again. Before parting ways, the war-captain told the young English traveler "that *James* had sent Knots to all the Indians thereabouts, for every Town to send in 10 Skins, meaning Captain *Moore*, then Governor of *South-Carolina*."[61] The news must have reached all the towns along the Trading Path in the Piedmont of what is now North Carolina—Waxhaws, Esaw, Keyauwees, Saponi, Occaneechi, and Adshusheer. In most of these towns, many different nations had gathered for protection from the dangers of the slave trade.

Their headmen, men like Adshusheer's Enoe-Will, who hired himself out as a guide to traders and travelers, kept the path open to Virginians and the Carolinians, accepting commissions from Virginia's governor and sending presents of skins to South Carolina's.[62] The political situation in the Piedmont was not much different than the one in towns across the region—from the Yamasee town of Pocotaligo to Tugaloo among the Lower Cherokees—that Carolina claimed as its subjects. In Virginia, Englishmen called a demand for "10 Skins" tribute. In the coy idiom of Carolina, the deerskins Moore requested were "presents." But the intention was much the same. For Enoe-Will and for many a headman in towns across the Southeast, accepting colonial commissions or giving presents to visiting traders did not mean subjection. Theirs was an alternative vision to the dreams of orderly empire reigning in colonial capitals. Enoe-Will at least had the advantage of some distance from Charles Town's reach. Other towns were not so lucky.

By the winter of 1700–1701, Carolina was growing in strength, threading together the largest constellation of towns in the region's history. The Yamasees were the cornerstone of the alliance system. Within a few years, Carolina's network would include four towns of refugee Apalachees forcibly removed from Florida. Rather than a complicated nexus of alliances, imperialists like Thomas Nairne boasted how Carolina had acquired "the greatest quantity of Indians Subject to this Government of any in all America."[63] The problem, as men like Nairne saw it, would be how exactly to govern them—and in a time of unrelenting war at that. For the Native "subjects" in the patchwork of towns that traded with Carolina, the problem was exactly the reverse. The talk in their council-houses was about what to do with the traders and officials from Charles Town and how to govern them. The predicament was even more dangerous because, at every step of the process of building their alliance, Carolinians and their Native partners like the Yamasees used ambiguous terms that disguised their intentions.

The arrival of James's "Knots" in town squares across the South was the herald of shifting political currents and another bout of imperial warfare. A scene much like the one the Society for the Propagation of the Gospel missionary John Talbot beheld in 1703 must have unfolded in other Indigenous towns all over eastern North America. "When we brought over the News that King William was dead and Queen Anne reigned in his Stead," Talbot wrote, "The Indians wonder'd what was come to the English that they should have a Squaw Sachem as they said a Woman King," but they did not shirk and still "sent her a Present."[64] The war of the "Woman King" fit conveniently in the wars Natives were then waging, and gave them a little added impetus.

In Charles Town the news of Anne's accession and that England was at war with Spain and France, led the Commons House of Assembly to make plans for the invasion of San Agustín late in 1702, a campaign that eventually foundered in a two-month siege. Outside the legislators' chamber, along the wharves lining the Bay (as the street by the quayside was known), stood the masts of scores of merchant vessels stacked like lances in a floating palace-at-arms.[65] The Commons House impressed the lot of them for the expedition. The invading force was two-pronged. By land went Colonel Robert Daniell, pillaging and burning the remaining Guale missions of Santa Maria, San Felipe, and Tupiqui.[66] By sea, in his makeshift fleet of pressed ships, went Governor Moore. The army included a few hundred colonial militia who marched with as many as six hundred Indigenous warriors of various nations, notably the Yamasees, many of whom had likely heeded the call for "10 Skins" from Governor Moore.[67]

The rock of the Castillo de San Marcos checked the onrush of Carolinian expansion momentarily in 1702. But the wave of carnage washed around it, sweeping through the vulnerable Native provinces, including Apalachee, lifting a portion of their inhabitants like flotsam, and pulling them back with the tide to the north and east. In 1703, at Moore's instigation, the Commons House approved a plan to invade Florida again and bring back as many Apalachees as he could, either as subjects or slaves. The Commons House voted on 15 September 1703 to "Advise" the new governor, Sir Nathaniel Johnson, in favor of a campaign into Apalachee "for the confirmation of our Friendly Indians to our interest."[68] In one swoop, the colony would shore up support among the Ocheses and Apalachicolas who were wavering in their loyalty—so the English thought—and would succeed in "gaining others," the Apalachees, to their side as well.[69]

Parsing the terms that Carolinians and their Indigenous allies used to describe the larger strategic picture during wartime reveals the tensions in the relationship between Charles Town and the Native peoples who were supposedly its subjects. Carolinians often fell back on language that was more agreeable to Native ideas of alliance, including describing the relationship as a state of "Amity."[70] South Carolinians of the era tended to speak of Indigenous peoples as "in our interest," and its use was an exercise in strategic ambiguity. The term "interest" in this sense implied a faction or following.[71] The Commons described the Apalachees in 1703 as "inclinable" to the English interest much as a faction in the House might be inclined to vote on one measure or another.[72] The Carolinians saw themselves as Natives' patrons, offering favor and protection to their dutiful if often surly "clients."[73] When John Lawson, for instance, fantasized about civilizing "a great many other Nations of the Savages, and" thereby "daily add to our Strength in Trade, and Interest" he understood "Interest" in that sense.[74] Friendly Natives would join as members in a great English party, as it were, able "to conquer or maintain our Ground, against all Enemies to the Crown of *England* in *America*, both

Christian and Savage."[75] What Englishmen like Lawson thought of as empire-building most of Carolina's Native allies saw as a mutual enterprise that profited them and did not compromise their independence.

The term "interest" implied considerable freedom of choice on Natives' part, something they could approve. "Trade and acquaintance" only had brought the Yamasees and other Native peoples into the English interest.[76] Equating trade with peace and alliance was not solely a European concept but accorded with the Native peoples' own theory of the law of nations, which placed trade relations on a level with friendship and alliance.[77] Yet, Carolinians believed that trade had a coercive power of its own, far beyond mere influence over customers. "There is no nation of Indians which either by husbandry, produce, or by manufacture make Any Sort of provisions or Commodities which is not Common and proper to every other nation," James Moore once wrote.[78] In theory, Natives therefore depended on Carolina's goods and in the bargain came their allegiance. The Carolinians, wrote John Lawson, were the "absolute Masters over the *Indians* and carry so strict a Hand over such as are within," as he put it, "the Circle of their Trade."[79] Tellingly, when the Tuscaroras, a powerful Indigenous chieftaincy of dozens of towns, struck North Carolina in 1711, that colony's leaders appealed to South Carolina to bring an army of its "tributary Indians," implying that Charles Town's Indigenous trading partners and allies were really its obedient subjects.[80] Still, even in wartime, the English urged that the transfer of Native allegiance from the Spanish appear to occur with a minimum of coercion. Natives were supposed to be making a free choice to join the English interest. In its 1703 resolution, the Commons House required that Governor Johnson give James Moore "Instructions to endeavor to gain by all peaceable means possible the Apalachees to our interest."[81]

After gaining them to their "interest," Carolina's leaders next had to make sure that Natives kept up "their devotion" to the English, as their Spanish rivals put it.[82] From San Agustín, it looked as if Natives like the Apalachicolas had deserted their allegiance to Spain and come under the protection or, more evocatively, the "Shelter [*Abrigo*] of the English of Carolina."[83] The English took steps to make their shelter comfortable for new Indigenous allies. In the early years of the eighteenth century, the Commons House of Assembly, working together with Indigenous headmen, improvised a system for dealing with complaints. By redressing their grievances, colonial legislators thought the Yamasees and other nations who had abandoned Florida would feel "Easy in Our Neighborhood and friendship, So as that they may not have reason to return to the Spaniards."[84]

The Yamasees, some 1,200 strong, living in two sets of towns near Port Royal, were Carolina's most prominent allies and archaeological evidence tells us just how much they expected from their "Neighborhood and friendship" with Carolina. The Upper Towns were a collection of peoples mainly from the missions in Florida, especially Guale. The Lower Towns mostly comprised refugees from the interior chiefdoms of modern-day Georgia, and if the site of an important public building in the head town of Altamaha is any indication, the Yamasees never forgot their former glory.[85] Excavations in Altamaha uncovered what appears to be the chief's residence or the council-house near an abandoned Mississippian-era mound.[86] As they looked back on the past, the tools they used and the jewelry they wore displayed the prosperity of the present. Yamasee women treated deer hides with "glass hide-scraping tools" they made out of pieces of rum bottles.[87] Equally extravagant were the Yamasee men who wore plundered Franciscan rings on their fingers and gorgets made of old gunstocks around their necks.[88] Notorious in Florida for their "ungovernable" temperament and commitment to liberty, in South Carolina, Yamasee headmen and warriors were touchy about their own authority and dignity.[89] Chiefs held considerable sway in matters of war and peace and insisted on deciding who was allowed to trade in their towns.[90] The recovery of lost power, wealth, and prestige was by the eighteenth century the touchstone of Yamasee politics and the whole purpose of the alliance with Charles Town. In January 1702, when the Commons House ordered an investigation into the "Abuses to our neighbor and friendly Indians," the entire Yamasee political project was in danger.[91] The alliance with Carolina was not living up to its promises.

Aggrieved Yamasees told the Commons House how traders killed their hogs, burned houses full of gunpowder and corn, cheated them of deerskins, stole their canoes, and "forcibly took" guns from men and even, in one case, "an Indian Widow."[92] Guns were valuable, priced at thirty buckskins in 1716.[93] But so were canoes, which European colonists up and down the Eastern Seaboard relied on—and dearly coveted—as "water-horses."[94] Understanding the value of what the traders took, and the potential fallout, the House urged the governor to "Empower" one of its own members, none other than Thomas Nairne, "to see full Satisfaction made by the several persons to the Several Yamasee Indians."[95] Some Carolinians, especially Nairne, feared their colony lacked the means to hold Native peoples in their sway. The Carolinians were constantly on guard against Spanish attempts to "draw the said Indians to their Interest."[96] Meanwhile, the Yamasees leveraged the threat of bolting to the Spanish to limit English meddling in their internal affairs. As one English missionary wrote, the Yamasees "revolted to us from the Spaniards because they would not be Christians, and if we require it of them it's feared they may return again to the Spaniards."[97] As they had done since the breakdown of the chiefdoms, and as the Apalachees were doing as the raids on their lands intensified, as a last resort, Natives could simply walk away, establishing their towns over again in a place better suited to their ambitions. Or, more disturbingly to Europeans, Natives could behave in ways that belied fantasies of European mastery over them.

The tortures Apalachees and Spaniards endured at the hands of James Moore's Apalachicola allies during their raids in Florida, for example, reveal just how far Carolinians were from being "absolute Masters" over Native peoples. The problem was not confined to relations with the Yamasees. Near San Luís de Talimali, a Spanish soldier witnessed the Creeks torture Apalachee captives, tying them to stakes, and burning them alive. When Fray Angel de Miranda confronted Moore, it became clear that something more pressing than the laws of waging a just war had forced the Englishman's hands. "There were eighty Englishmen," Moore replied, "and fifteen hundred Indians, and he could not remedy it."[98] Moore did not deny the Creeks' behavior was a shocking violation of the laws of warfare. For a man with a career like Moore's, it would be easy to assume that his comments were mere expediency. Moore's strategy had a simple and cynical logic: claim the Indians and own their actions as occasion suited; when it did not, disclaim them. The tactic had a long history. South Carolina governor James Colleton had done much the same with the Yamasees twenty years before when he denied they were under his government.[99] Here was a selective recognition of Indigenous sovereignty. Moore had in one comment acknowledged that the Creeks were driving the wars in the early eighteenth century and the Carolinians were only riding along.[100] But perhaps James Moore—the cynical realist, the hardened veteran of political intrigue and of many military campaigns—was, for once, caught by surprise. The reality was dawning on him in that moment that Carolina's Indian "subjects" were beyond the colony's control. Moore's comments were an admission of failure in the midst of striking success. If Carolina were to survive its triumph, the Natives could live no longer without reason, or law, and at their own liberty—to put the colonizers' problem in the terms Alonso de Leturiondo once used in his *Memorial* to the king of Spain.

The difficulty of reining in their victorious allies resolved the Carolinians to invite the Creeks to pay homage to Queen Anne in order to clear up any misunderstanding about the Indians' place in England's empire. On 5 August 1705, Sir Nathaniel Johnson accepted the "humble submission" of several Indian "Kings, Princes, Generals &c. to the Crown of England."[101] The "humble submission" was redolent of the by-then venerable tradition of America's "natural lords" bowing in obedience to a distant, European crown as befit Indian vassals. But in these Native leaders, European colonial fantasies met some of their savviest opponents yet. For later historians, the document Johnson drew up that day was no submission at all but one of the first European records of a formidable indigenous political entity, whom the English then knew by a rather harmless—perhaps careless—name, the "Indians on Ochese Creek."[102] But as these Creeks conquered Florida's republic of Indians, they simultaneously strengthened the independence of their own towns, each one a "petty republic."[103] And their independence further emboldened allied Natives like the Yamasees. In the guise of an Indigenous chieftaincy—a network of allied towns built on "Trade and acquaintance," something the Creeks could understand and perhaps endorse—Carolina was struggling to raise a massive empire of what it hoped would be compliant, tributary subjects.[104]

Carolina's designs put the colony at odds with Indigenous ambitions all over the Southeast. In the Piedmont, along the Trading Path, most headmen were content to keep their options open, trading with whomever they pleased. Closer to the hub of trade, the Yamasees dreamed of using the Carolinians in their own quest to recover lost power and secure their independence from all comers, Indigenous and European alike. Even so, Yamasee leaders often resorted to the familiar techniques of petitioning learned during their unhappy days in the missions of Florida. Fears that their "Indian subjects" might defect to the allegiance of other European powers softened the ways English colonizers discussed subjecthood and obliged them to try to redress Indigenous grievances. But colonial reformers still imagined subservient Indigenous subjects—looking to Spain for a model either to follow or avoid. Their efforts at reform met willing partners in the Apalachees who streamed into Carolina beginning in 1704 after Moore's incursions. Natives like the exiled Apalachees from Florida would help guide Carolina's reformers, tempering their pretensions to absolute rule, and placing law and justice at the center of politics if only for a moment.

The Regulation of the Savages

In the train of James Moore's army on its return from Florida were, all told, some 1,300 free Apalachees, driving oxcarts full of their belongings or carrying everything they had on their backs. These refugees avoided enslavement by "compounding" terms of surrender with Moore. Their arrival in Carolina as "free Indians" and "Indian subjects" coincided with a general realization among the colony's leaders that Carolina must rein in the Natives or lose its dominance. The migrations, the upheavals, the ambitions of some, the desperation of others made the years from the fall of Apalachee Province through the Yamasee War a restless and creative time in the history of political thought in the Southeast. Stretching the reach of their institutions up the trading paths, feeling their waxing strength, Carolinians freely borrowed colonial models from the Spaniards even as they routed them. Refugee Apalachees and the Yamasees, both of whom had endured Spanish colonialism, became the major targets of grandiose plans for what one English imperialist termed "the Regulation of the Savages."[105]

Before they could put any such plans into motion, Carolina's officials had first to formalize the transfer of the Apalachees' allegiance from vassals of Spain to subjects of England. Once the migrants entered Carolina's bounds—and not before—the Commons House resolved that the free Apalachees "brought in by Colonel Moore, be taken into the protection of this Government."[106] Until the governor followed the House's advice and extended the colony's legal and political protection over the free Apalachees, they were still revolted Spanish vassals. As such, they had forfeited all their goods and lands. In San Agustín, Governor Zúñiga decreed that all horses, cattle, swine, agricultural fields "and other things that were left by the Indians who went of their own free will with the enemy" were proclaimed "lost and seized."[107] The proceeds of the rebels' seized estates he ordered to be converted to serve "the essential needs of the province and its defense."[108] Still, the path back to Florida was yet open to any "Indian vassals of the King who went voluntarily and are now remorseful, desiring to come back under the Catholic law they once avowed."[109] The king of Spain would pardon all their transgressions and all their goods would come back into their hands or they would receive replacements at royal expense.[110]

Once the free Apalachees were under Carolina's protection, colonial officials took steps to maintain order among them, put their backs to use in carrying for the long-distance deerskin trade as well as their arms in defense of the colony's southwestern frontiers. The Carolinians recognized they would need better techniques of surveillance along with better ways to redress Indigenous grievances, thus keeping disturbances at least to a minimum. Heralding the high-handed approach to come, instead of an inspection tour like the Spanish visitations of old, in April 1704, the Commons House of Assembly commanded that "both the Caciques of our friendly Indians, among whom they are settled, and the Caciques of the Apalachees be sent for," and an "inquiry be made whether they live in Amity, one with the other."[111] Whatever the state of the Apalachees' relations with their neighbors—recent historians have characterized the migrants as "hostages" to the Creeks—the bigger problem was the principal work the Carolinians expected the exiles to perform.[112]

Although they came to Carolina as "free Indians," colonial officials had clear plans for the role they would play, advising—on the very day that they urged the government's protection over them—"that the Apalachee Indians be not employed as Burtheners by the Traders no further than the Savana Town."[113] Apalachees despised burdening in Florida, going all the way back to the long winter of 1539–1540, when their warriors freed Hernando de Soto's chained Indigenous porters.[114] Burdening for Spaniards even at a time when horses were plentiful had surely contributed to making Apalachees "inclinable" to an English alliance. Now the Carolinians were already loading them like packhorses. When Apalachee burdeners bolted off with "several Guns" and a share of Colonel Moore's plunder on the path from Coweta in the Lower Creek Nation, it was just a hint of troubles to come.[115] The government resolved that restitution for the thefts would come out of the public treasury, "the Apalachee Indians being but lately reduced and come into us" and unable to make Colonel Moore "satisfaction."[116] The point was that the free Apalachees were not yet sufficiently reorganized politically for the colonial government to hold them accountable, much less to compensate Moore for the damages. Nor were they loyal enough in colonial eyes. The Commons House urged the governor that "a free trade for Guns and Ammunition shall not be granted them, till we are better assured of their sincerity to us and that we may not lie open to such [barbarous] cruelty as hath been committed by some of them."[117] Being "but lately reduced," the Apalachees challenged Carolina officials to figure out the best way to bring them back to polity and order.

Carolina's imperialists were unashamed to adapt some Spanish colonial ideas to govern their newfound empire of "Indian subjects," even while rejecting others. Borrowing from what he believed were the most effective Spanish techniques of colonial governance, Thomas Nairne proposed that Carolina construct a *república de Indios* of its own, complete with religious missions, protectors to represent Native interests, and with clear political channels for Indigenous petitions. Although historians have characterized his politics as that of a Whig devoted to liberty, Nairne was just as concerned with the demands of order when it came to the Natives whom he claimed as Britain's "subjects."[118] On 20 August 1705, Nairne spelled out his vision to the Reverend Edward Marston, and through him, the SPG. Out of the human wreckage tallied in "numbers killed and sold for slaves," the Carolinians had "brought about 1600 Souls to settle among our Indians and be Subject to our Government."[119] Yet, the Franciscans managed to hold the "fidelity and friendship" of their Indian charges even as "they saw their Countries all fired and themselves daily killed and carried away Slaves by other Indians."[120] The perceptions of Franciscan influence, the vision of William Owen at the beginning of Carolina's history, seared certain lessons in Nairne's mind.

With the "tyranny" of the friars over at last, and with nothing to fear from them, Nairne urged his countrymen to learn from their example. In stating the reasons why, Nairne inadvertently echoed his Spanish opponents like Alonso de Leturiondo and Governor Zuñiga who despaired of losing so many souls that the Crown of Spain had won at such great expense. "What a good fight have we been fighting," Nairne pleaded, "to bring so many people from something of Christianity to downright Barbarity and Heathenism."[121] After the Spaniards had converted them, the Carolinians could not allow formerly missionized Natives to backslide into their old beliefs and customs. With good, stout missionaries in the mold of the Franciscans, Nairne believed the Carolinians could govern their new Native subjects effectively and hold their loyalty while saving their souls. Nairne's ideas were not idle speculation or merely plans for the future. Many of his ideas ended up in a later act to regulate the deerskin and slave trade, which the Commons House hoped would "Ease the Oppressions the Indian Lie under and have hitherto unsuccessfully Complained of."[122]

While Nairne urged a return to the instruments of colonial power that had held the republic of Indians in league with the republic of Spaniards in Florida, his contemporary John Lawson criticized the model of two republics and proposed his own plan for the "Regulation of the Savages" that would bring Native people under "the same Ecclesiastical and Civil Government we are under."[123] Spanish methods did not always lead to lasting conversions or lasting loyalties, Lawson claimed. "We find," he wrote in 1709, "that the *Fuentes* and several noted Indian families about *Mexico*, and in other parts of *New Spain*, had given several large Gifts to the Altar, and outwardly seem'd fond of their new Religion; yet those that were the greatest Zealots outwards, on a strict Enquiry, were found guilty of Idolatry and Witchcraft."[124] Separation for the sake of saving Indian bodies from the abuses of Spaniards had instead imperiled their souls. Would it not be the same if the English kept traders and settlers away from Native towns?

The story of the Fuentes family came from Central America, not New Spain, and was one of many tales from the notorious English Dominican Thomas Gage, whose oft-reprinted book Lawson may have read in its 1699 edition, but the lesson he drew points to the fault lines of political debate in the Carolinas. Instead of "Mexico" Lawson meant "Mixco" in Guatemala where Gage was a priest to the local Indigenous peoples. Among the Native "dissemblers" Gage confronted in Mixco "were four Brothers called Fuentes" who "were outwardly very fair tongued, liberal, and free handed to the Church, much devoted to the Saints, great feasters upon their day, and yet in secret great Idolaters."[125] Gage kept the discovery of the brothers' adherence to the old religion secret, waiting until he had gathered the town together in church to reveal that he had taken the idol, and then burn it at the altar. The zealous Gage wrote the president of the *audiencia* (local high court) and to the bishop for advice on how further to proceed. "And as touching the Indian Idolaters their counsel unto me was," Gage recorded, that he should "endeavor to convert them to the knowledge of the true God by fair and sweet means, shewing pity unto them for their great blindness, and promising them upon their repentance pardon from the Inquisition, which considering them to be but new plants, useth not such rigor with them, which it useth with Spaniards, if they fall into such horrible sins."[126] John Lawson, reading the passage decades later, used a similar horticultural metaphor but to different ends.

Drawing on his own observations and from Gage's, Lawson offered a trenchant critique of the two republics and an unexpected consequence of its principle of protecting Natives from Spaniards. The reason for Indigenous converts' backsliding, Lawson observed, with Gage's tale of the Fuentes family in mind, "seems to proceed from their Cohabiting, which, as I have noted before, gives Opportunities of Cabals to recall their ancient pristine Infidelity and Superstitions."[127] Citing Scriptural precedents, including the book of

Romans, Lawson imagined grafting Indians permanently to the English olive tree rather than imagining their commonwealths as separate plants, growing side-by-side as neighbors. Lawson favored "the *Indians* Marrying with the Christians, and coming into Plantations with their *English* Husbands, or Wives, [whereby] they would become Christians, and their Idolatry would be quite forgotten, and, in all probability, a better Worship come in its Stead; for were the *Jews* engrafted thus, and alienated from the Worship and Conversation of *Jews*, their Abominations would vanish, and be no more."[128] For the majority of the Natives that Carolina claimed as subjects, their isolation from Charles Town or from the settlements on Albemarle Sound meant that they too could maintain "their ancient pristine Infidelity," free to plan against the day they could rise up when the English became too oppressive. Lawson and Nairne propounded two distinct views of the lessons Spanish colonial governance offered for the English, but theirs were not the most important ones.

Another group of leaders—who had much greater experience with molding Spanish colonial institutions to serve their needs—were busy in their own campaign to reform Carolina. The refugee Apalachees who resettled on the Savannah River near the bustling and gritty trading outpost known as Savano Town, may have been hostages at first but they did not act like it for long. The Apalachees, who once bore the reputation of model vassals of Spain, came to Carolina with bitter memories of how Spaniards in Florida had failed them. Instead of waiting for English officials to do something about the lawlessness all around them, Apalachee leaders took the lead in skillfully pressing the Charles Town government, at every opportunity, to change its ways.

Rebuilding the Republic of Indians

While English imperialists debated, the "free" Apalachees of Carolina tested the institutions of the colonial state—the Commons House, the fledgling SPG missions, the governor, and council—to renegotiate with the English a version of the colonial compact they once enjoyed with the Spanish. The Apalachees who followed Moore to Carolina carried expectations from Florida about the proper colonial relationship and they voiced these ideas through lobbying and petitioning. To ease the way for their complaints, they curried favor with sympathetic Carolinians much as they had done with influential Spaniards in Florida. They worked, they fought, and they carried deerskins and trade goods hundreds of miles on their backs, all for Carolina. In return, the Apalachees demanded protection for their towns, their persons, and their souls. Within five years of their forced removal to the colony, the Apalachees reportedly "behaved themselves very submissive to the Government," but their actions said otherwise.[129] Throughout the years that they lived under Carolina's authority, the Apalachees boldly pressured English officials, clerics, and traders to help them rebuild the republic of Indians as best they could.

Carolina's colonial system imposed many of the same obligations upon the Apalachees as Florida's republic of Indians—and the Apalachees expected colonial officials to protect them in exchange. The town they established on the Savannah River put the Apalachees directly on the main trading path to the interior, all the better to serve Carolina's Indian traders as long-distance burdeners. In a report to the Lords Commissioners of Trade and Plantations in 1708, the governor and council reported that the Apalachees who "had deserted the Spaniards" now inhabited "a Considerable Town" on Savannah River, which, as planned, was "seated very advantageous for Carrying our Trade."[130] The distances Apalachee burdeners covered were as far-reaching as the colonial ambitions of Carolina. Back in Florida, carrying supplies might have meant a round trip of two weeks, but Apalachees in Carolina were traveling on journeys far longer.[131] "Indians seated upwards of seven hundred miles off are supplied with Goods by our White men that Transport them from this River upon Indian's backs," the governor boasted.[132] That same year roughly ten percent of an estimated "two hundred and fifty men" living at the Apalachees' new town went burdening on a journey of several hundred miles.[133] When Thomas Nairne traveled the path to the Chickasaw Nation, he went in company of "25 Apalachees that were burdeners" for a Carolina trader.[134] Apalachees performed other work besides burdening and participated actively in the trading economy, carrying messages for traders and colonial officials.[135] Such grueling physical labor in the trading economy was hardly the only service the Apalachees—reputed as fearsome warriors by the English—would perform.

The most important obligation Apalachees, Yamasees, and other Native subjects had was to fight for Carolina during wartime. Colonial officials eventually trusted enough in the fidelity and ability of Native warriors such as the Apalachees, that they regularly summoned them to Charles Town in times of alarm. In April 1709, the Commons and the Council sent for Indian warriors as part of a defensive levy, including "100 from the Savannah's And Apalachees and Tohagolico."[136] By then the colony had no reservations about the allegiance of the relatively new arrivals. There were even plans to garrison "two hundred Indians of what Nations" the governor believed best suited

Figure 9. Detail of Apalachee towns in Florida and South Carolina by William Hammerton, 1732; map of the southeastern part of North America, 1721. Yale Center for British Art, Gift of the Acorn Foundation, Inc., Alexander O. Vietor, Yale BA 1936, President, in honor of Paul Mellon.

for the purpose, a list that likely would have included the Apalachees by this point, "to be placed in the settlement where they may be ready to March to Town in Twelve hours' time."[137] Their service did not go unnoticed. One Yamasee man won a military pension in 1712, after his commander, Colonel John Barnwell, secured an order from the Commons House to "pay out of the Public Treasury unto Francisco a Yamasee Indian the sum of twenty Shillings per annum for five years . . . towards his support and maintenance, being disabled by a shot on his right hand on the late expedition against the Tuscaroras."[138] Colonial dependence on their fighting prowess and loyalty gave Native leaders some leverage with the English. As Governor Craven put it in 1712, Carolina must "have a particular regard for the Indians to protect them from insults, and by all manner of ways engage them to our interest, their friendship is so necessary to the wellbeing of this Province that 'tis obvious even to the meanest capacity."[139]

For the Apalachees, an important requirement for keeping them in the English interest was caring for their spiritual welfare. During their time in Carolina, the Apalachees sought priests to minister to their religious needs, giving them the unusual distinction of being one of the few Indigenous people in league with South Carolina who sought out missionaries. The Apalachees' arrival in Carolina coincided roughly with the 1701 foundation of the Society for the Propagation of the Gospel in Foreign Parts (SPG), a missionary arm of the Anglican Church with a charter to convert Native Americans within the empire.[140] Rather than convert "heathens" to Christianity, the primary objective of the early SPG missions in the Southeast was "to convert the Roman Catholic Indians" such as the Apalachees and some Yamasees to Protestantism.[141] One unnamed Apalachee *cacique* told the SPG's Francis Le Jau how, back in their homeland, they "had a Priest in every Town" and that "they maintain'd their Clergy very well."[142] Speaking to the Apalachees' persistence and savviness in navigating colonial political channels, the same Apalachee leader who importuned Le Jau had already "applied himself to the Governor for a Minister to live among them," the priest reported, adding that "they are baptized and were formerly subject to the Spaniards."[143]

Some towns went even further in their pursuit of spiritual aims. Much as the Spanish had educated the children of Native elites in Florida, the SPG sent the nephew of a Yamasee leader from the town of Euhaw to Britain, where the bishop of London baptized him "George" and officials celebrated him as the "Yamasee Prince."[144] The depth of his religious conversion is debatable. What is not in question is that Yamasees and Apalachees believed religious ties and religious ministers could help them achieve their political objectives. In his case, young George managed to turn the dogged SPG commissary, Gideon Johnston, into a somewhat effective advocate for his diplomatic mission in England.[145] George's story illustrates one reason the Apalachee leaders asked for priests in their towns—they wanted them to be their advocates in colonial and imperial councils.

The Apalachees' and Yamasees' history with the Spanish missions encouraged the SPG to publish the New Testament in a language it was believed they would understand. While Francis Le Jau continued to search for the linguistic key to converting Native Americans, his superiors concluded that it was Spanish.[146] Sometime around 1709, the SPG accepted a "Spanish Testament" that its leaders hoped would aid the society's mission along the "Borders of Florida and other Spanish Plantations to convert the Yamasee Indians Natives of those Parts."[147] In his petition to the SPG, its translator wished "that the dispersing of these Testaments amongst the Spaniards and Indians will prove by the Blessing of God an Instrument for Promoting Evangelical Truth."[148] In the end, the Society's original hopes for the Spanish Testaments did not fail entirely. Although few ministers proved willing to preach among the allied Natives using the testaments, they nevertheless saw use in another field of the SPG's purported mission in Carolina—ministering to Catholic Spaniards from Florida. In 1711, Commissary Gideon Johnston reported to the SPG's secretary that he had "given some of them to several Spanish Prisoners, that were brought into this place by the Privateers."[149] If religious missions to the Apalachees and Yamasees had mixed results, the effort to build institutions to safeguard their rights advanced even as the task facing those institutions proved daunting.

After five years and much political wrangling, Carolina responded to calls for reform, and impaneled a board of planters and traders to hear Natives' complaints. Pursuant to the "Act of Assembly for regulating the Indian Trade and making it safe to the Public," Ralph Izard gaveled to order the first meeting of the Board of Commissioners of the Indian Trade on 20 September 1710.[150] The board commissioned roving agents to inquire into relations between Englishmen and Natives much as visitors did in Spanish Florida. Native leaders and their Carolinian partners had largely replaced Florida's *república de Indios* with a fledgling experiment in Native governance of their own. On the second day of the board's existence, representatives of the "free" Apalachee Indians poured into the room in Charles Town where the commissioners were meeting. The complaints the Apalachees made to the commissioners reveal that they faced the same problems they had in Florida, especially a worrisome leveling of the status of chiefs with that of commoners.

In Carolina, colonists looked on the Apalachees as part of a ready pool of labor, regardless of rank, just as Spaniards in Florida had done near the end. Among other grievances, the Apalachees petitioned against Captain John Musgrove that he "demanded Indians to go and hoe his Corn."[151] Musgrove threatened the Apalachees that "if they did not answer his Demands he would beat them."[152] The Apalachees had tangled with Musgrove before. In December 1706, after he "hindered" the efforts of the "free people of the Apalachees" to "Set down Somewhere on the Savannah River," the "Caciques did Complain or were Coming to Complain to the Governor" against him.[153] John Musgrove's attitude toward the Apalachees was little different than the Florencia family's, who forced the residents of San Luís de Talimali to work without pay and "against their will."[154]

What was most offensive to the Apalachee leaders was the total disregard for chiefly privileges and prerogatives that Musgrove and so many others, from traders to officials, displayed with their demands for labor. Apalachee chiefs were always free from manual labor, complaining quickly—and at times violently—if the Spaniards infringed on their privileges. Apalachee elites tolerated few affronts to their control over their vassals' labor. In later years, accusations flew from Virginia traders about the abuses their Carolina rivals had committed against the Natives. One stands out as particularly galling to the Apalachees. The Virginia trader David Crawley alleged that Carolina's agent John Wright forced "Great numbers only to wait on and Carry his Luggage and packs of Skins from one town to another purely out of Ostentation saying in my hearing he would make them Honor him as their Governor and would be often threatening them and purpose to make them present him with Skins."[155] In short, Wright had usurped the rightful authority of *caciques* and headmen. Yet again, as in Florida, the Apalachees' leaders found themselves in an inferior position and without much hope of improving it. They expected the visiting agent, the Commons House, and the Board of Indian Commissioners to respond, as Thomas Nairne put it, "as the Spaniards always have done," not as the Spaniards like the Florencias had become accustomed in the days before the fall of the missions.

The chances that Carolina would honor its obligations were dwindling by 1715. In the census conducted that year "of all the Indian Nations that were subject to The Government of South Carolina and solely traded with them," 638 Apalachee men, women, and children were living in four towns—in the very midst of their erstwhile Native enemies—140 miles west of Charles Town.[156] A good distance from Charles Town, the Apalachees were not "Mixt with the English Settlements," though that did not prevent English settlers from troubling them.[157] If they were indeed hostages to the surrounding Native nations, the Apalachees did not always behave as such. Despite the distance, Apalachee leaders regularly went to Charles Town and petitioned the colony's leaders for redress.

The campaign the Apalachees waged to reform Carolina had garnered few gains in the decade since they arrived. From the start, the exiled Apalachee *caciques* demanded that the English agree to the terms of the "colonial compact" they had once enjoyed with the Spanish. That the "free" Apalachees repeatedly pursued their demands through legal and political channels may have been a legacy of their Florida past. But the difficult, menial labor Carolinians expected of them, especially long-distance burdening, made ordinary Apalachee men bitter and defiant. Apalachee leaders, desperate to keep up their numbers as the toll from runaways mounted, shared with South Carolina officials their "desire that their People may be restrained from leaving their own Town and going to reside at the Assapallago Town."[158] Some Apalachees, who when they first arrived had boldly absconded with trade goods and killed several slaves of the man who had dragged them to Carolina, were keeping the spirit of resistance alive. Piancho, "an Apalachee Indian," convinced an enslaved Indian boy "to run away" from his master in 1713.[159] Despite ten years of effort to rebuild an ideal of the republic of Indians in Carolina, the lives of Apalachees there were rife with the same abuses and hardships they had left in Florida—only worse. When the time came for a different kind of redress, the Apalachees who remained in Carolina would be ready to fight.

No People Keeps Indians in Such Subjection as the Spaniards

Their chance came in April 1715. The Yamasee War began, appropriately enough, with an unresolved Indigenous petition. That month, a complaint from a Yamasee man, along with dark hints of coming violence, led the traders who heard it to promise "that anything would be done to give them Satisfaction."[160] Messengers from South Carolina Governor Charles Craven soon followed announcing that a delegation of some of the colony's "Chief Men" was on its way to the Upper Yamasee town of Pocotaligo, "to hear and redress their Complaints and Greivances."[161] The governor dispatched James Wright and Thomas Nairne, colonial Indian Agents and inveterate rivals whose contradictory statements and blustery threats at last persuaded the Yamasee council that the only course was to go to war.[162] Florida's governor, Francisco Córcoles y Martínez, meanwhile, heard a very different story from "four ambassadors" who arrived in San Agustín that July.[163] Far from intending to resolve their grievances, "the Governor of San Jorge," in anticipation of a Native uprising, sent his agents "to seek out the Heads and do Justice on them."[164] Natives knowledgeable of "the English idiom" picked up the rumor that Carolina traders planned "to dispose of them, killing the strong men of the great towns."[165] The women and children they would sell to the West Indies, to recoup the debts the Yamasees owed for everything from shotguns to clothes.[166] On Good Friday, 15 April 1715, the Yamasees got a jump on the English. A party of warriors slew the governor's men, including Thomas Nairne.[167] Disagreements about the war's origins led to fresh appraisals of English applications of Spanish colonial models—and in Florida, a turn toward policies reminiscent of English colonizers.

The shock of the Natives' sudden uprising brought hand-wringing and recriminations among the English, especially between Virginians and Carolinians locked since the late seventeenth century in a vicious rivalry for dominance in the deerskin and slave trades.[168] Virginians accused the Carolinians of bringing on the war with their miserliness and rough treatment of their Native allies. The Carolinians fired back that the Virginians had "Encouraged our Indians to Do what they have Done" by pledging to "Supply them at a much Easier Rate than our Indian Traders Did And that they would Give them much better Treatment," including having packhorses to carry the goods.[169] In their debate with the Virginians, Carolinians revealed that their real goal was always the "Subjection" of Natives whom they said were "Naturally Proud."[170] Carolinians defended their perverse semblance of the republic of Indians, where ill-treated Natives carried the weight of colonial ambitions by arguing that "No People keeps their Indians in so much Subjection as the Spaniards and only by Keeping them Poor."[171]

Through with the poverty of colonial subjection, the Apalachees who remained in Carolina fought tenaciously once the war began, giving them a reputation far greater than their numbers alone would seem to merit. For them as for many of their Indigenous comrades in arms, the Yamasee War was no revolt but rather a kind of revolution against colonialism. The abuse of Natives' labor, particularly as long-distance burdeners, received blame as one of the major motivations of the war and no doubt contributed to the Apalachees' choice to fight. "[W]hen they had any Goods to be brought to them out of Carolina or Skins Carried thither they would demand so many men as was able to Do it and if they Refused would beat them," wrote Virginia trader David Crawley.[172] "Burdens they made up for them to Carry were Generally 70 or 80 and some 100 pound weight to Carry 3 or 4 sometimes 500 miles and," in a further violation of the customary rules about burdening, the traders "pay very Little for it."[173] Burdening under heavy loads for hundreds of miles for little pay came to symbolize everything Native men hated about colonial subjection. After a century of such treatment, first from Spaniards and now from Englishmen, the Apalachees were through.

Apalachee warriors endured extreme privation for the cause, living throughout the war only on "a little parched Corn and puddle water."[174] Instead of carrying burdens for Carolina traders, they now "carry all their Estates with them, and are never from home or out of their way."[175] The self-denial of Native warriors that once inspired admiration from Englishmen terrified them now. Such meager sustenance, one Carolinian wrote anxiously, still "fattens them like hogs."[176] Apalachees fought in the war's major campaigns, joining the allied Native coalition in the destruction of dozens of plantations.[177] After ransacking a church, one troop of warriors mysteriously spared it from the torch. The lone building stood amid the ruins of South Carolina as a testament, perhaps, to the Apalachees' restraining hand over their comrades in arms.[178] The Apalachees in Carolina still had faith, just not in any Englishman—or Spaniard, for that matter. The Apalachees of Carolina soon deserted the colony.

The allied warriors' success in the countryside left the colony trembling in terror just as George, the young headman from the Yamasee town of Euhaw, returned from London to Charles Town in September 1715. In many ways the living embodiment of South Carolina's experiment in supplanting Spanish Florida's republic of Indians, George returned to a shattered world. Frightened refugees from the surrounding countryside crowded inside the city's walls as he disembarked. Enemy Native forces raided so close to the city that the inhabitants could not "be supplied with Provisions but by Sea."[179] George hoped to reunite with his family. In a 1716 letter, Francis Le Jau said George's "uncle-father" actively opposed the war and had favored a closer relationship with the English.[180] But rumors soon circulated that "the Yamasees had kill'd 25 of their own Men who would not declare against us, among whom is the honest Father to the young Prince the Commissary carried to England."[181] When the truth arrived, the news was worse. The prince's "uncle-father," who had relocated to San Agustín, was now a slave of the English.[182] With this, the "Yamasee Prince" faded from the historical record. Perhaps, like so many other Natives in the war, George was killed or enslaved. Or he joined with other refugees who left Carolina and resettled near San Agustín and remade himself yet again—this time into a loyal vassal of the king of Spain.[183] If so, he would have met with Spanish officials who harbored very different attitudes toward the king's Indigenous vassals than was the case even a decade before.

The Yamasee War buoyed Spanish hopes of recovering their lost Native vassals and prompted a change in imperial policy toward the same hands-off methods for which they had once criticized the English.[184] In April 1716, King Felipe V issued a decree spelling out the terms of the new colonial compact with the people of the "161 Towns" who had purportedly sworn him allegiance the previous spring. The ambassadors brought a very different form of supplication—a string of knots representing the towns making the request. The knotted string was a material repudiation of the usual kinds of Indigenous petitions to European officials. From hard experience, the Spaniards had finally learned the measure of Native Southerners and the request received an attentive hearing.

The king warned the governor to keep in mind "that the nature of these Indians is very different from that of the rest, for in no part of the Indies are found others of their fortitude, Valor, industry, sagacity, and dexterity in the handling of firearms."[185] For this reason, he commanded that the Natives be "treated with gentleness and sweetness without obligating them to the payment of Tributes."[186] Nor were they to be relocated into missions or subject to harsh correction at the hands of any Spaniard, lay or religious, as in the past. Rather than force the Natives to work, the king ordered an increase in the royal subsidy to Florida to provide the hatchets, cloth, and other goods they coveted. Eventually, the Spaniards hoped their new vassals to settle, where else but in the old Province of Apalachee, "that is the richest and superabundant in fruits and cattle."[187] Instead, most of the Creek and other towns that purportedly swore allegiance to Spain stayed where they were. Many of the people who did move to Florida, including large numbers of Yamasees, lived huddled together on the outskirts of San Agustín, under the walls of the Castillo de San Marcos. For the next half-century, Yamasees, in communities like La Punta on the southern end of the city, fell back on the traditions of the old republic of Indians to survive.[188]

In June 1716, with the future very much in doubt, Carolina's Major James Cochran traveled to the *presidio* to recover property that the Yamasees had plundered and sold to the Spaniards. In the city's marketplace, he met "Several of his own Slaves . . . as also Several other Slaves who told him they belong'd" to the English.[189] They informed Cochran that they "were Carried and Sold to the Spaniards by the . . . Indians—Begging him to Redeem them."[190] Cochran also saw several small boats "which he was informed belonged to his Majesties Subjects."[191] Impatient to fulfill his mission, Cochran went to the house of Florida's governor and "made a Demand according to the Powers Given him" for the restitution of stolen English property.[192] Rather than assist him, the authorities in San Agustín "told him . . . that they had writ to the King of Spain for Directions how to Dispose of" the slaves and other property "and that they could not part with them till they had an Answer."[193] In the eyes of many Carolina officials, the Yamasee War was a revolt—the treacherous act of lawful subjects against their rightful rulers. The Spaniards' "Evasive answers" convinced Cochran of the truth of what many Carolinians suspected—"that the Spanish Government at St. Augustine Did Entice, Stir up and Encourage the Yamasees and other Nations of Indians" to rebel against the English.[194]

An exploration of the deeper political roots of the conflict shows that Cochran and other Carolinians were right—the Spanish did indeed contribute to the outbreak of the Yamasee War —but not in the way that the English believed.[195] At the start of the eighteenth century, even as they destroyed the Spanish missions and enslaved their inhabitants, the English also envied the Spanish method for governing Natives. The English took more than Indigenous slaves and communion plates during their campaign against the missions. They took ideas. Even after repeated petitions, Natives received no redress from colonial officials, but only answers that were sometimes worse than the problems themselves. English dreams of order based on Spanish models of governance would clash directly with Native political aspirations for sovereignty. Native peoples like the Apalachees, who had endured both Spanish and English colonialism and their often-hollow promises of justice, were exasperated with both by 1715, and ready to push them aside.

Conclusion: They Made Us Their Tributaries

The repercussions of the Yamasee War, the great revolution the Apalachees had joined, reverberated up and down eastern North America. Virginia's tributary Natives felt the tremors. When the war broke out, Lieutenant Governor Alexander Spotswood was in the middle of overhauling the colony's tributary regime. Spotswood envisioned a multigenerational plan to establish a republic of Indians on the frontier, with Native peoples from far afield dutifully becoming royal subjects and Christians. Combining missionary education with the strategy of reducing tributary Natives into new towns under closer English surveillance, Spotswood's plans resembled elements of both contemporary Spanish colonialism in Florida and of Thomas Nairne's ill-starred plans for Carolina. Indeed, the plan to make missionaries into roving justices of the peace in order to resolve conflicts between tributary Natives and settlers was precisely along the lines Nairne once proposed.[196] Unlike his fellow English imperialists, Thomas Nairne or John Lawson in the Carolinas, Spotswood managed to put most of his ideas into practice—at least until controversies over which colonists would benefit from Virginia's Indian trade squelched them. At Fort Christanna on the southwestern edge of Virginia, Spotswood posted a missionary and built a school for the children of Native tributary leaders.[197] Although the lieutenant governor has received most of the credit and the blame for this scheme, the Virginia reforms were as much of a cocreation between the English and Virginia Native peoples as the short-lived developments in Carolina had been.[198] Some Indigenous leaders embraced tributary status for the first time as a way to protect themselves from dispossession and slavery.[199] Even so, the relationship between Virginia and the tributaries was tense at times, especially when it came to giving up their children to English tutelage.[200] When a nation like the Nottoways sought protection, they did not surrender their rights, and were quick to let the English know it.

Fears that the Yamasee War would turn into a general "Indian Revolt" gave Spotswood an excuse to curtail the tributaries' privileges.[201] "I have upon some just Suspicions of one of the most Considerable Nations of our Tributaries," he alerted Secretary Stanhope back in England, "who keep a Correspondence with foreign Indians, found it necessary to have them disarmed, which will be speedily put in Execution."[202] Spotswood's heavy hand did not go unchallenged. The Nottoways, for one, chided the House of Burgesses in

August 1715 for the ill treatment they received. For the "trust reposed in us" the Nottoways had "always been at variance and envied almost by all nations of Indians and reduced to a Small Number, wholly relying on this Government for their favor and protection."[203] The Nottoways hoped the "House will take our Distressed Condition into Consideration and grant us all our former Rights and privileges and that we may be admitted to live on and hold our Lands according to law."[204]

While tributary Natives like the Nottoways would cling ever tighter to the promises of the protective tributary relationship in enclaves across the South, the Yamasee War shattered long-held English aspirations for an empire of Native subjects in the Southeastern interior. Whether the Indigenous towns of the interior really saw themselves as part of some larger polity with the English before the Yamasee War is difficult to tell—and perhaps unlikely. For most of the "Eight and twenty thousand" Indigenous peoples said to be "Subject to the Government of South Carolina in 1715," the answer was almost certainly no.[205] Nor were the Creeks who purportedly proffered their obedience to the Spanish king much inclined to vassalage. The Cherokees, who eventually allied with Charles Town against the colony's enemies, including the Creeks, showed little deference either. The Carolinians felt this fact acutely as the Native "Rebellion" dragged on into its second year. As they contemplated the price of peace, the Carolinians felt the sting of their fall from imperial heights. The gifts that Carolinians would need to seal an alliance with the Cherokees against the colony's Indian enemies were enough to complete the colonial overthrow. "For the last time the Cherokees were here, they Insulted us to the last degree, And Indeed by their demands (with which were forced to comply)," worst and most telling of all, "they made us their Tributaries."[206]

In the aftermath of the war, the only Indigenous vassals and subjects left in Florida, the Carolinas, and Virginia lived relatively close to European settlements. During the eighteenth century, the condition of Natives surrounding San Agustín and the "settlement Indians" in Carolina and Virginia were most alike. Smaller in numbers, poorer, usually meeting little but contempt in the glances of their colonial neighbors, they were also survivors whose stories have long been overshadowed by the rise of the larger Southern Native nations like the Creeks and Cherokees. After 1715, it was these Native peoples—Guales, Yamasees, Chowans, Nottoways, Pamunkeys—who kept the traditions of the republic of Indians alive.

This fact leads us to a monumental historical irony: after 1764, when the Spanish evacuated San Agustín, relocating surviving "mission Indians" to

Cuba, the few places where the principles of the "Republic of Indians" lived on in the Southeast were not in Spanish Florida, but in Tidewater Virginia and northeastern North Carolina where Native tributaries still invoked them in their petitions. The tradition lives on to this day, when every November, leaders of the Pamunkey and Mattaponi nations present the governor of Virginia their "tribute-tax," in keeping with the treaties of 1646 and 1677 and in service to the ideal of distinct sovereign commonwealths joined under a shared law.[207]

The Authors of Their Sovereignty

One morning, in about the year 1730, Thomas Hoyter rose before sunup in his cabin near Bennett's Creek. Hoyter donned the scarlet coat of a military officer, earned in one of "Eight expeditions against the Indian Enemies" of North Carolina.[1] His "Soldiers red Coat, Waistcoat, and Breeches" Hoyter reserved for grand occasions and the times when business called him southward through Chowan precinct to Edenton, the colonial capital.[2] He put on that uniform maybe once or twice in a year—more often when Hoyter needed to sell land or sue a troublesome neighbor. For Hoyter, the journey that day was a "State Visit" with his whole family—wife, brothers, children, and kin—joining him on his progress to trade deerskins in town "for *Blankets, Guns, Powder, Shot, Ball*, and other Necessaries."[3] Since time out of mind, the easiest way to travel was by boat. Paddling a dugout canoe or sailing a shallow-draft periauger down the Chowan River, Hoyter and his kin might have spied the imposing plantation seats—including Colonel William Maule's, who once surveyed Hoyter's lands—that stood overlooking the shore. But by the 1730s, the ancient precincts of North Carolina were crisscrossed with narrow, sandy roads, rickety wooden bridges, and, over the wider rivers, ferries. From his cabin inland on a fork in the creek, Hoyter could take the road that linked "Chowan to Nansemond in Virginia" straight to town.[4]

Riding the public highway to Edenton, Thomas Hoyter would have beheld the profound changes in the land north of Albemarle Sound since the first Englishmen began to colonize there in earnest during the middle of the seventeenth century. For one thing, there were more Englishmen, many more, and all of them clambering for plots of their own. North of the road was the Blanchards' place and farther along, the Spiveys'. As he nosed his mount into the highway, perhaps Captain Hoyter cast a sour glance their way. The Blanchards had coveted Hoyter's land for years. They had squatted on it and, at the beginning of the century, they had come to blows over it. In 1702, the boundary dispute broke into open fighting. Benjamin Blanchard and Thomas Spivey—with a gang of neighboring planters—accused Hoyter's people of "menacing and threatening" them and "destroying their Stocks burning their houses and other hostilities."[5] Hoyter and his kin shot back that the lands were theirs and nobody else's. Even fifteen years after, the feud still ran hot. Two more of the Blanchard clan—Ephraim and Aaron—had tried to carve out a piece of Hoyter's land for themselves in 1717, pretending to the government that they had the owner's leave to take it.[6]

On the road south, Hoyter would have passed an Anglican "Chapel," one of the "chapels of ease" that served Tidewater planters there and in Virginia, perhaps recalling long theological discussions he had had with its one-time minister.[7] During the Tuscarora War, when men and women had huddled together into blockhouses for shelter from their "Indian Enemies," a multitude had crowded the chapel to hear a sermon from the Anglican missionary, Giles Rainsford. They had found no solace in his words and "expressed very little or rather no devotion in time of divine Service."[8] The preoccupations of war, not the style of the parson, were likely to blame. "I like the Country far better than any I have hitherto seen," Rainsford wrote later to his superiors in London, "and certainly by nature tis one of the best in the world and were but the Inhabitants freed from the dangers of the War they might enjoy the blessings of plenty as well as all other comforts of life."[9] The Hoyters eventually took the stranger in and let him live with their people on Bennett's Creek for five months after the war with the Tuscarora ended.[10] They passed the time arguing over sacred history, recounting the origins of mankind and the story of Noah's flood. Now, as Hoyter's party traveled onward past the chapel, the road ran straight and narrow and even the most experienced travelers found it rough going. The roads were paved with sand, and the hooves of Hoyter's mounts would have slipped and sunk into the roadway or stumbled on hidden roots.[11] Even on the main road, there was little to guide them, not even the crudest mile markers to tell them the decreasing distance to the capital.[12]

Hoyter and his family at last entered Edenton, where a "Dirty Slash" traced the bounds of the colonial capital. In the summers, the ditch was a "foul annoyance, and furnishes abundance of that Carolina Plague, Mosquitos."[13] Travelers deplored the town's unhealthy climate, describing Edenton as a "regular fever nest and lies very low."[14] In the malarial lowlands between the "Dirty Slash" and Albemarle Sound stood maybe fifty houses "most of them Small, and built without Expense." William Byrd II, who came

through town in 1728, observed that, in Edenton, a man's neighbors counted
it a great extravagance should he have "Ambition enough to aspire to a Brick-
chimney."[15] Public buildings were few. The council and assembly met on a
rotating basis in the homes of the colony's leading men. "Justice herself is but
indifferently Lodged," Byrd noted, "the Court-House having much the Air of
a common Tobacco House."[16] Life in Edenton was not without its excitements
or its pageantry. Thomas Hoyter's entrance to town that day was a spectacle
for the curious bystander. The captain's errand was no ordinary visit and he
was no ordinary man.

Hoyter was the headman, and to the English, the "king" of the Chowan
Indians. John Brickell, an Irish traveler and physician, watched as Hoyter
arrived at the governor's house with "his *Queen, Children, Physician, Captains of War*, and his *Guards*" in train.[17] The "Guards were well Armed, with
each Man a Gun, good store of Powder and Ball, and a *Tamahawk* by his side,
which is a kind of small *Hatchet*."[18] Hoyter's "Retinue" befitted his station.[19]
At the governor's house, he rendezvoused with the other "*Indian Kings* in
this Province, who are civilized" and who had brought their own attendants
dressed in garb just as dazzling.[20] Together they delivered deerskins as tribute
and joined the governor for dinner. The "small Tribute," Brickell explained,
was "an Acknowledgment of their Subjection."[21] After dinner, the "Kings"
rejoined their companions and went to trade in town. On the street, Hoyter
and the Chowan delegation performed what Brickell called "the *Indian War*
[dance] . . . Hooping and Hollowing . . . while stamping altogether like Mad-
men."[22] The Chowans and the other tributary Natives present were likely
demonstrating the military skills they used during the war and making
a show of unity with the colonial government. It was a pledge of renewed
loyalty and an affirmation of their duty as defenders of the colonists, "ready
upon all occasions to assist them when ever they are required so to do."[23]

Thomas Hoyter was one of many Southern Native leaders—like the
Pamunkey queens Anne and Betty or the *cacique* of Nombre de Dios Chiquito, Don Francisco Jospogue—who kept the traditions of the republic of
Indians alive long after the main fighting in the Yamasee War ended in 1717.
All of them continued to be political players even as they lived in shrinking enclaves amidst the English and Spanish or as residents themselves
inside colonial towns.[24] By the eighteenth century, the condition of tributary
Natives or so-called "Settlement Indians" in the English colonies and the lives
of the Guales, Yamasees, and other Natives living by the walls of San Agustín
were virtually the same, as were their political strategies. Hoyter and the

other leaders who stuck fast to their status as tributaries, subjects, and vassals within wider empires did not take that legal condition for granted. In court appearances, conferences with governors, and especially in their numerous petitions they defined their subjecthood in terms more copious than colonial officials sometimes might have wished. Natives wielded petitions not just to fight off trespassers, squatters, and poverty, but they used them to argue about their place in the colonial world. In so doing, Southern Native petitioners continued to influence and even shape the policies that came to govern relations between themselves and the colonists.[25]

Eighteenth-century Southern Native petitioners took part in a wider regional culture of Native pleas, one that cut across colonial jurisdictions and Indigenous political boundaries to share forms and strategies in common. In the hands of Native people, even long after the era of the Yamasee War, petitioning served to hone political and legal thought, change policies and laws, and, ultimately, define ties such as the tributary relationship in ways more beneficial to themselves. Long after the republic of Indians was overthrown in Florida, the Chowans and Natives like them kept some of the old principles alive.

Of all the memorials the Chowans presented, none was as forceful or more revealing as the "humble petition of John Hoyter Indian," dating to sometime between 1703 and 1705, to have his people's land resurveyed and properly bounded.[26] John Hoyter, Thomas Hoyter's predecessor as Chowan "king," closed his plea by reminding the council—whose seat stood on the banks of a river and in a precinct that bore the name of his people, in a land he was pledged to defend—that "he is not a stranger nor a foreigner but in his own Native place."[27]

John Hoyter's 1705 plea fits into the larger pattern for Indigenous petitions in the southern colonies by striking a pose of humility, presenting his demands as a return on the services he and his people rendered the colony, and proposing specific legislative or executive action—in his case, an order from North Carolina's Executive Council to survey and establish the boundaries of the Chowans' land. Hoyter's petition was conventional in many ways, resounding with language familiar from other petitions from people in similar circumstances at the time. In 1728, Don Francisco Jospogue of the Guale refugee town of Nombre de Dios Chiquito placed himself figuratively "at Your Majesty's Royal Feet," adding how he had "grown old" in the service of his king.[28] Such rhetoric is unsurprising in Spanish-language Indigenous petitions, but it was common in English-language ones too. The Pamunkey

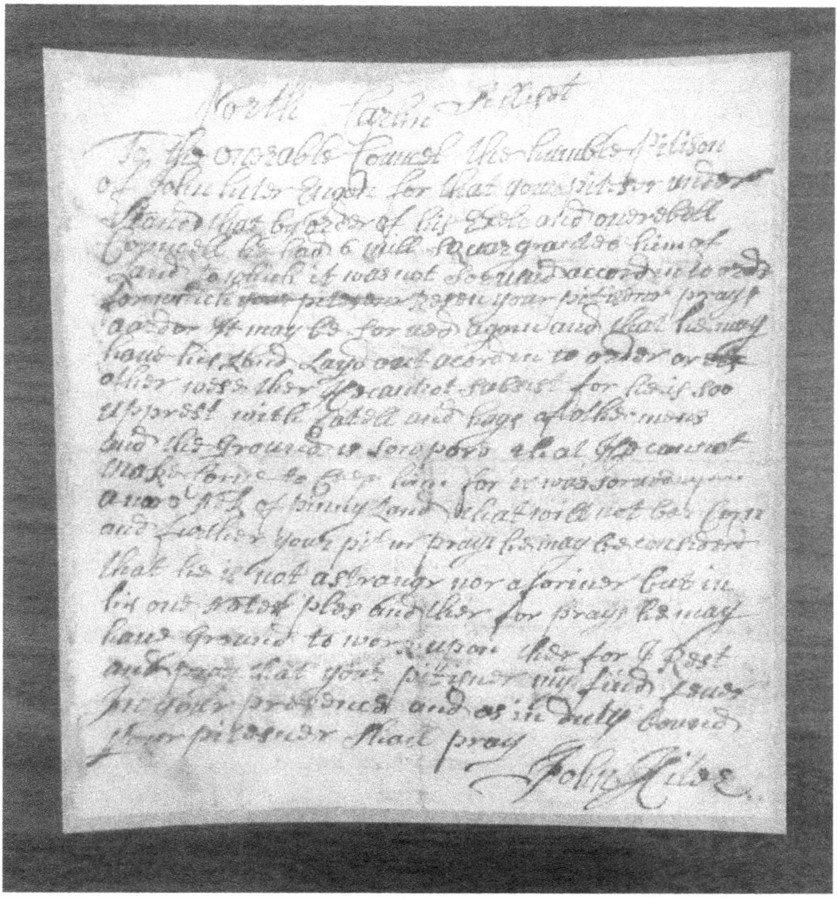

Figure 10. The Petition of John Hoyter, ca. 1705, CCR 187, North Carolina State Archives.

queen and "Great men" petitioned in 1708 for a reduction in their annual tribute "with all humility and submission."[29] In 1715, the Pamunkeys again wrote that they were but "a small poor nation" who "wholly leave ourselves to your Honor's Justice, Counsel and favor."[30] But they made demands all the same. Tributary Indians and Spanish Indigenous vassals of the era both had lost much in service to the republic of Indians. The Chowans' fields and fruit trees were ravaged during the Tuscarora War while they were out fighting the enemy.[31] In Florida, Don Francisco Jospogue fared even worse. Don

Francisco's petition for a soldier's *plaza* for himself and his heirs recounted a life of harrowing service and sacrifice "from the age of twenty-five years" all spent "fighting . . . the infidel enemy Indians who, led by the English, intended to destroy" Florida.[32] While out "on campaign with my people," enemy Natives attacked his town and captured his wife and four children.[33] After failing to entice Jospogue to their side, his enemies "sold my wife and children to distant nations, where they perished."[34] With its insistence on receiving justice for the hardships they had endured, the Chowans' 1705 petition followed the pattern, but differed in the terms Hoyter invoked to describe his status.

The Chowan leader did not choose his terms lightly and each one— *stranger, foreigner, native*—had deep historic meanings for Natives and colonizers, stretching back centuries. The choice Hoyter made stems from deeper conceptions of identity that sprang from the Chowans' connections with the land and their history, ties that he may have believed superseded other legal distinctions. In their petitions, they tried to hold colonists to a higher standard of justice, one that did not dismiss Natives as "strangers" and "foreigners" but included them as equal subjects in their "own Native place."[35] Although Hoyter's words resound now, they did not make much impression on the colonists of his day.

To colonial officials and to generations of the colonists' descendants, the Chowans seemed to have dwindled away, leaving only a name behind. By the mid-eighteenth century, Governor Arthur Dobbs, searching for Native warriors to serve in the war with the French, learned that there was "but one Indian Nation in Chowan County . . . But their Strength is Nothing, and their Condition very Deplorable By the Artifice and Cunning of Some of their Neighbors."[36] Dobbs's report had it right that the "Artifice and Cunning" of the surrounding settlers had proved impossible to restrain. Colonial North Carolina remained too uncivilized for "Civilized *Indians*."[37] In 1755, another report suggested that there were only seven Chowans left—two men and five women.[38] In 1792, the last of the reservation lands were sold. According to the petition of the white buyers who were seeking the North Carolina General Assembly's approval for the sale, William Lewis and Samuel Harrell, the Chowans "did in the late contest with Great Britain behave themselves as good and faithful soldiers in behalf of this and the United States."[39] Such sales should have been the purview of the federal government, but states in the new United States often assumed or claimed sole jurisdiction over Native peoples like the Chowans whose nations fell within their boundaries.[40] Ten years before, the Robbins family purchased thirty acres of land, holding it communally with other Chowans and Chowan descendants, and which local Anglo-American residents called "Indian Town."[41] The family and their fellow Chowans held possession of "Indian Town" until 1821, when an adverse court ruling in a case forced the land's sale at auction.[42] The story of the Chowans, however, was hardly over. From the nineteenth century to the present, Chowan descendants continued to live in the region, well aware of their Native heritage, and still fighting for their rights, just as John and Thomas Hoyter did.[43] Recently, members of the Chowanoke Nation purchased 146 acres of land on the former reservation near Bennett's Creek.[44]

The descendants of the people who dispossessed them forgot the history of the Chowans and the republic of Indians they struggled to maintain. Instead, in 1912, white residents engraved a marble plaque with fanciful stories about the "faithful friends and allies of the whites" who "migrated" to live with the Haudenosaunee.[45] The monument still stands inside the Chowan County courthouse in Edenton. The courthouse, completed in 1767, is today one of the oldest public buildings still in use in the United States. The Georgian facade, topped with a cupola and clock, was a stately replacement for the "common Tobacco House" of yesteryear.[46] The slab of marble honoring Chowan County's Indigenous namesakes was the work of Tribe no. 12 of the Improved Order of Red Men (a white fraternal society) who dedicated the plaque to the "Chowanock Indians always faithful friends and allies of the whites."[47]

Neither "friends" nor "allies" adequately captured the fullest sense of the relationship between the Chowans and the colony of North Carolina—or indeed, of the relationship other tributaries, subjects, and vassals had with colonizers across the region and through the centuries. They had, in fact, attempted to forge a mutual order in which their lands and political authority would be respected. The Chowans and English may not have established all the ties that Natives, or English, for that matter, believed were necessary to bind peoples together most effectively. They had not intermarried extensively, it was true. But in the seventeenth and eighteenth centuries, they had nevertheless joined together in a new and larger community, making them into something far more than strangers or foreigners. At a time when such possibilities were supposedly foreclosed, the Chowans and other tributary Natives had demanded the protection of law as subjects while retaining their distinct polities and liberties.

The traces of that history and what it meant were difficult to discern by the twentieth century. As one writer put it a year after the plaque honoring

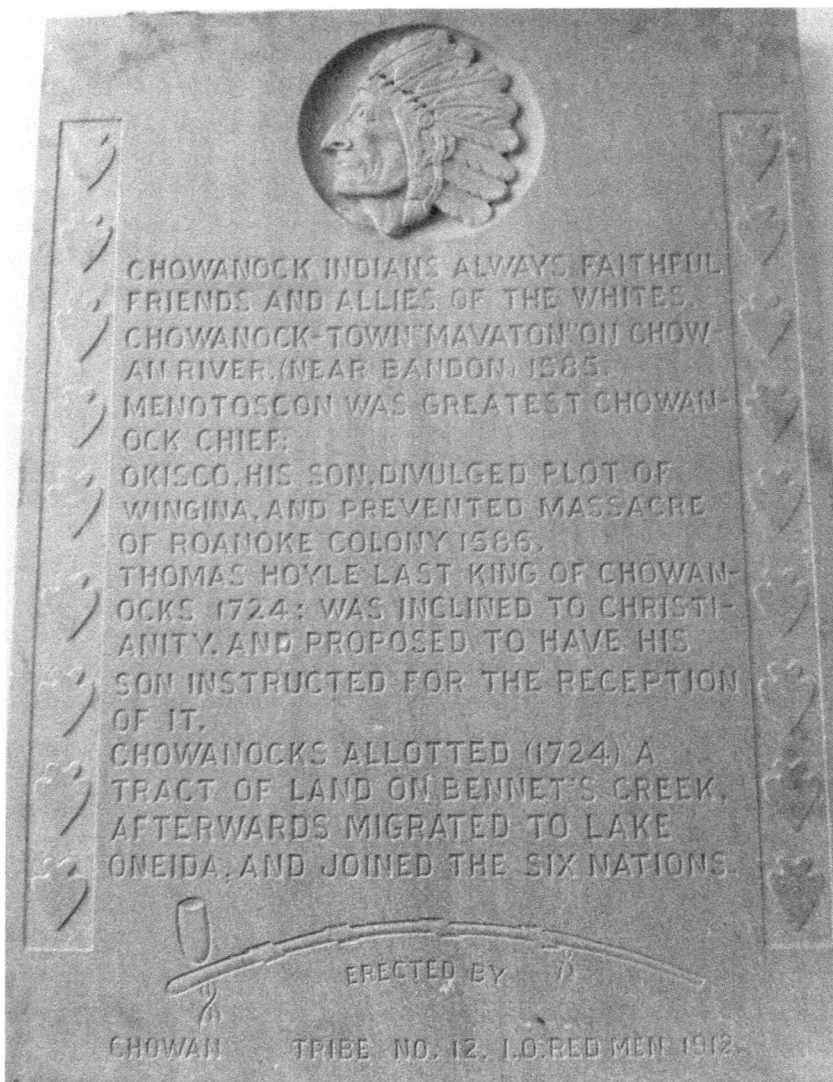

Figure 11. The Chowan Plaque, Chowan County Courthouse. Photograph by Kim Caroselli Dixon.

the Chowan Nation went up in the Chowan County courthouse, "the American mind could conceive a republic but not an Indian."[48] Others saw the history differently if still only partially, for all of their good intentions. Writing in the midst of World War II, Felix M. Cohen, legal architect of the Indian New Deal, looked to the history of imperial competition between Britain and Spain for the source of the principles—self-government, equality, federal sovereignty, and protection—he believed ran through federal Indian law.[49] Cohen's monumental *Handbook of Federal Indian Law* was a book worthy of the great seventeenth-century jurists Antonio de León Pinelo and Juan de Solórzano y Pereira, who had tried to systematize their own "maze" of royal decrees into an organized body, a truly comprehensive *Derecho Indiano* for the Spanish Empire. The *Handbook* became more than a United-Statesian *Recopilación*, instead serving as the guide for a generation of American Indians who studied it "by kerosene light in log cabins" and became "as competent in the niceties of legal fictions as most attorneys."[50] In an article in 1942, Cohen claimed "that the humane principles which guide our own law in Indian affairs all faithfully follow the teachings of Spanish theologians and the edicts of Spanish kings."[51] He left out the other people whose counsels swayed the kings.

This book began by equating the work of writing history to an imperial performance review, a Spanish-style *residencia*, not for the living but for the dead. History is a kind of *residencia* for the dead and the witnesses never get any rest. Cohen summoned them to find the origins of what he thought was "humane" in federal Indian law. Numerous scholars and historians after him have assumed the answer to the question depended upon the actions of settlers, the decrees of kings, and the exalted language of papal bulls. I was one of them. When I set out to conduct my *residencia* for the dead, I laid a number of charges specifically at the feet of European colonizers. I understood the matter in terms of what colonizers—especially the English—had done or failed to do, how they had excluded Natives from full membership in the body politic, how they had curbed Native political participation, or never truly regarded any Indian as a subject with rights. What I found instead was that Indigenous leaders were the decisive actors and they refused to be shoved aside.

Time and again, even in the face of the evidence of broken promises, high-handed treatment, and downright lies, Indigenous leaders in the South kept coming back, kept holding colonizers to the letter of the law. Although

its contours became virtually invisible during the eighteenth and early nineteenth centuries, Native leaders like Cockacoeske of Pamunkey and Santiago
of Tolomato forged a political tradition that included Indians in some of the
rights of citizenship as the early modern world defined them. Petitioning, a
right precious to Englishmen and Spaniard alike, became a powerful instrument in the hands of Native Americans who used formal complaints to protect hard-won privileges and even to create new ones in law. Treaties, "articles
of peace," capitulations, and ceremonies of allegiance, rather than symbols of
submission were in fact constitutions, the founding documents—written or
remembered—for shared systems of politics and law.

   If American Indian law embodies any humane principles, they are the
ones Indigenous people engraved into it with their words. If any empire had
a claim to benevolence, it was only to the extent that its Indigenous subjects
rewrote its laws. When they said their lands came from their forefathers,
they were reminding colonists that theirs were not mere claims to land but
established ownership through generations back to time immemorial. When
they appealed to distant kings as the source of their privileges, liberties, and
immunities, they were placing those treasured legal gains on a higher plane,
beyond the reach of grasping settlers. The thinkers who gave the concept of
sovereignty its fullest meaning in the seventeenth and early eighteenth centuries were "exiguous" nations of tributaries, loyal vassals of Spain, and "royal
subjects" of England's Crown. They never used the word as we would today.
Petitioners instead wrote in terms of inviolable ties to their homes, ties that
came with the right to govern themselves. God gave us these lands, said the
caciques of *Nombre de Dios* in Florida. We lived free in the old days under
our own laws, wills, and order, declared the Chickahominy *manguys*. I am
in my own native place, wrote the Chowan headman John Hoyter. Among
the authors of modern tribal sovereignty were Indigenous petitioners whom
European empires seldom considered to be sovereigns at all.

ABBREVIATIONS

AGI	Archivo General de Indias, Seville
CO 1	The Colonial Papers
CO 5	Colonial Letterbooks and Entry Books
CRNC	William L. Saunders et al., eds., *The Colonial and State Records of North Carolina* (Raleigh: 1886–1907).
CRSF	Jeanette Thurber Connor, trans., *The Colonial Records of Spanish Florida: Letters of Governors and Secular Persons*, 2 vols. (Deland, FL: The Florida Historical Society, 1925).
EC	Escribanía de Cámara
EJCCV	H. R. McIlwaine et al., eds., *Executive Journals of the Council of Colonial Virginia* (Richmond: Virginia State Library, 1925–1966).
INDIFERENTE	Indiferente General
JCHA	Alexander S. Salley, ed., *The Journals of the Commons House of Assembly of South Carolina* (Columbia, SC: 1907–1949).
JCIT	W. L. McDowell, ed., *Journals of the Commissioners of the Indian Trade, September 20, 1710–August 29, 1718* (Columbia: South Carolina Archives Department, 1955).
JHBV	H. R. McIlwaine, ed., *Journals of the House of Burgesses of Virginia* (Richmond: 1905–1915).
JHC	John H. Hann Collection
JTCC	Jeanette Thurber Connor Collection
JWC	John E. Worth Collection
MEX	México
PARES	Portal de Archivos Españoles
PKY	P. K. Yonge Library of Florida History, The University of Florida, Gainesville

RECNC	Robert J. Cain, ed., *Records of the Executive Council, 1664–1734* (Raleigh, NC: Division of Archives and History, 1984).
RVC	Susan Myra Kingsbury, ed., *The Records of the Virginia Company of London* (Washington, DC: Government Printing Office, 1906–1935).
SC	The John B. Stetson Collection
SCBPRO	A. S. Salley, Jr., ed., *Records in the British Public Record Office Relating to South Carolina*, 37 vols. (Atlanta, GA: Printed for the Historical Commission of South Carolina by Foote & Davies Company, 1928–1955).
SCDAH	South Carolina Department of Archives and History, Columbia
SD	Santo Domingo
Statutes	W. W. Hening, ed., *The Statutes at Large; Being a Collection of all the Laws of Virginia* [. . .] (New York: 1819–1823).
UKNA	The United Kingdom National Archives, Kew
VMHB	*The Virginia Magazine of History and Biography*
WBP	Warren M. Billings, ed., *The Papers of Sir William Berkeley, 1605–1677* (Richmond: Library of Virginia, 2007).
WLC	Woodbury Lowery Collection

NOTES

Prologue

1. Whenever possible, I have consulted the original sources. Translations are my own unless otherwise noted. Despite personally reveling in the variations of early modern language, for the sake of clarity and so that the Spanish translations and English quotations are all on the same footing in the reader's mind, I have modernized all English spelling, substituted "and" for "&," and expanded all abbreviations including the letter thorn, represented as "y." The only "archaic" forms I have retained are the quirks of capitalization and the italics found in printed books of the time. Titles of documents, when provided and used in the notes, retain their original spellings. All references to materials housed in the Archivo General de Indias in Seville have been converted to the post-1929 numbering system according to the guidelines provided in Paul E. Hoffman, "Table for Converting the Legajo Numbers Found on Photostats of the John B. Stetson, Jr., Collection of Documents Relating to the History of Spanish Florida" (unpublished manuscript, Gainesville, FL: [s.n.], 1968).

2. Hening, ed., *Statutes*, 1: 402; The Richahecrians became better known as the Westos. For more, see Eric E. Bowne, *The Westo Indians: Slave Traders of the Early Colonial South* (Tuscaloosa: University of Alabama Press, 2005), 72–75.

3. Throughout, my spellings for the names of peoples and places in Tsenacomacoh follow those found in Martin D. Gallivan, *The Powhatan Landscape: An Archaeological History of the Algonquian Chesapeake* (Gainesville: University Press of Florida, 2016), xxii.

4. For more on Totopotomoy's motivations, see Hayley Negrin, "Cockacoeske's Rebellion: Nathaniel Bacon, Indigenous Slavery, and Sovereignty in Early Virginia," *William and Mary Quarterly*, vol. 80, no. 1 (January 2023): 56; Martha McCartney, "Cockacoeske, Queen of Pamunkey: Diplomat and Suzerain," in *Powhatan's Mantle: Indians in the Colonial Southeast*, ed. Gregory A. Waselkov, Peter H. Wood, and Tom Hatley (Lincoln: University of Nebraska Press, 2006), 245; For the commemoration, see Frederic W. Gleach, *Powhatan's World and Colonial Virginia: A Conflict of Cultures* (Lincoln: University of Nebraska Press, 1997), 189–190.

5. For descriptions and analyses of the Timucua Revolt of 1656, see Alejandra Dubcovsky, *Informed Power: Communication in the Early American South* (Cambridge, MA: Harvard University Press, 2016), 68–96; Jerald T. Milanich, *Laboring in the Fields of the Lord: Spanish Missions and Southeastern Indians* (Washington, DC: Smithsonian Institution Press, 1999), 128, 161–164; John E. Worth, *The Timucuan Chiefdoms of Spanish Florida*, 2 vols. (Gainesville: University Press of Florida, 1998), 2: 38–65; Amy Turner Bushnell, *Situado and Sabana: Spain's Support System for Florida*, Anthropological Papers of the American Museum of Natural History 74 (New York: American Museum of Natural History, 1994), 128–133; John H. Hann, *Apalachee: The Land Between the Rivers* (Gainesville: University of Florida Press, 1988), 18–23.

6. Fray Juan Gómez to Fray Francisco Martínez, 13 March 1657, AGI SD 225, PKY, SC, reel 12.

7. Gómez to Martínez, 13 March 1657, AGI SD 225, PKY, SC, reel 12.

8. Fray Juan Gómez to Fray Francisco Martínez, 4 April 1657, AGI SD 225, PKY, SC, reel 12.

9. Gómez to Martínez, 13 March 1657, AGI SD 225, PKY, SC, reel 12.

10. Queen Cockacoeske to Francis Moryson, 29 June 1678, UKNA CO 1/42, no. 101, fol. 273r.

11. "*Swanne's Point* in *Virginia, June* 11," *London Gazette*, no. 1221 (30 July–2 August 1677). Original in the John Carter Brown Library.

12. Dubcovsky, *Informed Power*, 80–82.

13. Religious of Florida to the King, 10 September 1657, AGI SD 235, PKY, WLC, vol. 7, microfilm copy; John H. Hann translates this evocatively as "he also held a residencia for the dead." John H. Hann, trans., "Visitations and Revolts, 1656–1695," *Florida Archaeology* no. 7 (1993): 14.

14. For more, see Dubcovsky, *Informed Power*, 83–84.

15. Hening, ed., *Statutes*, 1: 422.

16. Adrian Masters has shown that ordinary people, notably Native petitioners, were effectively lawmakers within the Spanish Empire. This insight has broader applications to other regimes, including the English colonies. Adrian Masters, "A Thousand Invisible Architects: Vassals, the Petition and Response System, and the Creation of Spanish Imperial Caste Legislation," *Hispanic American Historical Review*, vol. 98, no. 3 (August 2018), 377–406.

17. The petite nations of Louisiana offer another useful point of comparison with Natives living "behind the frontier" in the English and Spanish colonies. Daniel H. Usner, "Chitimacha Diplomacy and Commerce in Colonial Louisiana," *Louisiana History: The Journal of the Louisiana Historical Association*, vol. 62, no. 2 (Spring 2021): 133–176; Elizabeth N. Ellis, "The Natchez War Revisited: Violence, Multinational Settlements, and Indigenous Diplomacy in the Lower Mississippi Valley," *William and Mary Quarterly*, 3d ser., vol. 77, no. 3 (July 2020): 441–472; Elizabeth N. Ellis, "Petite Nation with Powerful Networks: The Tunicas in the Eighteenth Century," *Louisiana History: The Journal of the Louisiana Historical Association*, vol. 58, no. 2 (Spring 2017): 133–178. The phrase "behind the frontier" comes from Daniel R. Mandell, *Behind the Frontier: Indians in Eighteenth-Century Massachusetts* (Lincoln: The University of Nebraska Press, 1996).

18. Numerous works have invited historians to think of key sites in North American history as part of either a Spanish periphery or (Spanish-dominated) circum-Caribbean. The trend was accelerating even as I finished the book. See the joint issue, "Colonial Roots/Routes in North America and Latin America" of the *William and Mary Quarterly*, vol. 80, no. 2 (April 2023) and the *Hispanic American Historical Review*, vol. 103, no. 2 (May 2023). See also the essays in Jorge Cañizares-Esguerra, ed., *Entangled Empires: The Anglo-Iberian Atlantic, 1500–1830* (Philadelphia: University of Pennsylvania Press, 2018); Anna Brickhouse, "Hemispheric Jamestown," in *Hemispheric American Studies*, ed. Robert S. Levine and Caroline Field Levander (New Brunswick, NJ: Rutgers University Press, 2008), 18–35; Eliga H. Gould, "Entangled Histories, Entangled Worlds: The English-Speaking Atlantic as a Spanish Periphery," *American Historical Review*, vol. 112, no. 3 (June 2007): 764–786; J. H. Elliott, "The Iberian Atlantic and Virginia," in *The Atlantic World and Virginia, 1550–1624*, ed. Peter C. Mancall (Chapel Hill: University of North Carolina Press, 2007), 541–557; Jorge Cañizares-Esguerra, *Puritan Conquistadors: Iberianizing the Atlantic, 1550–1700* (Stanford, CA: Stanford University Press, 2006),

esp. 215–233; April Lee Hatfield, "Spanish Colonization Literature, Powhatan Geographies, and English Perceptions of Tsenacommacah/Virginia," *Journal of Southern History*, vol. 69, no. 2 (May 2003), 245–282.

19. In the time between defending my dissertation and revising this book, scholars have challenged and reconceptualized the classic "two republics" model usually associated with Magnus Mörner, and, in the process, have revolutionized how we think about lawmaking in the Spanish Empire—indeed, in all empires. Adrian Masters, *We, the King: Creating Royal Legislation in the Sixteenth-Century Spanish New World* (New York: Cambridge University Press, 2023); Karen Graubart, *Republics of Difference: Religious and Racial Self-Governance in the Spanish Atlantic World* (New York: Oxford University Press, 2022). For a review of the multiplicity of ways sixteenth- and seventeenth-century Spaniards described the "republics" of the Americas and for more on the "Mörner Thesis" and its critics, see Adrian Masters, "The Two, the One, the Many, the None: Rethinking the Republics of Spaniards and Indians in the Sixteenth-Century Spanish Indies," *Americas*, vol. 78, no. 1 (January 2021), 3–36. For the rise of communal sovereignty among Andeans that also redefined the meaning of republic, see S. Elizabeth Penry, *The People Are King: The Making of an Indigenous Andean Politics* (New York: Oxford University Press, 2019); Max Deardorff, "Republics, Their Customs, and the Law of the King: Convivencia and Self-Determination in the Crown of Castile and its American Territories, 1400–1700," *Rechtsgeschichte – Legal History*, vol. 26 (2018), 162–199. An important influence on my understanding of the republic of Indians remains Amy Turner Bushnell, "Ruling 'the Republic of Indians' in Seventeenth-Century Florida," in *Powhatan's Mantle*, ed. Waselkov, Wood, and Hatley, 195–213.

20. "Narragansett Sachems and 'Squa Queen' of the Narragansetts," UKNA CO 1/44, no. 49.

21. For a similar legacy of political participation in another portion of what is now the continental United States, see Maurice Crandal, *These People Have Always Been a Republic: Indigenous Electorates in the U.S.-Mexico Borderlands, 1598–1912* (Chapel Hill: University of North Carolina Press, 2019).

22. This is ultimately where I come down in the debate concerning the nature of the republics in the Spanish Empire. There was a larger republic of Indians distinct from the republic of Spaniards and that larger republic of Indians was comprised of many little republics. See Graubart, *Republics of Difference*, 137; Masters, "Two, One, Many, None," *Americas*, 35 (quotation); For towns, see Deardorff, "Republics," passim. See also Bushnell's comment on the recent historiography in Amy Turner Bushnell, "Debitage of the Shatter Zone: Indoctrination, Asylum, and the Law of Towns in the Provinces of Florida," in *Petitioning in the Atlantic World, c. 1500–1840: Empires, Revolutions and Social Movements*, ed. Miguel Dantas da Cruz (New York: Palgrave Macmillan, 2022), 151 and n. 9.

23. In the Spanish Empire, this process usually played out through *gracia* petitions, when vassals sought special favors or exemptions. See Masters, "Two, One, Many, None," *Americas*, 29.

24. George Webb, *The Office and Authority of a Justice of Peace: And Also The Duty of Sheriffs, Coroners, Churchwardens, Surveiors of Highways, Constables, and Officers of Militia. Together with Precedents of Warrants, Judgments, Executions, and other legal Process, issuable by Magistrates within their respective Jurisdictions, in Cases Civil or Criminal. And The Method of Judicial Proceedings, before Justices of Peace, in Matters within their Cognisance out of Sessions. Collected from the Common and Statute Laws of England, and Acts of Assembly, now in Force; And adapted to the Constitution and Practice of Virginia* (Williamsburg, VA: 1736), 183; See also my earlier comparison of Florida and Virginia, Bradley Dixon, "'Darling Indians' and 'Natural Lords': Virginia's Tributary Regime and Florida's Republic of Indians in the Seventeenth

Century," in *Justice in New World: Negotiating Legal Intelligibility in British, Iberian, and Indigenous America*, ed. Brian P. Owensby and Richard J. Ross (New York: NYU Press, 2018), 183–212.

25. For the use of the concept of "emergent properties" as a way of connecting seemingly disparate events across empires and continents, see Margaret Ellen Newell, "'The Rising of the Indians': or, The Native American Revolution of (16)'76," *William and Mary Quarterly*, vol. 80, no. 2 (April 2023), 291–292.

26. As Joseph M. Hall, Jr. demonstrates, Indigenous people remade Spanish, English, and French colonial outposts in ways that suited their goals. Joseph M. Hall, Jr., *Zamumo's Gifts: Indian-European Exchange in the Colonial Southeast* (Philadelphia: University of Pennsylvania Press, 2009), 9.

27. James H. Merrell, *The Indians' New World: Catawbas and Their Neighbors from European Contact Through the Era of Removal* (Chapel Hill: University of North Carolina Press for the Institute of Early American History and Culture, 1989); Richard White, *The Middle Ground: Indians, Empires, and Republics in the Great Lakes Region, 1650–1815* (New York: Cambridge University Press, 1991; repr. 2011).

28. Moreover, White's "middle ground," as Dylan Ruediger, one of the most perceptive historians of the tributary regime in Virginia puts it, describes the relatively equal power relations on the "edge of empire rather than . . . within the churning core of the settler colony." Russell Dylan Ruediger, "Tributary Subjects: Affective Colonialism, Power, and the Process of Subjugation in Colonial Virginia, c. 1600–c. 1740" (PhD diss., Georgia State University, 2017), 11, accessed 11 May 2023, https://doi.org/10.57709/9979636. For creative misunderstandings, see White, *Middle Ground*, xxvi; For the violent outcomes of misunderstandings in the early South, see Seth Mallios, *The Deadly Politics of Giving: Exchange and Violence at Ajacan, Roanoke, and Jamestown* (Tuscaloosa: University of Alabama Press, 2006).

29. Masters, *We, the King*, 39 (quotation). The concept of the co-creation of law in a process of interchange between Indigenous vassals/subjects and the Crown is a key component of recent studies of the Spanish Empire. Karen Graubart concludes that the "political forms of the Spanish empire" were "concurrently established rather than imposed" on Indigenous republics. Graubart, *Republics of Difference*, 9; Masters, "Two, Many, One, None," *Americas*, 30. Some historians have embraced the idea in discussions of the tributary regime in Virginia, especially around the creation of the treaties of 1646 and 1677. Negrin, "Cockacoeske's Rebellion," 56, 80; Kruer, *Time of Anarchy*, 156–163; Ruediger, "Tributary Subjects," 22.

30. For the uses Indigenous peoples made of petitioning, see Adrian Masters and Bradley Dixon, "Indigenous Petitioning in the Early Modern British and Spanish New World," in *Petitioning in the Atlantic World*, ed. Dantas da Cruz, 105–136; Jenny Hale Pulsipher *Swindler Sachem: The American Indian Who Dropped Out of Harvard, Sold His Birthright, and Conned the King of England* (New Haven, CT: Yale University, 2018); Craig Yirush, "Claiming the New World: Empire, Law, and Indigenous Rights in the Mohegan Case, 1704–1743," *Law and History Review*, vol. 29, no. 2 (May 2011): 333–373; Craig Yirush, "'Chief Princes and Owners of All': Native American Appeals to the Crown in the Early-Modern British Atlantic," in *Native Claims: Indigenous Law Against Empire, 1500–1920*, ed. Saliha Belmessous (Oxford: Oxford University Press, 2011), 129–151; Jenny Hale Pulsipher, *Subjects unto the Same King: Indians, English, and the Contest for Authority in Colonial New England* (Philadelphia: University of Pennsylvania Press, 2005).

31. Elsewhere, notably in my dissertation, I have called this arrangement a "neochiefdom," to suggest that it was the result of a merger of the Indigenous "chiefdom" with European colonial

states to create a new form of polity. Chiefdom, however, carries too much baggage from its neoevolutionary origins, and I have used the term sparingly. See Timothy Pauketat, *Chiefdoms and Other Archaeological Delusions* (Lanham, MD: AltaMira Press, 2007). The challenge of what terms to use for Native American polities is ongoing. Amy Turner Bushnell proposes using "town" to describe what we have previously thought of as chiefdoms. Bushnell, "Debitage of the Shatter Zone," in *Petitioning in the Atlantic World*, ed. Dantas da Cruz, 137; Peter Olsen-Harbich argues for the importance of "petty kingship" as a category both for understanding Native polities in eastern North America and subsequent attempts by Europeans to "vassalize" Natives. Peter Jakob Olsen-Harbich, "A Meaningful Subjection: Kingly Government, Coercive Inequality, and Diplomacy in the North American Eastern Woodlands, 1000–1625 A.D.," (PhD diss., The College of William and Mary, 2021). Other notable recent works have pointed to the centrality of towns as a political unit, including Elizabeth N. Ellis, *The Great Power of Small Nations: Indigenous Diplomacy in the Gulf South* (Philadelphia: University of Pennsylvania Press, 2023), 17–44; Aubrey Lauersdorf has transformed our understanding of Apalachee politics by focusing on towns as "the center of Apalachee political life." Aubrey Lauersdorf, "An Apalachee Revolt?: Reconceptualizing Violence in Seventeenth-Century Apalachee," in "Indigenous Florida," ed. Denise I. Bossy and Andrew K. Frank, special issue, *The Florida Historical Quarterly*, vol. 100, no. 1 (Summer 2021): 27; For the importance of towns in Ossomocomuck, the land of Carolina Algonquians, see Michael LeRoy Oberg, "Tribes and Towns: What Historians Still Get Wrong About the Roanoke Ventures," *Ethnohistory*, vol. 67, no. 5 (October 2020): 579–602. Despite these shifts in historians' attitudes, the term "chiefdom" is practically unavoidable, especially when discussing the Powhatan polity, a multiethnic political formation that spanned the Tidewater. For recent uses of "chiefdom" to describe this polity, see Matthew Kruer, *Time of Anarchy: Indigenous Power and the Crisis of Colonialism* (Cambridge, MA: Harvard University Press, 2021), 22–23; Dylan Ruediger, who has carefully theorized the workings of the Powhatan polity, also uses "chiefdom" to describe Tsenacomacoh, rightly describing it as "more imperial than federative." See Dylan Ruediger, "'Neither Utterly to Reject Them, Nor Yet to Drawe Them to Come In': Tributary Subordination and Settler Colonialism in Virginia," *Early American Studies: An Interdisciplinary Journal*, vol. 18, no. 1 (Winter 2020): 6. For a classic description of chiefdoms in Florida, see Worth, *Timucua Chiefdoms*, 1: 1–18. Native nations, in some cases, could be the dominant party in hybrid polities with other nations, much as the Susquehannocks' were over New Sweden. See Cynthia J. Van Zandt, *Brothers Among Nations: The Pursuit of Intercultural Alliances in Early America, 1580–1660* (New York: Oxford University Press, 2008), 166–186. And, as we will see, Native leaders sought the position of paramount chief—albeit nested within and partially supported by colonial authority—at various times during the colonial era.

32. For treaties as constitutions, see Robert A. Williams, Jr., *Linking Arms Together: American Indian Treaty Visions of Law and Peace, 1600–1800* (New York: Routledge, 1999), 98–123. For the creation of Indigenous custom, see Yanna Yannakakis, *Since Time Immemorial: Native Custom and Law in Colonial Mexico* (Durham, NC: Duke University Press, 2023). For more on treaties and colonial claims, see Jeffrey Glover, *Paper Sovereigns: Anglo-Native Treaties and the Law of Nations, 1604–1664* (Philadelphia, PA: University of Pennsylvania Press, 2014).

33. Amy Turner Bushnell, "'These People Are not Conquered like Those of New Spain': Florida's Reciprocal Colonial Compact," *Florida Historical Quarterly*, vol. 92, no. 3 (Winter 2014): 551; Amy Turner Bushnell, "Spain's Conquest by Contract: Pacification and the Mission System in Eastern North America," in *The World Turned Upside-Down: The State of Eighteenth-Century Studies at the Beginning of the Twenty-First Century*, ed. Michael V. Kennedy and

William G. Shade (Bethlehem, PA: Lehigh University Press, 2001), 289; Amy Turner Bushnell, *Situado and Sabana*, 34–35 and 64.

34. For the treaties of 1646 and 1677, see discussions in Chapters 2 and 3 below.

35. Bradley J. Dixon, "'His One Netev Ples': The Chowans and the Politics of Indian Petitioning in the Colonial South," *William and Mary Quarterly*, 3d ser., vol. 76, no. 1 (January 2019), 50–52.

36. Robin Beck, *Chiefdoms, Collapse, and Coalescence in the Early American South* (New York: Cambridge University Press, 2013), 196.

37. Beck *Chiefdoms, Collapse, and Coalescence*, 238.

38. Ruediger, "Tributary Subordination," passim and 28; J. Leitch Wright, on the other hand, argued that tributaries were "considered sovereign, but statutes and treaties had spelled out their subordinate status in detail." J. Leitch Wright, Jr., *The Only Land They Knew: The Tragic Story of the American Indians in the Old South* (New York: The Free Press, 1981), 97.

39. The debate over what Indigenous subjecthood amounted to, whether in theory or in practice, has run the gamut from those scholars who conclude that subjecthood was meaningful to those who argue that it was practically meaningless. Most agree that the protections afforded tributaries in English colonies were not without qualifications. Dylan Ruediger has described the contradictions of tributary status as the result of what he argues was its role in both promoting Indian rights and managing Indian dispossession. Ruediger, "Tributary Subordination," 4 ("flexible"), 18, and 29; Matthew Kruer notes that tributary protections were serious but limited. Kruer, *Time of Anarchy*, 38, 44–45, 48, 153; Kruer elsewhere has argued that tributary Indians were part of the colonial "body politic." Matthew Kruer, "Bloody Minds and Peoples Undone: Emotion, Family, and Political Order in the Susquehannock-Virginia War," *William and Mary Quarterly*, 3rd ser., vol. 74, no. 3 (July 2017): 401–436, ("body politic," 411); Kristofer Ray, "Constructing a Discourse of Indigenous Slavery, Freedom and Sovereignty in Anglo-Virginia, 1600–1750," *Native South*, vol. 10 (2017): 19–39; Kristalyn Marie Shefveland, *Anglo-Native Virginia: Trade, Conversion, and Indian Slavery in the Old Dominion, 1646–1722* (Athens: University of Georgia Press, 2016); Ethan Schmidt, *Divided Dominion: Social Conflict and Indian Hatred in Early Virginia* (Boulder: University Press of Colorado, 2015); Daragh Grant describes the position of Indigenous subjects within English colonial states as that of "interior exclusion," meaning they live under the state's authority but were considered outside the "moral community" of persons for whom the state itself was constituted to serve. For more, see Daragh Grant, "On the 'Native Question': Understanding Settler-Colonialism's Logics of Domination" (PhD diss., University of Chicago, 2012), 7; Aziz Rana argues that subject status was little more than the suspension of colonial warfare against Indigenous peoples who swore allegiance to the Crown and carried few real protections. Aziz Rana, *The Two Faces of American Freedom* (Cambridge, MA: Harvard University Press, 2010), 33; Michelle LeMaster, "In the 'Scolding Houses': Indians and the Law in Eastern North Carolina, 1684–1760," *North Carolina Historical Review*, vol. 83, no. 2 (April 2006): 193–232; Michael Leroy Oberg, *Dominion and Civility: English Imperialism and Native America, 1585–1685* (Ithaca, NY: Cornell University Press, 1999); Gleach, *Powhatan's World and Colonial Virginia*; Helen C. Rountree, *Pocahontas's People: The Powhatan Indians of Virginia Through Four Centuries* (Lincoln: University of Nebraska Press, 1990); Wright, *The Only Land They Knew*; W. Stitt Robinson, Jr., "Tributary Indians in Colonial Virginia," *Virginia Magazine of History and Biography*, vol. 67, no. 1 (January 1959): 49–64; W. Stitt Robinson, Jr., "The Legal Status of the Indian in Colonial Virginia," *Virginia Magazine of History and Biography*, vol. 61, no. 3 (July 1953): 247–259.

40. Recently, Amy Turner Bushnell has reconstructed an Indigenous "ius municipium," or Law of Towns at work among Native Americans in the South, especially in Florida. The law of towns was "based upon local customs, precedents, and petitions and dignified by a tradition of debate and consensus" and governed such matters as the adoption of refugees, regulation of trade, the creation of new towns, and the relocation of old ones. See Bushnell, "Debitage of the Shatter Zone," in *Petitioning in the Atlantic World*, ed. Dantas da Cruz, 138 (quotation). For more on the principles of Indigenous law in the eastern North America generally, see Katherine A. Hermes, "The Law of Native Americans, to 1815," in *The Cambridge History of Law in America*, ed. Michael Grossberg and Christopher Tomlins (Cambridge, UK: Cambridge University Press, 2008), 32–62; John Philip Reid, *A Better Kind of Hatchet: Law, Trade, and Diplomacy During the Early Years of European Contact* (University Park, PA: Pennsylvania State University Press, 1975); John Philip Reid, *A Law of Blood: The Primitive Law of the Cherokee Nation* (DeKalb: Northern Illinois University Press, [1970] 2006).

41. The distinctions between English and Spanish colonialism go back at least to Captain John Smith. During the eighteenth century, writers refined them. See, for instance, books 9 and 10 of William Robertson, *The History of America* (London: 1796), notably 30, 54 and William Robertson, *The History of America*, 2 vols. (London: 1777), 2: 375; William Douglass, *A Summary, Historical and Political, of the First Planting, Progressive Improvements, and Present State of the British Settlements in North-America*, 2 vols. (London: 1755), 1: 205–206; John Campbell, *A Compleat History of Spanish America* (London: 1742).

42. James Adair, *The History of the American Indians; Particularly Those Nations adjoining to the Mississippi, East, and West Florida, Georgia, South and North Carolina, and Virginia . . . With a new Map of the Country referred to in the History* (London: 1775), 202.

43. Adair, *History of the American Indians*, 202.

44. Adair, *History of the American Indians*, 407.

45. "In so far as a 'republic of Indians' was to be found in British America," J. H. Elliott declared, "it was to be found in the praying towns of New England." J. H. Elliott, *Empires of the Atlantic World: Britain and Spain in America, 1492–1830* (New Haven, CT: Yale University Press, 2007), 85 (quotation) and 87. Elsewhere, Elliott has argued that "in spite of the so-called 'settlement Indians,' the true 'republic of Indians' in British America lay outside the areas of European settlement." J. H. Elliott, *Spain, Europe, & the Wider World, 1500–1800* (New Haven, CT: Yale University Press, 2009), 169.

46. Richard J. Ross, "Spanish American and British American Law as Mirrors to Each Other: Implications of the Missing *Derecho Británico Indiano*," in *New Horizons in Spanish Colonial Law: Contributions to Transnational Early Modern Legal History*, ed. Thomas Duve and Heikki Pihlajamäki (Berlin: Max Planck Institute for European Legal History, 2015), 9–28.

47. Bushnell, "Conquest by Contract," 311 ("wards of any Crown"); Patricia Seed, *American Pentimento: The Invention of Indians and the Pursuit of Riches* (Minneapolis: University of Minnesota Press, 2001), 72–90; Anthony Pagden, *Lords of All the World: Ideologies of Empire in Spain, Britain and France c. 1500–1800* (New Haven, CT: Yale University Press, 1995), 65; James Muldoon, *The Americas in the Spanish World Order: The Justification of Conquest in the Seventeenth Century* (Philadelphia: University of Pennsylvania Press, 1994), 4 ("only the Spanish"); Lewis Hanke, *Aristotle and the American Indians: A Study in Race Prejudice in the Modern World* (Bloomington: University of Indiana Press, 1959); Lewis Hanke, *The Spanish Struggle for Justice in the Conquest of America* (New York: Little, Brown and Company, [1949] 1965).

48. J. H. Elliott's monumental comparative history tellingly begins with Hernando Cortés and Christopher Newport, separated by thousands of miles of distance and a century of time. Elliott, *Empires of the Atlantic World*, 3–28. A notable recent exception to such sweeping comparisons is James D. Rice's effort to incorporate Spanish Florida into the larger story of the American South's history. James D. Rice, "Contact, Conflict, and Captivity in the Seventeenth-Century South," in *A New History of the American South*, eds. W. Fitzhugh Brundage, assoc. eds., Laura F. Edwards and Jon Sensbach (Chapel Hill: The University of North Carolina Press, 2023), 46–82. The "layered" approach of Dan Richter, which included a comparison of neighboring English, Dutch, French, and Spanish colonies in North America was framed to highlight the "oddity" of Chesapeake colonial societies. Daniel K. Richter, *Before the Revolution: America's Ancient Pasts* (Cambridge, MA: Harvard University Press, 2011), 212–238, 220 ("oddity"). For a brilliant yet compartmentalized approach to comparison that also tends to emphasize differences in the long run, see Alan Taylor, *American Colonies* (New York: Viking, 2001).

49. Masters, "A Thousand Invisible Architects," *HAHR*, 98:3, 379; a similar "bottom-up" process is evident in the process of defining freedom and race among people of African descent in the Americas. See Alejandro de la Fuente and Ariela Gross, *Becoming Free, Becoming Black: Race, Freedom, and Law in Cuba, Virginia, and Louisiana* (New York: Cambridge University Press, 2020).

50. For the centrality of "cultures of violence" in the early South, see Matthew Jennings, *New Worlds of Violence: Cultures and Conquests in the Early American Southeast* (Knoxville: University of Tennessee Press, 2011).

51. Violence was inherent in all of these colonial systems, as were deliberate efforts to erase Indigenous histories within the archives. See Rebecca Anne Goetz, "The Nanziatticos and the Violence of the Archive: Land and Native Enslavement in Colonial Virginia," *Journal of Southern History*, vol. 85, no. 1 (February 2019): 33–60.

52. They are the forebears of modern Indigenous activists who wielded law to "enable Native people to live as members of both particular indigenous communities and a large, democratic nation." Frederick Hoxie, *This Indian Country: American Indian Political Activists and the Place They Made* (New York: The Penguin Press, 2012), 5.

53. For "chieftaincy," see Beck, *Chiefdoms, Collapse, and Coalescence*, 195.

54. Charles W. Arnade, *Florida on Trial, 1593–1602*, ed. R. S. Boggs, University of Miami Hispanic American Studies 16 (Coral Gables, FL: University of Miami Press, 1959).

55. Juan Menéndez Marqués, "Description of Florida," 7 June 1606, AGI Patronato 19, fol. 1v, 2v, PARES, accessed 2 October 2021.

56. William M. Kelso, *Jamestown, the Truth Revealed* (Charlottesville: University of Virginia Press, 2017), 15–18.

Chapter 1

1. Amy Turner Bushnell, *Situado and Sabana: Spain's Support System for Florida*, Anthropological Papers of the American Museum of Natural History 74 (New York: American Museum of Natural History, 1994), 93; For a picture of life in the city during the seventeenth century, see Susan Richbourg Parker, "St. Augustine in the Seventeenth-Century: Capital of La Florida," in, "500 Years of Florida History—The Seventeenth Century," ed. Jane Landers, special issue, *Florida Historical Quarterly*, vol. 92, no. 3 (Winter 2014): 554–576. Deliberations about Florida's future lasted until 1608, when King Felipe III decided unequivocally in favor of keeping San

Agustin. White, *Cold Welcome*, 85–86; David J. Weber, *The Spanish Frontier in North America* (New Haven, CT: Yale University Press, 1992), 88–89.

2. "Testimony of Andrés López de Simancas," 25 June 1606, in "Información de D. Gaspar . . . ," 11 November 1607, AGI SD 232, PKY, SC, reel 8, fol. 232v. Transcription and translation of the document comes from the Stetson version; however, the folio numbers are those found on the copy of Don Gaspar's documents in PKY, JWC, reel 7.

3. "Testimony of Andrés López de Simancas," 25 June 1606, in "Información de D. Gaspar . . . ," 11 November 1607, AGI SD 232, PKY, SC, reel 8, fol. 232v; San Sebastián was what Amy Bushnell called a "service town" or "client community" and was deliberately relocated nearer the presidio in order to support it. See Bushnell, *Situado and Sabana*, 118–121, esp. 119–120.

4. "Testimony of Andrés López de Simancas," 25 June 1606, in "Información de D. Gaspar . . . ," 11 November 1607, AGI SD 232, PKY, SC, reel 8, fol. 233v ("did not know"), fol. 232v ("welcomed").

5. "Petition of Don Gaspar Marqués to the King," in "Información de D. Gaspar . . . ," 11 November 1607, AGI SD 232, PKY, SC, reel 8, fol. 223r.

6. "Petition of Don Gaspar Marqués to the King," in "Información de D. Gaspar . . . ," 11 November 1607, AGI SD 232, PKY, SC, reel 8, fol. 223v.

7. The request is in the petition of Don Gaspar Marqués to the King, in "Información de D. Gaspar . . . ," 11 November 1607, AGI SD 232, PKY, SC reel 8, fol. 223v. For the bishop's certification, see Juan de las Cabezas Altamirano, 28 June 1606, in "Información de D. Gaspar . . . ," 11 November 1607, AGI SD 232, PKY, SC, reel 8, fol. 234v.

8. Alden T. Vaughan, *Transatlantic Encounters: American Indians in Britain, 1500–1776* (New York: Cambridge University Press, 2006), 45 and 46 (quotation).

9. "L. Zuñiga to Philip III," 16 June 1608, in Alexander M. Brown, ed., *The Genesis of the United States* [. . .] (Cambridge, MA: The Riverside Press, 1897), 1: 172; Jeffrey Glover, *Paper Sovereigns: Anglo-Native Treaties and the Law of Nations, 1604–1664* (Philadelphia: University of Pennsylvania Press, 2014), 60–63.

10. The map followed conventions of Indigenous cartography, including representing towns as circles. Martin D. Gallivan, *The Powhatan Landscape: An Archaeological History of the Algonquian Chesapeake* (Gainesville: University Press of Florida, 2016), 33–38. The map also represented an intelligence coup for the Spanish. William S. Goldman, "The Spanish and the Founding of Jamestown," *William and Mary Quarterly*, vol. 68, no. 3 (July 2011): 439–441. For more on the map, see William P. Cumming, *The Southeast in Early Maps*, 3rd ed., Revised and Enlarged by Louis De Vorsey, Jr. (Chapel Hill: The University of North Carolina Press, 1998), 136–137.

11. Eliga H. Gould, "Entangled Histories, Entangled Worlds: The English-Speaking Atlantic as a Spanish Periphery," *American Historical Review*, vol. 112, no. 3 (June 2007): 769. For the cosmopolitan character of Virginia's early colonizers and the wider contexts surrounding the venture, see Alison Games, *The Web of Empire: English Cosmopolitans in an Age of Expansion, 1560–1660* (New York: Oxford University Press, 2008); Karen Ordahl Kupperman, *The Jamestown Project* (Cambridge, MA: Harvard University Press, 2007); Peter C. Mancall, ed., *The Atlantic World and Virginia, 1550–1624* (Chapel Hill: University of North Carolina Press, 2007).

12. For exchanges of children and captives, see Karen Ordahl Kupperman, *Pocahontas and the English Boys: Caught Between Cultures in Early Virginia* (New York: NYU Press, 2019). For Native American education in Virginia, see Margaret Connell Szasz, *Indian Education in the*

American Colonies, 1607–1783 (Lincoln: University of Nebraska Press, 2007), 46–62. After plans for a Jesuit college in Havana were discontinued, some Native leaders' children were "raised in the governor's house." Bushnell, *Situado and Sabana*, 105.

13. James Horn, *1619: Jamestown and the Forging of American Democracy* (New York: Basic Books, 2018), 150–151; James Horn, *A Land as God Made It: Jamestown and the Birth of America* (New York: Basic Books, 2005), 250–252. For more on Thorpe's background and legacy, see Eric Gethyn-Jones, *George Thorpe and the Berkeley Company: A Gloucestershire Enterprise in Virginia* (Gloucester, UK: Alan Sutton Publishing Limited, 1982). For a discussion of Thorpe, and a comparison of Spanish and English conversion efforts, see J. Leitch Wright, Jr., *The Only Land They Knew: The Tragic Story of the American Indians in the Old South* (New York: The Free Press, 1981), 64–66.

14. April Lee Hatfield notes that after 1622 the English in Virginia began to embrace "the more violent aspects of Spanish colonization." April Lee Hatfield, "Spanish Colonization Literature, Powhatan Geographies, and English Perceptions of Tsenacommacah/Virginia," *Journal of Southern History*, vol. 69, no. 2 (May 2003): 278–281 ("violent aspects," 281). Hereinafter cited as *JSH*, vol., no.

15. Gallivan, *Powhatan Landscape*, 171–172. For the etymology of the term "weroance" and the chief's function in Powhatan society and political economy, see Margaret Holmes Williamson, *Powhatan Lords of Life and Death: Command and Consent in Seventeenth-Century Virginia* (Lincoln: University of Nebraska Press, 2003), 137 and 148.

16. Frederic W. Gleach, *Powhatan's World and Colonial Virginia: A Conflict of Cultures* (Lincoln: University of Nebraska Press, 1997), 3.

17. Seth Mallios, *The Deadly Politics of Giving: Exchange and Violence at Ajacan, Roanoke, and Jamestown* (Tuscaloosa: University of Alabama Press, 2006).

18. Lisa Brooks, *The Common Pot: The Recovery of Native Space in the Northeast* (Minneapolis: University of Minnesota Press, 2008); Nancy Shoemaker, *A Strange Likeness: Becoming Red and White in Eighteenth-Century North America* (New York: Oxford University Press, 2004), 86–87.

19. Don Gaspar wished to make himself a bigger player in regional politics. John E. Worth, *The Timucuan Chiefdoms of Spanish Florida*, 2 vols. (Gainesville: University Press of Florida, 1998), 1: 25.

20. The town was gone from the records within just a few years of Don Gaspar's petition. Worth, *Timucuan Chiefdoms*, 1: 62. Tocoy survived into the 1620s at least, when it was the site of an unsanctioned marketplace for maize. Joseph M. Hall, Jr., *Zamumo's Gifts: Indian-European Exchange in the Colonial Southeast* (Philadelphia: University of Pennsylvania Press, 2009), 59.

21. Worth, *Timucuan Chiefdoms*, 2: 1–26.

22. Aubrey Lauersdorf, "An Apalachee Revolt?: Reconceptualizing Violence in Seventeenth-Century Apalachee," in "Indigenous Florida," ed. Denise I. Bossy and Andrew K. Frank, special issue, *Florida Historical Quarterly*, vol. 100, no. 1 (Summer 2021): 28–29.

23. Luís Gerónimo de Oré, *Account of the Martyrs in the Provinces of La Florida*, ed. and trans. Raquel Chang-Rodríguez and Nancy Vogeley (Albuquerque: University of New Mexico Press, 2017), 145.

24. For example, John Chamberlain styled him "Powhatan a king or cacique of that country." John Chamberlain to Sir Dudley Carleton, 22 June 1616, in *The Letters of John Chamberlain*, ed. Norman Egbert McClure (Lancaster, PA: Lancaster Press for the American Philosophical Society, 1939), 12.

25. Amy Turner Bushnell, "Ruling 'the Republic of Indians' in Seventeenth-Century Florida," in *Powhatan's Mantle: Indians in the Colonial Southeast*, ed. Gregory A. Waselkov, Peter H. Wood, and Tom Hatley (Lincoln: University of Nebraska Press, 2006), 200.

26. Timothy Pauketat, *Cahokia: Ancient America's Great City on the Mississippi* (New York: Penguin, 2009), 2.

27. Juliana Barr, "There's No Such Thing as 'Prehistory': What the Longue Durée of Caddo and Pueblo History Tells Us about Colonial America," *William and Mary Quarterly*, vol. 74, no. 2 (April 2017): 205; Charles R. Cobb and Adam King, "Re-Inventing Mississippian Tradition at Etowah, Georgia," *Journal of Archaeological Method and Theory*, vol. 12, no. 3 (September 2005), 168 ("cycles"); Adam King, *Etowah: The Political History of a Chiefdom Capital* (Tuscaloosa: The University of Alabama Press, 2003); Marvin T. Smith, *Coosa: The Rise and Fall of a Southeastern Mississippian Chiefdom* (Gainesville: University Press of Florida, 2000).

28. Fidalgo de Elvas, "The Account by a Gentleman from Elvas," in *The De Soto Chronicles: The Expedition of Hernando de Soto to North America in 1539–1543*, ed. Lawrence A. Clayton, Vernon James Knight, Jr., and Edward C. Moore, 2 vols. (Tuscaloosa: The University of Alabama Press, 1994), 1: 83. Hereinafter abbreviated as *DSC*.

29. The connection between religion and politics was so strong that the "Mississippian chiefdom political orders were true theocracies." Robbie Ethridge, *From Chicaza to Chickasaw: The European Invasion and the Transformation of the Mississippian World, 1540–1715* (Chapel Hill: University of North Carolina Press, 2010), 24. For a view of Mississippian cosmology and symbolism, see George E. Lankford, "Some Cosmological Motifs in the Southeastern Ceremonial Complex," in *Ancient Objects and Sacred Realms: Interpretations of Mississippian Iconography*, ed. F. Kent Reilly III and James F. Garber (Austin: University of Texas Press, 2008), 8–38.

30. Christina Snyder, *Slavery in Indian Country: The Changing Face of Captivity in Early America* (Cambridge, MA: Harvard University Press, 2010), 16; Kathleen DuVal, *The Native Ground: Indians and Colonists in the Heart of the Continent* (Philadelphia: University of Pennsylvania Press, 2006), 13–28.

31. For recent works that place the Mississippians within a larger "medieval world," see Timothy R. Pauketat and Susan M. Alt, eds., *Medieval Mississippians: The Cahokian World* (Santa Fe, NM: SAR Press, 2015). For a comparison of the two medieval worlds on the eve of their clash in North America, see Daniel K. Richter, *Before the Revolution: America's Ancient Pasts* (Cambridge, MA: Harvard University Press, 2011), 11–63.

32. Worth, *Timucuan Chiefdoms*, 1: 9.

33. Rodrigo Rangel, "Account of the Northern Conquest and Discovery of Hernando de Soto," in *DSC* 1: 267.

34. Marc Bloch, *Feudal Society*, trans. L. A. Manyon (Chicago: University of Chicago Press, 1961), 224–230; Bloch's analysis contrasts sharply with the views on vassalage found in Francis M. Jennings, *The Invasion of America: Indians, Colonialism, and the Cant of Conquest* (Chapel Hill: University of North Carolina Press, 1975), 105–127.

35. Ethridge, *Chicaza to Chickasaw*, 35.

36. For more on this political transformation generally, see Robin Beck, *Chiefdoms, Collapse, and Coalescence in the Early American South* (New York: Cambridge University Press, 2013). For the role of disease, see Paul Kelton, *Epidemics & Enslavement: Biological Catastrophe in the Native Southeast, 1492–1715* (Lincoln, NE: University of Nebraska Press, 2007). For the role of slave raids and Indian slavery generally, see Snyder, *Slavery in Indian Country* and Alan Gallay, *The Indian Slave Trade: The Rise of the English Empire in the South, 1670–1717* (New

Haven, CT: Yale University Press, 2002). For the role of exchange, see Hall, *Zamumo's Gifts* and Jessica Yirush Stern, *The Lives in Objects: Native Americans, British Colonists, and Cultures of Labor and Exchange in the Southeast* (Chapel Hill: University of North Carolina Press, 2017). For more on the role of information and networks, see Alejandra Dubcovsky, *Informed Power: Communication in the Early American South* (Cambridge, MA: Harvard University Press, 2016). Pulling many of these forces together into a synthetic whole is the concept of the "shatter zone." See Robbie Ethridge and Sheri M. Shuck-Hall, eds., *Mapping the Mississippian Shatter Zone: The Colonial Indian Slave Trade and Regional Instability in the American South* (Lincoln: University of Nebraska Press, 2009).

37. For Soto as a roving "foreign lord," see Ethridge, *Chicaza to Chickasaw*, 11; J. Michael Francis and Kathleen M. Kole, *Murder and Martyrdom in Spanish Florida: Don Juan and the Guale Uprising of 1597*, American Museum of Natural History Anthropological Papers 95 (New York: American Museum of Natural History, 2011), 29.

38. For more on the failed 1570 mission and the travels of Paquiquineo throughout the Spanish Atlantic world, see James Horn, *A Brave and Cunning Prince: The Great Chief Opechancanough and the War for America* (New York: Basic Books, 2021); Camilla Townsend, *Fifth Sun: A New History of the Aztecs* (New York: Oxford University Press, 2019), 175–177. For his significance in hemispheric history, see Anna Brickhouse, *The Unsettlement of America: Translation, Interpretation, and the Story of Don Luis de Velasco* (New York: Oxford University Press, 2015).

39. Paul Hoffman, *Florida's Frontiers* (Bloomington: Indiana University Press, 2002), 57.

40. Hoffman, *Florida's Frontiers*, 53.

41. "Pacification of the Caciques of the Province of Guale," 18 May 1600, AGI SD 224, PKY, JTCC, box 12, folder 54-5-9, microfilm copy.

42. Francis and Kole, *Murder and Martyrdom*, 89–93.

43. Don Juan, *mico* of San Pedro, to the King, 16 January 1598, AGI SD 231, in Francis and Kole, *Murder and Martyrdom*, 93.

44. Bushnell, *Situado and Sabana*, 46.

45. Hall, *Zamumo's Gifts*, 53; "Florida was not so much" a colony as a "community of interdependent" peoples. Worth, *Timucuan Chiefdoms*, 1: xviii; see also John E. Worth, "Spanish Missions and the Persistence of Chiefly Power," in *The Transformation of the Southeastern Indians, 1540–1760*, ed. Robbie Ethridge and Charles Hudson (Jackson: University Press of Mississippi, 2002), 52.

46. Amy Turner Bushnell argues that the similarities between English treaties, specifically that of 1646 in Virginia, and Spanish-Indigenous agreements, arise from their "feudal overtones." Bushnell, *Situado and Sabana*, 34. See my in-depth discussion in Chapter 2 below.

47. "Pacification of the Caciques of the Province of Guale," 18 May 1600, AGI SD 232, PKY, JTCC, box 15, folder 54-5-17, microfilm copy.

48. Pedro de Ibarra, "Relation of the Journey that was made by Pedro de Ybarra . . . to visit . . . Guale," November-December 1604, AGI SD 224, in *Documentos Históricos de la Florida y la Luisiana, siglos XVI al XVIII*, ed. Manuel Serrano y Sanz (Madrid: Victoriano Suárez, 1912), 175.

49. Ibarra, "Relation," November-December 1604, AGI SD 224, in *Documentos Históricos*, 169.

50. Ibarra, "Relation," November-December 1604, AGI SD 224, in *Documentos Históricos*, 169.

51. "45. Ralph Lane's Discourse on the First Colony, 17 August 1585–18 June 1586," in *The Roanoke Voyages, 1584–1590; documents to illustrate the English voyages to North America under the patent granted to Walter Raleigh in 1584*, ed. David Beers Quinn, 2 vols. (London: The Hakluyt Society), 1: 279. Hereinafter abbreviated as *RV*. For a comparison between Juan Pardo's

entrada in the 1560s and the Roanoke voyages in the 1580s, see Michael Leroy Oberg and David Moore, "Voyages to Carolina: Europeans in the Indians' Old World," in *New Voyages to Carolina: Reinterpreting North Carolina History*, ed. Larry E. Tise and Jeffrey J. Crow (Chapel Hill: University of North Carolina Press, 2017), 41–59; Vaughan, *Transatlantic Encounters*, 28.

52. "Anonymous Notes for the Guidance of Raleigh and Cavendish," 1584–1585, in *RV*, 1: 138; Ralph Lane to Sir Philip Sydney, 3 September 1585, in *RV*, 1: 204 (quotation). For the history of violence in the Roanoke colony and its effects, see Michael Leroy Oberg, *The Head in Edward Nugent's Hand: Roanoke's Forgotten Indians* (Philadelphia: University of Pennsylvania Press, 2007). For Raleigh's imperial ideology, see Alan Gallay, *Walter Ralegh: Architect of Empire* (New York: Basic Books, 2019).

53. A notable exception being Camilla Townsend, *Pocahontas and the Powhatan Dilemma* (New York: Hill and Wang, 2004), 43; Andrew Fitzmaurice, *Humanism and America: An Intellectual History of English Colonisation, 1500–1625* (Cambridge, UK: Cambridge University Press, 2003), 141; Hatfield, "Spanish Colonization Literature," *JSH* 69:2, 245–282; Jorge Cañizares-Esguerra, *Puritan Conquistadors: Iberianizing the Atlantic, 1550–1700* (Stanford, CA: Stanford University Press, 2006); Gould, "Entangled Histories," 769; J. H. Elliott, "Learning from the Enemy," in *Spain, Europe, & the Wider World, 1500–1800* (New Haven, CT: Yale University Press, 2009), 38.

54. Peter Martyr, *The decades of the newe worlde or west India*, trans. Richard Eden (London: 1555), [10v].

55. Martyr, *Decades*, [10v].

56. Sebastian Münster, *A treatyse of the newe India*, trans. Richard Eden (London: 1553), [138].

57. Henry Hawks, "A relation of the commodities of Nova Hispania, and the maners of the inhabitants, written by Henry Hawks merchant, which lived five yeeres in the sayd country, and drew the same at the request of M. Richard Hakluyt Esquire of Eiton in the county of Hereford, 1572," in *The Principall Navigations*, by Richard Hakluyt, 3 vols. (London: 1600), 3: 463. Hereinafter abbreviated as *PN*.

58. Hawks, "Nova Hispania," in Hakluyt, *PN*, 3: 468.

59. Hawks, "Nova Hispania," in Hakluyt, *PN*, 3: 468.

60. Hawks, "Nova Hispania," in Hakluyt, *PN*, 3: 468.

61. Hawks, "Nova Hispania," in Hakluyt, *PN*, 3: 466.

62. "*A briefe Note written by Master Iohn Ellis, one of the Captaines with Sir Richard Hawkins, in his Voyage through the* Strait of Magellan, begunne the ninth of Aprill, 1593. *Concerning the said Straite, and certaine places, on the coast and Inland of* Peru," in *Hakluytus Posthumus or, Purchas His Pilgrimes*, by Samuel Purchas (London: 1625), 1416.

63. Jorge Cañizares-Esguerra and Bradley J. Dixon, "The Oversight of King Henry VII: Imperial Envy and the Making of British America," in *The World of Colonial America: An Atlantic Handbook*, ed. Ignacio Gallup-Diaz (New York: Routledge, 2017), 49; David Armitage, *The Ideological Origins of the British Empire* (New York: Cambridge University Press, 2000), 8.

64. John F. Scarry, "The Apalachee Chiefdom: A Mississippian Society on the Fringe of the Mississippian World," in *The Forgotten Centuries: Indians and Europeans in the American South, 1521–1707* ed. Charles Hudson and Carmen Chaves Tesser (Athens: University of Georgia Press, 1998), 156–178; John H. Hann, *Apalachee: The Land Between the Rivers* (Gainesville: University Press of Florida, 1988), 96–117.

65. Lauersdorf, "Apalachee Revolt," 27–28.

66. Horn, *Brave and Cunning Prince*, 57–80; Karen Ordahl Kupperman, *Facing Off: Englishmen and Indians in Early America* (Ithaca, NY: Cornell University Press, 2004), 36–39.

67. Williamson, *Powhatan Lords of Life and Death*, 206.

68. For a helpful discussion of the "instability" of the Powhatan chiefdom, see Daniel K. Richter, "Tsenacommacah and the Atlantic World," in *Atlantic World and Virginia*, ed. Mancall, 33–36.

69. For more on the Chickahominies and the linguistic roots of the word, see Gallivan, *Powhatan Landscape*, 104–140; James D. Rice, "Escape from Tsenacommacah: Chesapeake Algonquians and the Powhatan Menace," in *Atlantic World and Virginia*, ed. Mancall, 101–102.

70. Some have argued that the unpromising nature of the Powhatans led Spanish officials to discount the chances of the Jamestown colony's success. I argue that Spanish officials understood the basic similarities between Powhatan and, for instance, Apalachee or Timucua social and political organization. That said, Townsend and others are right that it seems the Spanish opted to allow Jamestown to fall on its own, rather than to dislodge it. For the argument that Spanish officials thought the Powhatans unsuitable for colonization, see Camilla Townsend, "Mutual Appraisals: The Shifting Paradigms of the English, Spanish, and Powhatans in Tsenacomoco, 1560–1622," in *Early Modern Virginia: Reconsidering the Old Dominion*, ed. Douglas Bradburn and John C. Coombs (Charlottesville: University of Virginia Press, 2011), 57–89.

71. Lauersdorf, "Apalachee Revolt," 26.

72. Bushnell, *Situado and Sabana*, 33–34.

73. Fray Francisco de Pareja and Fray Alonso de Peñaranda to the King, 6 November 1607, AGI SD 224, PKY, SC, reel 8.

74. Maynard Geiger, "Biographical Dictionary of the Franciscans in Spanish Florida and Cuba (1528–1841)," *Franciscan Studies*, no. 21 (1940), 90.

75. Worth, *Timucuan Chiefdoms*, 1: 57.

76. Worth, *Timucuan Chiefdoms*, 1: 17.

77. Worth, *Timucuan Chiefdoms*, 1: 40.

78. Oré, *Martyrs of Florida*, 142.

79. Oré, *Martyrs of Florida*, 142.

80. Oré, *Martyrs of Florida*, 143.

81. Oré, *Martyrs of Florida*, 143.

82. Oré, *Martyrs of Florida*, 144.

83. "Document 46: Discourse of Western Planting by Richard Hakluyt, 1584," in *The Original Writings & Correspondence of the Two Richard Hakluyts*, ed. E. G. R. Taylor, vol. 2 (London: The Hakluyt Society, 1935), 215 and see note 1.

84. Virginia Company, *The Trve Declaration of the estate of the Colonie in Virginia, With a confutation of such scandalous reports as haue tended to the disgrace of so worthy an enterprise. Published by aduise and direction of the Councell of Virginia* (London: 1610), 6–7.

85. Oré, *Martyrs of Florida*, 146.

86. Oré, *Martyrs of Florida*, 146.

87. Virginia Company, *Trve Declaration*, 7.

88. Gallivan, *Powhatan Landscape*, 55, 57, 178.

89. Gallivan beautifully recreates the experience of visiting Werowocomoco in Gallivan, *Powhatan Landscape*, 173.

90. Gallivan, *Powhatan Landscape*, 46.

91. Gallivan, *Powhatan Landscape*, 44, 48, 50–51; Gleach, *Powhatan's World*, 115–116.

92. William Strachey, *The Historie of Travell into Virginia Britannia*, ed. Louis B. Wright and Virginia Freund (London: The Hakluyt Society, 1953), 57.

93. John Smith, "The Proceedings of the English Colonie in Virginia . . . ," in *Captain John Smith: Writings and other Narratives of Roanoke, Jamestown, and the First English Settlement of America*, ed. James Horn (New York: Literary Classics of the United States, 2007), 84.

94. Smith, "The Proceedings," in *Captain John Smith*, ed. Horn, 73.

95. Smith, "The Proceedings," in *Captain John Smith*, ed. Horn, 74.

96. For examples, see "The famous voyage of Sir Francis Drake into the South sea, and therehence about the whole Globe of the earth, begun in the yeere of our Lord, 1577," in Hakluyt, *PN*, 3: 738; Thanks to Jim Muldoon for pointing out the similarities in legal and political forms between Irish and Native American submissions since the Middle Ages. For more, see "4. The Treaty of Windsor, 1175, Between Henry II and Rory O'Conor, High King," in *Irish Historical Documents, 1172–1922*, ed. Edmund Curtis and R. B. McDowell (London: Methuen & Co., Ltd., 1943), 22–24; "18. Conditions of Submission Offered to Conn Bacach O'Neill, 1541," in *Irish Historical Documents*, ed. Curtis and McDowell, 107–109. For more on surrender and regrant, see Hans Pawlisch, *Sir John Davies and the Conquest of Ireland: A Study in Legal Imperialism* (Cambridge, UK: Cambridge University Press, 1985).

97. Smith, "The Proceedings," in *Captain John Smith*, ed. Horn, 73.

98. Brickhouse, *Unsettlement of America*, 26–37.

99. Garcilaso de la Vega, "La Florida," in *DSC*, 2: 144.

100. Richter, "Tsenacommacah and the Atlantic World," in *Atlantic World and Virginia*, ed. Mancall, 58–59.

101. Richter, "Tsenacommacah and the Atlantic World," in *Atlantic World and Virginia*, ed. Mancall, 54.

102. For Hakluyt's warnings and his prayer "worth of a conquistador's chaplain," see Cañizares-Esguerra and Dixon, "The Oversight of King Henry VII," in *The World of Colonial America: An Atlantic Handbook*, ed. Gallup-Diaz, 46.

103. Richard Hakluyt, *Virginia richly valu'd* (London: 1609), [7].

104. Hakluyt, *Virginia*, [7].

105. Hakluyt, *Virginia*, [7].

106. "754. August 3, 1598. Bartolomé de Argüelles reports to the King and the Council of the Indies on the situation in Florida," 3 August 1593, AGI 229, in David Beers Quinn, ed., *New American World: A Documentary History of North America to 1612*, vol. 5, *The Extensions of Settlement in Florida, Virginia, and the Spanish Southwest* (New York: Arno Press, 1979), 90. See the discussion of this document and the meaning of tributary relationships for Indigenous polities in Florida in Hall, *Zamumo's Gifts*, 49 and n. 36.

107. Smith, "The Proceedings," in *Captain John Smith*, ed. Horn, 64.

108. Smith, "The Proceedings," in *Captain John Smith*, ed. Horn, 95–96.

109. Peter Martyr, *De Nouo Orbe, or the historie of the west Indies*, trans. Michael Lok (London: 1612), 256v.

110. Andrew Lintott, *Imperium Romanum: Politics and Administration* (New York: Routledge, 1993), 18.

111. "Instructions orders and constitucons *** to Sr Thomas Gates knight Governor of Virginia," May 1609, *RVC*, 3: 18.

112. "Instructions orders and constitucons *** to Sr Thomas Gates knight Governor of Virginia," May 1609, *RVC*, 3: 18.

113. "Instructions orders and constitucons *** to Sr Thomas Gates knight Governor of Virginia," May 1609, *RVC*, 3: 18.

114. "Instructions orders and constitucons *** to Sr Thomas Gates knight Governor of Virginia," May 1609, *RVC*, 3: 19.

115. "Instructions orders and constitucons *** to Sr Thomas Gates knight Governor of Virginia," May 1609, *RVC*, 3: 19.

116. "Instructions orders and constitucons *** to Sr Thomas Gates knight Governor of Virginia," May 1609, *RVC*, 3: 19.

117. Gonzalo Mendez de Canzo, "Paragraphs from a letter from the Governor of Florida Gonzalo Mendez de Canzo, to His Majesty, about the Obedience and Submission of Various Caciques," 24 February 1598, in *Documentos históricos*, 136.

118. Mendez Canzo, "Paragraphs," 24 February 1598, in *Documentos históricos*, 136.

119. Francisco de Pareja, *Confessionario en lengua Castellana y Timuquana con algunos consejos para animar al penitente* (México: 1613), fol. 183v (my translation). A published translation of the *Confessionario* is also available. See Jerald T. Milanich and William C. Sturtevant, eds., *Francisco Pareja's 1613 Confessionario: A Documentary Source for Timucuan Ethnography*, trans. Emilio F. Moran (Tallahassee: Division of Archives, History, and Records Management, Florida Department of State, 1972), 34. The long-term Timucua-language recovery project of Alejandra Dubcovsky and linguist George Aaron Broadwell has shown just how different the words would have been in Timucua owing to Pareja's weak grasp of the language's grammar and the work of many Timucua informants in the compilation of the confessional. Alejandra Dubcovsky and George Aaron Broadwell, "Writing Timucua: Recovering and Interrogating Indigenous Authorship," *Early American Studies: An Interdisciplinary Journal*, vol. 5, no. 3 (Summer 2017): 409–441, esp. 432.

120. "Instructions orders and constitucons *** to Sr Thomas Gates knight Governor of Virginia," May 1609, *RVC*, 3: 19.

121. Strachey, *Virginia Britannia*, 81.

122. John Smith, *A map of Virginia: VVith a description of the countrey, the commodities, people, government and religion* (London: 1612), 36.

123. Pareja, *Confessionario*, 183v–184r.

124. William Symonds, *Virginia: A Sermon Preached at White-Chappel, In the presence of many, Honourable and Worshipfull, the Aduenturers and Planters for Virginia. 25. April. 1609* (London: 1609), 10.

125. Symonds, *Virginia*, 10.

126. Andrew Fitzmaurice points out that for English promoters the justice of colonization was something to be accounted for on the way to more "practical" concerns. There was no great open-ended debate. See Fitzmaurice, *Humanism and America*, 148. What debate occurred, says Leitch Wright, took place in the early seventeenth century. Wright, *Only Land They Knew*, 61–62.

127. Ralph Hamor, *A Trve Discovrse of the Present Estate of Virginia, and the successe of the affaires there till the 18 of Iune. 1614. Together. With a Relation of the severall English Townes and forts, the assured hopes of that countrie and the peace concluded with the Indians. The Christening of Powhatans daughter and her marriage with an English-man* (London: 1615), 2.

128. Smith, "The Proceedings," in *Captain John Smith*, ed. Horn, 57.

129. Smith, "The Proceedings," in *Captain John Smith*, ed. Horn, 89.

130. Smith, "The Proceedings," in *Captain John Smith*, ed. Horn, 49.

131. Virginia Company, *Trve Declaration*, 67.

132. Virginia Company, *Trve Declaration*, 8–9.

133. Virginia Company, *Trve Declaration*, 10.

134. William Strachey, "To the constant, mighty, and worthie friends, the Committies, Assistants vnto his Maiesties Councell for the Colonie in Virginea-Britannia," in *For the Colony in Virginea Britannia: Lavves Diuine, Morall and Martiall, &c.* (London: 1612), [7].

135. For Strachey's legal training, see S. G. Culliford, *William Strachey, 1572–1621* (Charlottesville: The University Press of Virginia, 1965), 31–32.

136. Laws 9 and 16, Strachey, *Lavves Diuine, Morall and Martiall*, 5 and 7.

137. Law 45, Strachey, *Lavves Diuine, Morall and Martiall*, 33.

138. Strachey, "A Praier duly said Morning and Euening vpon the Court of Guard, either by the Captaine of the watch himselfe, or by some one of his principall officers," in *Lavves Diuine, Morall and Martiall*, [7].

139. "Testimony Regarding the Arrival of Several Chiefs," 21 April 1609, AGI SD 224, PKY, SC, reel 9.

140. "Testimony," 21 April 1609, AGI SD 224, PKY, SC reel 9.

141. "Testimony," 21 April 1609, AGI SD 224, PKY, SC reel 9, ("garments"); Governor Pedro de Ibarra to the King, 30 April 1609, AGI SD 224, PKY, SC reel 9, ("doctrina").

142. Ibarra to the King, 30 April 1609, AGI SD 224, PKY, SC, reel 9 (quote); the cross he received is mentioned in "Testimony," 21 April 1609, AGI SD 224, PKY, SC reel 9.

143. Ibarra to the King, 30 April 1609, AGI SD 224, PKY, SC, reel 9.

144. For the entire exchange, see William Strachey, "A True Repertory," in *Captain John Smith*, ed. Horn, 1031–1032.

145. For the significance of 1612 in Virginia, specifically the Virginia Company's dire financial predicament, see Bernard Bailyn, *The Barbarous Years: The Conflict of Civilizations, 1600–1675* (New York: Alfred A. Knopf, 2012), 77–78.

146. Religious of Florida to the King, 16 October 1612, AGI SD 232, PKY, SC, reel 9.

147. Religious of Florida to the King, 16 October 1612, AGI SD 232, PKY, SC, reel 9.

148. Governor Juan Fernández de Olivera to the King, 13 October 1612, AGI SD 225, PKY, SC, reel 9.

149. Religious of Florida to the King, 16 October 1612, AGI SD 232, PKY, SC, reel 9.

150. Religious of Florida to the King, 16 October 1612, AGI SD 232, PKY, SC, reel 9.

151. Robert Johnson, *The New Life of Virginea: Declaring the Former Svccese and present estate of that plantation, being the second part of Noua Britannia; Published by the authoritie of his Maiesties Counsell for Virginea* (London: 1612), [40].

152. Robert Johnson, *Nova Britannia: Offring Most Excellent fruites by Planting in Virginia; Exciting all such as be well affected to further the same* (London: 1609), [16].

153. Admittedly, the context suggests that they probably meant "beasts," rather than "deer." Yet the comparison of Indigenous people to deer was a common European trope and I think my translation is a better choice. Religious of Florida to the King, 16 October 1612, AGI SD 232, PKY, SC, reel 9. In contrast to my translation, David Beers Quinn's rendered "*venados*" as "wild animals." See "775.October 16, 1612. The Franciscans of Florida to Philip III," in Quinn, ed., *New American World*, 5: 140.

154. Smith, *Map of Virginia*, 34.

155. Alexander Whitaker, *Good nevves from Virginia* (London: 1613), 26.

156. Religious of Florida to the King, 16 October 1612, AGI SD 232, PKY, SC, reel 9.

157. Religious of Florida to the King, 16 October 1612, AGI SD 232, PKY, SC, reel 9.

158. Virginia Company, *Trve Declaration*, 11.

159. "CLVII. Velasco to Philip III," 22 March 1611, in Brown, ed., *Genesis*, 1: 456.

160. Johnson, *New Life*, [17–18].

161. Velasco to Philip III, 22 March 1611, in Brown, ed. *Genesis*, 1: 456.

162. Religious of Florida to the King, 16 October 1612, AGI SD 232, PKY, SC, reel 9.

163. Religious of Florida to the King, 16 October 1612, AGI SD 232, PKY, SC, reel 9.

164. Religious of Florida to the King, 16 October 1612, AGI SD 232, PKY, SC, reel 9.

165. Religious of Florida to the King, 16 October 1612, AGI SD 232, PKY, SC, reel 9.

166. Johnson, *New Life*, [34].

167. Samuel Purchas, "Notes of the West Indies, gathered out of Pedro Ordonnes de Ceuallos a Spanish Priest, his larger obseruations," in *Purchas His Pilgrimes*, by Purchas, 1421.

168. Johnson, *New Life*, [36–37].

169. Johnson, *New Life*, [40].

170. Johnson, *New Life*, [42].

171. Strachey, *Virginia Britannia*, 87.

172. Strachey drew inspiration from John Ellis's account of his voyage to Peru late in the last century. Strachey, *Virginia Britannia*, 87–88.

173. Strachey, *Virginia Britannia*, 86–87.

174. Strachey, *Virginia Britannia*, 87.

175. William Vaughan, *The golden-grove, moralized in three bookes: a worke very necessary for all such, as would know how to governe themselves, their houses, or their countrey* (London: 1600), book 3, ch. 19.

176. Vaughan, *The golden-grove*, 3: 19.

177. Helen C. Rountree, *Pocahontas, Powhatan, Opechancanough: Three Indian Lives Changed by Jamestown* (Charlottesville: University of Virginia Press, 2005), 158–167; Townsend, *Pocahontas and the Powhatan Dilemma*, 85–134, 126 ("two nations").

178. The phrase is Jeffrey Glover's. See Glover, *Paper Sovereigns*, 3.

179. What sort of future the treaty heralded is the subject of debate. For the ways that the treaty of 1614 reflects Indigenous political ideas concerning subordination, tribute, and autonomy, see Dylan Ruediger, "'Neither Utterly to Reject Them, Nor Yet to Drawe Them to Come In': Tributary Subordination and Settler Colonialism in Virginia," *Early American Studies: An Interdisciplinary Journal*, vol. 18, no. 1 (Winter 2020): 8–10; Matthew Kruer, *Time of Anarchy: Indigenous Power and the Crisis of Colonialism in Early America* (Cambridge, MA: Harvard University Press, 2021), 24; James Horn emphasizes the expectations the English had of the Chickahominies' subordination in feudal terms. Horn, *Land as God Made It*, 220; Frederic W. Gleach points out that the agreement was predicated on equality—even if that term was understood differently by the parties involved. Gleach, *Powhatan's World*, 136–138.

180. Hamor, *A Trve Discovrse*, 11.

181. Hamor, *A Trve Discovrse*, 11.

182. Hamor, *A Trve Discovrse*, 15.

183. Hamor, *A Trve Discovrse*, 13.

184. Hamor, *A Trve Discovrse*, 13.

185. Hamor, *A Trve Discovrse*, 13.

186. Hamor, *A Trve Discovrse*, 14.

187. Hamor, *A Trve Discovrse*, 12.

188. See Amy Turner Bushnell, "'These People Are Not Conquered like Those of New Spain': Florida's Reciprocal Colonial Compact," *Florida Historical Quarterly*, vol. 92, no. 3 (Winter 2014): 551.

189. James D. Rice, "These Doubtfull Times, Between Us and the Indians: Indigenous Politics and the Jamestown Colony in 1619," in *Virginia 1619: Slavery & Freedom in the Making of English America*, ed. Paul Musselwhite, Peter C. Mancall, and James Horn (Chapel Hill: University of North Carolina Press for Omohundro Institute for Early American History and Culture, 2019), 217–219.

190. Oré, *Martyrs of Florida*, 152.

191. For the life of Oré, see the introduction in *Martyrs of Florida*, 1–59.

192. Oré, *Martyrs of Florida*, 152.

193. Oré, *Martyrs of Florida*, 152.

194. Oré, *Martyrs of Florida*, 155.

195. Oré, *Martyrs of Florida*, 154.

196. Lorenzo Martinez to the King, 14 September 1612, AGI SD 232, PKY, SC, reel 9.

197. Oré, *Martyrs of Florida*, 157.

198. Oré, *Martyrs of Florida*, 157.

199. Counseil for Virginia, *A Briefe Declaration of the present state of things in Virginia* (London: 1616), 5.

200. Hamor, *A Trve Discovrse*, 42.

201. Townsend, *Pocahontas*, 141–142.

202. Smith, "The Generall Historie," in *Captain John Smith*, ed. Horn, 442.

203. Robert Beverley, *The History & Present State of Virginia*, ed. Susan Scott Parrish (Chapel Hill: University of North Carolina Press for Omohundro Institute for Early American History and Culture, 2013), 47.

204. For more on the commonwealth idea as it applies to Virginia at the time, see James Horn, *1619: Jamestown and the Forging of American Democracy* (New York: Basic Books, 2018), 119–152.

205. "A reporte of the manner of proceeding in the General assembly," 1619, CO 1/1, no. 39, fol. 141v.

206. Rice, "Doubtfull Times," in *Virginia 1619*, ed. Musselwhite, Mancall, and Horn, 215–235.

207. Alexander Haskell, *For God, King, and People: Forging Commonwealth Bonds in Renaissance Virginia* (Chapel Hill: University of North Carolina Press for Omohundro Institute for Early American History and Culture, 2017), 196–198.

208. "Petition setting forth the needs of the church in St. Augustine," 15 January 1621, AGI SD 235, PKY, SC, reel 10.

209. "Petition setting forth the needs of the church in St. Augustine," 15 January 1621, AGI SD 235, PKY, SC, reel 10.

210. Francisca Ramirez to the King, 24 April 1622, AGI SD 232, PKY, SC, reel 10.

211. Francisca Ramirez to the King, 24 April 1622, AGI SD 232, PKY, SC, reel 10.

212. Fray Luís Gerónimo de Oré to the King, 1618, AGI SD 235, PKY, JTCC, box 15, folder 54-5-20, microfilm copy.

213. George Thorpe and John Pory to Edwin Sandys, 15–16 May 1621, in *RVC*, 3: 446.

214. "Instructions to the Governor and Council," 24 July 1621, in *RVC*, 3: 470.

215. Edward Waterhouse, *A Declaration of the State of the Colony and Affaires in Virginia* (London: 1622), 27.

216. Waterhouse, *Declaration*, 31.

217. Waterhouse, *Declaration*, 32.

218. Waterhouse, *Declaration*, 32.

219. Cañizares-Esguerra, *Puritan Conquistadors*, 65.

220. George Abbot, *A Briefe Description of the whole Worlde*, 3rd ed. (London: 1608), 134; April Hatfield pointed out this time lag, noting the curious respect the English had for Oviedo's history from the previous century. See Hatfield, "Colonizing Literature," *JSH* 69: 2, 280.

221. "VIII. The Adelantado, Pedro Menéndez, Reports the Damages and Murders Caused by the Coast Indians of Florida," *CRSF*, 1: 79.

222. Connor, trans., *CRSF*, 1: 33.

223. Connor, trans., *CRSF*, 1: 63.

224. Connor, trans., *CRSF*, 1: 35.

225. Connor, trans., *CRSF*, 1: 35.

226. Connor, trans., *CRSF*, 1: 35.

227. Waterhouse, *Declaration*, 13, 19.

228. Waterhouse, *Declaration*, 12.

229. Waterhouse, *Declaration*, 11.

230. Waterhouse, *Declaration*, 24.

231. Waterhouse, *Declaration*, 23.

232. Waterhouse, *Declaration*, 25.

233. Waterhouse, *Declaration*, 26.

234. Oré, *Martyrs of Florida*, 131.

235. Horn, *Brave and Cunning Prince*, 208–209.

236. William L. Shea, *The Virginia Militia in the Seventeenth Century* (Baton Rouge: Louisiana State University Press, 1983), 41–42.

237. Ian K. Steele, *Warpaths: Invasions of North America* (New York: Oxford University Press, 1994), 47.

238. William Perse, "A relation in generall of the present state of his Maties Colony in Virginia, by Captain William Perse, an antient planter of twenty yeares standing there," 1629, UKNA CO 1/5, fol. 69r.

239. Perse, "Relation," UKNA CO 1/5, fol. 69v.

240. Perse, "Relation," UKNA CO 1/5, fol. 69r.

241. See Worth, *Timucuan Chiefdoms*, 1: xviii.

242. Andrés Rodriguez Villegas to the King, 27 December 1630, AGI SD 225, fol. 112r, PARES, accessed 15 February 2021.

243. Rodriguez Villegas to the King, 27 December 1630, AGI SD 225, fol. 112r.

244. Rodriguez Villegas to the King, 27 December 1630, AGI SD 225, fol. 112v.

245. Clark Spenser Larsen et al., "Frontiers of Contact: Bioarchaeology of Spanish Florida," *Journal of World Prehistory*, vol. 15, no. 1 (March 2001): 98–100; see also Worth, *Timucuan Chiefdoms*, 2: 15.

246. Specifically, they were refusing baptism on account of burdening, said the friars. Fray Juan de Santander, O. F. M., Commissary General of the Indies to Don Fernando Ruíz de Contreras, 14 October 1630, AGI SD 235, PKY, JTCC, box 15, folder 54-5-20, microfilm copy.

247. Larsen et al., "Frontiers of Contact," 75.

248. For more on the political effects of demographic collapse on Indigenous peoples, see Worth, *Timucuan Chiefdoms*, 1: 79.

Chapter 2

1. "Luis Horruytiner to the King relative to the English," 15 November 1633, AGI SD 225, PKY, SC, reel 10.

2. "Mèritos, Luis Orruitiner," 1640, AGI INDIFERENTE 111, PARES, accessed 18 January 2021.

3. "Luis Horruytiner to the King relative to the English," 15 November 1633, AGI SD 225, PKY, SC, reel 10.

4. "Luis Horruytiner to the King relative to the English," 15 November 1633, AGI SD 225, PKY, SC, reel 10.

5. "Luis Horruytiner to the King relative to the English," 15 November 1633, AGI SD 225, PKY, SC, reel 10.

6. "Luis Horruytiner to the King relative to the English," 15 November 1633, AGI SD 225, PKY, SC, reel 10.

7. See Helen C. Rountree and E. Randolph Turner III, *Before and After Jamestown: Virginia's Powhatans and their Predecessors* (Gainesville: University Press of Florida, 2002), 157, figure 5.11.

8. Martin D. Gallivan, *The Powhatan Landscape: An Archaeological History of the Algonquian Chesapeake* (Gainesville: University Press of Florida, 2016), 182. Recent scholarship challenges the riverine plantation model of the Chesapeake, arguing for a continuous effort by officials to establish towns. Paul Musselwhite, *Urban Dreams, Rural Commonwealth: The Rise of Plantation Society in the Chesapeake* (Chicago: University of Chicago Press, 2019). For the interconnectedness of seventeenth-century Virginia via waterways, see April Lee Hatfield, *Atlantic Virginia: Intercolonial Relations in the Seventeenth Century* (Philadelphia: University of Pennsylvania Press, 2004). For Florida's waterborne expansion, see Amy Turner Bushnell, *Situado and Sabana: Spain's Support System for Florida*, Anthropological Papers of the American Museum of Natural History 74 (New York: American Museum of Natural History, 1994), 113.

9. "Act V. An Act for Tradesmen to worke on their trades," in *Statutes*, 1: 208.

10. Arthur Pierce Middleton, *Tobacco Coast: A Maritime History of Chesapeake Bay in the Colonial Era* (Baltimore, MD: Johns Hopkins University Press, [1953] 1984).

11. The note about the treaty is dated 30 September 1632. H. R. McIlwaine, ed., *Minutes of the Council and General Court of Virginia, 1622–1632, 1670–1676: With Notes and Excerpts from Original Council and General Court Records, Into 1683, Now Lost* (Richmond, VA: 1924), 480.

12. Governor Harvey to the Privy Council, 20 February 1633, UKNA CO 1/6, no. 73, fol. 195r.

13. 5 June 1633, in McIlwaine, ed., *Minutes of the Council and General Court*, 480.

14. Damián Vega Castro y Pardo to the King, 9 July 1643, AGI SD 225, PARES, accessed 21 January 2021.

15. In New England, such appeals were more common throughout the colonial era. See Craig Yirush, "Claiming the New World: Empire, Law, and Indigenous Rights in the Mohegan Case, 1704–1743, *Law and History Review*, vol. 29, no. 2 (May 2011): 333–373; Craig Yirush, "'Chief Princes and Owners of All': Native American Appeals to the Crown in the Early-Modern British Atlantic," in *Native Claims: Indigenous Law Against Empire, 1500–1920*, ed. Saliha

Belmessous (Oxford: Oxford University Press, 2011). Natives understood clearly how to navigate the "ladders of authority" in the English Atlantic world. Jenny Hale Pulsipher, *Subjects unto the Same King: Indians, English, and the Contest for Authority in Colonial New England* (Philadelphia: University of Pennsylvania, 2005), 56–57. From the South, Mary Musgrove petitioned the Crown and the Board of Trade in the eighteenth century. Steven C. Hahn, *The Life and Times of Mary Musgrove* (Gainesville: University Press of Florida, 2012), 167–168, 203–231.

16. Tamar Herzog has used the terms "insiders" and "outisders" in a far more sophisticated manner than here, essentially describing a process whereby colonizers "indigenized" or "naturalized" themselves. By "insiders" I simply mean Indigenous vassals or subjects who were in effect part of the larger colonial and imperial political system; "outsiders" were those who were not. Tamar Herzog, "The Appropriation of Native Status: Forming and Reforming Insiders and Outsiders in the Spanish Colonial World," *Rechtsgesechichte / Legal History*, vol. 22 (2014): 140–149.

17. "Luis Horruytiner to the King relative to Florida matters," 15 November 1633, AGI SD 225, PKY, SC, reel 10.

18. "Luis Horruytiner to the King relative to Florida matters," 15 November 1633, AGI SD 225, PKY, SC, reel 10.

19. "Mèritos, Luís Orruitiner," 1640, AGI INDIFERENTE 111, PARES, accessed 18 January 2021.

20. Damián Vega Castro y Pardo to the King, 22 August 1639, AGI SD 225, fol. 170r, PARES, accessed 6 February 2021.

21. For more on the dynamics between Apalachee towns, see Aubrey Lauersdorf, "An Apalachee Revolt?: Reconceptualizing Violence in Seventeenth-Century Apalachee," in "Indigenous Florida," ed. Denise I. Bossy and Andrew K. Frank, special issue, *Florida Historical Quarterly*, vol. 100, no. 1 (Summer 2021): 27.

22. Luis Horruytiner to the King, 12 September 1638, AGI SD 225, fol. 155v, PARES, accessed 3 February 2021.

23. See John H. Hann, *Apalachee: The Land Between the Rivers* (Gainesville: University of Florida Press, 1988), 13–14.

24. Samuel Matthews to Sir John Wolstenholme, 25 May 1635, UKNA CO 1/8, no. 65, fol. 178r.

25. Matthews to Wolstenholme, UKNA CO 1/8, no. 65, fol. 178r.

26. For discussions of Harvey's fall and Indian policy, see Alfred A. Cave, *Lethal Encounters: Englishmen and Indians in Colonial Virginia* (Santa Barbara, CA: Praeger, 2011); 131–132; Michael Leroy Oberg, *Dominion and Civility: English Imperialism and Native America, 1585–1685* (Ithaca, NY: Cornell University Press, 1999), 179. See also J. Mills Thornton III, "The Thrusting out of Governor Harvey: A Seventeenth-Century Rebellion," *Virginia Magazine of History and Biography*, vol. 76, no. 1 (January 1968): 24.

27. Matthews to Wolstenholme, UKNA CO 1/8, no. 65, fol. 178v.

28. Matthews to Wolstenholme, UKNA CO 1/8, no. 65, fol. 178v.

29. Matthews to Wolstenholme, UKNA CO 1/8, no. 65, fol. 178v.

30. Matthews to Wolstenholme, UKNA CO 1/8, no. 65, fol. 179r.

31. Matthews to Wolstenholme, UKNA CO 1/8, no. 65, fol. 178r.

32. "Two Indians, Agustín and Juan, complain of the treatment accorded them," 2 July 1636, AGI SD 27, PKY, SC, reel 11.

33. "Two Indians, Agustín and Juan, complain of the treatment accorded them," 2 July 1636, AGI SD 27, PKY, SC, reel 11.

34. "Two Indians, Agustín and Juan, complain of the treatment accorded them," 2 July 1636, AGI SD 27, PKY, SC, reel 11.

35. "Names of the Chief Mutineers in Virginia," ca. December 1635, UKNA CO 1/8, no. 85, fol. 220r.

36. "Chief Mutineers in Virginia," UKNA CO 1/8, no. 85, fol. 220r.

37. "Consulta del consejo relative to Indians of Florida held prisoner in Havana," 7 October 1637, AGI SD 6, PKY, SC, reel 11.

38. "Consulta del consejo relative to Indians of Florida held prisoner in Havana," 7 October 1637, AGI SD 6, PKY, SC, reel 11.

39. Oberg, for instance, argues convincingly that this conflict played out again and again in American history. Oberg, *Dominion and Civility*, 217–227, esp. 226–227.

40. Alexander B. Haskell, *For God, King, and People: Forging Commonwealth Bonds in Renaissance Virginia* (Chapel Hill: University of North Carolina Press, 2017), 253 and 269–270.

41. Haskell, *For God, King, and People*, 250.

42. Despite Stuart pretensions to absolutism during Charles I's personal rule and the first stirrings of imperial centralization, Harvey's position may not have been as strong as historians have tended to think. L. H. Roper, *The English Empire in America, 1602-1658: Beyond Jamestown* (New York: Routledge, 2016), 110–115, esp. 112.

43. "Consulta del consejo relative to Indians of Florida held prisoner in Havana," 7 October 1637, AGI SD 6, PKY, SC, reel 11.

44. Luis Horruytiner to the King, 24 June 1637, AGI SD 225, fol. 153r, PARES, accessed 7 March 2021.

45. Luis Horruytiner to the King, 24 June 1637, AGI SD 225, fol. 153r-v, PARES, accessed 7 March 2021.

46. Fray Juan Gómez de Palma to the King, [1637], British Museum Add. MSS. 13976, PKY, JTCC, box 23, microfilm copy, p. 4.

47. Luis Horruytiner to the King, 24 June 1637, AGI SD 225, fol. 153v, PARES, accessed 7 March 2021.

48. Luis Horruytiner to the King, 12 September 1638, AGI SD 225, fol. 155v, PARES, accessed 3 February 2021.

49. Damián Vega Castro y Pardo to the King, 22 August 1639, AGI SD 225, fol. 169v, PARES, accessed 6 February 2021.

50. Damián Vega Castro y Pardo to the King, 22 August 1639, AGI SD 225, fol. 169v, PARES, accessed 6 February 2021.

51. Damián Vega Castro y Pardo to the King, 22 August 1639, AGI SD 225, fol. 169v, PARES, accessed 6 February 2021.

52. Christopher M. Stojanowksi, *Mission Cemeteries, Mission Peoples: Historical and Evolutionary Dimensions of Intracemetery Bioarchaeology in Spanish Florida* (Gainesville: University Press of Florida, 2013), 259.

53. For the first deployment of soldiers, see Hann, *Apalachee*, 14; For the governor's motives concerning the royal jurisdiction and trade duties, see Damián Vega Castro y Pardo to the King, 9 July 1643, AGI SD 225, PARES, accessed 21 January 2021.

54. Lauersdorf, "Apalachee Revolt," 37, 39–40.

55. A common strategy and one that alarmed Europeans. Joseph M. Hall, Jr., *Zamumo's Gifts: Indian-European Exchange in the Colonial Southeast* (Philadelphia: University of Pennsylvania Press, 2009), 21, 62–63.

56. Lars C. Adams, *Breaking the House of Pamunkey: The Final Powhatan War and the Fall of an American Indian Empire* (Crofton, KY: Backintyme Publishing, 2017), 39–40.

57. 14 December 1640, in McIlwaine, ed., *Minutes of the Council and General Court*, 478.

58. William Castell, *A Short Discoverie of the Coasts and Continent of America, From the Equinoctiall Northward, and the adjacent Isles* (London: 1644), 3.

59. Castell, *Short Discoverie*, 20–21. For more on Castell and his plans to channel English aggression into American conquest and colonial expansion, see Evan Haefeli, *Accidental Pluralism: America and the Religious Politics of English Expansion, 1497–1662* (Chicago: The University of Chicago Press, 2021), 212–213.

60. Castell, *Short Discoverie*, 21.

61. Castell, *Short Discoverie*, 29 and 32.

62. "Cada día ba en mucho augmento," 29 August 1644, "Damián de Vega Castro y Pardo, Governor of Florida, to the King, referring to the lack of situado, repair of the fort, etc.," AGI SD 225, PKY, SC, reel 11.

63. "Damián de Vega Castro y Pardo to the King," 29 August 1644, AGI SD 225, PKY, SC, reel 11.

64. "Damián de Vega Castro y Pardo to the King," 29 August 1644, AGI SD 225, PKY, SC, reel 11.

65. "Damián de Vega Castro y Pardo to the King," 29 August 1644, AGI SD 225, PKY, SC, reel 11.

66. "Act IV" of the February 1645 session made the day a "yearly" day of thanksgiving. *Statutes*, 1: 290.

67. For more on the events of 1644, see James Horn, *A Brave and Cunning Prince: The Great Chief Opechancanough and the War for America* (New York: Basic Books, 2021), 219–232. For the only book-length treatment of the uprising of 1644–1646, see Adams, *Breaking the House of Pamunkey*.

68. Ferdinando Gorges, *America Painted to the Life* (London: 1658), 227–228. Anonymous, *A Perfect Description of Virginia: Being, A Full and true Relation of the present State of the Plantation, their Health, Peace, and Plenty . . . With the manner how the Emperor Nichotowance came to Sir William Berckley, attended with five petty Kings, to doe Homage, and bring Tribute to King Charles.* [. . .] (London: 1649), 10.

69. Lionel Gatford, *Publick Good without Private Interest: or, A Compendious Remonstrance of the Present Sad State and Condition of the English Colonie in Virginea* (London: 1657), 6.

70. Gallivan, *Powhatan Landscape*, 182–183.

71. Richard Kemp to Sir William Berkeley, 27 February 1645, in *WBP*, 65.

72. *Mercurius Civicus: Londons Intelligencer or, Truth impartially related from thence to the whole Kingdome, to prevent mis-information*, no. 104, [Thursday, May 15 to Thursday, May 22] 1645, 929.

73. Warren M. Billings, *Sir William Berkeley and the Forging of Colonial Virginia* (Baton Rouge: Louisiana State University Press, 2004), 32–36.

74. Robert Beverley, *The History and Present State of Virginia*, ed. Susan Scott Parrish (Chapel Hill: University of North Carolina Press, 2013), 47.

75. Thomas Ludwell to Lord Arlington, "A Discription of the Government of Virginia," 17 September 1666, UKNA CO 1/20, 125.i, fol. 220r.

76. Ludwell to Arlington, "Discription of Virginia," 17 September 1666, UKNA CO 1/20, 125.i, fol. 220r.

77. Detail from Augustine Herrman and William Faithorne, *Virginia and Maryland As it is planted and Inhabited this present Year 1670*, 1673, original in the John Carter Brown Library, Brown University.

78. Beverley, *History*, 47.

79. Hann, *Apalachee*, 15, 197–198.

80. "Testimony of Witness, the captain, Joachím de Florencia," 9 July 1709, in "The Juana Cathalina Florencia Document of 1709: The Tallahassee Area's First European Settlers," PKY JHC, p. 36.

81. "Royal officials to the King relative to the murder of three religious by the Indians of Apalachee; and requesting an increase for the garrison," 18 March 1647, AGI SD 229, PKY, SC, Reel 11.

82. Lauersdorf, "Apalachee Revolt," 45.

83. "Testimony of Juan Francisco," 8 July 1709, in "The Juana Cathalina Florencia Document of 1709: The Tallahassee Area's First European Settlers," PKY, JHC, p. 24.

84. "Testimony of Witness, the captain, Joachím de Florencia," 9 July 1709, in "The Juana Cathalina Florencia Document of 1709: The Tallahassee Area's First European Settlers," PKY, JHC, p. 37.

85. Lauersdorf, "Apalachee Revolt," 46.

86. Lauersdorf, "Apalachee Revolt," 28; "Royal officials to the King relative to the murder of three religious by the Indians of Apalachee; and requesting an increase for the garrison," 18 March 1647, AGI SD 229, PKY, SC, reel 11.

87. "Royal officials to the King relative to the murder of three religious by the Indians of Apalachee; and requesting an increase for the garrison," 18 March 1647, AGI SD 229, PKY, SC, reel 11, 1.

88. "Royal officials to the King relative to the murder of three religious by the Indians of Apalachee; and requesting an increase for the garrison," 18 March 1647, AGI SD 229, PKY, SC, reel 11, 2.

89. "Royal officials to the King relative to the murder of three religious by the Indians of Apalachee; and requesting an increase for the garrison," 18 March 1647, AGI SD 229, PKY, SC, reel 11, 2.

90. Lauersdorf, "Apalachee Revolt," 46 and 48–49.

91. "Royal officials of Florida to the King announcing that the insurrection among the Apalachees has been quelled," 28 July 1647, AGI SD 235, PKY, SC, reel 11, p. 1.

92. Historians debate the motives and objectives of the 1644 attack. Lars Adams argues that Opechancanough intended to retake "the whole of Virginia." Adams, *House of Pamunkey*, 61–62. Others have argued that the attack had more limited objectives. Helen C. Rountree, *Pocahontas, Powhatan, Opechancanough: Three Indian Lives Changed by Jamestown* (Charlottesville: University of Virginia Press, 2005), 231–235. Frederic W. Gleach, *Powhatan's World and Colonial Virginia: A Conflict of Cultures* (Lincoln: University of Nebraska Press, 1997), 175–176.

93. Lauersdorf, "Apalachee Revolt," 46–47.

94. As the decade of war after 1622 proved. Dylan Ruediger, "'Neither Utterly to Reject Them, Nor Yet to Drawe Them to Come In': Tributary Subordination and Settler Colonialism in Virginia," *Early American Studies: An Interdisciplinary Journal*, vol. 18, no. 1 (Winter 2020): 30; Cave, *Lethal Encounters*, 136.

95. Lauersdorf, "Apalachee Revolt," 49–50.

96. The phrase appears in Horn, *Brave and Cunning Prince*, 219–232.

97. Samuel Purchas, *Hakluytus Posthumus or, Purchas His Pilgrimes* (London: 1625), 1841.

98. Beverley, *History*, 47.

99. Beverley, *History*, 48.

100. Beverley, *History*, 48.

101. Beverley, *History*, 48.

102. Necotowance wanted to set the agenda by negotiating a larger treaty with the English and thereby maintain Pamunkey influence. Hayley Negrin, "Cockacoeske's Rebellion: Nathaniel Bacon, Indigenous Slavery, and Sovereignty in Early Virginia," *William and Mary Quarterly*, vol. 80, no. 1 (January 2023): 56; For Necotowance's relationship to Opechancanough, see Adams, *House of Pamunkey*, 197–198.

103. Helen C. Rountree, *Pocahontas's People: The Powhatan Indians of Virginia Through Four Centuries* (Norman: University of Oklahoma Press, 1990), 86–87.

104. For more on Berkeley's political ideas, see Haskell, *For God, King, and People*, 289–307.

105. Jeffrey Glover, *Paper Sovereigns: Anglo-Native Treaties and the Law of Nations, 1604–1664* (Philadelphia: University of Pennsylvania Press, 2014), 3.

106. For the view of the treaty of 1646 as more of an English imposition, see Kristalyn Marie Shefveland, *Anglo-Native Virginia: Trade, Conversion, and Indian Slavery in the Old Dominion, 1646–1722* (Athens, GA: University of Georgia Press, 2016), 8–9.

107. The submission may have accorded with Indigenous rules for ending conflicts. The fact that the submission came with "symbolic delivery of exotic goods," in this case beaver pelts, suggests that as bad as the war was, the defeat may have been considered less severe. See Wayne E. Lee, *The Cutting-Off Way: Indigenous Warfare in Eastern North America, 1500–1800* (Chapel Hill: UNC Press, 2023), 190–191.

108. The treaty was codified into statute as the first act of the October 1646 session of the Grand Assembly. *Statutes*, 1: 323.

109. My emphasis. *Statutes*, 1: 323.

110. Again, Virginia's practice in this regard was similar to that in the Spanish world. Karen Graubart, *Republics of Difference: Religious and Racial Self-Governance in the Spanish Atlantic World* (New York: Oxford University Press, 2022), 145.

111. The establishment of *cabildos* elsewhere in the empire ostensibly served "to curtail the authority of Indigenous nobles." Graubart, *Republics of Difference*, 139. For the discussion on *cabildos* (or their absence) among Spanish *vecinos* in Florida, see John H. Hann, "Evidence Pertinent to the Florida Cabildo Controversy and the Misdating of the Juan Marquez Cabrera Governorship," *Florida Historical Quarterly*, vol. 79, no. 1 (Summer 2000): 68–83.

112. "Order from Governor Benito Ruíz de Salazar Vallecilla," 11 July 1650, in Antonio de Argüelles to the King, 1662, AGI SD 23, fol. 15r, PARES, accessed 27 June 2021.

113. *Statutes*, 1: 323.

114. There were Indigenous precedents for the Florida *repartimiento*, with local chiefs sending laborers to work for other chiefs, often as burdeners. By this light, the aftermath of the Apalachee uprising allowed the Spanish to "propose" such an arrangement instead of imposing it. See Lauersdorf, "Apalachee Revolt," 35–36, 50 (quotation). Others have argued that the labor draft was imposed or grudgingly accepted. Robert C. Galgano, *Feast of Souls: Indians and Spaniards in the Seventeenth-Century Missions of Florida and New Mexico* (Albuquerque: University of New Mexico Press, 2005), 93–94; Bushnell, *Situado and Sabana*, 128.

115. For the best argument for the Algonquian and European natural-law roots of the tributary system, see Ruediger, "Tributary Subordination," 1–31. One recent work claims the terms of the treaty of 1646 resembled an *encomienda*. Shefveland, *Anglo-Native Virginia*, 6 and 11.

116. *Statutes*, 1: 323.

117. Juan de Solórzano y Pereira, *Política Indiana* (Madrid: 1648), 170.

118. Solórzano, *Política Indiana*, 170.

119. Solórzano, *Política Indiana*, 171.

120. Matthew Kruer calls this kind of arrangement the "patriarchal compact," and argues that emotions like love were at the heart of political discourse for Native peoples and the English during the seventeenth century. Matthew Kruer, *Time of Anarchy: Indigenous Power and the Crisis of Colonialism in Early America* (Cambridge, MA: Harvard University Press, 2021), 13–14, 19–21.

121. And who skillfully shifted the bother of a Spanish ranch onto their Yustaga allies while reaping the political capital from the venture. Lauersdorf, "Apalachee Revolt," 40.

122. Gallivan, *Powhatan Landscape*, 112.

123. Gallivan, *Powhatan Landscape*, 184–190.

124. See the terms of the treaty in *Statutes*, 1: 323–326.

125. Stanley Pargellis, "An Account of the Indians of Virginia," *William and Mary Quarterly*, vol. 16, no. 2 (April 1959): 241.

126. "Letters came now this March, 1648, relate further," in *Perfect Description of Virginia*, 13.

127. "Letters," in *Perfect Description of Virginia*, 13.

128. "Letters," in *Perfect Description of Virginia*, 13. For Berkeley's bodyguard see *Statutes*, 1: 354–355.

129. "Letters," in *Perfect Description of Virginia*, 13. See also Adams, *House of Pamunkey*, 205–206.

130. Graubart argues that rather than grafting themselves onto existing Indigenous empires, Spaniards actively dissolved them into their constituent parts, which were, in turn, made dependent on the Crown in Spain. Graubart, *Republics of Difference*, 8. For views on the collapse, breakup, or destruction of the chiefdom, see Negrin, "Cockacoeske's Rebellion," 55; Shefveland, *Anglo-Native Virginia*, 17–18; Ethan A. Schmidt, *The Divided Dominion: Social Conflict and Indian Hatred in Early Virginia* (Boulder: University Press of Colorado, 2015), 126 and 154. For the suggestion that the collapse was the result of deliberate colonial strategy, see Martha McCartney, "Cockacoeske, Queen of Pamunkey: Diplomat and Suzeraine," in *Powhatan's Mantle: Indians in the Colonial Southeast*, ed. Gregory A. Waselkov, Peter H. Wood, and Tom Hatley (Lincoln: University of Nebraska Press, 2006), 244; Rountree, *Pocahontas's People*, 86–87. For a differing conclusion, see Dylan Ruediger who calls the move not a breakdown but an Indigenous "act of resistance" by the constituent nations of the Powhatan polity. Russell Dylan Ruediger, "Tributary Subjects: Affective Colonialism, Power, and the Process of Subjugation in Colonial Virginia, c. 1600–c. 1740" (PhD diss., Georgia State University, 2017), 161–162, accessed 11 May 2023, https://doi.org/10.57709/9979636.

131. Robin Beck, *Chiefdoms, Collapse, and Coalescence in the Early American South* (New York: Cambridge University Press, 2013), 102.

132. For the origin of the phrase "house of Pamunkey," see McCartney, "Cockacoeske," 258.

133. "Act the 19th Concerninge Pattents to the Indians Kings" (10 October 1649), in Warren M. Billings, "Some Acts Not in Hening's 'Statutes': The Acts of Assembly, April 1652,

November 1652, And July 1653," *Virginia Magazine of History and Biography*, vol. 83, no. 1 (January 1975): 65. Billings identifies Ossakican as leader of the Piankatanks. Billings, "Some Acts Not in Hening's," 65 and n. 126. Rountree, with better evidence, argues he was Chiskiak. See Rountree, *Pocahontas's People*, 91 and n. 7.

134. Billings, "Some Acts not in Hening's," 65.

135. Billings, "Some Acts not in Hening's," 65.

136. Graubart, *Republics of Difference*, 153 and 167; Allan Greer, *Property and Dispossession: Natives, Empires and Land in Early Modern North America* (New York: Cambridge University Press, 2018), 359–367; Billings, "Some Acts not in Hening's," 66.

137. Billings, "Some Acts not in Hening's," 66.

138. Billings, "Some Acts not in Hening's," 66.

139. "Act the 8th Concerninge granting Indians land in the first place," 10 November 1650, in Billings, "Some Acts not in Hening's," 68.

140. Billings, "Some Acts not in Hening's," 68.

141. Shefveland, *Anglo-Native Virginia*, 9.

142. See, also, Ruediger, "Tributary Subordination," 20.

143. Kruer, *Time of Anarchy*, 38 and 44–45; Ruediger, "Tributary Subordination," 3; Shefveland, *Anglo-Native Virginia*, 18–19.

144. Kruer, *Time of Anarchy*, 48 and 153 (quotation).

145. Amy Turner Bushnell, "Ruling 'the Republic of Indians' in Seventeenth-Century Florida," in *Powhatan's Mantle: Indians in the Colonial Southeast*, ed. Gregory A. Waselkov, Peter H. Wood, and Tom Hatley (Lincoln: University of Nebraska Press, 2006), 203.

146. "Petition of Fr. Pedro Morena Ponce de Leon relative to the insurrection in Apalachee, and asking aid," 3 August 1648, AGI SD 235, PKY, SC, reel 11.

147. "Petition of Fray Pedro Moreno Ponce de Leon, procurador general of Florida and Havana, relative to the insurrection in Apalachee," 9 July 1648, AGI SD 235, PKY, SC, reel 11.

148. "Petition of Fray Pedro Moreno Ponce de Leon," 9 July 1648, AGI SD 235, PKY, SC, reel 11.

149. William Bullock, *Virginia impartially examined, and left to publick view, to be considered by all iudicious and honest men* (London: 1649), 55.

150. Bullock, *Virginia impartially examined*, 55.

151. "Governor Diego de Villalva to the King relative to the pacification of Apalachee and the need for religious," 22 March 1648, AGI SD 235, PKY, SC, reel 11.

152. Joseph M. Hall, Jr. observes that San Agustin and Havana were rivals for Apalachee affections—and commerce—during the mid-seventeenth century. Hall, *Zamumo's Gifts*, 65.

153. "Villalva to the King," 22 March 1648, AGI SD 235, PKY, SC, reel 11.

154. "Royal cédula to Governor Diego de Villalva," 1648, AGI SD 235, PKY, JTCC, box 15, folder 54-5-20, microfilm copy.

155. "Royal cédula addressed to the Governor and Royal Officials of Florida relative to the Indians," 8 August 1648, AGI SD 834, PKY, SC, reel 11.

156. "Royal cédula," 8 August 1648, AGI SD 834, PKY, SC, reel 11.

157. C. S. Everett, "'They Shalbe Slaves for Their Lives': Indian Slavery in Colonial Virginia," in *Indian Slavery in Colonial America*, ed. Alan Gallay (Lincoln: University of Nebraska Press, 2009), 67–108.

158. Bullock, *Virginia impartially examined*, 59.

159. Thomas Thorowgood, *Ievves in America, Or, Probabilities That the Americans are of that Race* (London: 1650), 74.

160. Hamon L'Estrange, *Americans are no Iewes, or Improbabilities that the Americans are of that Race* (London: 1652), 72.

161. George Gardyner, *A Description of the New World* (London: 1651). A manuscript copy of the American portion of Gardyner's work is among the Colonial Papers in the UK National Archives. "Generall Description of America or the new World," 1665, UKNA CO 1/19, no. 147.

162. Gardyner, *Description*, 136.

163. Gardyner, *Description*, 104.

164. Gardyner, *Description*, 102.

165. Joseph Acosta, *The Naturall and Morall Historie of the East and West Indies* (London: 1604), 471–472.

166. Gardyner, *Description*, 33–35.

167. Gardyner, *Description*, 33–35.

168. Gardyner, *Description*, 34.

169. Gardyner, *Description*, 102.

170. Thomas Gage, *The English-American his travaill by sea and land* [. . .] (London: 1648), [4]; Bartolomé de Las Casas, *The Tears of the Indians* [. . .] (London: 1656), [18].

171. Las Casas, *Tears of the Indians*, [30].

172. For more on the "Western Design," especially its impact on domestic politics in England, see Paul Lay, *Providence Lost: The Rise & Fall of Cromwell's Protectorate* (London: Apollo, 2022). For the fallout of Cromwell's plans in Jamaica, see Carla Gardina Pestana, *The English Conquest of Jamaica: Oliver Cromwell's Bid for Empire* (Cambridge, MA: Harvard University Press, 2017).

173. Gatford, *Publick Good*, 8; *Statutes*, 1: 402.

174. For more on the Westos and their origins, see Eric E. Bowne, *The Westo Indians: Slave Traders of the Early Colonial South* (Tuscaloosa: University of Alabama Press, 2005).

175. *Statutes*, 1: 402.

176. *Statutes*, 1: 402.

177. *Statutes*, 1: 403.

178. *Statutes*, 1: 403.

179. Gatford, *Publick Good*, 8.

180. Gatford, *Publick Good*, 8.

181. Gatford, *Publick Good*, 7.

182. John E. Worth, *The Timucuan Chiefdoms of Spanish Florida*, 2 vols. (Gainesville: University Press of Florida, 1998), 2: 45–46.

183. "Order from Rebolledo," 10 March 1655, in Antonio de Argüelles to the King, AGI SD 23, fol. 22v, PARES, accessed 27 June 2021.

184. "Order from Rebolledo," 10 March 1655, in Antonio de Argüelles to the King, AGI SD 23, fol. 22v, PARES, accessed 27 June 2021.

185. "Order from Rebolledo," 10 March 1655, in Antonio de Argüelles to the King, AGI SD 23, fol. 22v, PARES, accessed 27 June 2021.

186. "Order from Rebolledo," 10 March 1655, in Antonio de Argüelles to the King, AGI SD 23, fol. 23r, PARES, accessed 27 June 2021.

187. The deeper causes were complex but together reflected, as John E. Worth argues, "the erosion of chiefly power and the loss of political autonomy." Worth, *Timucuan Chiefdoms*, 2: 38.

188. Fray Juan Gómez to Fray Francisco Martínez, 4 April 1657, AGI SD 225, PKY, SC, reel 12.

189. Negrin, "Cockacoeske's Rebellion," 58.

190. *Statutes*, 1: 422–423.

191. *Statutes*, 1: 415.

192. *Statutes*, 1: 415.

193. Gatford, *Publick Good*, 6.

194. Hayley Negrin postulates that Cockacoeske came of age during the Second Anglo-Powhatan War of 1644–1646 and its aftermath, putting her birthdate sometime in the 1630s perhaps. Hayley Negrin, "Cockacoeske's Rebellion: Nathaniel Bacon, Indigenous Slavery, and Sovereignty in Early Virginia," *William and Mary Quarterly*, vol. 80, no. 1 (January 2023): 56.

195. Kristalyn M. Shefveland, "Cockacoeske and Sarah Harris Stegge Grendon: Bacon's Rebellion and the Roles of Women," in *Virginia Women: Their Lives and Times*, ed. Cynthia A. Kierner and Sandra Treadway Goia, vol. 1 (Athens: University of Georgia Press, 2015), 33–54.

196. Gatford, *Publick Good*, 7.

197. Gatford, *Publick Good*, 7.

198. Gatford, *Publick Good*, 6.

199. Gatford, *Publick Good*, 6.

200. Gatford, *Publick Good*, 5.

201. Fray Juan Gómez to Fray Francisco Martinez, 4 April 1657, AGI SD 225, PKY, SC, reel 12.

202. Gómez to Martinez, 4 April 1657, AGI SD 225, PKY, SC, reel 12.

203. Gómez to Martinez, 4 April 1657, AGI SD 225, PKY, SC, reel 12.

204. Religious of Florida to the King, 10 September 1657, AGI SD 235, PKY, WLC, reel 8.

205. Caciques of Guale to the King, 16 October 1657, AGI SD 235, PKY, WLC, reel 8.

206. Caciques of Guale to the King, 16 October 1657, AGI SD 235, PKY, WLC, reel 8.

207. Negrin, "Cockacoeske's Rebellion," 58; Ethan A. Schmidt, "Cockacoeske, Weroansqua of the Pamunkeys, and Indian Resistance in Seventeenth-Century Virginia," *American Indian Quarterly*, vol. 36, no. 3 (Summer 2012): 306–307; McCartney, "Cockacoeske," 255; Rountree, *Pocahontas's People*, 112.

208. Negrin, "Cockacoeske's Rebellion," 59 and 73; Schmidt, "Cockacoeske," 307.

209. "Roya cédula," 24 February 1660, enclosed in Alonso de Aranguiz y Cotes to the King, 15 November 1661, AGI SD 225, fol. 468r-v, PARES, accessed 22 January 2021.

210. "Roya cédula," 24 February 1660, enclosed in Alonso de Aranguiz y Cotes to the King, 15 November 1661, AGI SD 225, fol. 468v, PARES, accessed 22 January 2021.

211. Santiago, *Mico* of Tolomato, to the King, 21 March 1658, AGI SD 233, PKY, JTCC, box 15, folder 54-5-18, microfilm copy.

212. Bushnell, *Situado and Sabana*, 119.

213. Santiago to the King, 21 March 1658, AGI SD 233, PKY, JTCC, box 15, folder 54-5-18, microfilm copy.

214. Santiago to the King, 21 March 1658, AGI SD 233, PKY, JTCC, box 15, folder 54-5-18, microfilm copy.

215. Santiago to the King, 21 March 1658, AGI SD 233, PKY, JTCC, box 15, folder 54-5-18, microfilm copy.

216. "Roya cédula," 24 February 1660, enclosed in Alonso de Aranguiz y Cotes to the King, 15 November 1661, AGI SD 225, fol. 468v, PARES, accessed 22 January 2021.

217. Jamestown had dramatically shrunk in size during the previous decade. Musselwhite, *Urban Dreams*, 110. The project to rebuild James City in brick during Berkeley's second administration had not yet begun. Billings, *Berkeley*, 174–184.

218. Jon Kukla, *Political Institutions in Virginia, 1619–1660* (New York: Garland Publishing, Inc., 1989), 60.

219. For an overview of the procedure for hearing petitions and for the case of John Custis, who tried to suppress them, see Philip Alexander Bruce, *Institutional History of Virginia in the Seventeenth Century: An Inquiry into the Religious, Moral, Educational, Legal, Military, and Political Condition of the People Based on Original and Contemporaneous Sources*, 2 vols. (Gloucester, MA: Peter Smith, [1910] 1964), 2: 480–484.

220. H. R. McIlwaine, ed., *Journals of the House of Burgesses of Virginia, 1659/60–1693* (Richmond: 1914), 11, henceforth *JHBV 1659/60-1693*.

221. McIlwaine, ed., *JHBV 1659/60-1693*, 12.

222. McIlwaine, ed., *JHBV 1659/60-1693*, 8.

223. McIlwaine, ed., *JHBV 1659/60-1693*, 8.

224. McIlwaine, ed., *JHBV 1659/60-1693*, 11.

225. McIlwaine, ed., *JHBV 1659/60-1693*, 11.

226. Alonso de Aranguiz y Cotes to the King, 15 November 1661, AGI SD 225, fol. 466v, PARES, accessed 22 January 2021. Letter-writing Indigenous leaders may not have been so uncommon, as Alejandra Dubcovsky points out in her recent book. Alejandra Dubcovsky, *Talking Back: Native Women and the Making of the Early South* (New Haven, CT: Yale University Press, 2023), 48–49. Amy Turner Bushnell argues that *mico* Santiago's petition was the "final missive in the Franciscan barrage" against Governor Rebolledo, who was by then off the scene, making the Tolomato appeal "overkill." Bushnell, *Situado and Sabana*, 132.

227. John Hammond, *Leah and Rachel, Or, the Two Fruitfull Sisters Virginia, and Mary-Land* (London: 1656), 6 and 13.

228. Hammond, *Leah and Rachel*, 13.

229. Francis Moryson, comp., *The Lawes of Virginia Now in Force* (London: 1662), [5–6].

230. *Statutes*, 1: 547.

231. *Statutes*, 1: 547.

232. King of Great Britain, *Articles of Peace Between the Most Serene and Mighty Prince Charles II . . . And Several Indian Kings and Queens* [. . .] (London: 1677), 8. For the provision's appearance in the statute book, see Moryson, comp., *Lawes of Virginia*, 78.

233. For more on "oral petitions" and "hearsay" in Florida, see Amy Turner Bushnell, "Debitage of the Shatter Zone: Indoctrination, Asylum, and the Law of Towns in the Provinces of Florida," in Miguel Dantas da Cruz, ed., *Petitioning in the Atlantic World, c. 1500–1840: Empires, Revolutions and Social Movements* (New York: Palgrave Macmillan, 2022), 139.

234. *Statutes*, 1: 467.

235. Gatford, *Publick Good*, 7.

236. Gatford, *Publick Good*, 7 ("believed"); Moryson, comp., *Lawes of Virginia*, 77 ("Wild-Fruits").

237. Hening, *Statutes*, 1: 481.

238. Hening, *Statutes*, 1: 481–482.

239. Although historian Laura M. Stevens has argued that the term "poor Indians" was only an expression of "imperialist pity," in fact, it had much the same legal meaning in Virginia as it did in the Spanish Empire. Native petitioners used the term themselves in Virginia just as they did in places like colonial Mexico to demand the special attention and consideration of colonial officials and the Crown. Laura M. Stevens, *The Poor Indians: Missionaries, Native Americans, and Colonial Sensibility* (Philadelphia, PA: University of Pennsylvania Press, 2004), 19–20. For more on the term's usage in the Spanish Empire, see Brian P. Owensby, *Empire of Law and Indian Justice in Colonial Mexico* (Stanford, CA: Stanford University Press, 2006), 55–56.

240. Solórzano, *Política Indiana*, 66.

241. Moryson, comp., *Lawes of Virginia*, 76.

242. Moryson, comp., *Lawes of Virginia*, 76.

243. Colony of Virginia, *Acts of Assembly, Passed in the Colony of Virginia, From 1662, to 1715*, 2 vols. (London: 1727), 1: 65.

244. Moryson, comp., *Lawes of Virginia*, 76 and 40.

245. Ian K. Steele, *Warpaths: Invasions of North America* (New York: Oxford University Press, 1994), 49 (quotation).

246. G. R., *Virginia's Cure* (London: 1662), 6.

247. Moryson, comp., *Lawes of Virginia*, 78. In the early Spanish Antilles, Indians received badges to signify that they had paid their required tribute. Luis Weckmann, *La herencia medieval del México*, vol. 2 (Mexico City: El Colegio de México, 1983), 433.

248. Moryson, comp., *Lawes of Virginia*, 78.

249. Virginia, *Acts of Assembly*, 1: 63.

250. G. R., *Virginia's Cure*, 12–13.

251. Moryson, comp., *Lawes of Virginia*, 79.

252. Caciques of Guale to the King, 16 October 1657, AGI SD 235, PKY, WLC, reel 8.

253. Moryson, comp., *Lawes of Virginia*, 78.

254. Gatford, *Publick Good*, 23.

255. For example, see "Order 2: Guerra y Vega to Alcayde de Castro, January 17, 1665," in John E. Worth, *The Struggle for the Georgia Coast* (Tuscaloosa: University of Alabama Press, 2007), 71.

256. *A Collection of the Laws of Virginia* (London: 1684), 135. After the death of Cockacoeske, Queen of Pamunkey, for example, her nation petitioned to have her successor recognized as legitimate. See 1 July 1686, in H. R. McIlwaine, ed., *Executive Journals of the Council of Colonial Virginia*, vol. 1 [June 11, 1680—June 22, 1699] (Richmond: The Virginia State Library, 1925), 79.

257. Benito, *cacique* of Santa Elena de Machava, to the King, 1676, AGI SD 234, fol. 96r, PKY, JWC, reel 6. For a recent reappraisal of Benito's case and the significance of his descent from a leading Timucuan woman, see Dubcovsky, *Talking Back*, 47–52.

258. Benito, *cacique* of Santa Elena de Machava, to the King, 1676, AGI SD 234, fol. 96r, PKY, JWC, reel 6.

259. Ludwell to Arlington, "Discription of Virginia," 17 September 1666, UNKA CO 1/20, no. 125i., fol. 221r-v.

260. Santiago to the King, 21 March 1658, AGI SD 233, PKY, JTCC, box 15, folder 54-5-18, microfilm copy.

261. The invocation of royal symbolism and Indigenous leaders' strategic adherence to the Crown continued well into the eighteenth century. See Negrin, "Cockacoeske's Rebellion," 85; Ruediger, "Tributary Subjects," 245–246.

262. "Order 2: Guerra y Vega to Alcayde de Castro, January 17, 1665," 71a.

263. Governor Francisco de la Guerra y de la Vega to the King, 16 September 1666, AGI SD 225, fol. 495r, PARES, accessed 26 March 2021.

264. Governor Guerra y Vega to the King, 16 September 1666, AGI SD 225, fol. 495r, PARES, accessed 26 March 2021.

265. "Juan Fernandez de Olivera to the King relative to the ceremonies held at St. Augustine because of the death of the queen," 13 October 1612, AGI SD 225, PKY, SC, reel 9.

266. For the importance of the last Habsburg monarch in the metropolitan drive against Indian slavery, see Andrés Reséndez, *The Other Slavery: The Uncovered Story of Indian Enslavement in America* (Boston, MA: Houghton Mifflin Harcourt, 2016), 125–148.

267. John Lederer, *The Discoveries of John Lederer, in three several Marches from Virginia, to the West of Carolina, And other parts of the Continent* [. . .] (London: 1672), 15.

268. Moryson, *Lawes of Virginia*, 79.

269. 12 May 1699, in H. R. McIlwaine, ed., *Legislative Journals of the Council of Colonial Virginia*, vol. 1 (Richmond, VA: 1918), 262–263.

270. Gardyner, *Description*, 102.

Chapter 3

1. In San Luis de Talimali the ballgame field was in the heart of town near the main public buildings. John H. Hann, *Apalachee: The Land Between the Rivers* (Gainesville: University of Florida Press, 1988), 207. For the regular sweeping of the main plaza in town, see Bonnie G. McEwan, "Colonialism on the Spanish Florida Frontier: Mission San Luis, 1656–1704," in "500 Years of Florida History—The Seventeenth Century," special issue, *Florida Historical Quarterly*, vol. 92, no. 3 (Winter 2014): 603.

2. For more on regular *cacina* consumption and the method of the drink's preparation among the Apalachees, see Hann, *Apalachee*, 130–131. Apalachee consumption likely followed the pattern of Creek men in the eighteenth century who spent the mornings talking over the business of the town while drinking *cacina*. Kathryn E. Holland Braund, *Deerskins & Duffels: Creek Indian Trade with Anglo-America, 1685–1815* (Lincoln: University of Nebraska Press, 1993), 16.

3. Charles Hudson, *The Southeastern Indians* (Knoxville: The University of Tennessee Press, 1976), 298.

4. Tobacco production was a long and grueling process that included removing by hand excess growths called "suckers" that would otherwise detract from the size of the all-important leaves. For the best account of the growing and harvesting of tobacco in the colonial era, see T. H. Breen, *Tobacco Culture: The Mentality of the Great Tidewater Planters on the Eve of the Revolution* (Princeton, NJ: Princeton University Press, 1985).

5. For more on Ana Estasia and the abandonment of Tupiqui, see John E. Worth, *The Struggle for the Georgia Coast* (Tuscaloosa: University of Alabama Press, 2007), 23.

6. Although scholars (including me) draw different conclusions about whether Apalachees—and other Indigenous leaders in Florida—were Catholic converts in the sense the Franciscans meant or thought of themselves truly as vassals of the Crown in the Spanish sense, there can be little doubt now about their enduring power in the region. The best argument for

Apalachee, rather than Spanish dominance well into the 1670s is Aubrey Lauersdorf, "Apalachee Diplomacy, Politics, and Power, 1528–1678" (PhD diss., University of North Carolina, 2020), 176–206, accessed 8 June 2023. Thanks to Alejandra Dubcovsky for pointing me toward Lauersdorf's work. For recent discussions on conversion and acculturation in Florida, arguing that both were limited, see Denise I. Bossy, "Guns for Godliness: The Yamasees in Saint Augustine," in *Facing Florida: Essays on Culture and Religion in Early Modern Southeastern America*, ed. Timothy J. Johnson and Jeffrey M. Burns (Oceanside, CA: The Academy of American Franciscan History, 2021), 104–106; Jennifer Baszile rightly describes this generation as "an exceptional cadre of leaders," although she doubts the level of acculturation among these men and their fellow townspeople. Jennifer Baszile, "Apalachee Testimony in Florida: A View of Slavery from the Spanish Archives," in *Indian Slavery in Colonial America*, ed. Alan Gallay (Lincoln: University of Nebraska Press, 2009), 187 (quotation), 192–193.

7. "Certification by Andrés Perés," 23 June 1674, AGI SD 235, in John H. Hann, trans., "Visitations and Revolts, 1656–1695," *Florida Archaeology* no. 7 (1993): 75.

8. Thomas Mathew, "The Beginning, Progress, and Conclusion of Bacon's Rebellion, 1675–1676 [1705]," in Charles M. Andrews, ed., *Narratives of the Insurrections, 1675–1690* (New York: Charles Scribner's Sons, 1915), 15–16.

9. "Bacon's Manifesto," 1676, UKNA CO 1/37, no. 51, fol. 178v ("Darling Indians"); "Bacon's Declaracon in Virginia[:] The Declaration of the People," 1676, UKNA CO 1/37, no. 41, fol. 128r ("favored and Emboldened").

10. "Certification of the priests, fray Miguel de Valverde and fray Rodrigo de la Barrera," 10 September 1674, in John H. Hann, trans., "Visitations and Revolts, 1656–1695," *Florida Archaeology* no. 7 (1993): 35.

11. "Certification of the priests," 35.

12. "Certification of the priests," 35.

13. "Certification of the priests," 35.

14. See Amy Turner Bushnell, "'That Demonic Game': The Campaign to Stop Indian Pelota Playing in Spanish Florida, 1675–1684," *The Americas*, vol. 35, no. 1 (July 1978): 1–19.

15. Hann, *Apalachee*, 346.

16. The drastic reorganization of Timucua to service Spaniards on the *camino real*, along with the imposition of the *repartimiento* in Apalachee, were two examples of the authoritarian philosophy in action that gave outsiders pause before welcoming Spaniards, as Joseph M. Hall Jr. notes. Joseph M. Hall, Jr., *Zamumo's Gifts: Indian-European Exchange in the Colonial Southeast* (Philadelphia: University of Pennsylvania Press, 2009), 71.

17. Amy Turner Bushnell, *Situado and Sabana: Spain's Support System for Florida*, Anthropological Papers of the American Museum of Natural History 74 (New York: American Museum of Natural History, 1994), 145.

18. *Statutes*, 2: 274–275.

19. The weight of per capita labor burdens was already growing heavier by the 1650s. Hall, *Zamumo's Gifts*, 67.

20. See Matthew Kruer, *Time of Anarchy: Indigenous Power and the Crisis of Colonialism* (Cambridge, MA: Harvard University Press, 2021); Matthew Kruer, "Bloody Minds and Peoples Undone: Emotion, Family, and Political Order in the Susquehannock-Virginia War," *William and Mary Quarterly*, 3rd ser., vol. 74, no. 3 (July 2017): 401–436; Michael Leroy Oberg, *Dominion & Civility: English Imperialism & Native America, 1585–1685* (Ithaca, NY: Cornell University

Press, 1999), 195–198; Stephen Saunders Webb, *1676: The End of American Independence* (Syracuse, NY: Syracuse University Press, [1984] 1995), 23–24.

21. See Cynthia J. Van Zandt, *Brothers Among Nations: The Pursuit of Intercultural Alliances in Early America, 1580–1660* (New York: Oxford University Press, 2008), esp. 175 and 182.

22. Kruer, *Time of Anarchy*, passim.

23. Kruer, *Time of Anarchy*, 46.

24. "MÉRITOS: Gabriel Diaz de Vara Calderón," 30 January 1667 (and 1676), AGI INDIFERENTE 121, PARES, accessed 21 January 2021.

25. Bishop of Cuba to the Queen, 20 November 1675, AGI SD 151, [fol. 7r], PKY, JWC, reel 3. I have assigned folio numbers to the document.

26. Bishop of Cuba to the Queen, 1675, AGI SD 151, [fol. 3r], PKY, JWC, reel 3.

27. Bishop of Cuba to the Queen, 1675, AGI SD 151, [fol. 3r], PKY, JWC, reel 3.

28. Bishop of Cuba to the Queen, 1675, AGI SD 151, [fol. 4r], PKY, JWC, reel 3.

29. Report of the Chisca's Testimony, 23 May 1675 in Pablo de Hita Salazar to the Queen-Regent, 15 June 1675, AGI SD 855, PKY, JTCC, box 18, folder 58-2-5, microfilm copy, p. 6.

30. Chisca's Testimony, 23 May 1675 in Hita Salazar to the Queen-Regent, 15 June 1675, AGI SD 855, PKY JTCC, box 18, folder 58-2-5, microfilm copy p. 6.

31. Consulta from the Junta de Guerra to Her Majesty about evicting the English from the settlements that they have in the places of San Jorge and Santa Elena," 15 June 1674, AGI SD 863, PKY, JTCC, box 19, folder 58-2-14, microfilm copy, p. 1.

32. Hita Salazar to the Queen-Regent, 15 June 1675, AGI SD 855, PKY, JTCC, box 18, folder 58-2-5, microfilm copy, p. 3.

33. Mathew, "The Beginning, Progress, and Conclusion of Bacon's Rebellion," 16.

34. Sir William Berkeley to Nathaniel Bacon Jr., 14 September 1675, in *WBP*, 487.

35. Nathaniel Bacon Jr. to Sir William Berkeley, 18 September 1675, in *WBP*, 492.

36. Sir William Berkeley to Thomas Ludwell, 1 July 1676, in *WBP*, 537.

37. "Pablo de Hita Salazar," 1671, AGI Contratación 5437, PARES, accessed 9 June 2021.

38. Hita Salazar to the Queen, 20 January 1677, AGI SD 226, fol. 125r, PARES, accessed 8 May 2021.

39. Hita Salazar to the Queen, 24 August 1675, in John H. Hann, trans., "Visitations and Revolts, 1656–1695," *Florida Archaeology* no. 7 (1993): 43.

40. Andrés Perés to Governor Hita Salazar, 29 July 1675, AGI EC 156A, fol. 120r, PKY, reel 27I. In navigating the original source and to ensure accuracy, I consulted the definitive printed translation by John H. Hann. All translations are my own. For Hann's printed translation of selected records from the Hita Salazar residencia, including the documents related to the Chacato Revolt and the 1677–78 visitations of Guale, Mocama, Timucua, and Apalachee, see John H. Hann, trans., "Visitations and Revolts, 1656–1695," *Florida Archaeology* no. 7 (1993): 36–70 (Chacato Inquiry), 83–94 (Guale and Mocama visitation), 95–142 (Timucua and Apalachee visitation).

41. Fray Rodrigo de la Barrera to Andrés Perés, 26 July 1675, AGI EC 156A, fol. 122r, PKY, reel 27I.

42. "Confession of Juan de Diocsale," 20 October 1675, AGI EC 156A, fol. 139v, PKY, reel 27I.

43. "Third Witness, Nicolás, fiscal [of San Carlos]," 4 October 1675, AGI EC 156A, fol. 134r, PKY, reel 27I.

44. "Third Witness, Nicolás, fiscal [of San Carlos]," 4 October 1675, AGI EC 156A, fol. 134r, PKY, reel 271.

45. Barrera to Perés, 26 July 1675, AGI EC 156A, fol. 122r, PKY, reel 271.

46. "Fourth Witness, Carlos, *cacique principal* [of San Carlos]," 3 October 1675, fol. 135v, AGI EC 156A, PKY reel 271.

47. "*Auto* about the Uprising of the Chacatos," Juan Fernández de Florencia, 3 October 1675, AGI EC 156A, fol. 130r, PKY, reel 271.

48. "*Auto* about the Uprising of the Chacatos," Juan Fernández de Florencia, 3 October 1675, AGI EC 156A, fol. 130r, PKY, reel 271.

49. "*Auto* about the Uprising of the Chacatos," Juan Fernández de Florencia, 3 October 1675, AGI EC 156A, fol. 130v, PKY, reel 271.

50. Maynard Geiger, "Biographical Dictionary of the Franciscans in Spanish Florida and Cuba (1528–1841)," *Franciscan Studies*, no. 21 (1940): 32–33.

51. Quoted in Steven C. Hahn, *The Invention of the Creek Nation, 1670–1763* (Lincoln: University of Nebraska Press, 2004), 39.

52. For the concept of "secondary war," see Bushnell, *Situado and Sabana*, 35.

53. Andrés Perés to Governor Hita Salazar, 2 August 1675, AGI EC 156A, fol. 123v, PKY, reel 271.

54. Andrés Perés to Governor Hita Salazar, 2 August 1675, AGI EC 156A, fol. 123v, PKY, reel 271.

55. "Confession of Juan de Diozali," 20 October 1675, AGI EC 156A, fol. 140r, PKY, reel 271.

56. "Fifth Witness, Elena, wife of the *cacique* [of San Carlos]," 5 October 1675, AGI EC 156A, fol. 136r, PKY, reel 271.

57. Antonio Francisco de Herrara to Andrés Perés, 31 July 1675, AGI EC 156A, fol. 125r-v, PKY, reel 271.

58. The "tumults" of the Chacatos fit the model of an internal "coup" as developed by Lauersdorf for the events of 1647 in Apalachee. Diocsale and his confederates joined with the Chiscas in a similar sort of factional maneuver to change the direction of Chacato political life. Aubrey Lauersdorf, "An Apalachee Revolt?: Reconceptualizing Violence in Seventeenth-Century Apalachee," in "Indigenous Florida," ed. Denise I. Bossy and Andrew K. Frank, special issue, *The Florida Historical Quarterly*, vol. 100, no. 1 (Summer 2021): 45.

59. Alejandra Dubcovsky argues that the "so-called" revolt was about Franciscan interference in Chacato "gender conventions" and not an anticolonial rebellion as such. Alejandra Dubcovsky, *Talking Back: Native Women and the Making of the Early South* (New Haven, CT: Yale University Press, 2023), 57–58; John H. Hann, *The Native American World Beyond Apalachee: West Florida and the Chattahoochee Valley* (Gainesville: University Press of Florida, 2006), 31–38, 32 ("sexual mores").

60. Dubcosky notes correctly—and intriguingly, given the implications—that "Diocsale lived in their [the women's] dwelling, not the other way round." Thus, Franciscan meddling did not just offend the sensibilities of men, but the very property and domain of women. Dubcovsky, *Talking Back*, 58–59.

61. That said, Dubcovsky argues that the Chacatos "were not hostile to the Apalachees" and points out the fact that at least one of the Chacato conspirators, Ubabesa, had taken an Apalachee woman as a wife. Dubcovsky, *Talking Back*, 38–39, 60. The Chacato leaders who permitted the missionaries' entry respected Apalachee military power and initially must have allied with them for protection from mutual enemies. Aubrey Lauersdorf argues that the Apalachee

overtures in the region were predicated on making the security of their territory—through which valuable Spanish goods passed—vital to their Indigenous neighbors. The problem was that such moves stirred up opposition too. Lauersdorf, "Apalachee Diplomacy," 198–200.

62. "Declaration of Miguel, *cacique* [of San Nicolás]," 20 October 1675, AGI EC 156A, 140v, PKY, reel 271.

63. As Dubcovsky points out, Diocsale likely regarded the friars as little more than nuisances, certainly not "equal players." Dubcovsky, *Talking Back*, 59.

64. *Recopilación de las leyes de los reynos de Las Indias . . . tomo Segundo* (Madrid: por Iulian de Paredes, 1681), 6:7:1, 219v. Hereinafter cited as *Recopilación*, II, book:title:law, folio.

65. *Recopilación*, II, 6:7:1, 219v.

66. Barrera to Perés, 26 July 1675, AGI EC 156A, fol. 122r, PKY, reel 271.

67. The beating, not to mention the differential treatment, would have fueled discontent even further. Dubcovsky, *Talking Back*, 60.

68. *Recopilación*, II, 6:7:4, 219v.

69. Francis Moryson, comp., *The Lawes of Virginia Now in Force* (London: 1662), 78.

70. "Sentence of Diocsale," 21 October 1675, AGI EC 156A, fol. 142r, PKY, reel 271.

71. Junn was one of six enslaved "Indians" on Bacon's estate, mostly "boyes." UNKA CO 5/1371, pt. 2, fol. 233r, p. 455. What exactly Junn or the other enslaved people did on Bacon's estate is a matter of conjecture. James D. Rice paints a picture of a functioning tobacco plantation with enslaved people "working the fields or tending to the livestock." James D. Rice, *Tales from a Revolution: Bacon's Rebellion and the Transformation of Early America* (New York: Oxford University Press, 2012), 33. C. S. Everett, on the other hand, says Bacon "was no planter," but rather sought his fortune in the Indian trade. C. S. Everett, "'They Shalbe Slaves for Their Lives': Indian Slavery in Colonial Virginia," in *Indian Slavery in Colonial America*, ed. Alan Gallay (Lincoln: University of Nebraska Press, 2009), 84 (quotation), 85.

72. Nathaniel Bacon to Sir William Berkeley, May 1676, in *WBP*, 530.

73. Hayley Negrin rightfully emphasizes Bacon's legal education as a key to his thinking and a likely reason for his ability to rally a following. Hayley Negrin, "Cockacoeske's Rebellion: Nathaniel Bacon, Indigenous Slavery, and Sovereignty in Early Virginia," *William and Mary Quarterly*, vol. 80, no. 1 (January 2023): 68. For more on Bacon's early life, see Webb, *1676*, 27–28.

74. Royal Commissioners, "A True Narrative of the Late Rebellion in Virginia, by the Royal Commissioners, 1677," in Charles M. Andrews, ed., *Narratives of the Insurrections, 1675-1690* (New York: Charles Scribner's Sons, 1915), 110.

75. "Bacon's Manifesto," 1676, CO 1/37, no. 51, fol. 178v.

76. "Bacon's Manifesto," 1676, CO 1/37, no. 51, fol. 179r.

77. "Bacon's Manifesto," 1676, CO 1/37, no. 51, fol. 179r.

78. "Bacon's Manifesto," 1676, CO 1/37, no. 51, fol. 179r.

79. "Bacon's Manifesto," 1676, CO 1/37, no. 51, fol. 179r.

80. Dylan Ruediger, "'Neither Utterly to Reject Them, Nor Yet to Drawe Them to Come In': Tributary Subordination and Settler Colonialism in Virginia," *Early American Studies: An Interdisciplinary Journal*, vol. 18, no. 1 (Winter 2020): 25–26; Kristalyn Marie Shefveland, *Anglo-Native Virginia: Trade, Conversion, and Indian Slavery in the Old Dominion, 1646-1722* (Athens: University of Georgia Press, 2016), 45.

81. Natives "took the leap" toward the Crown, as Matthew Kruer aptly puts it. Kruer, *Time of Anarchy*, 162.

82. Negrin, "Cockacoeske's Rebellion," 55.

83. Negrin, "Cockacoeske's Rebellion," 58.

84. Richard Tuck believed the disputation between Roger Williams and John Cotton in 1630s Massachusetts Bay was "the English equivalent of the debate between Las Casas and Sepulveda." Richard Tuck, *The Rights of War and Peace: Political Thought and International Order from Grotius to Kant* (New York: Oxford University Press, 2001), 125.

85. For the example of William Byrd's rise and for Bacon's location nearby Byrd and other traders (apparently at Governor Berkeley's instigation, at least initially), see C. S. Everett, "'They Shalbe Slaves for Their Lives,'" 79–80, 84.

86. Royal Commissioners, "True Narrative," 110.

87. Royal Commissioners, "True Narrative," 111.

88. Royal Commissioners, "True Narrative," 110 ("melancholy"), 111 ("a Bacon"). A 1662 law against celebratory gunfire suggests Virginia's frontiersmen would have greeted Bacon accordingly. *Statutes*, 2: 126.

89. Mathew, "Bacon's Rebellion," 32.

90. "The Virginians Plea for Opposing ye Indians without ye Governors Order humbly Offer'd as ye Test of their utmost Intencons to clear & Vindicate them from all Misapprehensions of Disloyalty & Disobedience," 1676, UKNA CO 1/37, no. 14, fol. 29r.

91. "Virginians Plea," 1676, UKNA CO 1/37, no. 14, fol. 29r.

92. "Virginians Plea," 1676, UKNA CO 1/37, no. 14, fol. 29r.

93. Thomas Bacon to the King, June 1676, UKNA CO 1/37, no. 15, fol. 31r.

94. Thomas Bacon to the King, June 1676, UKNA CO 1/37, no. 15, fol. 31r.

95. James D. Rice says Thomas sent Nathaniel away to "escape prosecution" for a fraud he had committed in England. James D. Rice, *Tales from a Revolution: Bacon's Rebellion and the Transformation of Early America* (New York: Oxford University Press, 2012), 27.

96. Rice, *Tales from a Revolution*, 45–48.

97. Mathew, "Bacon's Rebellion," 27.

98. *Statutes*, 2: 336–338

99. Mathew, "Bacon's Rebellion," 27.

100. For the symbolism of Cockacoeske's accoutrements, see Negrin, "Cockacoeske's Rebellion," 73. For the original description of Cockacoeske's dress and appearance, see Mathew, "Bacon's Rebellion," 25–26.

101. Mathew, "Bacon's Rebellion," 25.

102. Mathew, "Bacon's Rebellion," 26.

103. Mathew, "Bacon's Rebellion," 25.

104. Mathew, "Bacon's Rebellion," 26.

105. Mathew, "Bacon's Rebellion," 26.

106. Mathew, "Bacon's Rebellion," 26.

107. The word is a guess based on John Smith's lexicon of Powhatan words. John Smith, *The Generall Historie of Virginia, New-England, and the Summer Isles* [. . .] (London: 1624), 40.

108. Mathew, "Bacon's Rebellion," 27.

109. Rice, *Tales from a Revolution*, 76–78.

110. Virginia Company, *The Trve Declaration of the estate of the Colonie in Virginia, With a confutation of such scandalous reports as haue tended to the disgrace of so worthy an enterprise. Published by aduise and direction of the Councell of Virginia* (London: 1610), 8–9.

111. William Sherwood to Sir Joseph Williamson, 1 June 1676, UKNA CO 1/37, no. 1, fol. 1r.

112. Lionel Gatford, *Publick Good Without Private Interest* [. . .] (London: 1657), 8.

113. "Declaration of the People," 1676, CO 1/37, fol. 128r.

114. For the 1667 statute, see *Statutes*, 2: 260. For "hereditary heathenism," see Rebecca Anne Goetz, *The Baptism of Early Virginia: How Christianity Created Race* (Baltimore, MD: The Johns Hopkins University Press, 2012), 3 and 10. Officially, tributary status amounted to a kind of religious toleration, despite such pronouncements as the *dicta* in Calvin's Case (1608) that non-Christians were always enemies of the Crown. A 1683 judicial decision in England concluded that conquered infidels could keep customs that were inoffensive to "the law of God." Craig Yirush, *Settlers, Liberty, and Empire: The Roots of Early American Political Theory* (New York: Cambridge University Press, 2011), 44. For Natives and religious toleration, see Evan Haefeli, *Accidental Pluralism: America and the Religious Politics of English Expansion, 1497–1662* (Chicago: The University of Chicago Press, 2021), 32; Richard W. Pointer, "Native Freedom? Indians and Religious Tolerance in Early America," in *The First Prejudice: Religious Tolerance and Intolerance in Early America*, ed. Chris Beneke and Christopher S. Grenda (Philadelphia: University of Pennsylvania Press, 2011), 169–194.

115. Thus providing an easy route to riches for smallholders in Virginia's nascent slave society. Negrin, "Cockacoeske's Rebellion," 50 and 77; Ruediger, "Tributary Subordination," 27. As April Lee Hatfield put it, Bacon's actions were "calculated" rather than merely expressions of "out-of-control racist anger." April Lee Hatfield, *Atlantic Virginia: Intercolonial Relations in the Seventeenth Century* (Philadelphia: University of Pennsylvania Press, 2004), 35.

116. "Cacique" was defined as "*Rex apud Indos*" in Robert Percival, *Bibliotheca Hispanica: Containing a Grammer; with a Dictionarie in Spanish, English, and Latine; gathered out of diuers good Authors: very profitable for the studious of the Spanish toung* (London: 1591). An even earlier definition of the word appeared in the glossary of Richard Eden's translation of Peter Martyr's *Decades*. He defined "Caciqui" as "kynges or gouernours." Peter Martyr, *The decades of the newe worlde or west India*, trans. Richard Eden (London: 1555), [8r]. For the relative absence of "king" and "queen" in Florida, see John H. Hann, "Political Leadership among the Natives of Spanish Florida," *Florida Historical Quarterly*, vol. 71, no. 2 (October 1992): 191.

117. *Recopilación*, II, 6:7:5, 220r.

118. For a thorough discussion on the use of the term "king" for Indigenous leaders in early North America, see Peter Jakob Olsen-Harbich, "A Meaningful Subjection: Kingly Government, Coercive Inequality, and Diplomacy in the North American Eastern Woodlands, 1000–1625 A.D.," (PhD diss., The College of William and Mary, 2021).

119. Historians have variously characterized Bacon's central grievance and motivations for overthrowing the tributary regime or, as Kristalyn Shefveland puts it, his "total disavowal of the entire tributary system." Shefveland, *Anglo-Native Virginia*, 49–50, 53 (quote). For some, the problem as Bacon and his followers saw it was that Berkeley and his cronies unjustly—and dangerously—"coddled" the Indians in their midst who instead should have been punished for their alleged lawlessness. Ruediger, "Tributary Subordination," 25; James D. Rice, "Bacon's Rebellion in Indian Country," *Journal of American History*, vol. 101, no. 3 (December 2014): 731. Others have seen Bacon's Indigenous targets as "scapegoats" in a "cathartic" war waged by the "losers" in Virginia's mad scramble for land and wealth. Kathleen M. Brown, *Good Wives, Nasty Wenches, and Anxious Patriarchs: Gender, Race, and Power in Colonial Virginia* (Chapel Hill: University of North Carolina Press, 1996), 161; Michael Leroy Oberg, *Dominion and Civility: English Imperialism and Native America, 1585–1685* (Ithaca, NY: Cornell University Press, 1999), 176 and 198–206; Helen C. Rountree, *Pocahontas's People: The Powhatan Indians of Virginia Through*

Four Centuries (Lincoln: University of Nebraska Press, 1990), 96–99; Edmund S. Morgan, *American Slavery, American Freedom: The Ordeal of Colonial Virginia* (New York: W. W. Norton & Co., 1975), 257.

120. "Declaration of the People," 1676, UKNA CO 1/37, no. 41, fol. 128r.

121. "Mr. Bacon's acct of their troubles in Virginia by ye Indians, June ye 18th, 1676," in "Bacon's Rebellion," *William and Mary Quarterly*, vol. 9, no. 1 (July 1900): 9.

122. Kruer, "Bloody Minds," 436.

123. "Bacon's Manifesto," 1676, UKNA CO 1/37, no. 51, fol. 178v. For the ranks of poor English rebels, their outrage against the tributaries stemmed in part from the perception that the Indians possessed greater rights than themselves. Ethan A. Schmidt, *Divided Dominion: Social Conflict and Indian Hatred in Early Virginia* (Boulder: University Press of Colorado, 2015), 129. Others may have seen Native tributaries as simply above the law. Lauren Benton, *A Search for Sovereignty: Law and Geography in European Empires, 1400–1900* (New York: Cambridge University Press, 2010), 99.

124. Anonymous, "The History of Bacon's and Ingram's Rebellion, 1676," in Charles M. Andrews, ed., *Narratives of the Insurrections, 1675–1690* (New York: Charles Scribner's Sons, 1915), 59.

125. "A True Narrative of the Rise, Progress, and Cessation of the late Rebellion in Virginia, Most humbly and Impartially Reported By His Majestyes Commissioners Appointed to Enquire into the Affairs of the said Colony," CO 5/1371, pt. 2, p. 390.

126. Mathew, "Bacon's Rebellion," 27.

127. 21 November 1674, in H. R. McIlwaine, ed., *Minutes of the Council and General Court of Virginia, 1622–1632, 1670–1676, With Notes and Excerpts from Original Council and General Court Records, into 1683, Now Lost* (Richmond, VA: 1924), 400.

128. Act III, in *Statutes*, 2: 352.

129. Bushnell, *Situado and Sabana*, 96.

130. "True Narrative," CO 5/1371, pt. 2, p. 389.

131. See Figure VI, in Negrin, "Cockacoeske's Rebellion," 79; "Personal Greivances of diuers Inhabitants within his Majesties Colony of Virginia . . . ," UKNA CO 5/1371, pt. 2, folio 181r, p. 357 (quote).

132. Rice, *Tales from a Revolution*, 90–96; Webb, *1676*, 57–65.

133. Anonymous, "Bacon's and Ingram's Rebellion, 1676," 74.

134. Anonymous, "Bacon's and Ingram's Rebellion, 1676," 74.

135. Anonymous, "Bacon's and Ingram's Rebellion, 1676," 75 (quotation); for the connection between Diocsale's confinement and Chisca attacks, see Hann, *Native American World Beyond Apalachee*, 38–41.

136. Sentencing of Diocsale, "*Auto*" from Governor Hita Salazar, 3 January 1677, AGI EC 156A, fol. 156v, PKY, reel 27I.

137. Hann, *Apalachee*, 347.

138. The heat inside Apalachee houses was reportedly sufficient to dispense with blankets. Hann, *Apalachee*, 209.

139. All translations my own from a scan of the original. Juan Mendoza, Matheo Chuba, and *Inija* Bentura, "Relation that was made before the Captain Juan Fernández de Florencia by the main heads that went to take the war to the Chiscas . . . ," enclosed in Governor Pablo de Hita Salazar to the King, 10 November 1678, AGI SD 226, fol. 150v, PARES, accessed 12 May 2021. There are two other translations available for reference. John H. Hann, "Apalachee

Leaders' Report on their 1677 Expedition Against the Chisca," MS 023, PKY, JHC; and John R. Swanton, *The Early History of the Creek Indians and their Neighbors*, Smithsonian Institution Bureau of American Ethnology, Bulletin 73 (Washington, DC: Government Printing Office, 1922), 299–304. For Serrano y Sanz's transcription of the Apalachee leaders' account, which was at times helpful in transcribing faded parts of the scan of the original manuscript, see "VIII. Letter from the Governor of Florida, Don Pablo de Hita Salazar, Giving Account of the War Against the Chiscas," San Agustín, 10 November 1678, in *Documentos Históricos de la Florida y la Luisiana, siglos XVI al XVIII*, ed. Manuel Serrano y Sanz (Madrid: Victoriano Suárez, 1912), 207–216.

140. Mendoza et al., "Relation," AGI SD 226, fol. 150r.

141. Mendoza et al., "Relation," AGI SD 226, fol. 150r-v.

142. Mendoza et al., "Relation," AGI SD 226, fol. 150v.

143. There must have been murmurings from ordinary Apalachees, who were vigorous spectators and participants in the games. Bushnell, "Demonic Game," 14–15.

144. Mendoza et al., "Relation," AGI SD 226, fol. 150v (quotation); "Diocsale is pardoned and remited to the Viceroy [of New Spain]," 5 July 1677, AGI EC 156A, fol. 158r-159r, PKY, reel 27I.

145. The governor described the Chisca fortification as a "*palenque*." Hita Salazar to the King, 10 November 1678, AGI SD 226, fol. 147r.

146. "Declaration of Pedro, [Diocsale's son]," 31 October 1676, AGI EC 156A, fol. 145v-146r, PKY, reel 27I.

147. Perés to Salazar, 29 July 1675, AGI EC 156A, fol. 120v, PKY, reel 27I.

148. Bushnell, *Situado and Sabana*, 210.

149. See Amy Turner Bushnell, "Ruling 'the Republic of Indians' in Seventeenth-Century Florida," in *Powhatan's Mantle: Indians in the Colonial Southeast*, ed. Gregory A. Waselkov, Peter H. Wood, and Tom Hatley (Lincoln: University of Nebraska Press, 2006), 205; Bushnell, *Situado and Sabana*, 173. See also the campaign synopsis in Hann, *Apalachee*, 185–187; Baszile's analysis says the deliberations were ongoing since "perhaps in 1675." See Baszile, "Apalachee Testimony," 192–193; Mendoza et al., "Relation," AGI SD 226, fol.150v.

150. Mendoza et al., "Relation," AGI SD 226, fol. 150v.

151. It seems clear that the *principales* were scrupulous about the legality of their expedition. I have translated the original text as "some said we will not be given license." Mendoza et al., "Relation," AGI SD 226, fol. 150v ("y algunas decian no se nos a de dar lizençia"). John Swanton's translator, working from Serrano y Sanz's 1912 transcription, translated this passage as "Some of them said, 'We need not be given leave to go.'" Swanton, *The Early History of the Creek Indians*, 303.

152. Bacon himself, of course, rather like the Timucua rebels of 1656, believed he was acting in the name of law, order, and the King. Goetz, *Baptism of Early Virginia*, 130.

153. Mendoza et al., "Relation," AGI SD 226, fol. 150v.

154. Mendoza et al., "Relation," AGI SD 226, fol. 150v-151r.

155. Mendoza et al., "Relation," AGI SD 226, fol. 151r.

156. Mendoza et al., "Relation," AGI SD 226, fol. 151r.

157. Mendoza et al., "Relation," AGI SD 226, fol. 151r.

158. Mendoza et al., "Relation," AGI SD 226, fol. 151r.

159. Mendoza et al., "Relation," AGI SD 226, fol. 151v.

160. Mendoza et al., "Relation," AGI SD 226, fol. 152r.

161. Mendoza et al., "Relation," AGI SD 226, fol. 152r.

162. Mendoza et al., "Relation," AGI SD 226, fol. 151r.

163. Mendoza et al., "Relation," AGI SD 226, fol. 152r.

164. "Fuimos a dormir al Rio lagino," Mendoza et al., "Relation," AGI SD 226, fol. 152r. According to John H. Hann, the word for the river meant "yellow." Hann, *Apalachee*, 406.

165. Mendoza et al., "Relation," AGI SD 226, fol. 152v.

166. The San Luís leaders said it was in Ivitachuco that the Apalachees confirmed that the perpetrators of the attacks were Chiscas, suggesting the men there took some of the raiders captive. Mendoza et al., "Relation," AGI SD 226, fol. 150r; Baszile argues the Apalachee towns that did not join were fearful of stirring up Chisca raids in retaliation. Baszile, "Apalachee Testimony," 194. Why province-wide participation was lacking is "unexplained in the report." Hann, *Apalachee*, 185. Although Hann later argued that Spanish officials had spurred San Luis and Escambe into making the assault. Hann, *Native American World Beyond Apalachee*, 61.

167. The *principales* of San Luís, not to mention the provincial lieutenant, clearly intended the document to bolster their collective influence with Spanish authorities. Baszile, "Apalachee Testimony," 197. For Fernández de Florencia's fluency in both Spanish and the Apalachee language, see Hann, *Apalachee*, 251.

168. Mendoza et al., "Relation," AGI SD 226, fol. 152v.

169. Mendoza et al., "Relation," AGI SD 226, fol. 152v.

170. Mendoza et al., "Relation," AGI SD 226, fol. 153r. This was "the name the Spaniards sometimes gave to the Apalachicola River." Hann, *Apalachee*, 47.

171. Mendoza et al., "Relation," AGI SD 226, fol. 153v.

172. Mendoza et al., "Relation," AGI SD 226, fol. 154v.

173. Mendoza et al., "Relation," AGI SD 226, fol. 155r.

174. Mendoza et al., "Relation," AGI SD 226, fol. 155v.

175. Mendoza et al., "Relation," AGI SD 226, fol. 155v.

176. Mendoza et al., "Relation," AGI SD 226, fol. 156r.

177. Mendoza et al., "Relation," AGI SD 226, fol. 156r.

178. Mendoza et al., "Relation," AGI SD 226, fol. 156r.

179. Mendoza et al., "Relation," AGI SD 226, fol. 157v.

180. Mendoza et al., "Relation," AGI SD 226, fol. 158v.

181. Mendoza et al., "Relation," AGI SD 226, fol. 158v.

182. The tactic of concentrating on a weak spot in the palisade and breaking through by force is reminiscent of the kind of northern warfare that the Westos learned from the Haudenosaunee and imported into the South. For more, see Dixie Ray Haggard, "The First Invasion of Georgia and the Myth of Westo Power, 1656–1684," *Journal of Military History*, vol. 86, no. 3 (July 2022): 552. John H. Hann notes that the "seriously outnumbered" Apalachees nevertheless possessed more firearms than their Chisca opponents, giving them an advantage. Hann, *Native American World Beyond Apalachee*, 61.

183. Mendoza et al., "Relation," AGI SD 226, fol. 158v.

184. Mendoza et al., "Relation," AGI SD 226, fol. 158v.

185. Mendoza et al., "Relation," AGI SD 226, fol. 158v.

186. Mendoza et al., "Relation," AGI SD 226, fol. 158v.

187. Mendoza et al., "Relation," AGI SD 226, fol. 158v-159r.

188. Mendoza et al., "Relation," AGI SD 226, fol. 159r.

189. Mendoza et al., "Relation," AGI SD 226, fol. 159r.

190. Mendoza et al., "Relation," AGI SD 226, fol. 159r.

191. Mendoza et al., "Relation," AGI SD 226, fol. 159v.

192. Mendoza et al., "Relation," AGI SD 226, fol. 159v.

193. Mendoza et al., "Relation," AGI SD 226, fol. 159v.

194. Mendoza et al., "Relation," AGI SD 226, fol. 159v ("from top to bottom"); Hita Salazar to the King, 10 November 1678, AGI SD 226, fol. 149r ("owners of the Field").

195. Mendoza et al., "Relation," AGI SD 226, fol. 160r.

196. Mendoza et al., "Relation," AGI SD 226, fol. 160v.

197. Mendoza et al., "Relation," AGI SD 226, fol. 161r.

198. Mendoza et al., "Relation," AGI SD 226, fol. 161r-v.

199. Mendoza et al., "Relation," AGI SD 226, fol. 161v. Conversion to Catholicism may have led Apalachee leaders to associate such conjuring with the Catholic Devil. Jorge Cañizares-Esguerra, "The Devil in the New World: A Transnational Perspective," in *The Atlantic in Global History, 1500–2000*, ed. Jorge Cañizares-Esguerra and Erik R. Seeman (New York: Routledge, 2007), 20–37.

200. Herbert Jeffreys to Sir Joseph Williamson, 11 June 1677, CO 1/42, no. 104, fol. 225r ("Guard-House"); "*Swanne's Point* in *Virginia, June 11*," *London Gazette*, no. 1221 (30 July–2 August 1677), John Carter Brown Library, Brown University, Providence, RI.

201. This phrase does not appear in the version in Kew but is found in the version transcribed and published in Michael Leroy Oberg, ed., *Samuel Wiseman's Book of Record: The Official Account of Bacon's Rebellion in Virginia, 1676–1677* (Lanham, MD: Lexington Books, 2005), 130.

202. For the tenor of the Green Spring Assembly, see Rice, *Tales from a Revolution*, 123 and 126; Webb, *1676*, 142–146.

203. H. R. McIlwaine, ed., *Journals of the House of Burgesses of Virginia, 1659/60–1693* (Richmond, VA: 1914), 89, henceforth *JHVB, 1659/60–1693*.

204. McIlwaine, ed., *JHVB, 1659/60–1693*, 89.

205. McIlwaine, ed., *JHVB, 1659/60–1693*, 89.

206. McIlwaine, ed., *JHVB, 1659/60–1693*, 89.

207. McIlwaine, ed., *JHVB, 1659/60–1693*, 90.

208. McIlwaine, ed., *JHVB, 1659/60–1693*, 90.

209. Herbert Jeffreys to Sir Joseph Williamson, 11 June 1677, UKNA CO 1/42, no. 104, fol. 225r.

210. Kruer, *Time of Anarchy*, 150. Jeffreys, for one, "personified the professional servants of the new state." Webb, *1676*, 137. See also Oberg, *Dominion and Civility*, 211; Charles M. Andrews, "Introduction" to "Narrative of the Commissioners," in Charles M. Andrews, ed., *Narratives of the Insurrections, 1675–1690* (New York: Charles Scribner's Sons, 1915), 101–102.

211. Kruer, *Time of Anarchy*, 150–152.

212. "A Particular Account how wee Your Majestyes Commissioners for the Affairs of Virginia haue obserued and Comply'd with our Instructions . . . ," UNKA CO 5/1371, pt. 2, fol. 185r, p. 365.

213. Queen Cockacoeske to Francis Moryson, 29 June 1678, CO 1/42, no. 101, fol. 273r.

214. Cockacoeske to Moryson, 29 June 1678, CO 1/42, no. 101, fol. 273r.

215. "Personal Greivances," UKNA CO 5/1371, pt. 2, fol. 181r, p. 357.

216. Rather than part of a necklace, this item has usually been described as a "frontlet" worn on the queen's brow as part of her traditional crown. Martha W. McCartney, "Cockacoeske, Queen of Pamunkey: Diplomat and Suzeraine," in *Powhatan's Mantle: Indians in the Colonial*

Southeast, ed. Gregory A. Waselkov, Peter H. Wood, and Tom Hatley (Lincoln: University of Nebraska Press, 2006), 264–265 and n. 42.

217. Herbert Jeffreys to Sir Joseph Williamson, 11 June 1677, CO 1/42, no. 104, fol. 225r.

218. Jeffreys to Williamson, 11 June 1677, CO 1/42, no. 104, fol. 225r.

219. Jeffreys to Williamson, 11 June 1677, CO 1/42, no. 104, fol. 225r.

220. Jeffreys to Williamson, 11 June 1677, CO 1/42, no. 104, fol. 225r.

221. Jeffreys to Williamson, 11 June 1677, CO 1/42, no. 104, fol. 225r.

222. Kruer calls the treaty a blueprint for a "multicultural commonwealth." Kruer, *Time of Anarchy*, 159.

223. Jeffreys to Williamson, 11 June 1677, CO 1/42, no. 104, fol. 225r.

224. King of Great Britain, *Articles of Peace Between the Most Serene and Mighty Prince Charles II . . . And Several Indian Kings and Queens* [. . .] (London: 1677), 4.

225. King of Great Britain, *Articles of Peace*, 5.

226. King of Great Britain, *Articles of Peace*, 8.

227. King of Great Britain, *Articles of Peace*, 8.

228. King of Great Britain, *Articles of Peace*, 14.

229. King of Great Britain, *Articles of Peace*, 13.

230. Kruer, *Time of Anarchy*, 161–162. See also discussion below and McCartney, "Cockacoeske," 254.

231. "Names and characters of & Prisints to ye Indians &c.," 1677, UKNA CO 5/1371, pt. 1, fol. 135v, p. 266.

232. Kruer, *Time of Anarchy*, 162.

233. "Names and characters," 1677, UKNA CO 5/1371, pt. 1, fol. 138r, p. 271.

234. "Names and characters," 1677, UKNA CO 5/1371, pt. 1, fol. 137r, p. 269.

235. "Names and characters," 1677, UKNA CO 5/1371, fol. 138r, p. 271.

236. "To the Kings Ma:[ty] most humble proposalls on behalf of the Indian Kings &c.," UKNA CO 5/1371, fol. 134v-135r, pp. 264–265.

237. "Most humble proposalls on behalf of the Indian Kings," UKNA CO 5/1371, fol. 135r, p. 265.

238. Shefveland, *Anglo-Native Virginia*, 57–58.

239. "Minutes of the Board of Trade," 18 October 1677, UKNA CO 391/2, pp. 130–131. For more on Major Bristow, see Oberg, ed., *Book of Record*, 284 and n. 58.

240. "Minutes of the Board of Trade," 18 October 1677, UKNA CO 391/2, p. 131.

241. "Minutes of the Board of Trade," 18 October 1677, UKNA CO 391/2, p. 131.

242. "The Agrievances of the Queen of Poemonkey and her Sonn: Capt. John West," UKNA CO 1/42, no. 88, fol. 177r.

243. "The Agrievances of the Queen of Poemonkey," UKNA CO 1/42, no. 88, fol. 177r.

244. "The Agrievances of the Queen of Poemonkey," UKNA CO 1/42, no. 88, fol. 177r.

245. The phrase "Cockacoeske's treaty" is Negrin's, who also links its significance to modern struggles for sovereignty. Negrin, "Cockacoeske's Rebellion," 54–55, 85.

246. The visitations of the Native towns of Florida and the meetings of the Virginia General Assembly were clearly very different. But they were similar in two key respects. Both convened to obtain subjects' consent to laws and regulations and both could settle disputes. For more on the General Assembly's early character, see the discussion in James Horn, *1619: Jamestown and the Forging of American Democracy* (New York: Basic Books, 2018), 65-83; see also Alexander Haskell's discussion of the assembly. Rather than making law, the first General Assembly, at

least, convened to advise on the suitability of the laws proposed to it by higher authority and then as John Pory put it, make a "humble petition" to have changed those that were unsuited. Alexander B. Haskell, *For God, King and People: Forging Commonwealth Bonds in Renaissance Virginia* (Chapel Hill: University of North Carolina Press, 2017), 198.

247. "Appointment of Antonio de Argüelles as Visitor," 29 November 1677, AGI EC 156A, fol. 519v, PKY, reel 271.

248. "Appointment of Antonio de Argüelles," 29 November 1677, AGI EC 156A, fol. 519r, PKY, reel 271.

249. Leturiondo had served more than thirty years in Florida by the time the governor appointed him. "MÉRITOS: Domingo de Leturiondo to the King," 16 November 1679, AGI INDIFERENTE 127, PARES, accessed 7 April 2021.

250. "Appointment of Antonio de Argüelles," 29 November 1677, AGI EC 156A, fol. 519r, PKY, reel 271; Charles II granted the commissioners process power to investigate the colony's grievances and "Report the same to Us" so that he could order what "Wee in Our Royall Wisdome shall think fitt and convenient." Oberg, ed., *Book of Record*, 35; "Appointment of Antonio de Argüelles," 29 November 1677, AGI EC 156A, fol. 519v, PKY, reel 271. For the commissioners' writ, see Oberg, ed., *Book of Record*, 186–188.

251. "Notary's Appointment and Installation of Notary," 29 November 1677, AGI EC 156A, fol. 523r-524r, PKY, reel 271. For Wiseman's oath, see Oberg, ed., *Book of Record*, 29–30.

252. Oberg, ed., *Book of Record*, 35.

253. "Royal cédula (copy)," 31 May 1676, AGI EC 156A, fol. 535v, PKY, reel 271.

254. "Auto, San Francisco [de Potano]," 5 January 1678, AGI EC 156A, fol. 609r, PKY, reel 271.

255. "Auto, San Francisco [de Potano]," 5 January 1678, AGI EC 156A, fol. 609r, PKY, reel 271.

256. "Auto, San Francisco [de Potano]," 5 January 1678, AGI EC 156A, fol. 609v, PKY, reel 271.

257. "General *Auto* of the Visitation," 20 December 1677, AGI EC 156A, fol. 525v, PKY, reel 271.

258. "General *Auto*," 20 December 1677, AGI EC 156A, fol. 525v, PKY, reel 271.

259. "Visitation of the place of San Joseph de Sapala," AGI EC 156A, fol. 526v, PKY, reel 271.

260. "Visitation of Sapala," AGI EC 156A, fol. 526v, PKY, reel 271.

261. "Visitation of Sapala," AGI EC 156A, fol. 526v, PKY, reel 271.

262. "Visitation of Sapala," AGI EC 156A, fol. 526v, PKY, reel 271.

263. "Visitation of Sapala," AGI EC 156A, fol. 527r, PKY, reel 271.

264. Bushnell, *Situado and Sabana*, 63.

265. "The Agrievances of the Queen of Poemonkey," 5 June 1678, UKNA CO 1/42, no. 88, fol. 177r.

266. Cockacoeske to Moryson, 29 June 1678, UKNA CO 1/42, no. 101, fol. 273r.

267. In 1675, Virginia's colonial council ordered the Chickahominies to restore a *manguy* they had deposed who was a "friend" to the English. 8 October 1675, in McIlwaine, ed., *Minutes of the Council and General Court*, 425.

268. *Recopilación*, II, 6:7:3, 219v.

269. Bushnell, *Situado and Sabana*, 144.

270. Gina M. Martino-Trutor, "'As Potent a Prince as Any Round About Her': Rethinking Weetamoo of the Pocasset and Native Female Leadership in Early America," *Journal of Women's*

History, vol. 27, no. 3 (Fall 2015): 37–60. For a larger discussion of female leadership in Indigenous polities across the Southeast, see Ruth Trocolli, "Elite Status and Gender: Women Leaders in Chiefdom Societies in the Southeastern U.S." (PhD diss., University of Florida, 2006).

271. Ethan A. Schmidt, "Cockacoeske, Weroansqua of the Pamunkeys, and Indian Resistance in Seventeenth-Century Virginia," *American Indian Quarterly*, vol. 36, no. 3 (Summer 2012): 305.

272. "*Auto* convening the General Assembly at Tomole," 20 December 1677, AGI EC 156A, fol. 540r, PKY, reel 271.

273. "*Auto*," 20 December 1677, AGI EC 156A, fol. 540v, PKY, reel 271.

274. "Apalachee General Assembly," 22 December 1677, AGI EC 156A, fol. 541v, PKY, reel 271.

275. "Apalachee General Assembly," 22 December 1677, AGI EC 156A, fol. 541v, PKY, reel 271.

276. "Apalachee General Assembly," 22 December 1677, AGI EC 156A, fol. 541v, PKY, reel 271.

277. "Apalachee General Assembly," 22 December 1677, AGI EC 156A, fol. 541v, PKY reel 271.

278. "Apalachee General Assembly," 22 December 1677, AGI EC 156A, fol. 542r, PKY, reel 271.

279. Bushnell, "'Demonic Game,'" 16–17.

280. Hudson, *Southeastern Indians*, 408–421.

281. "Apalachee General Assembly," 22 December 1677, AGI EC 156A, fol. 542r, PKY, reel 271.

282. "Apalachee General Assembly," 22 December 1677, AGI EC 156A, fol. 542r, PKY, reel 271. For more on the rank of *noroco*, achieved after slaying three enemies in battle, see Hann, *Apalachee*, 71 and 182.

283. Hita Salazar to the King, 10 November 1678, AGI SD 226, fol. 147r-147v ("hand of their King"), PARES, accessed 10 April 2021. The reference to the "painted linen, printed with bright colors" is in a note added on 5 September 1680, in Hita Salazar to the King, 10 November 1678, AGI SD 226, PARES, accessed 10 April 2021.

284. Hita Salazar to the King, 10 November 1678, AGI SD 226, PARES, accessed 10 April 2021.

285. King of Great Britain, *Articles of Peace*, 5–6, 13.

286. For example, at the installation of Miguel as chief of San Francisco de Potano. "Auto, San Francisco de Potano," 5 January 1678, AGI EC 156A, fol. 609v, PKY, reel 271.

287. As Antonio de Argüelles did at the conclusion of his visitation in Sapala. Visitation of Sapala, AGI EC 156A, fol. 527r, PKY, reel 271.

288. Regulations for Apalachee Province in "*Auto* to Remit to the Captain Juan Florencia, Ivitachuco," 10 January 1678, AGI EC 156A, fol. 565r, PKY, reel 271.

289. King of Great Britain, *Articles of Peace*, 9–10.

290. King of Great Britain, *Articles of Peace*, 10.

291. King of Great Britain, *Articles of Peace*, 10.

292. King of Great Britain, *Articles of Peace*, 11.

293. Bushnell, *Situado and Sabana*, 173.

294. King of Great Britain, *Articles of Peace*, 12.

295. King of Great Britain, *Articles of Peace*, 12.

296. King of Great Britain, *Articles of Peace*, 12.

297. "Visitation of the place of Santa Catalina," 21 December 1677, AGI EC 156A, fol. 526v, PKY, reel 27I.

298. Apalachee Regulations, "*Auto* to Captain Florencia," 10 January 1678, AGI EC 156A, fol. 564r, PKY, reel 27I.

299. Timucua Regulations, "*Auto* for Captain Andres Perés, Lieutenant of the [Province] of Timucua, to observe that which is contained within it," 26 January 1678, AGI EC 156A, fol. 611r, PKY, reel 27I.

300. Timucua Regulations, "*Auto* for Captain Perés," 26 January 1678, AGI EC 156A, fol. 611v, PKY, reel 27I.

301. Apalachee Regulations, "*Auto* to Captain Florencia," 10 January 1678, AGI EC 156A, fol. 564v, PKY, reel 27I. Timucua Regulations, "*Auto* for Captain Perés," AGI EC 156A, fol. 611v, PKY, reel 27I.

302. King of Great Britain, *Articles of Peace*, 7.

303. King of Great Britain, *Articles of Peace*, 7.

304. *Recopilación*, II, 6:3:21, fol. 200v.

305. *Recopilación*, II, 6:3:22, fol. 200v.

306. Article IV, in King of Great Britain, *Articles of Peace*, 6–7.

307. *Recopilación*, II, 6:3:20, fol. 200v.

308. Bushnell, "Ruling 'the Republic of Indians,'" 199.

309. "*Auto* Santa Cruz [de Ychutafun]," 6 January 1678, AGI EC 156A, fol. 558v, PKY, reel 27I.

310. King of Great Britain, *Articles of Peace*, 11.

311. King of Great Britain, *Articles of Peace*, 11.

312. King of Great Britain, *Articles of Peace*, 14.

313. King of Great Britain, *Articles of Peace*, 14–15.

314. Apalachee Regulations, "*Auto* to Captain Florencia," 10 January 1678, AGI EC 156A, fol. 564v, PKY, reel 27I.

315. King of Great Britain, *Articles of Peace*, 14.

316. King of Great Britain, *Articles of Peace*, 14.

317. Apalachee Regulations, "*Auto* to Captain Florencia," 10 January 1678, AGI EC 156A, fol. 564v-565r, PKY, reel 27I.

318. The original is "cada quatro meses." The literal translation seems odd in English. Apalachee Regulations, "*Auto* to Captain Florencia," 10 January 1678, AGI EC 156A, fol. 564v, PKY, reel 27I.

319. Philip Ludwell to Sir Joseph Williamson, 28 June 1678, Lee Family Papers, Mss1 L51 f 8, Virginia Historical Society (VHS), Richmond, p. 2.

320. Ludwell to Williamson, 28 June 1678, VHS, p. 2.

321. Cockacoeske to Moryson, 29 June 1678, UKNA CO 1/42, no. 101, fol. 273r.

322. For a discussion of Florida's language-based mission provinces, see Bushnell, *Situado and Sabana*, 19–20.

Chapter 4

1. Abraham Wood's servant, Gabriel Arthur, went along on raids with the Tomahitans and was outfitted with gun, hatchet, and shield. At one point, the party of some fifty warriors lay in wait by a "cart path" for a week in preparing an ambush. The group attacked one Native town

at dawn, a common practice. "Letter of Abraham Wood to John Richards, August 22, 1674," in *The First Explorations of the Trans-Allegheny Region by the Virginians, 1650–1674*, ed. Clarence Walworth Alvord and Lee Bidgood (Cleveland, OH: The Arthur H. Clark Company, 1912), 219 and 221.

2. The town was Santa Catalina de Ajoica. Juan Rodriguez Tisnado to Juan Marquez Cabrera, 16 March 1685, AGI SD 839, PKY, JTCC, box 16, folder 58-1-26, microfilm copy, p. 2.

3. Juan Rodriguez Tisnado to Juan Marquez Cabrera, 16 March 1685, AGI SD 839, PKY, JTCC, box 16, folder 58-1-26, microfilm copy, p. 2.

4. Robbie Ethridge coined the term in 2006. For more, see Robbie Ethridge, "Creating the Shatter Zone: Indian Slave Traders and the Collapse of the Southeastern Chiefdoms," in *Light on the Path: The Anthropology and History of the Southeastern Indians*, ed. Thomas J. Pluckhahn and Robbie Ethridge (Tuscaloosa: University of Alabama Press, 2006), 208–209.

5. John E. Worth, "Razing Florida: The Indian Slave Trade and the Devastation of Spanish Florida, 1659–1715," in *Mapping the Mississippian Shatter Zone: The Colonial Indian Slave Trade and Regional Instability in the American South*, ed. Robbie Ethridge and Sheri M. Shuck-Hall (Lincoln: University of Nebraska Press, 2009), 308.

6. "The Examination of Severall Yamassee Indians," 1685, UKNA CO 5/287, fol. 70v.

7. Kristalyn Marie Shefveland, *Anglo-Native Virginia: Trade, Conversion, and Indian Slavery in the Old Dominion, 1646–1722* (Athens: University of Georgia Press, 2016), 36. Francisco was enslaved by a Northumberland County planter named George Colclough. C. S. Everett, "'They Shalbe Slaves for Their Lives': Indian Slavery in Colonial Virginia," in *Indian Slavery in Colonial America*, ed. Alan Gallay (Lincoln: University of Nebraska Press, 2009), 76.

8. "Letter of Abraham Wood to John Richards, August 22, 1674," 218–219.

9. See Amy Turner Bushnell, "Living at Liberty: The Ungovernable Yamasees of Spanish Florida," in *The Yamasee Indians: From Florida to South Carolina*, ed. Denise Bossy (Lincoln: University of Nebraska Press, 2018), 27–53.

10. Laureano's Spanish original says only that the Apalachicolas "are not Vassals of that Government but of this." The English translator added "subjects." The quote refers to the English translation made in Charles Town of Don Alonso Laureano de Torres y Ayala to Governor Archdale, 24 January 1696, Doc. #10, Colonial Governor's Papers, CGP 1, North Carolina State Archives, Raleigh, NC.

11. Juan Rodriguez Tisnado to Juan Marquez Cabrera, 16 March 1685, AGI SD 839, PKY, JTCC, folder 58-1-26, microfilm copy, pp. 2–3. That said, the captives in the 1685 raid on Santa Catalina de Ajoica at least passed through the short-lived Scottish settlement of Stuart's Town, which Charles Town officials condemned for the whole affair. See Alan Gallay, *The Indian Slave Trade: The Rise of the English Empire in the South, 1670–1717* (New Haven, CT: Yale University Press, 2002), 79–80. For a detailed account of Carolina's plunge into the regional slave trade, see also Alan Gallay, "South Carolina's Entrance into the Indian Slave Trade," in *Indian Slavery in Colonial America*, ed. Alan Gallay (Lincoln: University of Nebraska Press, 2009), 109–146. John E. Worth states that some of the victims enslaved during the attack on Ajoica were sold "to a merchant from Charles Town, and the rest embarked on an Irish ship." John E. Worth, *The Timucuan Chiefdoms of Spanish Florida*, 2 vols. (Gainesville: University of Florida Press, 1998), 2: 140.

12. Indeed, one source describes the then ten-year-old English outpost as "Kaiawah sometimes called Charles towne." 1 June 1680, in *Journal of the Grand Council of South Carolina, August 25, 1671–June 24, 1680*, ed. A. S. Salley Jr. (Columbia, SC: The State Company, 1907),

84. For the *mico*, see "Mr. Carteret's Relation," in *The Shaftesbury Papers*, ed. Langdon Cheves (Charleston, SC: Home House Press, [1897] 2010), 168.

13. For the corn Sewee supplied to the English at Charles Town, see William Owen to Lord Ashley, 15 September 1670, in *Shaftesbury Papers*, ed. Cheves, 201. For more on how Indigenous people, especially the Sewees and Kiawahs, set Charles Town's location and shaped its development as a port—a "Native port" serving their interests—see Miller Wright, "A Native Port in a Native Market: How Indigenous Peoples Shaped the Foundation of Carolina, 1670–1710," in *Port Cities of the Atlantic World: Sea-Facing Histories of the US South*, eds. Jacob Steere-Williams and Blake C. Scott (Columbia: University of South Carolina Press, 2023), 17–33. My heartfelt thanks to Miller for sharing a pre-publication copy of his work after a conversation at Ethnohistory. Peter N. Moore argues that the decision to seek English "protection," with its implications of subordination, marked a real break in the history of coastal Carolina peoples who had long made their own independence the guiding principle of their politics. For this insight and for more on the deeper history of the peoples in the region known as Escamaçu to Spaniards, see Peter N. Moore, "Indigenous Power and Collapse on the Lower South Carolina Coast, Precontact-1684," *South Carolina Historical Magazine*, vol. 120, no. 1 (January 2019): 4–19, with discussion of the unprecedented request for English "protection," 8, 23–29. See also Joseph M. Hall Jr., *Zamumo's Gifts: Indian-European Exchange in the Colonial Southeast* (Philadelphia: University of Pennsylvania Press, 2009), 83. For the concept of kinship relations between towns, such as "mother" and "daughter," see Steven C. Hahn, *The Invention of the Creek Nation, 1670–1763* (Lincoln: University of Nebraska Press, 2004), 26.

14. See Alan Gallay, *The Indian Slave Trade: The Rise of the English Empire in the South, 1670–1717* (New Haven, CT: Yale University Press, 2002), 45–48.

15. Henry Woodward, "A Faithfull Relation of My Westoe Voiage, 1674," in *Narratives of Early Carolina, 1650–1708*, ed. Alexander S. Salley (New York: Charles Scribner's Sons, 1911), 126–134.

16. Gallay, *Indian Slave Trade*, 299.

17. Shefveland, *Anglo-Native Virginia*, 44.

18. Robert Sanford, "A Relation of a Voyage on the Coast of the Province of Carolina, 1666," in *Narratives of Early Carolina, 1650–1708*, ed. Alexander S. Salley (New York: Charles Scribner's Sons, 1911), 91.

19. Although Florida documents usually spell the word as "*bujio*."

20. William Hilton, *A relation of a discovery lately made on the coast of Floreda* [. . .] (London: 1664), 5. Original in the John Carter Brown Library.

21. Hilton, *Relation of a discovery*, 5.

22. John Lawson, *A New Voyage to Carolina* [. . .] (London: 1709), 38.

23. Sanford, "Relation of a Voyage," 91.

24. For towns as the key nodes in the "webs of empire"—and other political formations—see Hall, *Zamumo's Gifts*, 9.

25. In this respect, the world of the colonial era resembled the Mississippian world where towns vied with one another and built "networks of relationships" to expand their power. Towns remain central to Indigenous life to this day. Hall, *Zamumo's Gifts*, 6, 27.

26. Timothy Paul Grady, *Anglo-Spanish Rivalry in Colonial South-East America, 1650–1725* (New York: Taylor & Francis, 2010), 39; Steven J. Oatis, *A Colonial Complex: South Carolina's Frontiers in the Era of the Yamasee War, 1680–1730* (Lincoln: University of Nebraska Press,

2004); Verner W. Crane, *The Southern Frontier, 1670–1732* (New York: W. W. Norton, [1928] 1981).

27. For more on the possible location of Hickauhaugau, see Eric E. Bowne, *The Westo Indians: Slave Traders of the Early Colonial South* (Tuscaloosa: University of Alabama Press, 2005), 21–23.

28. For the principles behind Southeastern Native maps, see Gregory A. Waselkov, "Indian Maps of the Colonial Southeast," in *Powhatan's Mantle: Indians in the Colonial Southeast*, ed. Gregory A. Waselkov, Peter H. Wood, and Tom Hatley (Lincoln: University of Nebraska Press, 2006), 435–502. For Native maps more generally, see Mark Warhus, *Another America: Native American Maps and the History of Our Land* (New York: St. Martin's Press, 1997).

29. Sanford, "Relation of a Voyage," 91.

30. The signs of wealth, including fertile fields of maize that greeted English parties like Sanford's were, as Peter N. Moore points out, also signs of distress for coastal peoples who historically did not rely much on maize and were now too tightly bound by Westo incursions to follow their traditional patterns of subsistence. Moore, "Indigenous Power and Collapse," 25.

31. Owen to Ashley, 15 September 1670, in *Shaftesbury Papers*, ed. Cheves, 200.

32. Sanford, "Relation of a Voyage," 91.

33. Sanford, "Relation of a Voyage," 91.

34. Sanford, "Relation of a Voyage," 92.

35. Sanford, "Relation of a Voyage," 104.

36. Sanford, "Relation of a Voyage," 104.

37. Sanford, "Relation of a Voyage," 105.

38. Sanford, "Relation of a Voyage," 105.

39. Sanford, "Relation of a Voyage," 88. For the concept of "ceremonies of possession," see Patricia Seed, *Ceremonies of Possession in Europe's Conquest of the New World, 1492–1640* (New York: Cambridge University Press, 1995).

40. Sanford, "Relation of a Voyage," 105.

41. Sanford, "Relation of a Voyage," 105.

42. See Eric E. Bowne, "Dr. Henry Woodward's Role in Early Carolina Indian Relations," in *Creating and Contesting Carolina: Proprietary Era Histories*, ed. Michelle LeMaster and Bradford J. Wood (Columbia: University of South Carolina Press, 2013), 73–93 and especially 73–74 for more on Woodward's marriage and kinship networks.

43. Quoted in Bernard W. Sheehan, *Savagism and Civility: Indians and Englishmen in Colonial Virginia* (London: Cambridge University Press, 1980), 147.

44. Gentleman of Elvas, *A Relation of the Invasion and Conquest of Florida by the Spaniards* (London: 1686), [5]. Original in the John Carter Brown Library.

45. Peter Heylyn, *Cosmographie in Foure Bookes Contayning the Chorographie & Historie of the Whole World* (London: 1652), 117. Original in the John Carter Brown Library.

46. N. N., *America: or An Exact Description of the West-Indies* (London: 1655), 276–277. Original in the John Carter Brown Library.

47. For more on San Agustín in the 1660s and on Woodward's time there, see Diana Reigelsperger, "Pirate, Priest, and Slave: Spanish Florida in the 1668 Searles Raid," in "500 Years of Florida History—The Seventeenth Century," special issue, *Florida Historical Quarterly*, vol. 92, no. 3 (Winter 2014): 578, 589; Amy Turner Bushnell, *Situado and Sabana: Spain's Support System for the Presidio and Mission Provinces of Florida*, American Museum of Natural History, Anthropological Papers 74 (New York: 1994), 136.

48. Francisco de Sotolongo to the King, 4 July 1668, AGI SD 235, PKY, SC, reel 13. For more on the impact of Searles' raid, see Reigelsperger, "Pirate, Priest, and Slave," 577–590.

49. Sotolongo to the King, 4 July 1668, AGI SD 235, PKY, SC, reel 13.

50. Sotolongo to the King, 4 July 1668, AGI SD 235, PKY, SC, reel 13.

51. Sotolongo appears to have had legal training, which perhaps added force to his defense of the king's vassals. Reigelsperger, "Pirate, Priest, and Slave," 588.

52. "The Council to the Lords Proprietors," 11 September 1670, in *Shaftesbury Papers*, ed. Cheves,191.

53. For more on Woodward's kin connections that granted him an "'international' status," see Bowne, "Dr. Henry Woodward's Role," 74.

54. "The Council to the Lords Proprietors," 11 September 1670, in *Shaftesbury Papers*, ed. Cheves, 191.

55. "The Council to the Lords Proprietors," 11 September 1670, in *Shaftesbury Papers*, ed. Cheves, 191.

56. The 1668 attack marked a significant clash between Spanish and English ideas about subjecthood. It also followed the pattern of raids on missions for church ornaments and for human beings to enslave. Moreover, Woodward appears to have used his time in San Agustín deliberately to gather intelligence he could put to use later as "architect" of Carolina's alliance system with Native Americans. Reigelsperger, "Pirate, Priest, and Slave," 583 and 589–590.

57. "From the address of numerous letters, including Joseph West to Lord Ashley," 27 June 1670, in *Shaftesbury Papers*, ed. Cheves, 174.

58. Shaftesbury to Sir Peter Colleton, 27 November 1672, in *Shaftesbury Papers*, ed. Cheves, 416 (quotation).

59. William S. Powell, *The Proprietors of Carolina* (Raleigh, NC: State Department of Archives and History, [1963] 1968), 12–49.

60. Powell, *Proprietors*, 13–15.

61. Powell, *Proprietors*, 21–23.

62. Powell, *Proprietors*, 26–27.

63. Powell, *Proprietors*, 40 and 47.

64. Powell, *Proprietors*, 33; Warren M. Billings, *Sir William Berkeley and the Forging of Colonial Virginia* (Charlottesville: University of Virginia Press, 2004), 156–158.

65. "Instructions for Mr. Andrew Percivall," 23 May 1674, in *Shaftesbury Papers*, ed. Cheves, 443.

66. "Instructions to Governor Joseph West," UKNA CO 5/287, fol. 61v.

67. "Instructions to Governor Joseph West," UKNA CO 5/287, fol. 62v.

68. The seventeenth-century church was built sometime after 1604 when the site was reoccupied following the 1597 Guale Revolt. For more on the church and the site's archaeology, see David Hurst Thomas, "The Archaeology of Mission Santa Catalina de Guale: Our First 15 Years," in *The Missions of Spanish Florida*, ed. Bonnie G. McEwen (Gainesville: University Press of Florida, 1993), 9.

69. "Mr. Mathews' Relation," 1670, in *Shaftesbury Papers*, ed. Cheves, 169.

70. "Mr. Mathews' Relation," 169.

71. "Mr. Mathews' Relation," 169.

72. "Mr. Mathews' Relation," 169.

73. "Mr. Mathews' Relation," 169.

74. "Mr. Mathews' Relation," 169.

75. "Mr. Mathews' Relation," 169.
76. "Mr. Mathews' Relation," 169.
77. "Mr. Mathews' Relation," 169.
78. "Mr. Mathews' Relation," 170.
79. "Mr. Mathews' Relation," 170.
80. Joseph West to Lord Ashley, 27 June 1670, in *Shaftesbury Papers*, ed. Cheves, 174.
81. "Mr. Mathews' Relation," 170–171.
82. "Mr. Mathews' Relation," 171.
83. "Mr. Mathews' Relation," 171.
84. Juan Chicasle to Governor Pedro de Zuñiga y Cerda, 16 October 1700, AGI SD 858, PKY, JTCC, box 19, folder 58-2-8, microfilm copy.
85. For the corporate character of towns, see Amy Turner Bushnell, "Debitage of the Shatter Zone: Indoctrination, Asylum, and the Law of Towns in the Provinces of Florida," in *Petitioning in the Atlantic World, c. 1500–1840: Empires, Revolutions and Social Movements*, ed. Miguel Dantas da Cruz (New York: Palgrave Macmillan, 2022), 138; Bushnell, *Situado and Sabana*, 134; Kathryn E. Holland Braund, *Deerskins & Duffels: The Creek Indian Trade with Anglo-America, 1685–1815* (Lincoln: University of Nebraska Press, 1993), 15–18; John Phillip Reid, *A Law of Blood: The Primitive Law of the Cherokee Nation* (New York: New York University Press, 1970), 29–33.
86. Most of the coastal peoples of what is now South Carolina were already living in small towns governed by councils. Moore, "Indigenous Power and Collapse," 10. See also the discussion of the transformation from chiefly to conciliar government in Native polities in Robbie Ethridge, *From Chicaza to Chickasaw: The European Invasion and the Transformation of the Mississippian World, 1540–1715* (Chapel Hill: University of North Carolina Press, 2010), 82–84.
87. Heylyn, *Cosmographie*, 116.
88. For a succinct description of women's political and economic power in southern Indigenous societies, see Alejandra Dubcovsky, *Talking Back: Native Women and the Making of the Early South* (New Haven, CT: Yale University Press, 2023), 40. See also Theda Perdue, *Cherokee Women: Gender and Culture Change, 1700–1832* (Lincoln: University of Nebraska Press, 1999).
89. "The Council Journals," 10 March 1673, in *Shaftesbury Papers*, ed. Cheves, 421.
90. Thomas Colleton to Sir Peter Colleton, 23 November 1670, in *Shaftesbury Papers*, ed. Cheves, 240.
91. Council to the Proprietors, 9 September 1670, in *Shaftesbury Papers*, ed. Cheves, 180.
92. Council to the Proprietors, 9 September 1670, in *Shaftesbury Papers*, ed. Cheves, 180–181.
93. Florence O'Sullivan to Lord Ashley, 10 September 1670, in *Shaftesbury Papers*, ed. Cheves, 189.
94. Henry Brayne to Lord Ashley, 9 November 1670, in *Shaftesbury Papers*, ed. Cheves, 214.
95. Joseph West to Lord Ashley, September 1670, in *Shaftesbury Papers*, ed. Cheves, 203.
96. Capt. Brayne to Sir Peter Colleton, 20 November 1670, in *Shaftesbury Papers*, ed. Cheves, 235.
97. Henry Brayne to Lord Ashley, 9 November 1670, in *Shaftesbury Papers*, ed. Cheves, 214.
98. Henry Brayne to Lord Ashley, 9 November 1670, in *Shaftesbury Papers*, ed. Cheves, 214.
99. William Owen to Lord Ashley, 15 September 1670, in *Shaftesbury Papers*, ed. Cheves, 197; Joseph Dalton to Lord Ashley, 9 September 1670, in *Shaftesbury Papers*, ed. Cheves, 183 ("soldiers in a garrison").

100. "Coppy of Instruccons for Mr. West about o^r Plantacon," 27 July 1669, in *Shaftesbury Papers*, ed. Cheves, 126.

101. For a discussion of the concept, see Stephen A. Kowalewski, "Coalescent Societies," in *Light on the Path: The Anthropology and History of the Southeastern Indians*, eds. Thomas J. Pluckhahn and Robbie Ethridge (Tuscaloosa: University of Alabama Press, 2006), 94–122. For the classic case of the Catawba Nation and for the challenges of living together that faced all groups in early America, see James H. Merrell, "The Indians' New World: The Catawba Experience," *William and Mary Quarterly*, vol. 41, no. 4 (October 1984): 547–549.

102. Governor Sayle to Lord Ashley, 10 September 1670, in *Shaftesbury Papers*, ed. Cheves, 185.

103. Joseph Dalton to Lord Ashley, 9 September 1670, in *Shaftesbury Papers*, ed. Cheves, 183.

104. Stephen Bull to Lord Ashley, 12 September 1670, in *Shaftesbury Papers*, ed. Cheves, 194.

105. Stephen Bull to Lord Ashley, 12 September 1670, in *Shaftesbury Papers*, ed. Cheves, 193.

106. Joseph West to Lord Ashley, September 1670, in *Shaftesbury Papers*, ed. Cheves, 203.

107. Joseph West to Lord Ashley, 2 March 1671, in *Shaftesbury Papers*, ed. Cheves, 267.

108. Coastal Natives preferred living in dispersed settlements and practicing "seasonal mobility." Moore, "Indigenous Power and Collapse," 13. Indeed, Native peoples across the Southeast appear to have preferred dispersed settlement patterns as they were both better for agricultural production and healthier than crowded towns behind palisades. Paul Kelton, *Epidemics & Enslavement: Biological Catastrophe in the Native Southeast, 1492-1715* (Lincoln: University of Nebraska Press, 2007), 8–9.

109. Alejandra Dubcovsky has likened this English tendency to seeing the region through the lens of Spanish Florida. See Alejandra Dubcovsky, *Informed Power: Communication in the Early American South* (Cambridge, MA: Harvard University Press, 2016), 61–66.

110. "A List of all Such Masters, free passengers and servants which are now a board the Carolina now ridinge in the Downes," 10 August 1669, in *Shaftesbury Papers*, ed. Cheves, 135.

111. Joseph Dalton to Lord Ashley, 9 September 1670, in *Shaftesbury Papers*, ed. Cheves, 184.

112. Dalton to Ashley, 9 September 1670, in *Shaftesbury Papers*, ed. Cheves, 184

113. Dalton to Ashley, 9 September 1670, in *Shaftesbury Papers*, ed. Cheves, 183 (quote).

114. Dalton to Ashley, 9 September 1670, in *Shaftesbury Papers*, ed. Cheves, 183 (quote).

115. Owen to Lord Ashley, 15 September 1671, in *Shaftesbury Papers*, ed. Cheves, 197.

116. Owen to Lord Ashley, 15 September 1671, in *Shaftesbury Papers*, ed. Cheves, 197.

117. Owen to Lord Ashley, 15 September 1671, in *Shaftesbury Papers*, ed. Cheves, 198. Here, I think Cheves's transcription is mistaken. The word is not "language" but "tongue." William Owen to Lord Ashley, 15 September 1670, "Shaftesbury Papers," UKNA PRO 30/24/48, no. 37, fol. 99v.

118. Owen to Lord Ashley, 15 September 1671, in *Shaftesbury Papers*, ed. Cheves, 198.

119. Owen to Lord Ashley, 15 September 1671, in *Shaftesbury Papers*, ed. Cheves, 198.

120. Increase Mather, *A brief history of the war with the Indians in New-England, from June 24, 1675 (when the first Englishman was murdered by the Indians) to August 12, 1676* [...] (London: 1676), [3].

121. Mather, *A brief history of the war with the Indians*, [3].

122. Mather, *A brief history of the war with the Indians*, [3–4].

123. Joseph Dalton to Lord Ashley, 9 September 1670, in *Shaftesbury Papers*, ed. Cheves, 183.

124. Joseph Dalton to Lord Ashley, 9 September 1670, in *Shaftesbury Papers*, ed. Cheves, 183.

125. For a summary of the charges and responses from the Franciscan Commissary General of the Indies, Fray Miguel Avengoçar, see "About the *Doctrineros* of Florida," 10 September 1681, AGI SD 226, PKY, JTCC, box 13, folder 54-5-11, microfilm copy.

126. Francisco Pacheco to Governor Manuel de Cendoya, March 1672, in Jose Miguel Gallardo, trans., "The Spaniards and the English Settlement in Charles Town," *South Carolina Historical and Genealogical Magazine*, vol. 37, no. 2 (April 1936): 54–55.

127. Pacheco to Cendoya, March 1672, in Gallardo, trans., "Spaniards and the English Settlement," 55.

128. Lord Ashley to William Owen, 10 April 1671, in *Shaftesbury Papers*, ed. Cheves, 313.

129. See also the discussion about the proprietors' Indian policy in Barbara Arneil, *John Locke and America: The Defence of English Colonialism* (Oxford: Clarendon Press, 1996), 126–128.

130. For the name "Cassique," and the privileges that accompanied the title, see *The Fundamental Constitutions of Carolina* ([London, 1670]), 3–4.

131. James Horn, *A Land as God Made It: Jamestown and the Birth of America* (New York: Basic Books, 2005), 71.

132. The references to Niccoló Machiavelli and Thomas Hobbes alluded as much to his political acumen and learning as to his ruthlessness. J. G. Dunlop and Mabel L. Webber, "Letters from John Stewart to William Dunlop," *South Carolina Historical and Genealogical Magazine*, vol. 32, no. 2 (April 1931): 114.

133. Maurice Mathews to Lord Ashley, 30 August 1671, "Shaftesbury Papers," UKNA PRO 30/24/48, no. 55, fol. 44v.

134. The word "Topakin" does not appear in the *Oxford English Dictionary*. However, the words "toparch" and "toparchy" do. A toparch was "the ruler of a small district, city, or petty state; a petty 'king.'" A "toparchy" was "the small district or territory under the rule of a toparch." See "toparchy, n." and "toparch, n.," *OED Online*, accessed 4 May 2018, http://www.oed.com.ezproxy .lib.utexas.edu/view/Entry/203342?redirectedFrom=Toparchy. A 2008 online discussion via H-Net suggested that "Topakin" related either to a word for a Turkish palace or to "toparchs" and "toparchy." See the H-OIEAHC Discussion Logs by month, September 2008, http://h-net .msu.edu/cgi-bin/logbrowse.pl?trx=lx&list=H-OIEAHC&month=0809&user=&pw= (accessed 3 February 2017).

135. Thomas Amy, *Carolina; or A Description of the Present State of that Country* [. . .] (London: 1682), 36.

136. Maurice Mathews to Lord Ashley, 30 August 1671, in *Shaftesbury Papers*, ed. Cheves, 334.

137. Mathews to Ashley, 30 August 1671, in *Shaftesbury Papers*, ed. Cheves, 334.

138. Lord Ashley to Maurice Mathews, 20 June 1672, in *Shaftesbury Papers*, ed. Cheves, 399.

139. Ashley to Mathews, 20 June 1672, in *Shaftesbury Papers*, ed. Cheves, 399.

140. Lord Ashley to Stephen Bull, 19 August 1673, "Shaftesbury Papers," UKNA PRO 30/24/48, no. 55, p. 136.

141. Ashley to Bull, 19 August 1673, "Shaftesbury Papers," UKNA PRO 30/24/48, no. 55, p. 136.

142. Ashley to Bull, 19 August 1673, "Shaftesbury Papers," UKNA PRO 30/24/48, no. 55, p. 136.

143. For more on the practice during the early eighteenth century, see Hall, *Zamumo's Gifts*, 111–113.

144. F. R., *The Present State of Carolina with Advice to the Settlers* (London: 1682), 16.

145. F. R., *Present State*, 16.

146. Cacique Diego Huste and Juan Chicasle to the King, 1 March 1699, AGI SD 234, PKY, SC, reel 26.

147. "The Council Journals," 2 February 1674, in *Shaftesbury Papers*, ed. Cheves, 429.

148. "The Council Journals," 2 February 1674, in *Shaftesbury Papers*, ed. Cheves, 429.

149. Deposition of Bernardo de Medina, 17 October 1678, in Don Pablo de Hita Salazar to the King, 10 November 1678, AGI SD 839, PKY, SC, reel 15.

150. Deposition of Bernardo de Medina, 17 October 1678, in Hita Salazar to the King, 10 November 1678, AGI SD 839, PKY, SC, reel 15.

151. "Instructions for the Comission[rs] appointed to heare and determine differences between the Christians and the Indians," 17 May 1680, in *SCBPRO*, 1: 97–98.

152. "Instructions," 17 May 1680, *SCBPRO*, 1: 101.

153. Woodward, "A Faithfull Relation of My Westoe Voiage, 1674," in *Narratives*, ed. Salley, 132.

154. Woodward, "A Faithfull Relation of My Westoe Voiage, 1674," in *Narratives*, ed. Salley, 132.

155. Robin Beck, *Chiefdoms, Collapse, and Coalescence in the Early American South* (New York: Cambridge University Press, 2013), 195.

156. Thomas Newe, "Letters of Thomas Newe, 1682," in *Narratives*, ed. Salley, 182.

157. "Royal cédula to Governor Juan Marquez Cabrera," 15 January 1681, AGI SD 834, PKY, SC, reel 15.

158. For reports of a prolonged drought in the summer of 1671, see Maurice Mathews to Lord Ashley, 30 August 1671, in *Shaftesbury Papers*, ed. Cheves, 333.

159. "Council Journal," 27 September 1671, in *Shaftesbury Papers*, ed. Cheves, 341–342.

160. "Council Journal," 27 September 1671, in *Shaftesbury Papers*, ed. Cheves, 342.

161. "Carolina Memoranda—In Locke's Hand," 14 February 1672, in *Shaftesbury Papers*, ed. Cheves, 388.

162. "Mr. Carteret's Relation," 1670, in *Shaftesbury Papers*, ed. Cheves, 168.

163. "The Council Journals," 25 July 1674, in *Shaftesbury Papers*, ed. Cheves, 451.

164. "The Council Journals," 25 July 1674, in *Shaftesbury Papers*, ed. Cheves, 451.

165. "The Council Journals," 25 July 1674, in *Shaftesbury Papers*, ed. Cheves, 451.

166. Ashley to Owen, 10 April 1671, in *Shaftesbury Papers*, ed. Cheves, 313.

167. "Instructions to the Governor of Albemarle County from the Lords Proprietors of Carolina," 1676, Saunders et al, eds., *CRNC*, 1: 230.

168. See Lars C. Adams, "'Sundry Murders and Depredations': A Closer Look at the Chowan River War, 1676–1677," *North Carolina Historical Review*, vol. 90, no. 2 (April 2013): 149–172; Shannon Lee Dawdy, "The Meherrin's Secret History of the Dividing Line," *North Carolina Historical Review*, vol. 72, no. 4 (October 1995): 394.

169. Maurice Mathews to Lord Ashley, 30 August 1671, "Shaftesbury Papers," UKNA PRO 30/24/48, no. 55, folio 44v. Mathews to Ashley, 30 August 1671, in *Shaftesbury Papers*, ed. Cheves, 334.

170. "Royal cédula to Governor Hita Salazar," 15 October 1680, AGI SD 834, PKY, SC, reel 15.

171. Governor's letter to Merenciana enclosed in Juan Marquez Cabrera to the King, 25 January 1682, AGI SD 226, PKY, SC, reel 16.

172. Governor's letter to Merenciana Marquez Cabrera to the King, 25 January 1682, AGI SD 226, PKY, SC, reel 16 (quotation). For the similar 1694 agreement between the Apalachees in San Luis de Talimali and the refugee Chacatos, see Chapter 5 below, and the discussion in Dubcovsky, *Talking Back*, 39.

173. For more on Merenciana and how the governor "effectively circumvented the political power of the Mocama leadership," see John E. Worth, *The Struggle for the Georgia Coast: An Eighteenth-Century Spanish Retrospective on Guale and Mocama* (1995, repr.; Tuscaloosa: University of Alabama Press, 2007), 35.

174. Governor's letter to Merenciana enclosed in Juan Marquez Cabrera to the King, 25 January 1682, AGI SD 226, PKY, SC, reel 16.

175. "Document 18, Deed of Land by Kussoe Indians," in *Early American Indian Documents: Treaties and Laws, 1607–1789*, ed. Alden T. Vaughan, vol. 13, *North and South Carolina Treaties, 1654–1756*, ed. W. Stitt Robinson (Bethesda, MD: University Publications of America, 2001), 22.

176. Don Pablo de Hita Salazar to the King, 6 March 1680, AGI SD 226, PKY, SC, reel 15.

177. "Royal cédula to Governor Juan Marquez Cabrera," 15 January 1681, AGI SD 834, PKY, SC, reel 15.

178. "Royal cédula to Governor Juan Marquez Cabrera," 15 January 1681, AGI SD 834, PKY, SC, reel 15.

179. Lord Ashley to Sir John Yeamans, 18 September 1671, in *Shaftesbury Papers*, ed. Cheves, 343.

180. "The Council Journals," 20 December 1671, in *Shaftesbury Papers*, ed. Cheves, 368.

181. "To ye Governour & Counsell at Ashley River," 10 April 1677, in *SCBPRO* 1: 55.

182. "Commissions and Instructions for the government," 5 June 1682, in *SCBPRO* 1: 174.

183. "Commissions and Instructions for the government," 5 June 1682, in *SCBPRO* 1: 174.

184. Stephen Bull to Lord Ashley, 2 March 1671, in *Shaftesbury Papers*, ed. Cheves, 275.

185. Stephen Bull to Lord Ashley, 2 March 1671, in *Shaftesbury Papers*, ed. Cheves, 275.

186. "The Council Journals," 4 March 1673, in *Shaftesbury Papers*, ed. Cheves, 420.

187. "Auto by Juan Marquez Cabrera," 21 August 1684, AGI SD 226, PKY, JTCC, box 13, folder 54-5-11, microfilm copy, p. 5 ("infested"); Juan Marquez Cabrera to the King, 26 August 1684, AGI SD 226, PKY, JTCC, box 13, folder 54-5-11, microfilm copy, p. 3 ("Republic").

188. For more, see the discussion in Worth, *Struggle for the Georgia Coast*, 38–40.

189. Juan Marquez Cabrera to the King, 26 August 1684, AGI SD 226, PKY, JTCC, box 13, folder 54-5-11, microfilm copy, p. 2.

190. "Auto," 21 August 1684, AGI SD 226, PKY, JTCC, box 13, folder 54-5-11, microfilm copy, p. 7.

191. "Auto," 22 August 1684, AGI SD 226, PKY, JTCC, box 13, folder 54-5-11, microfilm copy, p. 10.

192. "Records of the Junta de Guerra in San Agustín," 21 August 1685, AGI SD 226, PKY, JTCC, box 13, folder 54-5-11, p. 7.

193. "Opinion of the Caciques," 22 August 1684, AGI SD 226, PKY, JTCC, box 13, folder 54-5-11, microfilm copy, p. 11.

194. Worth, *Struggle for the Georgia Coast*, 42.

195. Matthew Kruer, *Time of Anarchy: Indigenous Power and the Crisis of Colonialism* (Cambridge, MA: Harvard University Press, 2021), 162–163 and 176–177.

196. The terror of Iroquois raids, the rise of the Indian slave trade, and a growing dependence on enslaved labor in Virginia led English lawmakers there to curb the rights of Native
tributary subjects, though not without protests. Kruer, *Time of Anarchy*, 174–175, 218–219.

197. Helen C. Rountree, *Pocahontas's People: The Powhatan Indians of Virginia Through
Four Centuries* (Lincoln: University of Nebraska Press, 1990), 115–116; John H. Hann, *Apalachee:
The Land Between the Rivers* (Gainesville: University of Florida Press, 1988), 202–203.

198. Geoffrey Kimball, "An Apalachee Vocabulary," *International Journal of American Linguistics*, vol. 54, no. (October 1988): 388; For a partial translation of the Apalachee-language
version of the letter, see also Geoffrey Kimball, "A Grammatical Sketch of Apalachee," *International Journal of American Linguistics*," vol. 53, no. 2 (April 1987): 141. For more generally on
the Apalachee language, see Hann, *Apalachee*, 118–125; Hann also included among his papers
a purported translation of the Apalachee version of the letter by John Swanton. John Swanton
transcription and translation of Apalachee-language petition, 1688, Hann Collection, MS 048,
PKY JHC, 27–34.

199. Translated by the author from the Spanish version by Fray Marcelo de San Joseph,
using the Spanish version from the John Carter Brown Library, which is easily accessible online.
Buckingham Smith, "Documents in the Spanish and two of the early tongues of Florida (Apalachian and Timuquan)" [in Spanish], Codex Ind 38, Original in the John Carter Brown Library,
p. 11. The Stetson Collection also has a copy. See Diego Quiroga y Losada to the King, "Proceedings and Letters from the Caciques of Apalachee," 1 April 1688, AGI SD 839, PKY, SC, reel 19. I
am grateful to Michele Wilbanks of the P. K. Yonge Library of Florida History for scanning and
sending me a copy of this document during the pandemic before I was able to visit the library in
person. For more on Carlos II and his reign, see John Lynch, *Spain Under the Habsburgs*, vol. 2,
1598–1700 (New York: Oxford University Press, 1981); John Langdon-Davies, *Carlos: The King
Who Would Not Die* (Englewood Cliffs, NJ: Prentice-Hall, Inc., 1962).

200. Smith, [Documents], 11. Quiroga y Losada to the King, "Proceedings and Letters,"
1 April 1688, AGI SD 839, PKY, SC reel 19.

201. For the honorifics, see John H. Hann, "Political Leadership Among the Natives of
Spanish Florida," *Florida Historical Quarterly*, vol. 71, no. 2 (October 1992): 199.

202. Smith, [Documents], 11; "Proceedings and Letters," 1 April 1688, AGI SD 839.

203. Warren M. Billings, *Virginia's Viceroy, Their Majesties' Governor General: Francis Howard, Baron Howard of Effingham* (Fairfax, VA: George Mason University Press, 1991); Effingham
had left for England sometime around February of 1688. James Rice, *Tales from a Revolution:
Bacon's Rebellion and the Transformation of Early America* (New York: Oxford University Press,
2012), 173.

204. "Petition of the Chiefs of the Chickahominy Indians to Governor Francis Lord Howard, Baron of Effingham, 1689," 1689, Colonial Papers Collection, box 142, folder 6, microfilm
copy, Library of Virginia (LVA), Richmond.

205. "Petition of the Chiefs of the Chickahominy Indians," 1689, LVA, p. 1.

206. "Petition of the Chiefs of the Chickahominy Indians," 1689, LVA, p. 1.

207. Smith, [Documents], 12; "Proceedings and Letters," 21 January 1688, AGI SD 839,
PKY, SC, reel 19.

208. See the case of an enslaved Rappahannock Indian woman who argued she could not
be a slave since the "articles of peace" between the English and her nation forbade it. 5 March
1685, (Old) Rappahannock County, Orders (No. 1), 1683–1686 Transcript, Orders, 1686–1692,
reel 13, Library of Virginia, Richmond, pp. 77–78.

209. "Petition of the Chiefs of the Chickahominy Indians," 1689, LVA, p. 1.

210. "Petition of the Chiefs of the Chickahominy Indians," 1689, LVA, p. 1.

211. Smith, [Documents], 11; "Proceedings and Letters," 21 January 1688, AGI SD 839, PKY, SC, reel 19.

212. Alejandro Cañeque, *The King's Living Image: The Culture and Politics of Viceregal Power in Colonial Mexico* (New York: Routledge, 2004).

213. Bartolomé de Las Casas, *An Account of the First Voyages and Discoveries Made by the Spaniards in America* (London: 1699), [5]. Original in the John Carter Brown Library.

214. Las Casas, *Account*, [4].

215. "Cámara de Indias relative to the English of San Jorge," Madrid, 7 August 1693, AGI SD 6, PKY, SC, reel 23.

216. "Cámara de Indias," 7 August 1693, AGI SD 6, PKY, SC, reel 23.

217. "Cámara de Indias," 7 August 1693, AGI SD 6, PKY, SC, reel 23.

218. For an overview of Archdale's administration, see L.H. Roper, *Conceiving Carolina: Proprietors, Planters, and Plots, 1662-1729* (New York: Palgrave Macmillan, 2004), 115-116; for a biographical summary, see Powell, *Proprietors*, 51–52.

219. "Translation of Don Alonso Laureano de Torres y Ayala to Governor Archdale," 24 January 1696, doc. 10, Colonial Governor's Papers, CGP 1, North Carolina State Archives, Raleigh, NC.

220. For more on the migration, see Hahn, *Invention of the Creek Nation*, 49–52.

221. "Translation of Laureano de Torres y Ayala to Governor Archdale," doc. 10, Colonial Governor's Papers, CGP 1, North Carolina State Archives.

222. "Translation of Laureano de Torres y Ayala to Governor Archdale," doc. 10, Colonial Governor's Papers, CGP 1, North Carolina State Archives.

223. John Archdale to Laureano de Torres y Ayala, 4 April 1696, doc. 12, Colonial Governor's Papers, CGP 1, North Carolina State Archives, Raleigh, NC.

224. James Colleton to Diego Quiroga y Losada enclosed in Quiroga y Losada to the King, 1 April 1688, AGI SD 839, PKY, JTCC, box 16, folder 58-1-26, microfilm copy. For more on Colleton's attitudes see Bushnell, "Living at Liberty," in *Yamasee Indians*, ed. Bossy, 38–39.

225. John Archdale, *A New Description of that Fertile and Pleasant Province of Carolina* (London: 1707), 19. Original in the John Carter Brown Library; for Archdale and his Spanish counterpart, the objective was to prevent a general war between England and Spain. Hahn, *Invention of the Creek Nation*, 56–57.

226. Archdale, *New Description*, 19.

227. Archdale, *New Description*, 20; Richard Gergel and Belinda Gergel, "'A Bright New Era Now Dawns upon Us': Jewish Economic Opportunities, Religious Freedom, and Political Rights in Colonial and Antebellum South Carolina," in *The Dawn of Religious Freedom in South Carolina*, ed. James Lowell Underwood and W. Lewis Burke (Columbia: University of South Carolina Press, 2006), 98–99.

228. Archdale, *New Description*, 20.

229. Archdale, *New Description*, 20.

230. Archdale, *New Description*, 22.

231. Archdale, *New Description*, 22.

232. Archdale, *New Description*, 22.

233. Archdale, *New Description*, 29.

234. Diego Huste and Juan Chicasle to the King, 1 March 1699, AGI SD 234, PKY, SC, reel 26.

235. Diego Huste and Juan Chicasle to the King, 1 March 1699, AGI SD 234, PKY, SC, reel 26.

236. Diego Huste and Juan Chicasle to the King, 1 March 1699, AGI SD 243, PKY, SC, reel 26.

237. Don Patricio Hinachuba and Don Andrés to the King, 12 February 1699, AGI SD 234, PKY, JWC, reel 6.

238. Archdale to Laureano Torres y Ayala, 4 April 1696, Colonial Governors' Papers, CGP 1, doc. 12, North Carolina State Archives, Raleigh, NC.

239. Alonso de Leturiondo, *Memorial a El Rey Nvestro Señor En Sv Real Y Svpremo Consejo de las Indias, En Que Se da noticia de el estado en que se halla el Presidio de San Agustín de la Florida; de las cosas que necesita para su guarda, defensa, y conservación: para el buen gobierno, y puntual servicio de su Magestad en aquellas Provincia*, ca. 1700, AGI SD 853, fol. 8v, PKY, SC, reel 27.

240. Leturiondo, *Memorial*, fol. 8v.

241. Leturiondo, *Memorial*, fol. 8v.

242. Leturiondo, *Memorial*, fol. 8v.

243. Leturiondo, *Memorial*, fol. 9r.

244. Leturiondo, *Memorial*, fol. 9r.

245. Leturiondo, *Memorial*, fol. 8r.

Chapter 5

1. Alejandra Dubcovsky, "'All of Us Will Have to Pay for These Activities': Colonial and Native Narratives of the 1704 Attack on Ayubale," *Native South*, vol. 10 (2017): 7.

2. John H. Hann, trans., "Church Furnishings, Sacred Vessels and Vestments Held by the Missions of Florida: Translation of Two Inventories," *Florida Archaeology*, no. 2 (1986): 151–152.

3. For the best account of the assault on Ayubale, see Dubcovsky, "Attack on Ayubale," *Native South*, 1–18 and, for the motive of the attack, 10.

4. Antoine Simon Le Page Du Pratz, *The History of Louisiana or of the Western Parts of Virginia and Carolina: Containing a Description of the Countries that lie on both Sides of the River Mississippi: With an Account of the Settlements, Inhabitants, Soil, Climate, and Products* (New Orleans: Pelican Press, Inc., n.d. [1774]), 87.

5. Michael J. Heitzler, "Boochawee: Plantation Land and Legacy in Goose Creek," *South Carolina Historical Magazine*, vol. 111, no.1/2 (January–April 2010): 34–70.

6. For more on the siege of 1702, see William R. Adams et al., "Firestorm and Ashes: The Siege of 1702," *El Escribano*, vol. 39 (2002): 1–163; Charles W. Arnade, *The Siege of St. Augustine in 1702* (Gainesville: University of Florida Press, 1959).

7. John Ash, "The Present State of Affairs in South Carolina, 1706," in *Narratives of Early Carolina, 1650–1708*, ed. A. S. Salley (New York: Charles Scribner's Sons, 1911), 272.

8. An act of 1712 mentions that Moore was among the original library commissioners appointed in November 1700. Thomas Cooper, ed., *The Statutes at Large of South Carolina*, vol. 2 (Columbia, SC: A. S. Johnston, 1836), 374; Moore's second-in-command, Robert Daniell, ordered the burning of the library in San Agustín, but Moore surely approved. Rev. Edward

Marston to Dr. Thomas Bray, 2 February 1702, Records of the Society for the Propagation of the Gospel, Letter Books Series A, vol. I, no. 60, microfilm (quotation).

9. Edmund Bohun to James Petiver, 20 April 1700, in W. H. G. Armitage, ed., "Letters Upon Natural History of Carolina, 1700–1705," *South Carolina Historical Magazine*, vol. 55, no. 2 (April 1954), 65.

10. James Moore to Philip Ludwell and the Council of Virginia, 1692, Lee Family Papers, Mss 1L51f7 Lee, Virginia Historical Society (VHS), Richmond, p. 107.

11. Moore to Ludwell, 1692, Lee Family Papers, VHS, p. 107.

12. Moore to Ludwell, 1692, Lee Family Papers, VHS, p. 107.

13. Author's emphasis. Wednesday, 15 September 1703, in A. S. Salley Jr., ed., *Journals of the Commons House of Assembly of South Carolina for 1703* (Columbia, SC: The State Company, 1934), 121. Hereafter cited as Salley, ed., *JCHA 1703*.

14. B. R. Carroll, ed., *Historical Collections of South-Carolina; Embracing many Rare and Valuable Pamphlets, and Other Documents, Relating to the History of that State, from its First Discovery to its Independence in the Year 1776* (New York: AMS Press, Inc., [1836] 1973), 574.

15. Governor Pedro de Zuñiga y Cerda to the King, 30 March 1704, AGI SD 833 PKY, SC, reel 29.

16. This focus on Spanish failures obscured Native agency and choices. See Alejandra Dubcovsky, "Defying Indian Slavery: Apalachee Voices and Spanish Sources in the Eighteenth-Century Southeast," *William and Mary Quarterly*, 3rd ser., vol. 75, no. 2 (April 2018): 295–322.

17. Governor Pedro de Zuñiga y Cerda to the King, 30 March 1704, AGI SD 833 PKY, SC, reel 29.

18. Carroll, ed., *Historical Collections*, 574.

19. Thomas Nairne to Rev. Edward Marston, 20 August 1705, in Frank J. Klingberg, ed., "Early Attempts at Indian Education in South Carolina, a Documentary," *South Carolina Historical Magazine*, vol. 61, no. 1 (January 1960), 2.

20. Nairne to Marston, 20 August 1705, in Klingberg, ed., "Early Attempts," 2. Although the Jesuits may have been on Nairne's mind, the Spanish missions were arguably of greatest influence on early Carolinians and caught the attention of more than a few SPG officials too. For a consideration of both the Jesuit influence and the "legacy of the Franciscans," see Steven J. Oatis, *A Colonial Complex: South Carolina's Frontiers in the Era of the Yamasee War, 1680–1730* (Lincoln: University of Nebraska Press, 2004), 91–95.

21. Dubcovsky credits the rising power of Carolina's Native allies with the colony's waxing strength, a crucial insight necessary to understanding subsequent events and the outbreak of the Yamasee War. See Dubcovsky, "Attack on Ayubale," 12.

22. Nairne to Marston, 20 August 1705, in Klingberg, ed., "Early Attempts," 3.

23. Nairne to Marston, 20 August 1705, in Klingberg, ed., "Early Attempts," 3.

24. For the Yamasees, the legacy of the experience with Spanish colonialism was a commitment to rejecting heavy colonial demands, but they also surely learned techniques like petitioning during that time. Amy Turner Bushnell, "Living at Liberty: The Ungovernable Yamasees of Spanish Florida," in *The Yamasee Indians: From Florida to South Carolina*, ed. Denise Bossy (Lincoln: University of Nebraska Press, 2018), 27–53. While in the missions, the Yamasees formed a strong faction that "sought survival and autonomy on their own terms." Keith Ashley, "Yamasee Migrations into the Mocama and Timucua Mission Provinces of Florida, 1667–1683," in *Yamasee Indians*, ed. Bossy, 64. What Bradley Schrager called the "colonial education" of the Yamasees included learning how to avoid what the Spaniards demanded of their vassals, while in

Carolina, they made themselves indispensable to the colony's expansion, dumping both colonial regimes when the deal turned against them. Bradley Scott Schrager, "Yamasee Indians and the Challenge of Spanish and English Colonialism in the North American Southeast, 1660–1715" (Ph.D. diss., Northwestern University, 2001), 225. For the Apalachees who forcibly migrated to Carolina in the early eighteenth century, insofar as they had received a "colonial education," its lessons encouraged them to use legal channels, including petitions, to insist on more, not less colonial involvement as will be seen below.

25. Eric C. Poplin and Jon Bernard Marcoux, "Yamasee Material Culture and Identity: Altamaha/San Marcos Ceramics in Seventeenth- and Eighteen-Century Yamasee Indian Settlements, Georgia and South Carolina," in *Yamasee Indians*, ed. Bossy, 84.

26. Denise I. Bossy, "Spiritual Diplomacy: Reinterpreting the Yamasee Prince's Eighteenth-Century Voyage to England," in *Yamasee Indians*, ed. Bossy, 131–162.

27. Nairne to Marston, 20 August 1705, in Klingberg, ed., "Early Attempts," 3.

28. Don Antonio Ponce de León to the King, 29 January 1702 AGI SD 863, PKY, SC, reel 27.

29. "Royal Cédula to Remedy Guale Greivances," 9 June 1700, AGI SD 836, PKY, SC, reel 27.

30. "Royal Cédula to Remedy Guale Greivances," 9 June 1700, AGI SD 836, PKY, SC, reel 27.

31. Don Patricio and Don Andrés to the King, 12 February 1699, AGI SD 234, fol. 883r, PKY, JWC, reel 6.

32. For the life of Don Patricio, see Amy Turner Bushnell, "Patricio de Hinachuba: Defender of the Word of God, The Crown of the King, and the Little Children of Ivitachuco," *American Indian Culture and Research Journal*, vol. 3, no. 3 (1979), 1–21.

33. John H. Hann, trans., "The Quiñones-Caravajal Piece (1719–1721)," AGI EC 153, PKY, JHC, MS 012, p. 8.

34. Don Patricio and Don Andrés to the King, 12 February 1699, AGI SD 234, fol. 883v, PKY, JWC, reel 6.

35. Don Patricio and Don Andrés to the King, 12 February 1699, AGI SD 234, fol. 883v, PKY, JWC, reel 6.

36. Don Patricio and Don Andrés to the King, 12 February 1699, AGI SD 234, fol. 883v, PKY, JWC, reel 6.

37. Don Antonio Ponce de León to the King, 29 January 1702, AGI SD 863, PKY, SC, reel 27.

38. Don Antonio Ponce de León to the King, 29 January 1702, AGI SD 863, PKY, SC, reel 27.

39. Don Patricio Hinachuba to Don Antonio Ponce de León, 10 April 1699, enclosed in Don Antonio Ponce de León to the King, 29 January 1702, AGI SD 863, PKY, SC, reel 27.

40. The Council's summary in Don Antonio Ponce de León to the King, 29 January 1702, AGI SD 863, PKY, SC, reel 27.

41. Don Patricio Hinachuba to Don Antonio Ponce de León, 10 April 1699, AGI SD 863, PKY, SC, reel 27.

42. Don Patricio and Don Andrés to the King, 12 February 1699, AGI SD 234, fol. 883r-v, PKY, JWC, reel 6.

43. "Orders from Don Joseph de Zuñiga Captain Jacinto Roque Perez," 5 November 1700, AGI SD 858, PKY, JTCC, box 19, folder 58-2-8, microfilm copy, p. 3.

44. Don Patricio and Don Andrés to the King, 12 February 1699, AGI SD 234, fol. 883v, PKY, JWC, reel 6.

45. Don Patricio Hinachuba to Don Antonio Ponce de León, 10 April 1699, AGI SD 863, PKY, SC, reel 27.

46. "Orders from Don Joseph de Zuñiga Captain Jacinto Roque Perez," 5 November 1700, AGI SD 858, PKY, JTCC, box 19, folder 58-2-8, microfilm copy.

47. "*Auto* of the *Visitador* of Apalachee Province, Captain Juan de Ayala Escobar," 22 February 1701, AGI SD 858, PKY, JTCC, box 19, folder 58-2-8, p. 2, microfilm copy.

48. "*Auto* of the *Visitador* of Apalachee Province," 22 February 1701, AGI SD 858, PKY, JTCC, box 19, folder 58-2-8, p. 2, microfilm copy.

49. "*Auto* of the *Visitador* of Apalachee Province," 22 February 1701, AGI SD 858, PKY, JTCC, box 19, folder 58-2-8, microfilm copy.

50. "Governor Zuñiga to the King, Upon the raid into Santa Fé and the expedition upon which Captain Romo was sent" [30 September 1702], in *Here They Once Stood: The Tragic End of the Apalachee Missions*, ed. Mark F. Boyd, et al. (Gainesville: University of Florida Press, 1951), 37.

51. "Visitor's Orders for the Province to Promote Good Government," John H. Hann, trans., "Visitations and Revolts in Florida, 1656–1695," *Florida Archaeology*, no. 7 (1993): 190.

52. "Thomas Nairne's Memorial to Charles Spencer, Earl of Sunderland" [10 July 1708], in *Nairne's Muskhogean Journals: The 1708 Expedition to the Mississippi River*, ed. Alexander Moore (Jackson: University Press of Mississippi, 1988), 77.

53. Hann, trans., "The Quiñones-Caravajal Piece," AGI EC 153, PKY, JHC, p. 11.

54. For more on the politics of burdening, see Brad Dixon, "'In Place of Horses': Indigenous Burdeners and the Politics of the Early American South," *Ethnohistory*, vol. 70, no. 1 (January 2023): 1–23.

55. "Order from Governor Zuñiga," 14 March 1701, AGI SD 858, PKY, JTCC, box 19, folder 58-2-8, p. 2, microfilm copy.

56. "Order from Governor Zuñiga," 14 March 1701, AGI SD 858, PKY, JTCC, box 19, folder 58-2-8, p. 2, microfilm copy.

57. "Order from Governor Zuñiga," 14 March 1701, AGI SD 858, PKY, JTCC, box 19, folder 58-2-8, p. 2, microfilm copy.

58. "Governor Zuñiga to the King" [30 September 1702], in *Here They Once Stood*, ed. Boyd et al., 37.

59. "Governor Zuñiga to the King" [30 September 1702], in *Here They Once Stood*, ed. Boyd et al., 38.

60. Wednesday, 15 September 1703, in *JCHA 1703*, ed. Salley, 121.

61. John Lawson, *A New Voyage to Carolina* [. . .] (London: 1709), 42–43. According to the *Oxford English Dictionary* an archaic usage of "knot" was to signify "a bond or obligation; a binding condition; a spell that binds." In this case, the word perhaps signifies a bond to provide tribute.

62. Richard Traunter, "The Travels of Richard Traunter on the Main Continent of America from Appomattox River in Virginia to Charles Town in South Carolina. In two Journals; performed in the Years 1698: and 1699: Wherin is Contained the Quality & Nature of the Soyle, the Disposition of the Inhabitants, and the Reception I had amongst them; Also my making peace with several Nations of Indians, the great advantage of the Indian Traders in those parts, by opening away that had not been Travell'd before; with what else Remarkably

Occur'd in my way," Mss 5:9 T6945:1, Virginia Historical Society, Richmond, p. 20; Lawson, *New Voyage*, 57.

63. Nairne to Marston, 20 August 1705, Klingberg, ed., "Early Attempts," 3.

64. Mr. Talbot to the Secretary, 1 September 1703, no. 125, Records of the Society for the Propagation of the Gospel, Letter Books Series A, vol. I, no. 125, microfilm.

65. For more on old Charles Town's layout and architectural history, see, Katherine Saunders, "'As regular and fformidable as any such woorke in America': The Walled City of Charles Town," in *Another's Country: Archaeological and Historical Perspectives on Cultural Interactions in the Southern Colonies*, eds J. W. Joseph and Martha Zierden, foreword by Julia A. King (Tuscaloosa: The University of Alabama Press, 2002), 198–214.

66. "Unsigned Letter to the King," 5 November 1702, AGI SD 858, PKY, JTCC, box 19, folder 58-2-8, pp. 1–2, microfilm copy.

67. For more on the details of the invasion force and the possible numbers involved, see Arnade, *Seige of St. Augustine*, 5.

68. 15 September 1703, in *JCHA 1703*, ed. Salley, 121.

69. 15 September 1703, in *JCHA 1703*, ed. Salley, 121.

70. 15 May 1711, Journals of the Commons House of Assembly, October–June 1711, Green transcripts, no. 3, SCDAH, 552. All page numbers reference the modern pagination of the Green volumes in SCDAH.

71. Steven C. Hahn, discussing a case in the 1720s, explains the use of the term as referring to the force of Indigenous "public opinion" being behind one or another European power—or their proposals. Steven C. Hahn, *The Invention of the Creek Nation, 1670–1763* (Lincoln: University of Nebraska Press, 2004), 139.

72. Salley, ed., *JCHA 1703*, 121.

73. Wayne E. Lee notes that South Carolina's "client" relationship with Natives featured "independent operations with simultaneous pursuit of Indigenous and English interests." For more, see Wayne E. Lee, *The Cutting-Off Way: Indigenous Warfare in Eastern North America, 1500–1800* (Chapel Hill: UNC Press, 2023), 171–172.

74. Lawson, *New Voyage*, 237.

75. Lawson, *New Voyage*, 237.

76. As evidenced in concerns the South Carolinians expressed about the proximity of the French traders to the Tallabooses. See Salley, ed., *JCHA 1702*, 6. Of Natives, Europeans like Thomas Nairne believed trade and alliance "magically transformed them into subjects." Alan Gallay, *The Indian Slave Trade: The Rise of the English Empire in the South, 1670–1717* (New Haven, CT: Yale University Press, 2002), 176.

77. Kathryn E. Holland Braund, *Deerskins & Duffels: The Creek Indian Trade with Anglo-America, 1685–1815*, 2d. ed. (Lincoln: University of Nebraska Press, 1996), 27.

78. Moore to Ludwell, 1692, Lee Family Papers, VHS, p. 107.

79. Lawson, *New Voyage*, 4.

80. "Memorial of Christopher Gale to Governor Robert Gibbes of South Carolina," 2 November 1711, in *CRNC*, 1: 828.

81. Salley, ed., *JCHA 1703*, 121.

82. Francisco de Córcoles y Martínez to the King, 5 July 1715, AGI SD 843, PKY, SC, reel 36.

83. "Royal *cédula* Relieving the 161 Towns from Tribute," 17 April 1716, AGI SD 837, PKY, SC, reel 36.

84. Salley, ed., *JCHA 1702*, 6.

85. Archaeological evidence shows striking similarities in culture between eighteenth-century Yamasees and their Mississippian forebears. Alexander Sweeney, "Cultural Continuity and Change: Archaeological Research at Yamasee Primary Towns in South Carolina," in *Yamasee Indians*, ed. Bossy, 99.

86. Sweeney, "Cultural Continuity," 110–111.

87. Sweeney, "Cultural Continuity," 114.

88. Poplin and Marcoux, "Material Culture," 92–93.

89. Amy Turner Bushnell, "Living at Liberty: The Ungovernable Yamasees of Spanish Florida," in *Yamasee Indians: From Florida to South Carolina*, ed. Bossy, 27–53.

90. Sweeney, "Cultural Continuity," 102.

91. 26 January 1702, in *JCHA 1702*, ed. Salley, 19.

92. For the litany of Yamasee complaints, see Salley, ed., *JCHA 1702*, 21. William Ramsey, in his careful study of the Yamasee War, explored in depth the conduct of Indian traders and the cultural expectations surrounding the Indian trade. Ramsey identified three categories of native grievances—crimes against women that violated native gender norms, abuses of Indian and English notions of credit and debt, and violations of what he called the "rudimentary protocol" that governed the process of Indian enslavement. However, Ramsey also argued that Indian reports of trader misconduct "masked" deeper concerns that grew out of clashes between English norms and the cultures of the native South. William Ramsey, *The Yamasee War: A Study of Culture, Economy, and Conflict in the Colonial South* (Lincoln: University of Nebraska Press, 2008), 13, 16–17, 20–23 ("masked"), 29.

93. See "Prices of Indian Trading Goods (1716–1718)," in *The Southern Frontier, 1670–1732*, by Verner W. Crane (New York: W. W. Norton & Company, Inc., [1928] 1981), 332, Appendix B.

94. Andrew Lipman, *The Saltwater Frontier: Indians and the Contest for the American Coast* (New Haven, CT: Yale University Press, 2015), 72–76.

95. 26 January 1702, in *JCHA 1702*, ed. Salley, 22.

96. 20 January 1702, in *JCHA 1702*, ed. Salley, 10.

97. Marston to Bray, 2 February 1702, Records of the Society for the Propagation of the Gospel, Letter Books Series A, vol. 1, no. 60, microfilm.

98. "Juan de la Cruz, soldier," 9 June 1705, in "Report dated about the War of Ayubale, the death of the Religious missionaries, soldiers, and Indians that were killed and burned at the hands of the Infidel escorts of the English from San Jorge," 6 June 1705, AGI SD 863, PKY, JTCC, box 19, folder 58-2-14, microfilm copy, p. 9.

99. James Colleton to Diego Quiroga y Losada enclosed in Quiroga y Losada to the King, 1 April 1688, AGI SD 839, PKY, JTCC, box 16, folder 58-1-26, microfilm copy.

100. Hahn, *Invention of the Creek Nation*, 56, 62.

101. "The Humble Submission of the Kings, Princes, Generals, &c. to the Crown of England," 1705, North Carolina Collection, University of North Carolina at Chapel Hill, facsimile broadside.

102. "Humble Submission," 1705, North Carolina Collection, UNC, facsimile broadside (quotation). The Creeks were "promoting security without sacrificing autonomy." Joseph Hall, "Anxious Alliances: Apalachicola Efforts to Survive the Slave Trade, 1638–1705," in *Indian Slavery in Colonial America*, ed. Alan Gallay (Lincoln: University of Nebraska Press, 2009), 149.

103. Moore, ed., *Nairne's Muskhogean Journals*, 32.

104. For "chieftaincy," see Robin Beck, *Chiefdoms, Collapse, and Coalescence in the Early American South* (New York: Cambridge University Press, 2013), 195.

105. Lawson, *New Voyage*, 234.

106. 27 April 1704, JCHA, April–May 1704, Green Transcripts, SCDAH, no. 2, p. 232.

107. "Instructions and articles from Governor Zuñiga," n.d., AGI SD 858, PKY, JTCC, box 19, folder 58-2-8, microfilm copy, p. 1.

108. "Instructions from Zuñiga," n.d., AGI SD 858, PKY, JTCC, box 19, folder 58-2-8, microfilm copy, p. 1.

109. "Instructions from Zuñiga," n.d., AGI SD 858, PKY, JTCC, box 19, folder 58-2-8, microfilm copy, p. 2.

110. "Instructions from Zuñiga," n.d., AGI SD 858, PKY, JTCC, box 19, folder 58-2-8, microfilm copy, p. 3.

111. 27 April 1704, JCHA, April–May 1704, Green Transcripts, no. 2, SCDAH, p. 232.

112. See Ramsey, *Yamasee War*, 110–111; Gallay, *Indian Slave Trade*, 148, but with fuller discussion in 144–149.

113. 27 April 1704, JCHA, April–May 1704, Green Transcripts, no. 4, SCDAH, p. 232.

114. Charles M. Hudson, *Knights of Spain, Warriors of the Sun: Hernando de Soto and the South's Ancient Chiefdoms* (Athens: University of Georgia Press, 2013), 142.

115. 6 May 1704, JCHA, April–May 1704, Green Transcripts, no. 4, SCDAH, p. 246.

116. 29 April 1704, JCHA, April–May 1704, Green Transcripts, no. 2, SCDAH, p. 236; 6 May 1704, JCHA, April–May 1704, Green Transcripts, no. 2, SCDAH, p. 246–247.

117. 27 April 1704, JCHA, April–May 1704, Green Transcripts, no. 2, SCDAH, p. 232.

118. For Nairne's Whiggish political views, see Gallay, *Indian Slave Trade*, 168–170.

119. Nairne to Marston, 20 August 1705, in Klingberg, ed., "Early Attempts," 3–4.

120. Nairne to Marston, 20 August 1705, in Klingberg, ed., "Early Attempts," 2.

121. Nairne to Marston, 20 August 1705, in Klingberg, ed., "Early Attempts," 2.

122. Friday, 4 July 1707, in *Journal of the Commons House of Assembly of South Carolina, June 5, 1707–July 19, 1707*, ed. A. S. Salley (Columbia, SC: State Company, 1940), 79.

123. Lawson, *New Voyage*, 234, 237.

124. Lawson, *New Voyage*, 238.

125. Thomas Gage, *A Survey of the Spanish West-Indies* (London: 1699), 389. Thanks to Ken Ward of the John Carter Brown Library for helping me to figure out Lawson's source.

126. Gage, *Survey*, 397–398.

127. Lawson, *New Voyage*, 238.

128. Specifically, his language echoes Romans 11:24. Lawson, *New Voyage*, 237.

129. "Letter from the Governor and Council of Carolina," 17 September 1708, UKNA CO 5/1264, no. 86, folio 155r.

130. "Letter from Carolina," 17 September 1708, UKNA CO 5/1264, no. 86, folio 155r.

131. Amy Turner Bushnell, *Situado and Sabana: Spain's Support System for Florida*, Anthropological Papers of the American Museum of Natural History 74 (New York: American Museum of Natural History, 1994), 114.

132. "Letter from Carolina," 17 September 1708, UKNA CO 5/1264, no. 86, folio 155r.

133. "Letter from Carolina," 17 September 1708, UKNA CO 5/1264, no. 86, fol. 155r.

134. Moore, ed., *Nairne's Muskhogean Journals*, 51.

135. 17 August 1713, in *JCIT*, ed. McDowell, 48.

136. 23 April 1709, JCHA, February–May 1709, Green Transcripts, no. 3, SCDAH, p. 419.

137. 28 April 1709, JCHA, February–May 1709, Green Transcripts, no. 3, SCDAH, p. 423.

138. 17 November 1712, JCHA, November–December 1712, Green Transcripts, no. 4, SCDAH, p. 113.

139. 2 April 1712, JCHA, April 1712, Green Transcripts, no. 4, SCDAH, p. 2.

140. For recent interpretations of the origins of the SPG, see Brent S. Sirota, *The Christian Monitors: The Church of England and the Age of Benevolence, 1680–1730* (New Haven, CT: Yale University Press, 2014); Travis Glasson, *Mastering Christianity: Missionary Anglicanism and Slavery in the Atlantic World* (New York: Oxford University Press, 2012).

141. John Oldmixon, "From the History of the British Empire in America, by John Oldmixon, 1708," in *Narratives of Early Carolina, 1650–1708*, ed. A. S. Salley (New York: Charles Scribner's Sons, 1911), 364.

142. Le Jau to the Secretary, 22 April 1708, in Le Jau, *Carolina Chronicle, 1706–1717*, ed. Frank M. Klingberg (Berkeley: University of California Press, 1956), 39.

143. Le Jau to the Secretary, 22 April 1708, in Le Jau, *Carolina Chronicle*, 39.

144. For the best account of the "Yamasee Prince," see Bossy, "Spiritual Diplomacy," 131–162.

145. Bossy, "Spiritual Diplomacy," 144–145.

146. For more on Le Jau's linguistic quest, see Gallay, *Indian Slave Trade*, 235–236.

147. "Petition of Sebastian van der Eycken," *Microfilm Publication of the Papers of the Society for the Propagation of the Gospel in the Lambeth Palace Library, 1701–1750*, vol. 8: *Correspondence: British Isles, July 1707-undated*, 245.

148. "Petition of Sebastian van der Eycken Petition," *Microfilm Publication*, 245.

149. "Comry Johnston to the Secry, 27th Janry 1710/11," in *Carolina Chronicle: The Papers of Commissary Gideon Johnston, 1707–1716*, ed. Frank J. Klingberg (Berkeley: University of California Press, 1946), 82.

150. McDowell, ed., *JCIT*, 3.

151. Thursday, 21 September 1710, in *JCIT*, ed. McDowell, 4.

152. Thursday, 21 September 1710, in *JCIT*, ed. McDowell, 4.

153. Wednesday, 11 December 1706, in *Journal of the Commons House of Assembly of South Carolina, November 20, 1706–February 8, 1706/7*, ed. A. S. Salley, (Columbia, SC: The State Company, 1939), 22.

154. John H. Hann, *Apalachee: The Land Between the Rivers* (Gainesville: University of Florida Press, 1988), 232–233.

155. David Crawley to the Lords Commissioners of Trade and Plantations, 30 July 1715, UKNA CO 5/1265, no. 2, fol. 2r.

156. Sir Nathaniel Johnson, 12 January 1720, UKNA CO 5/1265, no. 144, fol. 383r.

157. Sir Nathaniel Johnson, 12 January 1720, UKNA CO 5/1265, no. 144, fol. 383r.

158. 21 September 1710, in *JCIT*, ed. McDowell, 4.

159. 25 March 1713, in *JCIT*, ed. McDowell, 41.

160. Governor Charles Craven to Viscount Townshend, 23 May 1715, UKNA CO 5/1264, no. 147(ii), 295r.

161. Craven to Townshend, 23 May 1715, UKNA CO 5/1264, no. 147(ii), 295r.

162. Ramsey, *Yamasee War*, 96–97.

163. Francisco de Córcoles y Martínez to the King, 5 July 1715, AGI SD 843, PKY, SC, reel 36. For more on the networks that brought this information, see Alejandra Dubcovsky,

"One Hundred Sixty-One Knots, Two Plates, and One Emperor: Creek Information Networks in the Era of the Yamasee War," *Ethnohistory*, vol. 59, no. 3 (Summer 2012): 489–513.

164. Córcoles y Martínez to the King, 5 July 1715, AGI SD 843, PKY, SC, reel 36.

165. Córcoles y Martínez to the King, 5 July 1715, AGI SD 843, PKY, SC, reel 36.

166. Córcoles y Martínez to the King, 5 July 1715, AGI SD 843, PKY, SC, reel 36.

167. Oatis, *Colonial Complex*, 126; Gallay, *Indian Slave Trade*, 328.

168. Oatis, *Colonial Complex*, 74–78.

169. "Some Paragraphs of Letters from South Carolina," 19 June 1715, in "Extracts of Several Letters from Carolina relating to the Indian War and the Prejudice that Province has received from the Virginia Indian Traders," December 1716, UKNA CO 5/1265, #44(iii), fol. 91r.

170. "Some Paragraphs of Letters from South Carolina," 5 April 1715, in "Extracts," December 1716, UKNA CO 5/1265, #44(iii), fol. 91v.

171. "Some Paragraphs of Letters from South Carolina," 5 April 1715, in "Extracts of Several Letters from Carolina relating to the Indian War and the Prejudice that Province has received from the Virginia Indian Traders," December 1716, UKNA CO 5/1265, #44(iii), fol. 91v.

172. Crawley to the Commissioners of Trade and Plantations, 30 July 1715, UKNA CO 5/1265, fol. 2r.

173. Crawley to the Commissioners of Trade and Plantations, 30 July 1715, UKNA CO 5/1265, fol. 2r.

174. John Tate to Sir John Duddleston, 16 September 1715, UKNA CO 5/1265, no. 11.i, fol. 16r.

175. John Tate to Sir John Duddleston, 16 September 1715, UKNA CO 5/1265, no. 11.i, fol. 16r.

176. John Tate to Sir John Duddleston, 16 September 1715, UKNA CO 5/1265, no. 11.i, fol. 16r.

177. Ramsey, *Yamasee War*, 122.

178. Ramsey, *Yamasee War*, 122.

179. Alexander Spotswood to Secretary James Stanhope, 27 May 1715, UKNA CO 5/1264, no. 147.i, folio 293r.

180. Le Jau to the Secretary, 19 March 1715/16, in Le Jau, *Carolina Chronicle*, 175. The best explanation of the prince's family relations is Bossy, "Spiritual Diplomacy," 136–138.

181. Le Jau to the Secretary, 14 May 1715, in Le Jau, *Carolina Chronicle*, 155.

182. Bossy, "Spiritual Diplomacy," 156–157.

183. Bossy, "Spiritual Diplomacy," 157.

184. For more on these Native-inspired shifts and the demands for a "tangible" alliance in the form usually of firearms, see Denise I. Bossy, "Guns for Godliness: The Yamasees in St. Augustine," in *Facing Florida: Essays on Culture and Religion in Early Modern Southeastern America*, eds. Timothy J. Johnson and Jeffrey M. Burns (Oceanside, CA: The Academy of Franciscan History, 2021), 103–121. See also discussion of post–Yamasee War policy in Florida in Timothy Paul Grady, *Anglo-Spanish Rivalry in Colonial South-East America, 1650–1725* (New York: Taylor & Francis, 2010), 136–139. Indeed, one of the lessons of the Yamasee War for European imperialists was the dangers of the more "hands-on approach" that the Carolinians took in the decade or so before 1715. Oatis, *Colonial Complex*, 55.

185. "Royal cédula relieving the 161 Towns from Tribute," 17 April 1716, AGI SD 837, PKY, SC, reel 36.

186. "Royal cédula relieving the 161 Towns from Tribute," 17 April 1716, AGI SD 837, PKY, SC, reel 36.

187. "Royal cédula relieving the 161 Towns from Tribute," 17 April 1716, AGI SD 837, PKY, SC, reel 36 (quotation). For more on Spanish plans to repopulate Apalachee with Indigenous allies, see Hahn, *Invention of the Creek Nation*, 93.

188. Andrea P. White, "Refuge Among the Spanish: Yamasee Community Coalescence in St. Augustine After 1715," in *The Yamasee Indians: From Florida to South Carolina*, ed. Denise I. Bossy (Lincoln: University of Nebraska Press, 2018), 251–280.

189. "Copy of Robert Daniell's Certificate of James Cochran's Affidavit," 13 August 1716, UKNA CO 5/1265, folio 94r.

190. "Cochran Affidavit," 13 August 1716, UKNA CO 5/1265, folio 94r.

191. "Cochran Affidavit," 13 August 1716, UKNA CO 5/1265, folio 94r.

192. "Cochran Affidavit," 13 August 1716, UKNA CO 5/1265, folio 94r.

193. "Cochran Affidavit," 13 August 1716, UKNA CO 5/1265, fol. 94r.

194. "Cochran Affidavit," 13 August 1716, UKNA CO 5/1265, fol. 94r.

195. Direct Spanish involvement was unlikely, although the knowledge that they could potentially ally with the Spanish must have given them some confidence in the decision to wage war against the Carolinians. See Oatis, *Colonial Complex*, 130–131.

196. Kristalyn Marie Shefveland, *Anglo-Native Virginia: Trade, Conversion, and Indian Slavery in the Old Dominion, 1646–1722* (Athens: University of Georgia Press, 2016), 93.

197. See the full account of Spotswood's policies in Shefveland, *Anglo-Native Virginia*, 80–103.

198. For more on Indigenous attempts to revitalize the Virginia tributary regime, see Dylan Ruediger, "'In Peace with All, or at Least in Warre with None': Tributary Subjects and the Negotiation of Political Subordination in Greater Virginia, 1676–1730," in *The Specter of Peace: Rethinking Violence and Power in the Colonial Atlantic*, ed. Michael Goode and John Smolenski (Boston, MA: Brill, 2018), 64–94. For the central role of the Saponis, see Stephanie Gamble, "A Community of Convenience: The Saponi Nation, Governor Spotswood, and the Experiment at Fort Christanna, 1670–1740," *Native South*, vol. 6 (2013): 70–109.

199. Shefveland, *Anglo-Native Virginia*, 94, 102–103.

200. Shefveland, *Anglo-Native Virginia*, 91.

201. Spotswood to Stanhope, 27 May 1715, UKNA CO 5/1264, no. 147.i, folio 293r.

202. Spotswood to Stanhope, 27 May 1715, UKNA CO 5/1264, no. 147.i, folio 293r.

203. "Petition of the Nottoway Indians to the House of Burgesses," 4 August 1715, Mss 1 L51 661 Lee, Lee Family Papers, VHS.

204. "Petition of the Nottoway Indians," 4 August 1715, Mss 1 L51 661 Lee, Lee Family Papers, VHS.

205. Sir Nathaniel Johnson, 12 January 1720, UKNA CO 5/1265, no. 144, fol. 382r.

206. "Abstracts of Several Letters from Carolina relating to the State of that Province with regard to ye Indian War," 25 April 1717, UKNA CO 5/1265, no. 69, fol. 140r.

207. Kassidy Hammond, "344-Year-Old Tradition Continues at Virginia Governor's Mansion," WTVR, *ABC 8*, 24 November 2021, https://www.wtvr.com/news/local-news/indian-tax-tribute-ceremony-virginia-2021.

Epilogue

1. "Petition of John Hoyter to the Executive Council of North Carolina," 11 August 1714, *RECNC*, 48 (quotation). Thomas Hoyter may have participated in the expeditions referenced in

John Hoyter's petition or received the coat as an heirloom or a token of other services rendered to the colony.

2. John Brickell, *The Natural History of North-Carolina. With an Account of the Trade, Manners, and Customs of the Christian and Indian Inhabitants. Illustrated with Copper-Plates, whereon are curiously Engraved the Map of the Country, several strange Beasts, Birds, Fishes, Snakes, Insects, Trees, and Plants, & c.* (Dublin: James Carson, 1737), 283.

3. Brickell, *Natural History*, 284.

4. Edward Moseley's map of North Carolina from 1733 depicts the major landmarks that Hoyter and his companions would have passed along their route. An original copy reposes in Special Collections at the Joyner Library, East Carolina University, Greenville, NC. Edward Moseley, "A New and Correct Map of the Province of North Carolina (Moseley Map)," 1733, MC0017, East Carolina University Digital Collections, accessed 7 July 2023, https://digital.lib .ecu.edu/62315.

5. "The petition of Benjamin Blanshard John Campbell, Thomas Spivey Francis Rowntree, Robert Rountree, Robert Laciter, George Laciter and Nicholas Stallings" to the Executive Council, 28 March 1702, *RECNC*, 388–389.

6. "Complaint of John Hoyter to the Executive Council," 22 November 1717, *RECNC*, 70.

7. Rhys L. Isaac, *The Transformation of Virginia, 1740–1790* (Chapel Hill: University of North Carolina Press for Institute of Early American History and Culture, 1982), 58.

8. Giles Rainsford to John Chamberlain, Secretary of the SPG, 25 July 1712, *CRNC*, 1: 858.

9. Rainsford to Chamberlain, 25 July 1712, *CRNC*, 1: 860.

10. Rainsford reported speaking with "Thomas Hoyle." Rainsford to Chamberlain, 25 July 1712, *CRNC*, 1: 859; Giles Rainsford to John Chamberlain, Secretary of the SPG, 19 January 1715, *CRNC*, 2: 152.

11. For more on the state of the roads in the early eighteenth century, see Alan D. Watson, *Colonial Society in North Carolina* (Raleigh, NC: Division of Archives and History, 1996), 103.

12. Crude mile markers did not begin to appear on the main roads until after 1764. Watson, *Colonial Society*, 102.

13. Kevin Joel Berland, ed., *The Dividing Line Histories of William Byrd II of Westover* (Chapel Hill: University of North Carolina Press, 2013), 107.

14. "Journal of August Gottlieb Spangenberg's voyage to North Carolina to establish a Moravian Settlement [Translation]," 26 September 1752, *CRNC*, 5: 3.

15. Berland, ed., *Dividing Line Histories*, 107.

16. Berland, ed., *Dividing Line Histories*, 107–108.

17. Brickell, *Natural History*, 284.

18. Brickell, *Natural History*, 284.

19. Brickell, *Natural History*, 284.

20. Brickell, *Natural History*, 282–283.

21. Brickell, *Natural History*, 33.

22. Brickell, *Natural History*, 285.

23. Brickell, *Natural History*, 33.

24. Colin Calloway, *"The Chiefs Now Within This City": Indians and the Urban Frontier in Early America* (New York: Oxford University Press, 2021), 71–91; Susan Richbourg Parker, "Chief Francisco Jospogue: Reconstructing the Paths of a Guale-Yamasee Indian Lineage through Spanish Records," in *The Yamasee Indians: From Florida to South Carolina*, ed. Denise I. Bossy (Lincoln: University of Nebraska Press, 2018), 281–307.

25. For more on the Chowans and their petitions in this era, see Bradley J. Dixon, "'His One Netev Ples': The Chowans and the Politics of Native Petitions in the Colonial South," *William and Mary Quarterly*, vol. 76, no. 1 (January 2019): 41–74.

26. "Petition of John Hoyter," [1705], CCR 187, State Archives of North Carolina, Raleigh.

27. "Petition of John Hoyter," [1705], CCR 187, State Archives of North Carolina, Raleigh.

28. Don Francisco Jospogue to the King, 18 October 1728, AGI SD 2584, PKY, JWC, reel 3.

29. "Petition of Queen Ann of the Pamunkeys for relief from payment of tribute" [1710], in *Calendar of Virginia State Papers and Other Manuscripts, 1652–1781, Preserved in the Capitol at Richmond*, ed. W[illia]m P. Palmer (Richmond, VA: 1875), 1: 127–128 ("Great men," 1: 127). Henceforth *CVSP*.

30. "Petition of Ann, Queen of the Pamunk[e]ys, for redress and protection against trespasses upon the territory of her nation" [1715], in Palmer, ed., *CVSP*, 1: 185 (quotation).

31. Petition of John Hoyter to the Executive Council of North Carolina, Aug. 11, 1714, *RECNC*, 48.

32. Jospogue to the King, 18 October 1728, AGI SD 2584, PKY, JWC, reel 3.

33. Jospogue to the King, 18 October 1728, AGI SD 2584, PKY, JWC, reel 3.

34. Jospogue to the King, 18 October 1728, AGI SD 2584, PKY, JWC, reel 3.

35. "Petition of John Hoyter," [1705], CCR 187, State Archives of North Carolina, Raleigh.

36. James Craven to Arthur Dobbs, 7 December 1754, in *The State Records of North Carolina*, comp. and ed. Walter Clark, vol. 22 (Goldsboro, NC: 1907), 329.

37. Brickell, *Natural History*, 331.

38. "Report concerning the militia in each county of North Carolina," 1754, *CRNC*, 5: 162.

39. "General Assembly Session Records," November–December 1790, box 2, State Archives of North Carolina, quoted in Forest Hazel, "Looking for Indian Town: The Dispersal of the Chowan Indian Tribe in Eastern North Carolina, 1780–1915," *North Carolina Archaeology*, vol. 63 (October 2014): 37. For an online version, see Petition 11279002, Gates County, NC, 23 October 1790, quoted at "Race and Slavery Petitions Project," Digital Library on American Slavery, University of North Carolina, last updated January 19, 2008, http://library.uncg.edu/slavery/petitions/details.aspx?pid=635.

40. For the illegality of the sale, see Warren E. Milteer Jr., "From Indians to Colored People: The Problem of Racial Categories and the Persistence of the Chowans in North Carolina," *North Carolina Historical Review*, vol. 93, no. 1 (January 2016): 37–38. For how states often claimed jurisdiction over Native nations within their boundaries, see Deborah A. Rosen, *American Indians and State Law: Sovereignty, Race, and Citizenship, 1790–1880* (Lincoln: University of Nebraska Press, 2007), 51–79.

41. Milteer, "Indians to Colored People," 43–44.

42. Milteer, "Indians to Colored People," 45; Hazel, "Looking for Indian Town," 44–46.

43. For a remarkable account of the Chowans' survival from the nineteenth century to the present day, see Milteer, "From Indians to Colored People," 43–57.

44. Justin Petrone, "Chowanoke Descendants Reclaim Ancestral Land, Envision Cultural Center," *Indian Country Today*, 10 August 2016, https://newsmaven.io/indiancountry today/archive/chowanoke-descendants-reclaim-ancestral-land-envision-cultural-center -aka9RVXZaketpYBag7fpLg/.

45. Author's transcription of the Chowan plaque, Chowan County Courthouse, Edenton, North Carolina.

46. Berland, ed., *Dividing Line Histories*, 107–108.

47. Chowan plaque transcription, Chowan County Courthouse, Edenton, North Carolina. For more on this fraternal organization and others like it, see Philip J. Deloria, *Playing Indian* (New Haven, CT: Yale University Press, 1998), 38–70.

48. Joseph K. Dixon, *The Vanishing Race, the Last Great Indian Council* [. . .] (Garden City, NJ: Doubleday, Page & Company, 1913), 37.

49. Spanish ideas entered Anglo-American law through the process of imperial competition. Felix S. Cohen, "The Spanish Origin of Indian Rights in the Law of the United States," *Georgetown Law Journal*, vol. 31, no. 1 (November 1942): 3, 20. For the life and legacy of Felix S. Cohen, see Alice Beck Kehoe, *A Passion for the True and Just: Felix and Lucy Kramer Cohen and the Indian New Deal* (Tucson, AZ: The University of Arizona Press, 2014); Dalia Tsuk Mitchell, *Architect of Justice: Felix S. Cohen and the Founding of American Legal Pluralism* (Ithaca, NY: Cornell University Press, 2007).

50. Vine Deloria, Jr., *Custer Died for Your Sins: An Indian Manifesto* (Norman: University of Oklahoma Press, [1969] 1988), ix.

51. Cohen, "Spanish Origin," 9.

INDEX

Figures are indicated by page numbers followed by fig.

ACKNOWLEDGMENTS

A celebrated author of the eighteenth century once quipped that he had to turn over half a library to write one book. (Judging by the clutter of books and papers in my house, I would say on that point he was right.) But Dr. Johnson neglected to mention all the people who help you find those books, who critique what you write, who guide you along the way, and without whom no book would ever be finished.

For my part, I came to the study of history late in my undergraduate career but had excellent preceptors in college, especially Jim Clark, who was my professor and became my friend; Jim Crisp, who sold me on the lore of Texas before I knew I was headed there; John M. Riddle, who brought the High Middle Ages to life; and Holly Brewer for her encouragement, scholarly example, and her famous trips to Williamsburg.

Even so, I had no inkling of going to graduate school or history as a career until, one night in an introductory museology course, Judy Kertész, for what reason related to museums I can't recall, displayed the Catawba May of 1721. The map, with its vibrant Indigenous world of circles and paths at the center and the colonial world at its margins, captivated me. Judy rekindled my interest in Native American history and she was one of the first people who seriously suggested I might study history for a living. I will always cherish her good advice, humor, including her "splat" method of writing, and love of old maps. It was Judy who introduced me to Brent Sirota. A model of professionalism who had by that point, as the saying goes, simply forgotten more than I'll ever know, Brent's introductory historiography course remains one of the greatest classes I ever took. His deep knowledge and ability to cut to the core of any question were qualities I always admired. His example is always before me. (My U.S. survey students have him to thank for the day I spend talking about the English Civil Wars and Restoration.)

When the time came, Brent put me in touch with Bob Olwell at Texas, a scholar whose book I'd read in Holly's class, and thoroughly enjoyed. From there, Bob's—as he put it—"Yoda-like" advice steered me to Austin. Ever since, he has shown me great wisdom, patience, humor, and an extensive knowledge of early America. I will always cherish the portraits of the "Four Mohawk Princes" that look down on me as I write and are a constant reminder of his generosity and patience and all the meetings we had in his office. At the University of Texas, my interests and experiences broadened after meeting Jorge Cañizares-Esguerra. He opened up the world of the Iberian Atlantic to me and I am eternally grateful for that and everything he did to encourage my work at every step of the way. Jorge is a tireless advocate for his students, a passionate critic—in short, a good person to have in your corner—who always backed me even when I didn't back myself. I'll never have enough to repay him. Together, my supervisors, Jorge and Bob have been constant sources of inspiration and support. If I ever needed more, I could always walk down the hall to Julie Hardwick's office. Julie's enthusiasm for the beguiling early modern world was equaled only by her simple, calming advice. "Keep going," she would say. Or, another one I always liked: "Everything's a work in progress." Many others—also short walks down the hall—made my time in Austin much better. Through two semesters of serving as Neil Kamil's teaching assistant, I gained invaluable experience in the classroom and benefited from his perspective on early America and the Atlantic World. Thanks to Erika Bsumek for excellent suggestions for my work and for overseeing my Native American comps field; Alison Frazier for her dedication to student professionalization and for her good writing advice; Alan Tully for his generosity with books and conversation; James M. Vaughan for his friendship and enthusiastic suggestions for my work; Philippa Levine for her early guidance and writing savvy; and to Marilyn Lehman for helping me with so many details through the years that I would have otherwise neglected. My graduate student colleagues at UT have always been generous and a pleasure to work with. I want to thank the members of what started as our Native American Readings Group: Nakia Parker, Adrienne Sockwell, Brooks Winfree, Jesse Ritner, Maria Hammack, and Micaela Valadez. Although I have too many debts to my graduate student colleagues to name, I want to single out for special thanks Shery Chanis, Kristie Flannery, Nicolás González Quintero, Julia Gossard, Chloe Ireton, William Kramer, Adrian Masters, Kazushi Minami, Ernesto Mercado-Montero, Juan Carlos de Orellano, Jimena Perry, Samantha Rubino, and Christina M. Villareal. I have learned much from you all.

I am especially grateful to the Institute for Historical Studies and then-director Miriam Bodian, whose class on religious repression and toleration was also one of my favorites, for offering me a place to work and refine my ideas after defending my dissertation.

At the University of Memphis, I found a home in Mitchell Hall and am grateful to all my colleagues and to the Department of History for its support. I should especially thank Aram Goudsouzian and Dan Unowsky for their support as chairs and as readers. Thank you to Karen Bradley and Erika Feleg for everything you do. For support and comments on my work, thanks go to Dean Clement, Guiomar Dueñas-Vargas, Ben Graham, Brian Kwoba, Scott Marler, Caroline Peyton, Sarah Potter, Amanda Lee Savage, and Andrei Znamenski. I am grateful to the Marcus Orr Center for the Humanities for the semester I spent there finalizing this manuscript. Thanks especially to the director, Donal Harris, and the fellows, Gul Hos, Simramjit Khalsi, Heike Polster, Kathy Lou Schultz, and Jasper St. Bernard. Their sharp critiques of a last draft of Chapter 4 helped immeasurably.

I have been fortunate to receive critical feedback in a number of scholarly conferences and seminars, including the Allen Morris Forum at Florida State University, the Winthrop-King Institute for Contemporary French and Anglophone Studies, the Omohundro Institute Conference, Renaissance Society of America Conference, the Southern Historical Association Conference, the American Society for Ethnohistory Conference, the Institute for Historical Studies, the John Carter Brown Library, Early Americanists in Texas, and the Symposium on Comparative Early Modern Legal History at the Newberry Library, among others.

To me, the best part of the process of writing has been meeting the authors whose work has so influenced me through the years. Alejandra Dubcovsky and Robbie Ethridge read and critiqued—down to each line—the entire manuscript. Many other scholars have generously given their time and knowledge in various ways, whether as readers or commenters on my work at various times through the years at UT and beyond. Thanks to Brooke Bauer, Herman Bennett, Denise Bossy, Amy Turner Bushnell, Tessa Evans, Andrew K. Frank, Alan Gallay, Julia Gossard, Daragh Grant, Jack P. Greene, Evan Haefeli, Dixie Ray Haggard, April Lee Hatfield, Matthew Kruer, Katie LaBelle, Michelle LeMaster, Hayley Negrin, Michael LeRoy Oberg, Jerome Offner, Peter Olsen-Harbich, Brian Owensby, Barbara M. Parramore, Micah Pawling, Josh Piker, Mario Rewers, Dan Richter, Richard Ross, Kristalyn M. Shefveland, Michael Stoff, Anne Twinam, Larisa Veloz, Holly White, Miller Shores Wright, and Craig Yirush. I am also grateful to Evan Nooe and all the members of the

Native South Happy Hour for their friendship and warm welcome. At the University of Pennsylvania Press, my editor, Bob Lockhart has patiently worked with me every step of the way. Thanks to Lily Palladino for her endless patience and assistance on the final stretch of production. Thanks to Kate Blackmer of Blackmer Maps for designing the maps for the book.

Many institutions have supported this project at various stages from preliminary research to writing. This book was produced with the generous support of the Society of Colonial Wars Fellowship in Memory of Kenneth R. LaVoy Jr., established by the Society of Colonial Wars in the State of Florida and administered by Florida Atlantic University. The History Department provided a summer fellowship that supported in-depth research in the United Kingdom at the UK National Archives in Kew and at the British Library. The Archie K. Davis Fellowship from the North Caroliniana Society made possible research in the North Carolina State Archives and in the North Carolina Collection at the University of North Carolina at Chapel Hill. The concept of the dissertation grew thanks to the Social Science Research Council's Dissertation Proposal Development Fellowship. Thanks to all the participants in our workshop for their good-natured and spirited discussions. My work also benefited from a research stint at the Library Company of Philadelphia and the Historical Society of Pennsylvania thanks to a short-term fellowship. I would like to thank the library's director at the time, James Green, for his hospitality, as well as Connie King, for her invaluable help locating materials. A New England Regional Consortium Fellowship in 2016 broadened the context and deepened my understanding of the problems of Indian law throughout early America. The grant supported research in important collections for the history of Native Americans and the law, including the collections of the Connecticut Historical Society, the Rhode Island Historical Society, the Congregational Library, and Harvard University's Houghton Library.

The semester I spent at the John Carter Brown Library at Brown University in Providence, Rhode Island as a Paul W. McQuillen Fellow was one of the most memorable and gratifying experiences I had as a graduate student researcher. I wish to thank the staff of the JCB, especially Gabe Agnulo, Val Andrews, Scott Ellwood, Susan Newbury, Kim Nusco, Neil Safier, Meghan Sullivan-Silva, and Ken Ward for all of their kindness and help. I also thank our host that semester, Evelyn Lincoln. Special thanks to three of the library's research associates are also in order. Thank you to Jim Muldoon for lively discussions of everything from medieval canon law to Boston politics. And thanks again to Amy Turner Bushnell and Jack P. Greene for their hospitality, solid critiques, and for sharing their great knowledge of early America. I must again thank the History Department at the University of Texas at Austin for awarding me a writing fellowship for the 2017–2018 academic year in which I was able to complete my dissertation manuscript. Thank you to the Department of History at the University of Memphis for supporting my 2021 trip to the P. K. Yonge Library of Florida History at the University of Florida, Gainesville which the pandemic had significantly delayed. Special thanks to Jim Cusick and Michelle Wilbanks for their generous help in navigating the library's collection of Spanish colonial documents, and for sending me scans when I needed them. She also found an illustration right when I needed it. I am eternally grateful.

Parts of this book have appeared in various forms elsewhere. Some discussions of burdening and its effects were adapted from "'In Place of Horses': Indigenous Burdeners and the Politics of the Early American South," *Ethnohistory*, vol. 70, no. 1 (January 2023): 1–23. Parts of Chapter 3 appeared in "'Darling Indians' and 'Natural Lords': Virginia's Tributary Regime and Florida's Republic of Indians in the Seventeenth Century," in *Justice in a New World: Negotiating Legal Intelligibility in British, Iberian, and Indigenous America*, ed. Brian P. Owensby and Richard J. Ross (New York: NYU Press, 2018): 183-212. Parts of Chapters 4 and 5 appeared in "'As the Spaniards Always Have Done': The Legacy of Florida's Missions for Carolina Indian Relations and the Origins of the Yamasee War," in *Entangled Empires: The Anglo-Iberian Atlantic, 1500–1830*, ed. Jorge Cañizares-Esguerra (Philadelphia: University of Pennsylvania Press, 2018): 178–193. Parts of the epilogue appeared as "'His One Netev Ples': The Chowans and the Politics of Indian Petitioning in the Colonial South," *William and Mary Quarterly*, 3rd ser., vol. 76, no. 1 (January 2019): 41–74. Some of my earliest thoughts about the republic of Indians appeared in "Albion's Caciques: England and the Republic of Indians," *The Atlantic Millennium: An Academic Journal on Atlantic Civilization*, vol. 12 (2013–14): 1–16. I am grateful to Florida International University's Department of History Graduate Student Association for the opportunity to present the paper on which the article was based at their conference in April 2014.

So much has happened in the last few years—let alone the last decade—and I'm grateful for friends and family who have been with us through it all, whether the pandemic or raising a small child. Thanks to the RSPTL—Matt and Stephanie, Ryan and Lauren, Brett and Amy. For popping in every now and then with a funny text or email, thanks to Bao, Matt, Nathan, and Wes. Special thanks to Christina Brugnara Foster. Thanks especially to my parents,

Stan and Vanessa. If I had listened to them, I might have pursued this career much earlier. Thanks to my extended family, Patti, James, Emma, and Greg. Thanks to my in-laws Al, Chrissy, John, Sara, Vincent, and above all to Debra who introduced me to Stephen King. Thank you especially to my wife, Kim, for coming to Texas and for always helping me to see things clearly. My son, Samuel, has taught me a lot, including all the phases of the moon, and when to stop working. And thanks to Phoebe, Melville, and especially to Olive, who came to work every single day.

www.ingramcontent.com/pod-product-compliance
Lightning Source LLC
Chambersburg PA
CBHW020335100426
42812CB00029B/3137/J